Making B[illegible]

What makes bureaucracy w[illegible] s the world, countries have a[illegible] y education. Yet, policy implementation is uneven and not well under-stood. *Making Bureaucracy Work* investigates when and how public agencies deliver primary education in rural India. Through a multi-level comparative analysis and more than two years of ethnographic field research, Mangla opens the "black box" of Indian bureaucracy to demonstrate how differences in bureaucratic norms – informal rules that guide public officials and their everyday relations with citizens – generate divergent implementation patterns and outcomes. While some public agencies operate in a legalistic manner and promote compliance with policy rules, others engage in deliberation and encourage flexible problem-solving with local communities, thereby enhancing the quality of education services. This book reveals the complex ways bureaucratic norms interact with socioeconomic inequalities on the ground, illuminating the possibilities and obstacles for bureaucracy to promote inclusive development.

Akshay Mangla is Associate Professor of International Business at Saïd Business School at the University of Oxford. He specializes in comparative politics, political economy of development, public institutions, education, social welfare and South Asia.

CAMBRIDGE STUDIES IN THE COMPARATIVE POLITICS OF EDUCATION

Editor

Terry M. Moe, *Stanford University*

Education and its reform are matters of great political salience throughout the world. Yet as Gift and Wibbels observed, "It is hard to identify a community of political scientists who are dedicated to the comparative study of education." This series is an effort to change that. The goal is to encourage a vigorous line of scholarship that focuses squarely on the politics of education across nations, advances theoretical thinking, includes a broad swath of educational terrain – from elementary and secondary education to vocational education to higher education – and explores the impacts of education on key aspects of society. The series welcomes books of very different types. Some may be grounded in sophisticated quantitative analysis, but qualitative work is welcome as well, as are big-think extended essays that develop agenda-setting ideas. Work is encouraged that takes on big, important, inherently messy topics, however difficult they may be to study. Work is also encouraged that shows how the politics of education is shaped by power, special interests, parties, bureaucracies and other fundamentals of the political system. And finally, this series is not just about the developed nations, but encourages new work on developing nations and the special challenges that education faces in those contexts.

Books in the Series

The Comparative Politics of Education: Teachers Unions and Education Systems around the World
Edited by Terry M. Moe and Susanne Wiborg

A Loud but Noisy Signal?: Public Opinion and Education Reform in Western Europe
Marius R. Busemeyer, Julian L. Garritzmann and Erik Neimanns

The Politics of Comprehensive School Reforms: Cleavages and Coalitions
Katharina Sass

Making Bureaucracy Work

Norms, Education and Public Service Delivery in Rural India

AKSHAY MANGLA
University of Oxford

CAMBRIDGE
UNIVERSITY PRESS

CAMBRIDGE
UNIVERSITY PRESS

Shaftesbury Road, Cambridge CB2 8EA, United Kingdom

One Liberty Plaza, 20th Floor, New York, NY 10006, USA

477 Williamstown Road, Port Melbourne, VIC 3207, Australia

314–321, 3rd Floor, Plot 3, Splendor Forum, Jasola District Centre, New Delhi – 110025, India

103 Penang Road, #05–06/07, Visioncrest Commercial, Singapore 238467

Cambridge University Press is part of Cambridge University Press & Assessment, a department of the University of Cambridge.

We share the University's mission to contribute to society through the pursuit of education, learning and research at the highest international levels of excellence.

www.cambridge.org
Information on this title: www.cambridge.org/9781009258043

DOI: 10.1017/9781009258050

First published 2022
First paperback edition 2023

A catalogue record for this publication is available from the British Library

ISBN 978-1-009-25801-2 Hardback
ISBN 978-1-009-25804-3 Paperback

For my parents
Arun Kumar Mangla and Malti Mangla
who taught me the value of education

Contents

List of Figures *page* ix
List of Tables xi
Acknowledgments xiii
List of Abbreviations xix

PART I INTRODUCTION, PUZZLES AND THEORY

1 Introduction: Bureaucracy and the Politics of Implementing Primary Education 3
2 Bureaucratic Norms: A Theory of Implementation 34
3 The State and Primary Education in India 86

PART II IMPLEMENTING PRIMARY EDUCATION IN NORTHERN INDIA

4 How Legalistic Bureaucracy Generates Uneven Implementation 119
5 How Deliberative Bureaucracy Facilitates Adaptive Implementation 171
6 Norm Persistence: Exit, Voice and Bureaucratic Inertia 219
7 Norm Change: Conflict and Commitment on the Front Lines of Reform 261

PART III COMPARATIVE EXTENSIONS AND IMPLICATIONS

8 The Argument in Comparative Perspective 301
9 Conclusion: Reimagining Bureaucracy for Inclusive Development 327

Appendix: Researching Bureaucracy and Frontline Public Services 351
References 366
Index 405

Figures

1.1	Map of case study states in India	*page* 25
2.1	Taxonomy of administrative tasks in primary education	41
2.2	Primary schools (%) in compliance with RTE Act infrastructure standards	43
2.3	Summary of the argument	51
2.4	Mechanism 1: Bureaucratic understandings and behaviors	57
2.5	Mechanism 2: Societal feedback	62
3.1	Adult literacy rate (%) for males and females in India (1951–2011)	90
3.2	Adult literacy rate (%) for Scheduled Castes and Scheduled Tribes in India (1951–2011)	90
3.3	Public expenditure on education in India (1951–2011)	95
3.4	Indian central and state government shares (%) of total public expenditure on education (1992–2006)	107
3.5	Allocation of public expenditure (%) on education in India by level of education	108
4.1	Study map of Uttar Pradesh	120
4.2	Voting for national elections underway in a government primary school (Saharanpur, Uttar Pradesh)	136
4.3	New government primary school building (Saharanpur, Uttar Pradesh)	141
4.4	Government primary school classroom (Sitapur, Uttar Pradesh)	142
4.5	Women's association members preparing the midday meal (Saharanpur, Uttar Pradesh)	154
4.6	Unpaved path leading to village (Saharanpur, Uttar Pradesh)	160

5.1 Study map of Himachal Pradesh 172
5.2 Himachal Pradesh state assembly election results (1972–2017) 182
5.3 Temple for village deity (Theog, Himachal Pradesh) 184
5.4 Teacher training session underway (Koti, Himachal Pradesh) 191
5.5 Primary school in a Himalayan village (Mashobra, Himachal Pradesh) 196
5.6 Mother Teacher Association members (Shimla, Himachal Pradesh) 206
6.1 Study map of Uttarakhand 223
6.2 Teacher training center (Almora, Uttarakhand) 243
6.3 Aerial view of village terrace farms (Almora, Uttarakhand) 250
6.4 Women's association members performing ceremonial dance outside a preschool center (Dwarahat, Uttarakhand) 255
7.1 Study map of Bihar 279
9.1 Regimes of coproduction 335
A.1 Multilevel field research summary 352

Tables

1.1 Demographic indicators of case study states (2011) *page* 26
1.2 Socioeconomic indicators of case study states (1990–2011) 26
2.1 School access and input indicators (2012) 43
2.2 Student participation and teaching input indicators (2012) 44
2.3 Student learning indicators (2012) 45
2.4 Typology of bureaucratic norms 53
2.5 Varieties of bureaucratic norms and their predicted effects on policy implementation 77
3.1 Timeline of central government policies and judicial action for primary education (1950–2010) 98
3.2 Gross enrollment ratios for grades 1–8 in India (1951–2011) 101
3.3 Growth in primary school attendance and completion rates in India (1992–1999) 108
3.4 Program components of Sarva Shiksha Abhiyan 110
4.1 List of cabinet secretaries, Government of India (1950–2018) 126
4.2 Uttar Pradesh state government leadership (1952–2022) 129
4.3 Comparative socioeconomic indicators for Uttar Pradesh study districts (2011) 139
4.4 Panchal village: Socioeconomic indicators 159
5.1 Himachal Pradesh state government leadership (1971–2022) 181
5.2 Dharmaur village: Socioeconomic indicators 208
6.1 Public infrastructure in Uttar Pradesh and Uttarakhand (1991–1992) 226
6.2 Sarkot village: Socioeconomic indicators 250

A.1 Interviews in India 358
A.2 Focus group discussions in India 358
A.3 Local field sites in India 363
A.4 Study villages in India 363

Acknowledgments

The ideas for this book saw their first rays of light in the summer of 2006. As a United Nations Children's Fund (UNICEF) intern, I was researching child labor interventions in the carpet belt districts of Uttar Pradesh. I had not intended to write about India's primary school system. However, from fieldwork I learned that many children were neither engaged in work nor attending school, a residual category of "nowhere children," which the Government of India's decadal census fails to see. My conversations with households made it clear that parents had high hopes for their children and took significant steps to support their education. Yet, when visiting rural primary schools, I was struck by the chasm between citizens' aspirations and the actual services they received. To understand this disconnect, I consulted studies of rural state–society relations and social welfare, particularly Myron Weiner's *The Child and the State in India* and James Scott's *Weapons of the Weak*. The influence of these scholars reverberates throughout this book.

In the pages that follow, readers will encounter parents, schoolteachers, village leaders, women's association members, social activists and elected officials. Most of all, they will learn about civil servants, including officials from the Indian Administrative Service (IAS) as well as local bureaucrats, who hold the fate of so many children in their hands. These research participants, most of whom must go unnamed, provided raw materials for the book's arguments. They generously gave their time and candor during interviews. They shared meals and (too many) cups of *chai*, offering me a window into the social life of public institutions and village schools. The debts I have incurred to them are beyond repayment. I can only hope that this study does justice to their experiences.

This book began as a doctoral dissertation at the Massachusetts Institute of Technology (MIT). I was fortunate to have a distinguished group of scholars on my dissertation committee – Richard Locke, Suzanne Berger, Edward Steinfeld and Patrick Heller. Through her incisive comments, Suzanne Berger sharpened my theoretical lens while urging me not to miss the forest for the trees. Edward Steinfeld helped me think comparatively and weigh alternative explanations with due care. Patrick Heller guided my reading of India's political economy and set a standard for scholarship to which I aspire. My greatest debt is to my dissertation chair, Richard Locke, whose influence on this project was profound. An exemplary scholar and educator, he patiently heard my ideas, encouraged me at difficult moments and prodded me along when needed. Rick showed me what it means to do rigorous research that contributes to a just world.

Outside of my committee, I owe a special debt to Ashutosh Varshney and Devesh Kapur. I benefited greatly from Ashu's intellectual vitality, generous support and feedback throughout the project. I also thank him for leading the Brown-Harvard-MIT Seminar in South Asian Politics, a vibrant scholarly community. Devesh opened his academic treasure chest, brimming with questions, puzzles and insights. With his guidance, I improved my understanding of the Indian state, and his encouragement helped me cross the finish line.

I was privileged to make Harvard Business School my first professional home, a fruitful setting for refining the book's arguments. For their support and constructive engagement, I thank colleagues from the Business, Government & the International Economy Unit, including Rawi Abdelal, Raphael Di Tella, Catherine Duggan, Kristin Fabbe, Jeremy Friedman, Lakshmi Iyer, David Moss, Aldo Musacchio, Vincent Pons, Sophus Reinert, Forest Reinhardt, Meg Rithmire, the late Julio Rotemberg, Gunnar Trumbull, Richard Vietor, Matthew Weinzerl and Eric Werker. I am very grateful to Tarun Khanna for his mentorship and support under the Lakshmi Mittal and Family South Asia Institute.

Between MIT and Harvard, this book benefited from countless conversations and feedback from scholars. I thank the late Alice Amsden for encouraging me to study the state's role in development. I also thank Jackie Bhabha, Joshua Cohen, Archon Fung, Tarun Khanna, Uday Mehta, Dilip Mookherjee, Roger Petersen, Michael Piore, Lant Pritchett, Bish Sanyal, Ben Ross Schneider, Susan Silbey, Lily Tsai and Michael Walton. I am grateful to the late Judith Tendler, whose pathbreaking work on public services continues to inspire me. For their comments and enduring support, I thank my MIT graduate school peers, including Matthew Amengual, Rodrigo Canales, Nathan Cisneros, Salo Coslovsky, Greg Distelhorst, Kristin Fabbe, Jason Jackson, Gabi Kruks-Wisner, Reo Matsuzaki, Timea Pal, Seth Pipkin, Roberto Pires, Andrew Radin, Gustavo Setrini, Rachel Wellhausen and Adam Ziegfeld.

I am immensely grateful to South Asia scholars of my generation, whose work has taught me so much, including Amit Ahuja, Adam Auerbach, Tara Béteille, Rikhil Bhavnani, Rachel Brulé, Jennifer Bussell, Uday Chandra, Simon Chauchard, Emily Clough, Aditya Dasgupta, Emmerich Davies, Francesca Jensenius, Himanshu Jha, Gabrielle Kruks-Wisner, Dinsha Mistree, Sergio Mukherjee, Karthik Muralidharan, Garreth Nellis, Susan Ostermann, Prerna Singh, Pavithra Suryanarayan, Neelanjan Sircar, Paul Staniland, Sandip Sukhtankar, Tariq Thachil, Milan Vaishnav, Gilles Verniers and Adam Ziegfeld.

The manuscript was shaped by the wealth of advice given at an author's workshop at Brown University chaired by Patrick Heller, which brought together Tulia Falleti, Devesh Kapur, Andrew Schrank, Lily Tsai and Ashutosh Varshney. I am thoroughly grateful to have had these incredible scholars debate my arguments and offer constructive feedback.

At Cambridge University Press, I thank Sara Doskow and Rachel Blaifeder for their outstanding editorial guidance, and Jadyn Fauconier-Herry and Joshua Penney for seeing the manuscript through production. I thank Shyama Warner for proofreading the manuscript with care. Many thanks to Terry Moe for supporting this book project and including it in the Comparative Politics of Education series. I thank two anonymous reviewers for their excellent comments.

I received many helpful suggestions while presenting my research at Ashoka University, Azim Premji University, Brown University, Carnegie Endowment for International Peace, Centre for Policy Research (CPR) in New Delhi, Fudan University, Harvard University, National University of Singapore, Lucknow University, MIT, University of California Berkeley, University of Manchester, University of Oslo, University of Oxford, University of Pennsylvania's Center for the Advanced Study of India, Yale University's Modern South Asia Workshop, the Annual Conference on South Asia at the University of Wisconsin-Madison, as well as annual meetings of the American Political Science Association, Midwest Political Science Association, Political Studies Association and the Society for the Advancement of Socio-Economics. For comments on my presentations and working papers, I thank Yamini Aiyar, Rikhil Bhavnani, Quinlan Bowman, Kanchan Chandra, Pradeep Chhibber, Dia Da Costa, John Harriss, Barbara Harriss-White, Ron Herring,

Michael Hill, Merilee Grindle, Bethany Lacina, Karuna Mantena, Rahul Mukherji, Susan Ostermann, Jan Pierskalla, Roberto Pires, Dan Posner, Sanjay Reddy, Peregrine Schwartz-Shea, Aseema Sinha, Nicholas Rush Smith, Guillermo Toral, Yogendra Yadav and Dvora Yanow.

The final stages of writing took place at the University of Oxford's Saïd Business School, my current intellectual home. My gratitude to fellow members of the International Business Group, Mari Sako, Matthew Amengual, Marc Szepan and Eric Thun. I owe a special debt to Mari Sako, whose comparative political economy seminar stimulated my thinking as a graduate student. I am extremely fortunate to have her as a colleague and mentor. I am grateful to Tom Lawrence for organizing our faculty Write Club and generously commenting on my work. I thank our former dean, Peter Tufano, for his enthusiasm and support for my research. I thank other Oxford colleagues for helpful conversations, including Teppo Felin, Barbara Harriss-White, Raymond Loveridge, Steve New, Rafael Ramirez, Maya Tudor, Marc Ventresca and Martin Williams.

This book has benefited from the feedback of scholars in India. I am deeply grateful to Pratap Bhanu Mehta for his generous insights and mentorship. For their guidance, I thank Jean Drèze, Ram Guha and Yogendra Yadav. CPR has been a second academic home for me. A special thanks goes to Yamini Aiyar, whose research continues to shape my understanding of Indian bureaucracy. I thank other CPR colleagues for their advice, including Kiran Bhatty, Jishnu Das, Ambrish Dongre, Mekhala Krishnamurty, Partha Mukhopadhyay and Neelanjan Sircar.

This book has been enriched through numerous conversations with IAS officers, current and retired. I thank the late S.K. Alok, Srikant Baldi, Balamurugan Devaraj, Amit Kaul, Dr. Rakesh Kumar, Dhir Jingran, Santhosh Mathew, Jagdish Chandra Pant, Deepak Sanan, Naresh Saxena, Amarjeet Sinha, Abhimanyu Singh, C.P. Sujaya and Vrinda Swarup. I am eternally grateful to my dear friend, the late Keshav Desiraju, who taught me so much. Keshav's humane vision of public administration inspires these pages.

I have also learned immensely from civic agencies in India. I am grateful to Dr. Rukmini Banerji, whose leadership brings hope to India's primary education system. I thank Rukmini and the Pratham team for sharing their field experiences, granting me access to the Annual Status of Education Report datasets, and aiding my research in Agra, Delhi and Bihar. I thank Ashish Dhawan and colleagues at the Central Square Foundation for their engagement and support. I am indebted to my friend the late Girindre Beeharry, who shared his vision on education and took the Gates Foundation's education portfolio to new heights.

The fieldwork for this book benefited from the support of many individuals and institutions in India. In Uttar Pradesh, I thank Dr. Arvind Mohan at Lucknow University for his guidance. I am grateful to Dr. Rashmi Sinha and Mahila Samakhya Uttar Pradesh district teams, for their assistance in Saharanpur, Mathura and Sitapur. I thank UNICEF officers, including Rajib Ghoshal and Vinobajee Gautam, and local teams in eastern Uttar Pradesh and Bundelkhand. My warmest thanks to Sanjeev Goel and family for their hospitality in Saharanpur. In Bihar, I am grateful to Amarjit Sinha and Pratham field teams for their assistance.

In Himachal Pradesh, I benefited from Deepak Sanan's sage advice. For their guidance, I thank Rakesh Kanwar, Akshay Sood and Bansi Lal Shukla. I thank Chetan Singh for engaging my questions about Himalayan history. I am most grateful to Himachal Gyan Vigyan Samiti members, including Kuldip Tanwar, O.P. Bhuraita, Balveer Singh Kaushal and Pradeep Thakur. A warm thanks to Pradeepji and family for their hospitality in Theog. My research in Uttarakhand was supported by the late Keshav Desiraju and Dr. Rakesh Kumar. In Almora, I received generous support from Dr. Lalit Pande, Anuradha Pande and others at Uttarakhand Seva Nidhi. I am indebted to Mohan Chandra Kandpal for his guidance and hospitality in Dwarahat.

This book benefited from excellent research assistance by Melissa Patel, Padmini Baruah and Devarchan Banerjee. My research was financially supported by an American Institute for Indian Studies Junior Research Fellowship, National Security Education Program David L. Boren Fellowship, MIT Carroll L. Wilson Award, along with support from Harvard's Radcliffe Institute and the Lakshmi Mittal South Asia Institute.

This project was made possible by the love, support and blessings of my family and dear friends. I cherish the times with my late grandmother, Prabha Rani Mangla, who kept my bedroom ready in Soami Nagar and made sure that I was well fed. I thank Mama and Mami, Suresh Chandra Sharma and Pushpa Sharma, who provided a second home for me in Palam. A special thanks to my cousin, Aditya Sharma, whose support and good cheer carried me through my fieldwork. I am grateful to my Lucknow friends – Raghav Manocha, Ajit Pal Singh, Gagan Tandon and Pranav Sharma – for their warmth and revelry.

I dedicate this book to my parents, Arun Kumar Mangla and Malti Mangla. Their enduring love, unspoken sacrifices and commitment to education enabled me to find my path. I thank my siblings, Aditya and Mahima, and my dear friend Vikram for being there for me always. I thank Kratos and Toby for bringing us boundless joy.

I am extremely grateful to the Khosla family for welcoming me into their home. My heartfelt appreciation goes to the late Harish Khosla and the late Rajiv Khosla. I only wish they could have seen the book. For their love and blessings, I thank Suchinta Sahni, Amita Khosla and Madhav Khosla.

My gratitude to Radhika Khosla defies expression in words. This book would not have seen the light of day without her encouragement, resilience and unswerving faith in me. She kept me attuned to life's many riches, far away from the book. I am forever thankful to her for joining me on this walk.

Abbreviations

ASER	Annual Status of Education Report
BDO	Block Development Officer
BEO	Block Education Officer
BEP	Bihar Education Project
BGVS	Bharat Gyan Vigyan Samiti
BIMARU	Bihar, Madhya Pradesh, Rajasthan and Uttar Pradesh
BJP	Bharatiya Janata Party
BPL	Below Poverty Line
BSA	Basic Shiksha Adhikari (see DEO)
BSP	Bahujan Samaj Party
CPM	Communist Party of India (Marxist)
DC	District Collector
DEO	District Education Officer
DIET	District Institute of Education and Training
DISE	District Information System of Education
DM	District Magistrate
DPEP	District Primary Education Programme
GER	Gross enrollment ratio
GOI	Government of India
HGVS	Himachal Gyan Vigyan Samiti
HP	Himachal Pradesh
IMF	International Monetary Fund
INC	Indian National Congress
JDU	Janata Dal United
KGBV	Kasturba Gandhi Balika Vidyalaya
KSSP	Kerala Sastra Sahitya Parishad
MDGs	Millennium Development Goals
MDM	Midday Meal Programme

MHRD	Ministry of Human Resource Development
MSUP	Mahila Samakhya Uttar Pradesh
NCERT	National Council of Educational Research and Training
NFHS	National Family Health Survey
NGO	nongovernmental organization
NIEPA	National Institute of Education Planning and Administration
NPE	National Policy on Education
NPEGEL	National Programme for Education of Girls at Elementary Level
OBC	Other Backward Classes/Other Backward Castes
PRI	Panchayati Raj Institution
PROBE	Public Report on Basic Education
RJD	Rashtriya Janata Dal
RTE	Right to Education (Act)
SAP	Structural Adjustment Program
SC	Scheduled Caste
SCERT	State Council of Educational Research and Training
SDGs	Sustainable Development Goals
SHG	Self Help Group
SP	Samajwadi Party
SPD	State Project Director (for Sarva Shiksha Abhiyan)
SSA	Sarva Shiksha Abhiyan
ST	Scheduled Tribe
TaRL	Teaching at the Right Level
UKD	Uttarakhand Kranti Dal
UNICEF	United Nations Children's Fund
UP	Uttar Pradesh
UPBEP	Uttar Pradesh Basic Education Project
USN	Uttarakhand Seva Nidhi
VEC	Village Education Committee

PART I

INTRODUCTION, PUZZLES AND THEORY

1

Introduction

Bureaucracy and the Politics of Implementing Primary Education

It is ironic that bureaucracy is still primarily a term of scorn, even though bureaus are among the most important institutions in every nation in the world.

– Anthony Downs (1965, 439)

The most striking fact about the Indian state is how varied its performance has been, spanning the spectrum from woefully inadequate to surprisingly impressive.

– Devesh Kapur (2020, 31)

1.1 INTRODUCTION

What makes bureaucracy work, especially for the least advantaged? During a field visit to the Himalayan region in the spring of 2010, I was struck by an education official's answer to this question. Mr. Chauhan greeted me in his office in Shimla district, the capital of Himachal Pradesh (HP). Our conversation about India's primary education programming took an unexpected turn as he described a schooling initiative for children from the nomadic *Gujjar* community. A pastoral tribe, the Gujjars spent summer months in the Shimla foothills, where they reared buffalo, goats and other livestock. During winters, they migrated to the plains of Saharanpur, a nearby district in the state of Uttar Pradesh (UP), disrupting their children's education. Local education officials experimented by creating mobile schools. The Gujjars were joined by a caravan of volunteer teachers who taught remedial classes. After a few years, the first cohort of Gujjar children from Shimla had completed primary schooling. In Mr. Chauhan's words, "Local administration needed to mobilize teachers and parents to work side-by-side ... We had to uphold the policy structure (*dhancha*), but sometimes we let go of it. This way, the community felt it was our (*apna*) school."[1]

Mr. Chauhan articulated a vision of bureaucracy that was puzzling in many ways. Mobile schooling was costly and difficult for local agencies to administer. Parental participation was hardly guaranteed, as witnessed in the floundering of so many community-based development programs. The practical steps needed to make mobile schools operational were complex and politically fraught. District administration had recruited volunteers from among the Gujjars and later appointed them as contract-based teachers. Subsequently, they were promoted as regular teachers with civil service protections. These actions broke with administrative protocol and drew criticism from teacher unions. The Indian central government's policy framework for primary education stipulated, in minute detail, the responsibilities of state governments, but there was no mention of mobile schools or the regularization of volunteer teachers. Nor was the mobile schooling program an aberration. Similar initiatives had surfaced elsewhere in HP, often led by bureaucrats working around administrative rules.

What motivated these officials to allocate scarce resources for marginalized populations and face local resistance? Equally puzzling, I observed no comparable bureaucratic initiatives in Saharanpur, where Gujjars resided in larger numbers, possessed land and had electoral clout. Nor were bureaucrats in HP more inclined to beneficence. The administrative structures, resources and career incentives for bureaucrats across the two states were similar. My fieldwork in UP revealed that local administrators there too had tried experimenting with programs for marginalized communities. But whereas local adaptations flourished in HP, bureaucracy in UP was hamstrung by a commitment to rules, enabling some initiatives to take off, but stifling many others.

This book seeks to explain when and how bureaucracy works for disadvantaged citizens, to realize the promise of education for all. One does not have to travel to Himalayan villages to recognize the importance of these questions. To provide every child with an education is a basic duty of the modern state. Most countries have laws making primary education free, universal and compulsory. Many declare education a constitutional right. How well states fulfill these promises has a profound influence on

[1] Interview with an education official, Shimla, February 2, 2010.

the quality of life that people lead. In that regard, the stunning growth of publicly funded primary schooling systems in developing countries occasions optimism. The United Nations (UN) Millennium Development Goals (MDGs) program reported that primary school enrollments in developing countries climbed steeply in previous decades, reaching 91 percent of children by 2015 (UNDP 2015). The number of out-of-school children fell by almost a half, from an estimated 100 million children in 2000 to 55 million in 2015. Enrollment rates in sub-Saharan Africa rose to 80 percent, even as a staggering 40 percent of the population lives in extreme poverty. In South Asia, a region with stark gender disparities, less than seven girls attended primary school for every ten boys in the 1990s. The gender gap in enrollment has reduced considerably, reaching parity in many places.

The breathtaking expansion of primary schooling masks another disheartening trend. Millions of children remain out of school, or receive services of abysmal quality, and are effectively denied *education*.[2] Dilapidated school buildings, teacher absenteeism, dysfunctional classrooms, high dropout rates for girls, broken systems of monitoring and academic support, a lack of community engagement – these are the maladies afflicting government primary school systems across the world. And whereas wealthy households have exited the government system to seek private schooling, the least advantaged continue to bear the brunt of low-quality governmental services. In some places, the poor too have opted to exit, committing scarce household resources toward "low-fee" private schools, some decent, others of questionable repute (Tooley and Dixon 2006; Srivastava 2013).

The impressive gains, and equally alarming gaps, in primary education across developing countries provoke questions of when, why and how bureaucracies effectively deliver public services for the masses. These questions are of intrinsic importance. For observers of political life, they raise longstanding conundrums. A venerable line of thought, going as far back as ancient Greece, suggests that democracy enhances human well-being. Democratic mechanisms of popular participation, electoral competition and a free press are believed to empower citizens and make states responsive to their needs. "It is not surprising," Amartya Sen famously contends, that "no famine has ever taken place in the history of the world in a functioning democracy" (1999, 16). Democracy's "Third Wave" saw

[2] Lant Pritchett (2013) distinguishes between the delivery of "schooling" inputs and "education" services, with the latter being more closely connected to student learning.

countries in Africa, Asia and Latin America adopt democratic institutions. Democratic accountability may have led some governments to commit more public resources to primary education and other social policies, as evidenced by cross-national studies (Lake and Baum 2001; Brown and Hunter 2004; Ansell 2010). Yet, public spending, while critical, is hardly sufficient for producing high-quality public services (Filmer and Pritchett 1999; Nelson 2007).[3] Democracy, it appears, has not led states to acquire the bureaucratic capabilities needed to implement social programs effectively (Andrews, Pritchett and Woolcock 2017, 14–26). Famines may indeed be fewer, but illiteracy, chronic hunger and insecurity persist.

If we extend our analytic gaze beyond the high politics of state spending, to the mundane assignment of *implementing* public services, questions of state capacity come to the fore. Few developing country states are well endowed with what Mann (1984, 2008) calls "infrastructural power," the ability to project authority and implement policy decisions over their territories. Fewer still have institutions resembling Weberian bureaucracy (Rauch and Evans 2000). Institutional weakness creates an enormous gulf between the aims of public policy and its execution, between what citizens aspire to attain and what they actually get (Rothstein 2011). Institutional weakness also diminishes the credibility of the state's policy commitments, incentivizing politicians to channel resources in a particularistic fashion, to the neglect of programmatic services (Keefer 2007). These political dynamics are visible across the world, from Mexico to Brazil, Nigeria to South Africa, India to Indonesia and beyond. At the extreme, predatory bureaucracies license officials to extract public resources, but offer citizens few services in return. Yet, service delivery can also suffer when bureaucracies are coherent and public-minded, just as patronage politics can thrive even in well-established democracies (Piattoni 2001).

The dominant pattern in developing countries is not of outright failure, but of variation in state performance. Bureaucracies display large differences in their capabilities to implement policy, both between and within countries, across different policy functions, as well as across

[3] The economics of education literature shows that, beyond a minimum threshold, public spending has little noticeable impact on the quality of education services (Hanushek and Woessmann 2011; Woessmann 2016). Summarizing the findings from cross-national studies, Evans, Huber and Stephens (2017, 387) observe, "[l]evels of expenditure are only weakly correlated to even the crudest measures of outcome, levels of enrollment."

administrative tasks within a given function. There are also striking cases of effective public service delivery within developing countries (Uphoff 1994; Grindle 1997; Tendler 1997; Chand 2006). Public services do sometimes reach citizens, even where conventional theories least predict it. The uneven performance of public services in India and elsewhere motivates the central questions of this book: How does bureaucracy implement primary education, within the least likely settings? Why do some bureaucracies deliver education services more effectively than others? What, in short, makes bureaucracy *work* for the least advantaged?

My answer to these questions stems from the recognition that bureaucracies are collective agencies bound by norms (March and Olsen 1989; Ostrom 2000). Where formal institutions are weak or politicized, the implementation of public services may nonetheless vary depending on the informal norms that guide bureaucratic behavior. This book takes us inside the state. It casts light on the street-level bureaucracies that deliver education in rural India (Lipsky 1980). I argue that historical differences in bureaucratic norms have contributed to subnational variation in the delivery of primary education across northern Indian states. Conceived as the informal rules of the game, bureaucratic norms instruct public officials on how to interpret their policy mandates and the actions deemed appropriate in fulfilling them. Bureaucratic norms also influence how officials interact with individuals and groups in society, conditioning citizen expectations and collective action around public services.

Subject to the same national policy framework, as well as common political, legal and administrative institutions, I find that bureaucratic norms have evolved differently across Indian states, with material consequences for the delivery of primary schooling. Some Indian states have secured a commitment to *legalism*, norms encouraging a rule-based orientation. Legalism unleashes a protective dynamic, motivating officials to uphold rules, procedures and administrative hierarchies. Other states have norms committing officials to *deliberation*, which stimulates a problem-based orientation. Deliberation generates an organizational dynamic centered on solving problems, encouraging officials to interpret policies in a flexible manner. These distinct types of bureaucratic norms produce very different implementation patterns and outcomes for primary education. Legalism enables officials to secure compliance with policy rules and undertake less complex tasks, such as enrollment and infrastructure provision, but it weakens their ability to monitor schools and sustain community input over time, leading to uneven implementation of services.

On the other hand, deliberation enables the performance of more complex tasks, encouraging officials to adapt policy rules to local needs and sustain community monitoring, thereby improving the quality of services. I ground the argument historically, connecting the divergence in bureaucratic norms to the politics of subnational state-building. Bureaucratic norms are politically constructed and maintained through the collective strategies and relationships that have evolved between subnational politicians and bureaucratic elites, often in response to central administration.

I build and test this book's arguments in rural north India, a setting of endemic poverty, social divisions and political clientelism. Through a multilevel comparative analysis in four northern Indian states, I demonstrate that the divergence in bureaucratic norms is a causal driver of subnational differences in the implementation of primary education. On the basis of two and a half years of comparative field research, using ethnographic methods, including 507 interviews of senior officials and participant observation with street-level bureaucrats, I trace policy implementation across multiple levels of administration, from planning decisions in state capitals to routine monitoring by district administrations, down to village-level governance by schoolteachers, parents and wider communities.

In India and elsewhere, weak institutions are expected to render bureaucracy wholly subservient, captured, or corrupt. Bureaucrats are depicted as cogs who surrender their discretion to politicians. Rarely are they seen as having political authority of their own, let alone the ability to use discretion in productive ways. This book argues for a different approach, one that brings bureaucratic institutions back into the comparative political economy of developing countries. Against overwhelmingly pessimistic predictions, I find that bureaucracy in northern India can deliver primary education effectively in some cases. Yet, the quality of services varies substantially depending on the nature of bureaucratic norms that guide public officials. In demonstrating the different ways that bureaucracy works for disadvantaged groups in society, this book sheds new light on how states promote inclusive development.

1.2 FROM SOCIAL POLICIES TO CITIZEN WELFARE: STUDYING THE IMPLEMENTATION OF PRIMARY EDUCATION

The battle for welfare is often waged beyond the voting booth, at the local interfaces between citizens and the state: on school campuses, at the service counters of employment offices and inside the waiting rooms of medical clinics. Primary education occupies the empirical domain of this book, but the challenge of implementation stretches across a broader theoretical canvas. It raises more general questions regarding how states transform social policies into concrete services that improve societal well-being. Chapter 2 articulates the concept and measures of implementation used in this book. Here, I discuss the importance of studying primary education through the lens of comparative politics.

Few public institutions touch our lives more directly than primary schools. Primary education lays the groundwork for learning and skills acquisition, enlarging our life chances and prospects for mobility. Education is integral to the human capabilities that we strive to cultivate, not least of all the ability to lead a life of dignity (Sen 1999). At a societal level, primary education contributes to a country's stock of human capital, a recognized catalyst for productivity and economic growth (Goldin and Katz 2009; Barro and Lee 2015). Beyond the transmission of skills, schools impart civic lessons and help forge our relationship to the state (Gutmann 1999; Bruch and Soss 2018). Schools are formative political spaces, where children first encounter the "imagined community" of the nation (Anderson 1991). Schooling is a principal mode by which states broadcast territorial control, transmit ideologies and construct citizen identities. Mass public education, Ansell and Lindvall write, "marked the first profound extension of the state's powers to civilians" in nineteenth-century Europe and America (2013, 520). In France's Third Republic, the state consolidated its authority in the countryside through schools, transforming "peasants into Frenchmen" (Weber 1976).

Primary education also features prominently in political debates over redistribution and social welfare. "Full citizenship," in Marshall's (1950) classic statement, involves the progressive attainment of civil, political and social rights. The last of these rights is arguably the most difficult to realize. The provision of mass education has been an important ingredient in the protection of social rights, predating social insurance and other welfare measures (Iversen and Stephens 2008, 603). The American school reformer Horace Mann proclaimed that public education is "the great equalizer of the conditions of men," a pathway for social mobility.[4] Today, early child education is seen as a pivotal policy mechanism for combatting inequality (Chetty et al. 2011). Yet, education has also been a great discriminator within society, "hugely important," Bourdieu

4 As quoted in Monroe (1940), who examines the growth of public education in America.

observed, "in the affirmation of differences between groups and social classes, and the reproduction of those differences."[5]

For all of these reasons, primary education is a core public function and parameter for judging state performance. Yet, compared to other state functions, such as national security, regulation and industrial policy, we know far less about the politics of when, why and how states provide primary education. "The scholarly literature at this point is almost a *tabula rasa* on these scores," Moe and Wiborg (2017, 4) write. The status of education research in other social science disciplines offers a lesson in contrasts. The economics of education has made strides following the pioneering work of Schultz (1961) and Becker (1964), from macroeconomic studies of human capital growth to rigorous, microlevel evaluations of education policy.[6] Another fertile field, the sociology of education has illuminated the linkages between schooling and social stratification. Education research has spawned new sociological theories, such as social capital, influencing the study of politics and development.[7]

To be sure, the comparative politics of education is not an empty field.[8] Research under the "Varieties of Capitalism" rubric has explored national patterns of skill formation, demonstrating how systems of higher education and vocational training complement economic institutions and shape inequalities (Hall and Soskice 2001; Thelen 2004; Iversen and Stephens 2008; Busemeyer 2014). Yet, less is known about the politics of *primary* education, an institution that touches more lives and has its own distributional politics.[9] Moreover, attention to national systems and cross-national spending patterns has eclipsed subnational-level research on policy implementation. The need to study implementation is pressing, perhaps more so in developing countries, where the institutional challenges of providing quality services are enormous (Corrales 2005; World Bank 2018). Research from developing countries also reveals the

5 Interview of Bourdieu by Emily Eakin (2001) "The Intellectual Class Struggle," *New York Times*, January 6, 2001. Available at: www.nytimes.com/2001/01/06/arts/the-intellectual-class-struggle.html.

6 Education research has helped transform development economics, spearheaded by Nobel prize-winning scholarship at the MIT Poverty Action Lab. See, for example, Banerjee et al. (2015).

7 Bourdieu (1986) pioneered social capital theory in a volume on education. Coleman (1988) refined the concept in a seminal article examining high school dropout rates, hence the title "Social Capital in the Creation of *Human* Capital" (emphasis added).

8 See review articles by Busemeyer and Trampusch (2011) and Gift and Wibbels (2014).

9 Recent exceptions include Ansell (2010), Kosack (2012) and Paglayan (2021).

weak correlation between school spending and outcomes, such as student learning (Hanushek and Woessmann 2011; Pritchett 2013).

Problems of implementation are not, however, unique to developing countries. The United States enacted far-reaching education reforms in the early-twentieth-century Progressive Era, but it struggles to provide quality education till this day. A crowded menu of reforms for urban school districts has yielded modest results (Hess 1999). More than sixty years after the US Supreme Court declared racial segregation unconstitutional in its landmark decision on *Brown* v. *The Board of Education*, the legacy of racial discrimination continues to be felt in American schools. Resource disparities between school districts are an obstacle, but public spending patterns do not fully explain educational inequalities (Hanushek 2010). In the state of Connecticut, for instance, the towns of Bridgeport and Fairfield spent, respectively, \$14,000 and \$16,000 per student during the 2014–2015 academic year, above the national average of \$10,800. And, whereas 94 percent of high school students in Fairfield graduated on time that year, only 63 percent did so in Bridgeport.[10] These sharp differences between neighboring school districts within a single US state are a reminder that, even in wealthy countries, policy implementation can have profound consequences for social welfare and inequality.

1.3 THE PUZZLE: PRIMARY EDUCATION IN NORTHERN INDIA

This book investigates the delivery of primary education in rural north India, an unlikely setting for public services to function well. Chapter 2 presents comparative indicators to illustrate the large subnational differences in education within this region. India historically has earned accolades for its democracy, marked by competitive elections, high voter participation and smooth transfers of power. Stable democracy is an achievement given India's income level and extraordinary ethnic diversity (Varshney 2014). Between elections, however, citizen experiences of the state leave much to be desired (Corbridge et al. 2005; Gupta 2012; Kruks-Wisner 2018). Bureaucracy can be apathetic and capricious in its treatment of disadvantaged citizens, prompting scholars to ponder why India's poor even bother to vote (Ahuja and Chhibber 2012). Wearisome

[10] E. Harris and Hussey, K., "In Connecticut, a Wealth Gap Divides Neighboring Schools," *New York Times*, September 11, 2016, Available at: www.nytimes.com/2016/09/12/nyregion/in-connecticut-a-wealth-gap-divides-neighboring-schools.html.

encounters of the state are matched by dismal human development outcomes. India accounts for 15 percent of the world's population, but it is home to 37 percent of global illiterates (287 million people). Indian adults complete 5.4 years of schooling on average, less than citizens in poorer countries such as Haiti, Honduras, Nigeria and Zimbabwe. India's literacy rate of 74 percent in 2011 was surpassed by China more than twenty years prior, despite India having a lead at independence. India's woeful human development performance is not confined to education (Drèze and Sen 2013). The United Nations Development Program's (UNDP) Human Development Index (HDI) presents a composite measure of well-being based on indicators for education, health and per capita income. India's HDI ranking of 131 (out of 188 countries) places it between Namibia and Honduras, far below other BRICS – Brazil (84), Russia (52), China (85) and South Africa (114) – the large emerging economies with which it is often clubbed.[11]

India's failure to provide quality public services is not for want of resources. Illiteracy and hunger have persisted despite three decades of robust economic growth and notable reductions in poverty (Kohli 2012). Income disparities have also grown, leaving the country looking "more and more like islands of California in a sea of sub-Saharan Africa" (Drèze and Sen 2013, ix). Nor does an absence of political will explain these deprivations. With economic liberalization in the 1990s, state control of the economy receded, but social programming expanded, substantially in some areas. Public spending on education, a paltry 1 percent of GDP in the 1970s, reached 4 percent by the 1990s. In 2000, the central government enacted Sarva Shiksha Abhiyan, its flagship "Education for All" program, providing infrastructure and incentives to improve access in underserved areas. The Midday Meal Programme, the world's largest child nutrition intervention, provides a free daily meal in more than 2 million government schools. The 2010 Right to Education [RTE] Act places a legally enforceable duty on the state to guarantee free and compulsory education for all children of ages 6 to 14 years. Not all developing countries have such progressive social legislation.[12] Yet, the pervasive deficiencies in implementation have been well documented (PROBE 1999). According to a World

[11] Human Development Index 2020 Rankings, UNDP. Available at: http://hdr.undp.org/en/content/latest-human-development-index-ranking.

[12] Whereas in many countries guardians are legally mandated to ensure that children attend school, India's RTE Act places this legal responsibility on the state.

Bank study, 25 percent of government teachers are absent from school on a normal workday (Kremer et al. 2005).[13] A national survey reports that less than half of rural fifth graders can read from second grade textbooks, to say nothing of their comprehension or critical thinking skills (ASER 2015).

This bleak picture at the aggregate level masks substantial differences across Indian states. This book analyzes the puzzling variation in primary education outcomes in northern India's Hindi belt, a least-likely setting for programmatic policies to reach citizens. Social divisions and clientelistic politics are thought to emasculate service delivery within this region. Nevertheless, some states in the Hindi belt perform far better than expected, surpassing the educational performance of wealthier states in southern and coastal India, while others show sluggish and uneven progress. Subnational differences in implementation exist despite a common national policy and legal framework for primary education, as well as similar electoral institutions and administrative structures. A socioeconomic laggard, UP is among the places where conventional theories least expect public services to be well-implemented (Drèze and Gazdar 1996; Mehrotra 2006). Since the late-1990s, however, UP has experienced a dramatic upsurge in primary schooling, recording rapid growth in infrastructure, provision of the midday meal, and other inputs. By 2015, the enrollment rate in primary schools surpassed 95 percent. UP's literacy rate also grew substantially, from 56.3 percent in 2001 to 69.7 percent in 2011. Long considered a development failure, the state of Bihar has made surprising gains as well in primary school enrollments and infrastructure provision (Singh and Stern 2013). At the same time, services in UP and Bihar are irregular and the quality of education woefully inadequate, evidenced by poor learning outcomes.

The puzzles of this book extend to the Himalayan region, where the state of HP stands out as a leader in primary education within India. It lags only behind Kerala, a recognized model of social development in South Asia. HP's educational achievements are even more remarkable than Kerala's in many ways. HP's mountainous topography, harsh climate and low population density make the administration of services far more challenging. At independence, Kerala had a substantial lead in

[13] Chaudhury et al. (2006) report that teacher absence in India (25%) is higher than in Peru (11%), Ecuador (14%) and Bangladesh (16%) and slightly lower than in Uganda (27%).

literacy (47.2 percent) over the rest of India, whereas HP (at 8 percent) was among the least literate states in the country. Since the 1980s, HP has surged ahead of other states, with educational gains broadly shared by women, lower castes and tribal populations (World Bank 2007). The puzzle of HP's superior performance deepens when compared to other parts of the Himalayan region. The adjacent state of Uttarakhand, which has similar economic and sociocultural characteristics to HP, performs markedly worse in primary education, even though it had a substantially higher literacy rate (19 percent) around independence.

What explains the exceptional performance of primary schooling in HP? Why does Uttarakhand's education system fare much worse, despite its similar geographic, economic and sociocultural features, as well as an historic lead in literacy? What, moreover, explains the uneven implementation pattern in UP? Given UP's social inequalities, clientelism and fractured political commitment to primary education, how has the state managed to improve school access and infrastructure? Why do the same state institutions falter in providing quality services? And finally, what accounts for Bihar's notable gains in education? Why has robust political commitment for education in Bihar not also translated into quality services? These puzzles from India's primary education sector raise larger theoretical questions about state capacity and public service delivery in developing countries.

1.4 THE LIMITS OF EXISTING EXPLANATIONS

To make sense of the aforementioned puzzles, I consulted a vast political economy literature on the state and human development. According to a prominent school of thought, modernization and economic development lead to improvements in public service delivery and attendant social outcomes (Lipset 1959; Przeworski and Limongi 1997). As an economy develops, the state accumulates resources and citizens acquire new preferences and abilities to demand primary education (Meyer, Ramirez and Soysal 1992). Some posit a virtuous cycle between growing affluence and good governance. Economic growth, the logic goes, leads to increased social spending as well as improvements in bureaucratic quality (Kurtz and Schrank 2007). Though the direction of causality is much debated – does growth lead to good governance, or vice versa? – higher income polities are expected to enjoy more and better quality public services.

With the acceleration of economic growth, social spending in India increased significantly in the 1990s. However, implementation of social programs is uneven and services remain "yoked to local public administration with weak capabilities" (Kapur, Mukhopadhyay and Subramanian 2008, 38). Several lower-income states in India have made substantial gains in primary education and other aspects of human development, outperforming wealthier states (Drèze and Sen 2002, 2013). Income growth cannot account for why an economic laggard like UP made notable gains in enrollment and infrastructure provision, while performing quite inadequately on other dimensions of implementation. Nor does rising income explain why services in UP's more affluent western belt are no better than in poorer parts of the state. Likewise, modernization does not explain why HP, a subsistence-based agricultural economy with little industrial production, outperforms other states, including Uttarakhand, which has a similar level of income and *higher* levels of urbanization and industrial development.

A second line of thinking assigns causal weight to geography and the natural environment (Nunn and Puga 2012). Herbst (2000, 13) highlights the "challenges posed by political geography" in Africa, such as low population density and physical terrain, to explain the state's uneven capacity. O'Donnell likewise contends that in emerging democracies, "the authority of the state fades off as soon as we leave the national urban centers" (1993, 1358). Accordingly, Krishna and Schober (2014) analyze the spatial "gradient of governance" in India and observe that villages further away from urban centers perform worse on multiple dimensions of governance. Village population density has a positive effect on access to public goods, suggesting that "ease of delivery" is a criterion for state provision (Banerjee and Somanathan 2007, 304). Emphasizing administrative costs and political barriers for implementation in rural locales, this research reaffirms Bates' (1981) argument of an urban bias in development. Recognizing geography's importance, the empirical cases in this book were selected to control for terrain and population density. HP performs better than other states despite comparatively low urbanization and population density, scattered settlement patterns, unfriendly climate and terrain, making it costlier to provide services. The limits of geographic explanations become apparent in the case of Uttarakhand, which performs markedly worse than HP despite similar physical characteristics.

A third branch of scholarship argues for the causal primacy of institutions (Acemoglu and Robinson 2006). The formal structure of constitutions, electoral systems, rules of federalism and executive power help explain cross-national variation in social spending and welfare outcomes (Huber, Ragin and Stephens 1993). Yet, formal institutions cannot account for variation in the performance of subnational bureaucracies operating under a common legal, fiscal and electoral framework. A distinct strand of institutionalist literature studies the long-term effects of colonial rule on development. Acemoglu and Robinson (2006) find that variation in settlement patterns of European colonizers influenced the adoption of institutions, producing lasting effects on economic performance. On similar lines, Banerjee and Iyer (2005) observe the impact of India's colonial land institutions on the provision of health and education. Regions historically subjected to *zamindari*, a system granting upper caste landlords authority over revenue collection, perform worse than places under *ryotwari*, where revenues were drawn directly from cultivators. Landlord–peasant relations in zamindari regions display persistent caste conflict, hampering collective action for public goods.

This book's empirical strategy takes colonial institutional legacies into careful consideration. My comparative cases include localities with similar (and different) types of colonial land administration, a research design that yields unanswered puzzles. I compare districts of HP and Uttarakhand having *similar* histories of direct British rule and military recruitment, but different contemporary patterns of education service delivery. I also examine districts of UP with *different* colonial land tenure systems, but similar implementation patterns. This approach does not negate the importance of colonial land institutions. It does suggest, however, that implementation is not simply the byproduct of a colonial past but tied to political and administrative activities in the postcolonial period.[14]

In sum, while prominent explanations help us understand important aspects of bureaucracy and implementation, they do not adequately address the puzzles of this book. The factors considered briefly thus far – economic development, geography, formal institutions and colonial administrative legacies – are important, but they do not fully explain variation in how states in northern India implement primary education. A new theory is needed that moves past the distant correlates of state capacity to illuminate how bureaucracy works in practice and relates to citizens on the ground.

[14] On these lines, Banerjee and Somanathan (2007) report broad convergence in public goods across Indian districts from 1971 to 2001.

1.5 THE ARGUMENT IN BRIEF

What, then, allows bureaucracies to implement primary education (more or less) effectively? Chapter 2 presents the book's theory of implementation, connecting differences in bureaucratic norms to variation in policy implementation and related outcomes for primary schooling. Bureaucratic norms are unwritten rules governing the orientations and behaviors of state officials. I argue that bureaucratic norms drive policy implementation through two channels. First, they influence the collective understandings and behaviors of officials. Given resource constraints and multiple policy rules, norms allow bureaucrats to interpret policy problems in a practical sense and determine what it means to solve them. Second, bureaucratic norms stimulate societal feedback by shaping the ordinary interactions between frontline officials and citizens. As citizens gain exposure to the local state, their experiences condition future expectations and the collective monitoring of schools, impacting the quality of services.

Drawing inspiration from interdisciplinary literatures in institutional theory, public administration and political philosophy, I argue that differences in bureaucratic norms have varying material consequences for the implementation of public services. Chapter 2 develops an analytical typology of bureaucratic norms and theorizes their effects on policy implementation. I conceptualize policy implementation based on the tasks involved in delivering services like primary education. I demarcate tasks according to their varying degrees of administrative and political complexity and create a measurement scheme sensitive to the empirical context of education in rural India. I propose two ideal types of bureaucracy governed by different sets of norms, which I refer to as "deliberative" and "legalistic," and theorize the mechanisms whereby each ideal-typical bureaucracy influences policy implementation.

I develop and test the argument in Chapters 4–7. Based on empirical materials from northern India, I connect differences in bureaucratic norms to subnational variation in implementation processes and outcomes for primary education. My comparative field research shows that deliberative bureaucracy fosters a problem-based orientation among state officials, encouraging flexibility in the interpretation of rules and robust coordination across organizational boundaries. Lower-level bureaucrats learn to discuss problems collectively with senior officials, transmitting local knowledge into hierarchical decision-making. Legalistic bureaucracy, by contrast, encourages officials to adopt a rule-based orientation, maintaining a strict interpretation of policy and well-defined organizational boundaries. Lower-level officials treat policy rules as binding constraints and seek hierarchical guidance on how to apply policies in particular cases.

Against much received wisdom, I demonstrate that legalistic bureaucracy leads to uneven policy implementation. Bureaucratic commitment to rules enables state officials to challenge political interferences, facilitating gains in enrollment and infrastructure provision. However, the bureaucracy's emphasis on rule compliance undermines monitoring of services and other complex tasks, which involve contextual information and repeated state–society interactions. Legalistic bureaucracy supports societal participation in service delivery through official channels, such as administrative grievance procedures, enabling community oversight of schools. However, these channels create administrative burdens for marginalized groups and tend to reinforce inequalities. Over time, societal input tends to become episodic and fragmented, leading to lower quality services. By contrast, I show that deliberative bureaucracy enables officials to undertake complex tasks and adapt policies to varying local needs, which yields higher quality services. Deliberation encourages officials to identify pragmatic answers to policy problems. Deliberation also widens the scope for societal participation in service delivery by fostering public discussions in more diverse spaces, helping to integrate rural women, lower castes and other marginalized groups in the routine monitoring of schools. I develop these arguments through subnational comparative field research. Analyzing implementation in the Gangetic plains (Chapters 4 and 7) and the Himalayan foothills (Chapters 5 and 6), I demonstrate how the theoretical framework distinguishing legalistic and deliberative bureaucracy is robust to differences in agrarian economies, political party systems and caste and gender norms.

If divergent bureaucratic norms lead to variation in the delivery of primary schooling, what causes the divergence in bureaucratic norms? To answer this question, I examine the historical process of subnational state-building, tracing the political origins and persistence of bureaucratic norms across time. I argue that bureaucratic norms get consolidated in the state-building process based on the collective incentives and strategies of governing elites. Periods of relative political stability offer windows of opportunity for governing elites to establish bureaucratic norms. Once introduced, bureaucratic norms are reinforced through the emergent relations between political and bureaucratic leadership. Where subnational state politicians and bureaucratic elites had incentives to compete for authority and resources, legalism became the dominant mode of bureaucracy. Under the threat of subversion from political forces, bureaucrats used administrative rules to protect bureaucratic authority from political interference. On the other hand, where political and bureaucratic leadership had strong incentives to cooperate for authority and resources, norms encouraging deliberation took hold within the bureaucracy. Faced with the acute necessity to join hands, bureaucrats learned to deliberate to solve collective problems. The empirical cases in Chapters 4–6 show that the consolidation of bureaucratic norms happened *prior to* the introduction of universal primary education policies and was exogenous to the political decision to expand primary education.[15] Once established, I find that bureaucratic norms can withstand to political changes and shifting policy commitments. I also examine processes of norm change (Chapter 7), reveals the commitment of frontline agents and the conflicts they experience.

1.5.1 Building State Capacity for Inclusive Development

This book's arguments contribute to theoretical debates surrounding the question of how states promote inclusive development. The need to make development more inclusive finds expression in Sen's (1999) capability-centered approach. Sen challenges development theory's conventional emphasis on capital accumulation and reorients it toward the expansion of human capabilities, indicated by broad-based improvements in health, education and well-being. More than mere recipients of government services, marginalized citizens are conceived as agents having a political voice in the development process. This reorientation carries political implications for bureaucracies, who in addition to providing services must enable societal participation during service delivery (Evans and Heller 2015). Sen's normative formulation of what states *ought* to do needs to be complemented with an analytical framework for what states *can* do to make development more inclusive. Here, Ostrom's (1996) theory of "coproduction" elegantly brings state–society relations

[15] I do not suggest that primary education expansion has no impact on bureaucratic norms. As theorized in Chapter 2, the mechanism of societal feedback reinforces bureaucratic norms and augments their impact on service delivery.

to the fore, suggesting that states can draw productively from a constellation of non-state actors. Coproduction is not only a technique of governance but also a set of institutionalized relationships between the state and society, with attendant power differences and conflicts (Joshi and Moore 2004).

The "Sen-Ostrom vision" is transformative, Evans, Huber and Stephens (2017) suggest, but it raises questions about what kinds of bureaucratic arrangements support inclusive development. This book aims to help answer these questions. Bringing diverse scholarly traditions into conversation, my argument connecting bureaucratic norms to policy implementation advances literatures on state capacity, social welfare and public service delivery. Modern states are responsible for multiple policy functions. They have to protect external borders, maintain internal order and security, regulate the economy and provide public goods. As Skocpol writes, states must possess multiple "*capacities*" (emphasis in original), the study of which requires sector-specific analysis (1985, 17). In developing countries, Kohli (1987, 2004) adds, states need to facilitate income growth and poverty alleviation. Accordingly, the "developmental state" literature has shown how states promote industrial development and rapid growth (Haggard 2018). Autonomous, Weberian bureaucracies have played an integral part in this process. Along with autonomy, Evans (1995) suggests, developmental states are embedded in networks, facilitating coordination with industrial capitalists.

Developmental state scholarship has shed much-needed light on bureaucracy's contributions to economic growth. However, the inclusive development agenda calls attention to the welfare needs of mass publics, which present different challenges for the state. Bureaucracies have to penetrate hard-to-reach geographies and coordinate with society on a much larger scale. To sustain coproduction of services, bureaucracy cannot always rely on preexisting societal networks, which can be fragmented or exclusionary (Mansuri and Rao 2013). Instead, bureaucracy needs to seek out marginalized groups and counter entrenched inequalities to secure their participation. To undertake these tasks, state agencies have to motivate "street-level bureaucrats," who possess wide discretion over the interpretation of policy rules (Lipsky 1980).

Another vast literature, on clientelism and distributive politics, is less optimistic about bureaucracy's ability to promote inclusive development (Kitschelt and Wilkinson 2007; Hicken 2011). In contrast to high-powered agencies overseeing industrial policy, quotidian bureaucracies that deliver social services tend to lack Weberian characteristics and are more often enmeshed in particularistic exchanges (Grindle 2012; Brun and Diamond 2014). Rather than being a source of capability, bureaucratic discretion in the latter instances is associated with political interference and capture (Piore 2011). Institutional reforms designed to motivate frontline bureaucrats and curb malfeasance, through pecuniary rewards and monitoring, have shown mixed results (Pepinsky, Pierskalla and Sacks 2017).

To secure the kind of bureaucratic initiative that inclusive development requires, "getting the incentives right" is not enough (Levi and Sherman 1997, 332). Where formal authority structures are comparatively weak, the informal rules of the game can help bolster bureaucratic commitment (Helmke and Levitsky 2004). Bureaucratic norms bind officials to a common purpose. They provide a shared grammar to make sense of policy mandates and negotiate conflicts on the job, eliciting commitment to collective goals. The nature of these commitments can vary, however, and their efficacy depends on the administrative task at hand. Deliberative bureaucracy's advantages stem from its ability to solve complex problems, which call for repeated interactions between officials and coordination across different levels of the state.

State action is essential but insufficient for realizing inclusive development. My theorization of societal feedback arises from the need for "bottom up" collective action as well (Banerjee, Iyer and Somanathan 2007), which is particularly challenging to sustain in settings of inequality (Heller and Rao 2015). I build on the insights of the "policy feedback" literature, which suggests that policies can have varied political effects on citizen perceptions, interests and mobilization over time (Pierson 1993; Mettler 2002; Campbell 2005; Kumlin and Rothstein 2005; MacLean 2010). Showcasing how bureaucratic norms induce varied responses from society during *implementation*, my argument brings the literature on policy feedback into dialogue with public administration research on local state–society interactions (Moynihan and Soss 2014). I suggest that legalistic and deliberative bureaucracies offer different administrative channels for societal participation in service delivery. These channels create distinct learning opportunities for marginalized citizens (Lawless and Fox 2001), as well as administrative burdens when they attempt to monitor services (Herd and Moynihan 2018), which has ramifications in turn for how they "see" the state (Corbridge et al. 2005).

1.6 RESEARCH DESIGN AND METHODOLOGY

This book's theory was developed and tested using a multilevel comparative research design. I trace the implementation process from political centers down to rural districts, villages and primary schools. This section explains the rationale for multilevel comparisons and my case selection strategy. It gives an overview of the qualitative data collected from ethnographic fieldwork, including participant observation, in-depth interviews, oral histories and focus group discussions. A detailed exposition of field methods, including information on research sites and the selection of study respondents is contained in the Appendix.

1.6.1 Multilevel Comparative Analysis

Comparative scholarship on social policy has identified the state as the chief actor in service provision (Heclo 1974; Esping-Anderson 1990; Skocpol 1992).[16] While revealing important cross-national patterns, less attention has been accorded to subnational variation in the implementation of services. Yet, countries display large subnational differences in social welfare provision and outcomes. Studies have leveraged subnational comparative research designs fruitfully to explain these variations (Weitz-Shapiro 2014; Singh 2016). Subnational comparative research has shed light on wide-ranging phenomena, from economic development and public goods provision to voting behavior and ethnic violence (Snyder 2001).[17] Subnational comparison allows us to hold constant explanatory factors that are shared by subnational political units (e.g., regime type, constitutional-legal framework, national policies and formal state institutions) that can plausibly affect implementation. Taking subnational comparison one step further, this book's methodological approach embraces multilevel comparative analysis, which involves the theoretically guided study of decisions and actions at multiple jurisdictions of the state. Combining controlled comparisons with systematic process-tracing, it aims to uncover the causal mechanisms for multilevel processes, such as policy implementation, and explain variation in outcomes.

[16] See the review by Skocpol and Amenta (1986).

[17] India has provided fertile ground for subnational comparative research. See, for example, Varshney (2002), Chandra (2004), Thachil (2014), Singh (2016) and Ahuja (2019).

My approach answers the need to examine interrelationships between levels of the state, as well as between state and society. Bringing the *vertical* dimension of governance into focus, multilevel comparative analysis offers advantages for the study of policy implementation.[18] First, it addresses the empirical reality of public service delivery in much of the world. In recent waves of decentralization, countries have transferred political and administrative authority to lower-level jurisdictions. Yet, the intergovernmental balance of power is not settled by constitutional edict. Decentralization is politically contested, shifting and often incomplete (Falleti 2010). In a multilevel federation such as India, Sinha notes, "policy implementation is the product of intergovernmental interaction" (2003, 466).[19] Administrative processes operating across tiers of the state invite opportunities for coordination as well as conflict.

India's social policy sector is a prime example of contested decentralization. Federalism under India's constitution grants state (or provincial) governments primary authority to legislate and implement social policy. A constitutional amendment in 1976 placed education policy under the joint legislative jurisdiction of the central and state governments. Since then, India's central government has enlarged its bargaining power and administrative presence, using centrally sponsored programs, discretionary fiscal transfers and other mechanisms to gain political leverage over state governments (Chhibber, Shastri and Sisson 2004; Tillin 2016). State governments hold chief authority over the implementation of primary schooling, but they do not have free rein. They are constrained from above by central administrative oversight and resource allocations. They also depend on the cooperation of frontline bureaucracies. To reach citizens, social programs have to pass through the "eye of the needle," which is the local district administration (Kapur and Mukhopadhyay 2007).[20] In addition, the 73rd and 74th Amendments to India's constitution, enacted in 1992, devolved authority to Panchayati Raj Institutions, elected village and municipal councils, a new layer of local authority over public goods and services.[21]

18 As Snyder suggests, subnational comparison "can help us build theories that explain the dynamic interconnections among the levels and regions of a political system." (2001, 100).

19 For related work on multilevel governance, see Hooghe and Marks (2003) and Piattoni (2010).

20 By the 2011 Census, India had 709 districts with an average population of 1.7 million.

21 Panchayats vary in their efficacy, contributing to spatial differences in public goods provision. See Betancourt and Gleason (2000) and Besley, Pande and Rao (2007).

Multilevel comparison opens new theoretical and methodological avenues as well. The tension between "top-down" control and "bottom-up" discretion by frontline agents is a recurring theme in policy implementation research (O'Brien and Li 1999). In a parallel debate, the political economy literature explores the relative importance of state initiatives from above and societal collective action for public goods provision (Banerjee, Iyer and Somanathan 2007). These tensions reflect the fact that authority is situated in more than one place. The state has "many centers of decision-making that are formally independent of each other," but the extent to which they "actually function independently, or instead constitute an interdependent system of relations" is an empirical question (Ostrom, Tiebout and Warren 1961, 831). Studies concentrating on elite decisions, at the national (or subnational) level, risk overstating the power of the "center," omitting authority-holders in the "periphery" who can refashion policy in unanticipated ways. On the other hand, attention to the micro-politics of implementation risks neglecting the background institutions that can impact the work of street-level bureaucrats. Multilevel comparison calls attention to how different nodes of state authority interact to influence policies and politics. This *relational* treatment of the state also has methodological advantages. Investigating implementation over multiple tiers of the state increases the number of observations as well as the variety of sociopolitical contexts in which causal mechanisms are tested. Different observable implications of a theory can be probed, allowing multiple forms of evidence to corroborate or falsify causal hypotheses (Gerring 2004). Theory testing against rival explanations at different units of analysis helps to refine and strengthen the robustness of causal claims.

1.6.2 Case Selection

With these considerations in mind, I chose to investigate primary education in a small number of carefully selected states and rural locales in northern India. Existing studies have highlighted the differences between India's "backward" northern Hindi belt and the more "progressive" southern states (Mehrotra 2006; Singh 2016). However, meaningful variation exists within northern India, a region that has also seen important changes in recent decades. The four states selected for protracted investigation are HP, Uttarakhand, UP and Bihar (see map in Figure 1.1).

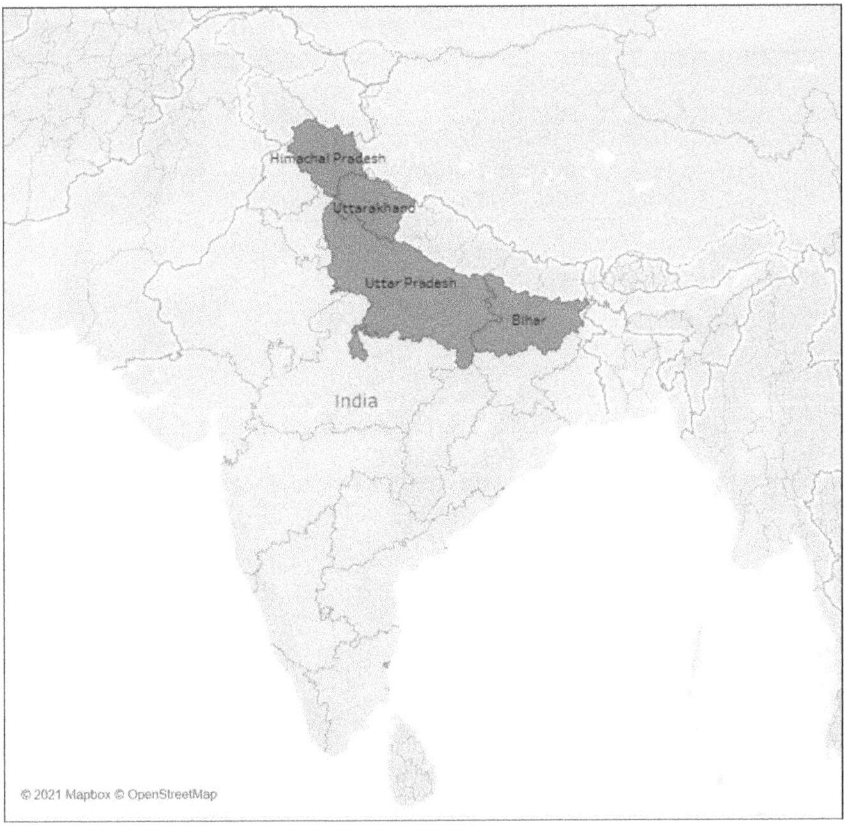

FIGURE 1.1 Map of case study states in India
Source: © Mapbox, © OpenStreetMap

These four states exhibit important similarities and differences on key demographic and socio-economic variables (see Tables 1.1 and 1.2). These states were selected to allow for rigorous theory testing through controlled comparisons, ensuring the internal validity of findings, while also permitting the construction of a general theory. Controlled comparisons are useful in qualitative, small-N research, permitting "intense theoretical engagement" with rival hypotheses to establish validity (Slater and Ziblatt 2013, 13). The states and local districts were chosen to probe my theory against alternative explanations for implementation.

Concentrating on these four states permits a close engagement with the politics and sociocultural context of northern India. Context is

TABLE 1.1 *Demographic indicators of case study states (2011)*

	Population (millions)	Annual population growth rate[1] (%)	Rural population (%)	Population density (pop. per km^2)	Scheduled castes (%)	Scheduled tribes (%)
Himachal Pradesh	6.9	1.4	90.2	109	25.2	5.7
Uttarakhand	10.1	1.8	69.8	159	18.8	2.9
Uttar Pradesh	199.8	2.1	77.7	690	20.7	0.06
Bihar	104.1	2.4	88.7	881	15.9	1.3

Note:
1. Population growth rate is the annualized average for 1991–2011.
Source: Census of India 1999, 2001 and 2011.

TABLE 1.2 *Socioeconomic indicators of case study states (1990–2011)*

	Income per capita[1] (₹)	Annual income growth[2] (%)	Poverty rate[3] (%)	Literacy rate[4] (%)	Sex ratio (females per 1,000 males)
Himachal Pradesh	37,078	5.2	25.9	82.8	972
Uttarakhand	32,934	5.7	27.4	78.9	963
Uttar Pradesh	14,430	2.6	35.5	67.7	912
Bihar	9,383	3.6	56.1	61.8	918

Note:
1. Income per capita is based on the Net State Domestic Product (NSDP) averaged over 2004–2010, at constant 2004–2005 prices.
Source: Planning Commission of India.
2. Income growth is the annual growth rate of per capita NSDP for 1993–2010.
Source: Kumar and Subramanian (2012, 49).
3. Poverty rate based on the Tendulkar Committee poverty estimation method, taken as the average rate over 1993–1994, 2004–2005 and 2009–2010.
Source: India Planning Commission.
4. Literacy rate and sex ratio are for the adult population.
Source: Census of India 2011.

critical in the study of implementation (Grindle 1980). The same policies can stimulate very different political meanings and conflicts across settings, which raises the inescapable challenge of analytical equivalence in comparative politics. The risk of neglecting differences in political meaning is recognized in cross-national comparative research (Locke and Thelen 1995). However, subnational comparisons are not immune to these pitfalls, especially in a country as large and culturally heterogeneous as India. For example, while caste and gender discrimination has pervaded India's education system, the nature of social norms and discrimination differs throughout the country (Drèze and Kingdon 2001). More generally, interdisciplinary research on governance and collective welfare suggests that local political dynamics and sociocultural practices influence how citizens participate in and experience public services (Rao and Walton 2004; Hall and Lamont 2009). Attention to these contextual differences improves the descriptive accuracy of cases and validity of comparisons. Equally, it facilitates the identification of causal relationships. As Falleti and Lynch propose, "causation resides in the interaction between the mechanism and the context within which it operates" (2009, 1145).[22] My selection of north Indian states permits a close exploration of meanings and other contextual factors operating alongside causal mechanisms to shape implementation.

Ensuring that cases vary on outcomes of interest is a cardinal principal of case selection (Gerring 2004). The states of HP, Uttarakhand, UP and Bihar exhibit wide variation in outcomes for primary schooling, as the data presented in Chapter 2 will demonstrate. The selection of states and localities also presents theoretical conundrums for existing literature. Mountainous and landlocked, HP is one of India's top-performing states in primary education. Uttarakhand exhibits markedly worse outcomes, despite having similar geographic, economic and sociocultural features to HP, as well as an historical lead in literacy. UP and Bihar are among India's weakest performers in primary education. However, against theoretical expectations, UP has made considerable progress in the last two decades, improving access, enrollment and infrastructure, though the quality of services remains poor. More recently, Bihar too has recorded noteworthy gains in enrollment and infrastructure provision, but the quality of services lags considerably, despite political commitment to education from the state government.

To discern causal mechanisms for implementation, the research design controls for certain explanatory factors, including formal institutions and colonial administrative legacies. The four study states have common political, bureaucratic and constitutional-legal structures. Formal bureaucratic systems and procedures are the same, enabling the identification of

[22] Also see George and Bennett (2005, 19–21).

differences in *in*formal bureaucratic norms. Government bureaucrats and schoolteachers are hired through common selection rules and have similar employment conditions, civil service protections, training and standards for pay and promotion. Officers in the Indian Administrative Service (IAS), the elite national civil service cadre, are recruited by competitive examination and assigned by lottery to states.[23] Once deployed, IAS officers work in the same state for most of their careers. Lower-level bureaucrats working in education and other social policy functions likewise get recruited by state-level public service commissions and do not move from their assigned states. However, bureaucrats can and do get transferred to different locations and administrative posts *within* their assigned states, sometimes for political reasons (Iyer and Mani 2011). These administrative conditions allow informal bureaucratic norms to vary and propagate differently across Indian states.

As with any inductive study, the research design must also confront difficulties of generalizability. To generalize over a country as large and diverse as India is a fraught enterprise. Guided by theory and political history, I chose cases that reflect important aspects of public administration in India. I began the study in UP, a state that could be the world's seventh largest country, more populous than Brazil or Nigeria. The case of UP brings out the challenge of implementation on a large scale.[24] UP's geography fluctuates from fertile Gangetic plains to drought-prone flatlands. Home to hundreds of castes, ethnolinguistic groups and a large Muslim population, UP is the political epicenter of the Hindi heartland. Its significance for national politics is unrivaled, having produced many prime ministers and national policymakers (Kudaisya 2002). Historically, UP adopted a "law and order" bureaucracy, once seen as a model for the rest of India (Kohli 1987). After a period of Congress Party dominance, UP state politics shifted to multiparty coalitions in the 1980s, a pattern followed by India's central government. To use Gerring's phrase, UP represents a "paradigm case" of legalistic bureaucracy in India, which can illuminate how legalism operates elsewhere in the country. It also constitutes a theoretically "least-likely case" for public service delivery. Explanations for implementation failure find their most favored terrain in UP. The colonial land revenue system in UP (zamindari) is associated with persistent inequality and the undersupply of public goods (Banerjee

23 The lottery system for IAS deployment helps ensure that Indian states have an equal chance of receiving high caliber officers. On IAS selection and posting rules, see Krishna (2010).

24 I thank Devesh Kapur for alerting me to the importance of scale for governance in India.

and Iyer 2005). UP is also the exemplar of Chandra's (2004) notion of "patronage democracy." Caste politics in UP is seen to exacerbate social divisions and corruption (Jeffrey 2002). If bureaucratic mechanisms are found to support implementation in UP, they have a strong chance of succeeding elsewhere. Within UP, I studied local districts (Saharanpur and Sitapur) in very different socioeconomic and cultural regions, helping to identify bureaucratic mechanisms operating across the state.

My arguments also leverage a matched-pair comparison of HP and Uttarakhand. These contiguous states in the Himalayan region were selected to hold several explanatory factors constant, such as geography, agrarian economy, social structure and party system. Less populous (by Indian standards), these states have income levels, poverty rates and other socioeconomic indicators that are comparable. The comparison of HP and Uttarakhand also controls for sociocultural norms, an important but understudied variable in public goods provision (Rao and Walton 2004). The hill-based (*Pahari*) communities in the two states share similar customs, languages and religious practices, such as deity (*devta*) worship. Crucially, they have similar caste and gender norms, which may influence access to education. To ensure valid local-level comparisons, I selected administrative districts (Shimla in HP and Almora in Uttarakhand) with similar geographies, agrarian economies, caste structures and political party systems. Historically, both districts were directly governed by the British and were prime locations for military recruitment, which may have increased the demand for education (Eynde 2016). Following field visits and interviews with state officials, I selected three villages in each district for prolonged research. Village case selection accounted for population size, caste composition and distance from town centers and major roads.[25] A further innovation in my research design, I exploit the fact that, prior to becoming a separate state in 2000, Uttarakhand was part of UP for more than five decades after independence. Despite their very different economic and socio-demographic indicators, UP and Uttarakhand are bound by a shared political and administrative history. The political rupture caused by Uttarakhand's separation presents a rare opportunity to test for whether and how bureaucratic norms persist and shape implementation within a new political environment. To strengthen the validity of local-level comparison, I studied districts on either side of the UP–Uttarakhand border (Saharanpur and Dehradun).

[25] See the Appendix for details on study districts and villages.

The multilevel comparative approach of this book demands this kind of rigorous attention to context. My main empirical findings suggest that bureaucratic norms persist and produce lasting effects on implementation, but I also investigate norm change through the analysis of institutional reforms in UP and the adjacent state of Bihar. Bihar's human development performance ranks at the bottom among Indian states and the state long suffered from lawlessness, corruption and divisive caste politics. However, a political turnaround took place in the early 2000s, ushering in a period of relative stability that brought new state leadership committed to improving governance and public goods provision. I study the implementation of institutional reforms for education in Bihar alongside reforms undertaken in UP. In the late-1990s, the central government launched the Mahila Samakhya program in UP. Like the Bihar reforms, the Mahila Samakhya program sought to increase school participation among disadvantaged girls and improve the quality of services. The comparison of reform implementation in Bihar and UP allows me to hone in on mechanisms of bureaucratic norm change in the least likely settings.

1.6.3 Data and Methods

This book examines the state up close. The findings are based on intensive qualitative field research, combined with analysis of official documents, administrative data and archival sources. The qualitative data was collected during twenty-eight months of fieldwork between 2007 and 2011 and between 2013 and 2014. I employed multiple field methods to open up the "black box" of the bureaucracy and examine local state–society interactions. These methods included in-depth interviews and focus groups discussions (in Hindi) of various state and societal actors in education, participant observation with frontline officials and ethnographies conducted at the village and school level. The Appendix details my qualitative methods and gives a summary of local field sites and the sample of interview respondents. Each method had its advantages and limitations, but triangulation across methods helped substantiate the presence of bureaucratic norms and rule out alternative explanations, strengthening the overall findings (Denzin 2012). For instance, the weaving together of interviews with participant observation of frontline bureaucrats allowed me to probe discrepancies between "what they say" and "what they do" (Brodkin 2008, 330). The inclusion of citizen perspectives on the state also presented an important check on the information given by bureaucrats.

I performed ethnographic fieldwork at multiple administrative levels, from subnational state capitals to administrative districts, and ultimately, village primary schools. In summary, I conducted 507 interviews of state actors (e.g. state and local bureaucrats, politicians and schoolteachers), 346 interviews with non-state actors (e.g., parents, village residents, unelected village leaders and civic agencies) and 103 focus group discussions with bureaucrats, teachers, parents and other village residents. Field research was supplemented by the systematic review of government documents (e.g. administrative reports and circulars), administrative data, media reports and a combination of primary and secondary historical sources. In all four states, I lived within or close to local field sites. My full-time presence in the field facilitated immersion into the social life of rural services, enabling a first-hand account of India's bureaucracy and primary school system.

1.7 PLAN OF THE BOOK

In seeking to explain subnational variation in the delivery of primary education in northern India, this book builds and tests a theory connecting differences in bureaucratic norms to varying patterns of implementation. The arguments are structured into three parts. Part 1 (Chapters 1–3) introduces the empirical puzzles and research design, theoretical arguments and institutional context for primary education in India. Chapter 2 presents my theoretical framework. I conceptualize policy implementation and introduce a measurement scheme that captures the variation in primary education outcomes in northern India. Next, I theorize bureaucratic norms and their influence on bureaucratic behavior. I develop the theoretical ideal types of legalistic and deliberative bureaucracy and delineate the causal mechanisms by which they produce differences in policy implementation. Moving up the causal chain, I theorize the political origins and propagation of bureaucratic norms, which I connect to historical processes of state-building. I then discuss my theory's scope conditions and consider alternative political explanations for observed differences in implementation. Chapter 3 sets the empirical stage for the study, exploring the Indian state's shifting involvement in primary education since independence, focusing on the recent period since economic liberalization. I examine the political currents behind the expansion of national education programming. I also introduce the formal administrative architecture for service provision, common across the four states that I studied, paving the way for an analysis of informal bureaucratic norms.

Part 2 (Chapters 4–7) presents the book's main empirical findings. I explore the political origins of bureaucratic norms within each state as well as the contemporary context of implementation. Next, I present empirical materials from multilevel comparative field research to show how bureaucratic norms operate and affect the delivery of primary schooling. Through nested case studies, cutting across state-, district- and village-level administration, I show how bureaucratic norms influence the performance of different administrative tasks, while testing for alternative explanations. Chapter 4 begins by analyzing legalistic bureaucracy in the Gangetic plains of UP. I trace the origins of legalism back to the late-nineteenth century colonial ideal of a "law and order" state, later reinforced by governing elites competing for state control. I then show how legalistic bureaucracy has facilitated gains in school infrastructure and enrollment, while concurrently producing low quality services. Village-level case studies reveal that while legalistic processes of grievance redressal encourage societal participation they systematically burden marginalized citizens and reinforce social inequalities, weakening community oversight of primary schooling.

Chapters 5 and 6 examine implementation in the Himalayan region, leveraging a matched-pair comparison of HP and Uttarakhand. Chapter 5 connects HP's improbable achievements in primary education to the establishment of a deliberative bureaucracy. I trace the origins of deliberation in HP to collective action by political and bureaucratic elites during the 1970s, spurred by the state's political marginalization and acute need for central government fiscal support. Next, I show how deliberation unfolds inside state agencies and helps officials overcome a series of governance challenges, allowing them to adapt primary education to meet local needs. Village case studies demonstrate how deliberative bureaucracy helps sustain community monitoring of schools, leading to better quality services. Chapter 6 examines the comparative case of Uttarakhand, which has similar economic and sociocultural characteristics but performs significantly worse in delivering education. I show that, despite the political separation of Uttarakhand from UP in 2000, legalistic bureaucracy has persisted in Uttarakhand, producing a pattern of uneven implementation. Village case studies reveal that, while households voiced demands for better public services, their efforts were stymied by administrative burdens, inducing some to exit the government system and seek private schooling.

Chapter 7 revisits the Gangetic plains region to study the implementation of institutional reforms in UP and Bihar. In UP, I show how Mahila

Samakhya, a central government program for women's empowerment, promoted deliberation among frontline workers, who in turn mobilized village women's associations to integrate disadvantaged girls into school. Fieldwork performed in three UP districts shows how deliberative bureaucracy manages social conflicts around girls' education under conditions of entrenched social inequality. By contrast, Bihar's institutional turnaround in the 2000s was initiated by the state's political leadership, which was committed to improving governance and public services. I show how a broad institutional conversion to legalism took place within the bureaucracy, contributing to improved enrollments, school access and teacher recruitment. However, efforts to enhance the quality of education faltered, despite state commitment and sharing of "best practices" by education experts. I argue that frontline officials and schoolteachers experienced conflicts between the rules-based orientation of legalistic bureaucracy and the flexibility required to adopt new, innovative classroom teaching practices.

Part 3 examines the wider implications of the book for theory and policy. Chapter 8 situates the book's arguments in a comparative perspective, examining cases beyond northern India. I explore a set of shadow cases, selected to cover a wide range of sociopolitical contexts: the south Indian state of Kerala, along with country-level cases of China, Finland and France. In Kerala, I show that deliberative bureaucracy has evolved alongside lower caste social movements, contributing to superior education outcomes within India. In the case of China, I explore how deliberative bureaucracy operates in a non-democratic environment, highlighting the adaptive and flexible models of bureaucratic governance that have shaped the delivery of education. Next, through a comparative assessment of school education in the advanced economies of Finland and France, I consider how divergent bureaucratic norms contribute to varying patterns of education service delivery, even in places with strong formal institutions. I conclude in Chapter 9 by examining the book's contributions to scholarship and implications for policy. The argument connecting bureaucratic norms to policy implementation advances our understanding of institutions, social welfare and local state–society relations. For policy, I suggest how institutional reforms may help stimulate deliberation to improve the quality of public services and promote inclusive development.

2

Bureaucratic Norms

A Theory of Implementation

> The central problem of planning is increasingly that of implementation, and the problems of implementation are essentially those of politics, social organization and cultural values ... The result is often a great hiatus between law and reality, between what is willed by the national leadership and what is done at the local level, between the high ideals in New Delhi and the cynicism in the mofussil towns.
>
> – Myron Weiner (1962, 239)

2.1 INTRODUCTION

In developing countries, the enactment of public policy is not the end of politics, but often just the beginning. Marginalized citizens struggle to obtain essential services, their experiences made contingent on the behavior of street-level bureaucrats. Chapter 1 introduced the contemporary challenge of implementing primary education in India. Implementation hurdles have long occupied India's state planners. In his pioneering studies of Indian politics, Myron Weiner (1962, 1991) observed striking deficiencies in the law's implementation, the hiatus between what he called the "rhetoric" of rights etched in the Indian Constitution and the "reality" of service delivery in the rural hinterlands. His explanation for these gaps emphasized cultural values rooted in the unequal social order of caste, which legitimated state inaction and dampened bureaucratic motivation to secure the welfare of disadvantaged children. The discriminatory structures of caste and patriarchy continue to have a pernicious influence in India. Yet, subaltern groups have mobilized in many places, demanding education and other social rights from the state (Heller 1999;

Kruks-Wisner 2018; Ahuja 2019; Auerbach 2019). India also displays large subnational differences in social service provision, which cultural arguments are hard-pressed to explain (Mehrotra 2006; Singh 2016).

Cultural explanations for the state's lackluster performance have given way to an emphasis on electoral incentives. Voter–politician relations in India are found to be clientelist, anchored on the exchange of targeted goods, disconnected from programmatic public services (Keefer and Khemani 2004). Indian elections are fought on ethnic lines and politicians appeal to narrow identities to compete for votes, rather than social policy platforms (Chandra 2004). Caught in the clutches of clientelism, bureaucrats are expected to surrender their discretion to political forces. Yet, social services do not flow like water from a tap, for politicians to turn on or off at will. Implementation operates through complex webs of institutional rules, resources and relationships, involving a constellation of state and societal actors. Moreover, programmatic services do sometimes reach citizens, despite great odds.

This chapter takes up the challenge of explaining how developing country states implement services like primary education, and why some do so more effectively than others. My argument casts light on the quotidian bureaucracies that interact with citizens regularly, transforming social policies into concrete services. I advance a theory centered on differences in bureaucratic norms, the unwritten rules of the game, that guide the internal behavior of bureaucrats and their external relations with society. Bureaucratic norms influence how state officials collectively interpret and enact their policy mandates. They also condition citizen expectations and collective strategies for monitoring services, thereby impacting the quality of services and associated outcomes. My framework proposes two ideal types, legalistic and deliberative bureaucracy, and theorizes the mechanisms through which they drive implementation to yield divergent outcomes for primary education. Whereas a venerable scholarship on bureaucracy and the rule of law recommends legalistic bureaucracy as an antidote to laxity and the surest path to effective implementation, I argue instead that deliberative bureaucracy has distinct advantages for the delivery of complex services like primary education. Drawing on disciplinarily diverse literatures on institutions, organizational theory and policy feedback, I argue that deliberative bureaucracy enables officials to undertake complex tasks and sustain societal monitoring, generating higher quality services.

In what follows, I first unpack the concept of policy implementation and operationalize it for the domain of public services like primary education. I then present comparative indicators that capture the varied performance of primary education across states in northern India, the empirical puzzle motivating this book. Next, I develop a theory that elucidates the differences in bureaucratic norms and the mechanisms by which they produce variation in implementation patterns and outcomes. I then examine the political origins of bureaucratic norms, which I argue, diverge depending on the historical processes of state-building at the subnational level and the incentives and strategies of governing elites in relation to the central state. I also highlight how my theoretical argument differs from prior approaches to bureaucracy and development. I then flesh out the scope conditions of the theory and contrast it with alternative political explanations for the implementation of public services.

Implementing primary education and other capability-enhancing services presents enormous challenges for developing country states (Evans and Heller 2015). I do not suggest that bureaucratic norms always constitute the best or only answer to these challenges. Nor should an appreciation of bureaucratic commitment blind us to bureaucracy's defects. Recognizing that bureaucracies are collective agencies bound by norms enlarges our theoretical vocabulary and suggests new institutional pathways for services to reach citizens.

2.2 POLICY IMPLEMENTATION: CONCEPTS AND MEASURES

The growing scholarship on state capacity and institutional performance in developing countries has spawned a lively debate on what it means to govern well.[1] Beyond academia, international development agencies like the World Bank have promoted a "good governance" agenda, commissioning studies and conferences around institutional efficiency, transparency and accountability (Kaufman 2005). Governance refers to the ability of the state to formulate and implement policy rules on society (Fukuyama 2013). This book deals with the latter process, though the line between policy choice and implementation is often ambiguous. In this section, I conceptualize policy implementation and then operationalize it for the policy domain of primary education. I also present comparative education indicators for the empirical context of northern India, showcasing the divergence in outcomes across states.

[1] See the literature reviews on state capacity and bureaucratic service delivery by Pepinsky, Pierskalla and Sacks (2017), Berwick and Christia (2018) and Khemani (2019).

2.2.1 Conceptualizing Implementation

Until recently, implementation captured little attention from the scholarship on institutions. Research was dominated by questions of institutional choice, how elites design the "rules of the game" to facilitate and constrain behavior (North 1990). Inspired by the New Institutional Economics, institutions were analyzed in relation to their influence over market failures and collective decisions (Williamson 2000). How institutions function on a quotidian basis, that is, how institutional agents interpret and enact the rules of the game, was accorded less attention. Expectations about strong formal institutions in advanced economies, "characterized by a tight coupling between formal rules and actual behavior," may have led scholars to eschew these questions (Levitsky and Murillo 2009, 117).[2] On the other hand, comparative and historical institutionalists have recognized that the rules of the game do not mechanically sustain themselves. Studies of institutional persistence and change have explored how agents make sense of the rules and negotiate conflicts over their interpretation (Mahoney and Thelen 2010). The assumption of tightly coupled rules and behavior, even in comparatively "strong" institutional environments, has been questioned. As Thelen writes, "rules are never 'simply' applied, they are always interpreted, enforced and enacted, and, of course, by actors who have divergent and conflicting interests" (2009, 490–491). Questions of rule interpretation are familiar to those holding a sociological lens to institutional analysis (DiMaggio and Powell 1983). Institutions are vested with meanings that fundamentally shape political interests and behavior (March and Olsen 1989, 48).

Implementation is of central concern to the literature on state capacity and social welfare. In developing countries, where institutions are comparatively weak and administrative resources limited, implementation is a political act with direct material consequences for citizens (Grindle 1980).[3] Building on Mann's (1984) notion of state infrastructural power, I define policy implementation as the series of tasks undertaken by individuals and groups for achieving the state's policy objectives over

[2] Hall and Taylor (1996) outline three schools of institutionalism: rational choice, historical and sociological. The "tight coupling between formal rules and actual behavior" is perhaps most salient in rational choice approaches, which theorize institutions as systems producing equilibrium order.

[3] Also see Van Meter and Van Horn (1975), Sabatier and Mazmanian (1979) and Pressman and Wildavsky (1984).

its territory. This definition presumes that policies are formulated and reflect the goals of the state.[4] The territorial dimension of implementations points to subnational differences in the state's ability to deliver services (Soifer and vom Hau 2008). Territorial unevenness and regional variation in state capacity is well recognized by scholars of comparative politics (O'Donnell 1993; Ziblatt 2008; Niedzwiecki 2018). Adding to this, I emphasize the multiplicity of tasks, following the work of public administration scholars. Brehm and Gates (1999, 63) suggest that tasks are "the fundamental unit of bureaucratic organization," an idea traceable to Adam Smith's conception of division of labor.[5] However, unlike Smith's hypothetical pin factory, which divided labor into a few discrete tasks (e.g., cutting the wire and assembling the pinhead), the implementation of services involves many interrelated tasks of varying complexity. The notion of task complexity builds on Simon's (1965) theoretical distinction between "programmable" and "nonprogrammable" decisions, which differ according to their cognitive and administrative complexity.

Attention to the multiplicity of tasks involved in public service delivery is also warranted in light of the *politics* of implementation. Fundamentally, implementation is a political process connecting policy decisions to concrete services and outcomes for citizens. As Kramon and Posner (2013) suggest, studies based on a single policy outcome indicator (e.g., rates of literacy or school enrollment) risk making incomplete or distorted conclusions about distributive politics. Restating their argument from a task-based perspective, because the political dilemmas of implementation vary between tasks, focusing on one task (or implementation indicator) limits our understanding of the wider politics at play. In education policy, the provision of primary, secondary or tertiary schooling presents distinct political tradeoffs for the state (Kosack 2012). Within the primary education arena, studies show that the politics of encouraging enrollments can differ from the politics of infrastructure provision (Harding and Stasavage 2014), which differs from the politics of schoolteacher management (Ramachandran et al. 2018), which again can differ from the

[4] Mann's concept of infrastructural power can be differentiated from Putnam's (1994, 8–9) notion of "institutional performance," which incorporates both policy formulation and implementation. For Mann, policy formulation is a separate activity, indicating the state's *despotic* power, that is, the ability to make autonomous decisions. Fukuyama (2013) sharpens the state autonomy–capacity distinction and explores its interrelationships. Also see the helpful discussion in Hanson and Sigman (2013).

[5] Brehm and Gates cite James Q. Wilson's formulation that "[p]eople matter, but organizations matter also, and tasks matter most of all" (1989, 173).

politics underlying quality-oriented school reforms (Bruns, Macdonald and Schneider 2019). A multidimensional perspective equips us to see the wider political forest and identify potential conflicts and tradeoffs that different tasks present for the state.

In addition to tasks, my understanding of implementation places the spotlight on the role of *society*. Recognizing that the boundary between the state and society can be porous, Evans (1995, 12) argues that state "embeddedness" in society improves industrial policymaking by creating "institutionalized channels for the continual negotiation and renegotiation of goals and policies." The notion of embeddedness may be even more applicable to the implementation of public services, which involves street-level bureaucrats, who regularly interact with citizens (Lipsky 1980).[6] Moreover, as Ostrom's (1996) agenda-setting work demonstrates, public services are not simply provided by state agencies but "co-produced" with societal groups. Studies suggest that institutionalized forms of coproduction can lead to better schools, more dependable health clinics and safer factories (Joshi and Moore 2004).

However, coproduction is more than an efficient technique of governance. It invites power differences and conflicts, among societal actors as well as between the state and society (Cornwall and Gaventa 2000). Primary schooling, for instance, requires joint effort by teachers, administrators, parents and children, as well as from the wider communities in which schools are embedded. The political interests and capabilities of these participants may vary and conflict. Teachers are more likely to organize themselves into unions, improving their bargaining position vis-à-vis parents.[7] In unequal societies, such as rural India, poor households, lower castes and rural women often face exclusionary norms that obstruct their full participation in service delivery (Heller and Rao 2015). Where patriarchy is pronounced, the educational interests of girls can take a back seat, even when societal participation is robust (Drèze and Kingdon 2001). Coproduction can also spawn elite backlash, as when policies challenge status quo norms in society. Applying a political lens to coproduction thus raises thornier questions of how bureaucracies relate to marginalized groups and whether frontline officials work to counter (or reinforce) power imbalances during implementation.

6 Evans (2004, 2015) has extended the embeddedness argument to cover human development. Bhavnani and Lee (2018) show that officer embeddedness in India's higher civil service improves public goods provision.

7 See the comparative literature on teacher unions and education reforms (Murillo 1999; Kingdon and Muzammil 2003; Moe 2011; Moe and Wiborg 2017; Schneider 2021).

2.2.2 Operationalizing Implementation

Focusing on administrative tasks and state–society interactions for primary schooling, I now operationalize the concept of implementation. Research in comparative politics has focused largely on cross-national differences in public education spending (e.g., budget shares and per-pupil expenditures) and aggregate outcomes, such as literacy rates.[8] Taking a more granular approach, development economists, such as Pritchett (2013), distinguish between "schooling" goals and "education" goals. Schooling relates to input provision, such as the construction of school buildings, and teacher recruitment and training. Schooling also includes student enrollment, attendance and completion rates. Education, meanwhile, points to the acquisition of cognitive skills, measured by learning outcomes. Relatedly, political scientists, such as Corrales (1999, 2005), have studied the "coverage" of school systems and the "quality" of education, measured respectively by enrollment rates and standardized test scores.

In line with these granular approaches, I propose a contextualized measurement scheme, grounded in the administrative tasks for primary education. Andrews, Pritchett and Woolcock suggest the need "to think analytically about the diverse range of tasks within a given sector" (2017, 110). These scholars categorize administrative tasks by their "transaction intensity," understood in technical and organizational terms. Additionally, I stress the political complexity of tasks, the power differences and conflicts arising in implementation. Figure 2.1 presents a taxonomy of tasks according to their degree of complexity. At the lower end of the complexity spectrum are *codifiable* tasks. These tasks involve routine decisions based on information that can be standardized and transmitted with relative ease. They include episodic, one-off activities, such as school enrollment campaigns. Codifiable tasks cover situations that are consistent in nature and require limited frontline agent discretion – the provision of infrastructure, textbooks and other "hard" inputs is one example.

At the middle range of the complexity spectrum, *intensive* tasks involve more difficult activities. They cover less predictable situations, calling for frontline judgment and contextual knowledge. Such tasks also summon interdependencies between state organs and society, raising the need for coordination and management of human relations, which is politically

[8] For example, Lake and Baum (2001), Brown and Hunter (2004) and Ansell (2010).

Complexity	Tasks		Administrative and political challenges
Low			
	• Student enrollment • Providing textbooks and materials • Building school infrastructure and facilities	*Codifiable tasks*	• Identifying out-of-school children • Bottlenecks in delivery of physical ("hard") inputs over a territory • Establishing common systems and procedures
	• School and academic planning • Posting teachers in difficult to reach schools • Providing teacher training	*Intensive tasks*	• Integrating less tangible ("soft") inputs • Coordination among local agencies and across geographic jurisdictions • Managing frontline worker (e.g., schoolteacher) resistance
↓	• Monitoring the quality of classroom teaching • Providing academic support to teachers • Promoting community engagement in school governance	*Complex tasks*	• Repeated coordination between local agencies, schools and community members • Managing community demands • Adjudicating conflicts between teachers and parents
High			

FIGURE 2.1 Taxonomy of administrative tasks in primary education

more challenging. Examples of intensive tasks include the posting of teachers to underserved schools and the provision of specialized services for disadvantaged students. State agents have to identify hard-to-reach populations and motivate teachers. The need for state–society coordination can also spark resistance, making it challenging for the state to depend on standardized procedures.

Finally, *complex* tasks are the most challenging from an administrative and political perspective. These tasks encompass open-ended problems and unpredictable situations, drawing on multiple agents whose decisions and actions generate feedback loops. State officials need to exercise a high degree of discretion and acquire even deeper contextual knowledge. Complex tasks include the family of "wicked problems" identified by public administration scholars (Weber and Khademian 2008; Peters 2017). These causally complex problems are difficult to plan for ex ante and create feedback loops between state and societal agencies. Examples include classroom teaching and routine monitoring of education services. These activities call for repeated, "thick" interactions between administrators, schoolteachers, children and parents. Politically, such tasks may breed conflicts, particularly when state and societal actors have competing interests and understandings.

2.2.3 Comparative Indicators for Primary Education

To measure implementation, I assemble context-sensitive indicators for the codifiable, intensive and complex tasks involved in primary education delivery in rural India. These indicators are mapped on to measures of coverage (or schooling inputs) and quality (or learning outcomes) commonly used in the development and education literature, but they go further in helping to discern the differences in implementation across school systems. I use data from a nationally representative education survey, the Annual Status of Education Report (ASER), administered by Pratham, a globally recognized education NGO that operates throughout India.[9]

Table 2.1 contains measures of codifiable tasks, which relate to school access and the provision of hard inputs. These include the student enrollment ratio and the percentage of schools that have received the annual development grant provided by India's Sarva Shiksha Abhiyan (SSA) program. Bearing in mind that primary schools also have responsibilities for child health and nutrition, the table includes the percentage of schools meeting the legal obligations to provide the midday meal, India's flagship school meal scheme and a critical safety net for poor households. Figure 2.2 presents data on infrastructure provision. It shows the percentage of government primary schools in compliance with infrastructure standards stipulated by India's Right to Education [RTE] Act.

Among the four states, Himachal Pradesh (HP) performs the best on dimensions of access and provision of inputs (Table 2.1), though it does not perform noticeably better on school infrastructure indicators (Figure 2.2). An exception is the provision of libraries, which are available in nearly all primary schools surveyed in HP. This exception is notable since, among the infrastructure stipulations of India's RTE Act, libraries are more directly related to student learning. Uttarakhand also performs relatively well on codifiable tasks, as demonstrated through access indicators, with the exception of providing the school development grant, which is below average for India. The two highly populous states in the Gangetic plains, Uttar Pradesh (UP) and Bihar do marginally

[9] The ASER survey is administered annually across rural India, covering all districts with a random sample of thirty schools per district. Information on the ASER survey's design and methodology is available at: www.asercentre.org/Wave/p/372.html.

TABLE 2.1 *School access and input indicators (2012)*

	Children aged 6–14 enrolled in school (%)	Schools that received SSA development grant (%)	Schools serving the midday meal (%)
Himachal Pradesh	99.0	90.9	98.0
Uttarakhand	97.0	76.5	95.1
Uttar Pradesh	93.9	69.7	95.0
Bihar	96.3	84.0	75.0
All-India average	96.7	78.8	87.4

Source: ASER (2013).

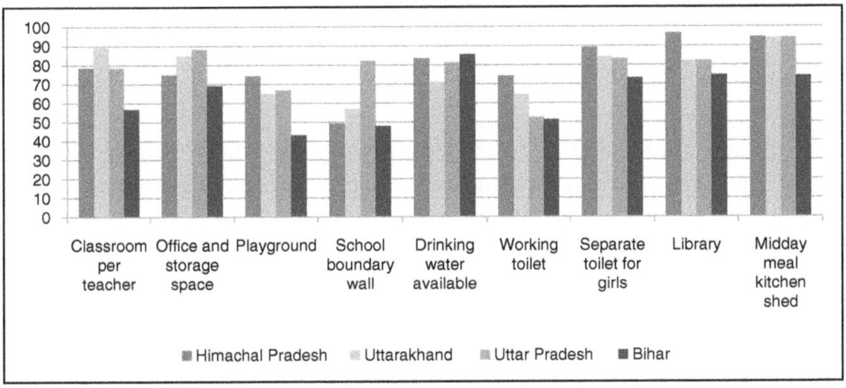

FIGURE 2.2 Primary schools (%) in compliance with RTE Act infrastructure standards
Note: Calculated as percentage of government primary schools in compliance with each infrastructure requirement.
Source: ASER (2013).

worse on codifiable tasks, though Bihar does far worse on midday meal provision.[10] UP performs almost as well as HP on meeting compliance with infrastructure standards in Figure 2.2, with markedly better provision of school boundary walls.

The indicators for intensive tasks, presented in Table 2.2, tell us how school systems function at a routine level and handle progressively more

[10] Qualitative research (Chapter 4) reveals that the midday meal in UP is often irregularly provided and of low quality.

TABLE 2.2 *Student participation and teaching input indicators (2012)*

	Attendance rate for children aged 6–14[1] (%)	Girls aged 11–14 out of school (%)	Single-teacher schools (%)	Teacher absence rate[2] (%)
Himachal Pradesh	89.9	1.8	6.1	14.9
Uttarakhand	81.9	3.8	12.9	13.2
Uttar Pradesh	54.9	11.5	7.5	20.0
Bihar	58.3	5.2	5.1	21.9
All-India average	71.9	6.0	9.0	14.8

Notes:
1. Attendance rate is the percentage of enrolled children present on the day of the survey team's school visit.
2. Teacher absence rate is the percentage of teachers absent for unofficial reasons on the day of the survey team's school visit.
Source: ASER (2013).

difficult activities. The rate of student attendance, which is more challenging than mere enrollment, indicates the regularity of child participation in school. The share of girls in the higher age bracket (11–14 years) who are out of school indicates the school system's ability to retain adolescent girls, a major challenge facing India's school system (Azam and Kingdon 2013). Table 2.2 also has two input-based indicators for teaching used by education researchers in India, the percentage of schools served by only a single teacher and the rate of schoolteacher absence. These tasks are intensive since they require state agencies to coordinate activities and overcome possible resistance from teachers.

HP and Uttarakhand perform comparatively well on student participation indicators, though HP does better overall in terms of out-of-school children and teaching inputs. Teacher absence in HP is slightly worse than in Uttarakhand, but the share of single-teacher schools in Uttarakhand is much higher, which means that absences in the latter case tend to be more disruptive for students. Despite having a similar geographic terrain as HP, Uttarakhand appears to be less successful in posting teachers to remote villages. UP and Bihar perform far worse on indicators of student participation. It appears that many enrolled children do not attend school regularly. In UP, more than one out of ten girls in the adolescent age cohort (11–14 years) are not in school, nearly twice

TABLE 2.3 *Student learning indicators (2012)*

	Students in fifth grade with basic reading skills[1] (%)	Students in fifth grade with basic arithmetic skills[2] (%)
Himachal Pradesh	72.8	48.7
Uttarakhand	58.4	35.0
Uttar Pradesh	42.7	21.1
Bihar	44.4	31.4
All-India average	46.8	24.8

Notes:
1. Basic reading ability is the percentage of students in fifth grade who can read from a second-grade textbook.
2. Basic arithmetic ability is the percentage of children in fifth grade who can perform simple division.
Source: ASER (2013).

the national average. Bihar does better on indicators of student participation, but teacher absence is comparatively worse.

Finally, Table 2.3 contains indicators for the complex tasks involved in providing quality education, measured by student learning outcomes. Pratham's ASER survey administers a reading and mathematics exam to rural fifth graders, which asks them to read from a second-grade textbook and perform simple arithmetic. Learning levels throughout rural India are far from adequate. Almost half of rural fifth graders cannot read and a quarter of them cannot perform basic arithmetic. Weak learning outcomes at the aggregate level mask the sizable variation across states. Learning levels in HP are much better than in other states, though there too there is much room for improvement.

Learning outcomes are conditioned by multiple factors, of course, including the socioeconomic background of students, such as household income, parental education attainment and at-home support for children (Hanushek and Woessmann 2011). Rural adult literacy in HP (81.9 percent) is above the national average (68.9 percent), and so some degree of student achievement can be attributed to higher parental education. Yet, student learning outcomes are considerably worse in Uttarakhand, even though it too has above-average rural adult literacy (76.3 percent). Some portion of the gap in student learning between HP and Uttarakhand can likely be attributed to state failures to provide adequate education services. Student learning outcomes in UP and Bihar are exceedingly low by comparison and closer to the all-India average. The weak performance of these states partly reflects the fact that many students enrolled in government schools are first-generation learners, whose parents may not have attended school. Having noted these caveats, it should be emphasized that the ASER survey tests for the most rudimentary skills in reading and arithmetic, skills that one reasonably expects all students to gain from school, irrespective of social background. To supplement the quantitative indicators here, Chapters 4–7 provide rich, qualitative evidence from fieldwork, further detailing the stark differences in how school systems function across the four states.

2.3 THE ARGUMENT

Having defined the concept of implementation and operationalized it for the context of primary education in northern India, I now present my theoretical argument centered on differences in bureaucratic norms. Subject to the same formal institutions, I argue, state agencies can have different informal bureaucratic norms, which generate variation in the implementation of primary education. In this section, I first define bureaucratic norms and situate the concept within a broad literature on institutions and public administration. I then introduce the mechanisms of my argument. Next, I construct an analytical typology of bureaucratic norms, anchored on the concepts of legalism and deliberation, and highlight their differences on various organizational dimensions. I theorize the mechanisms by which these two distinct forms of bureaucracy produce varied implementation patterns and outcomes.

2.3.1 Bureaucratic Norms

Scholars have long observed that bureaucracies operate according to norms (Barnard 1938; Kaufman 1967; Wilson 1978; DiIulio 1994). Weberian bureaucracy, whose hierarchical design and meritocratic structure has been the subject of many studies, is undergirded by a "bureaucratic ethos" rewarding competence, honesty and impartiality (Du Gay 2000). Before considering why bureaucratic norms matter for public service delivery, we should first be clear on what is meant by norms. Norms are informal rules of conduct that instruct agents on how to act within a social context. Social theorists, such as Elster (1989) and Ostrom (1990), maintain that models of instrumental rationality – an agent's choosing the course of action that produces the highest expected material payoff – although powerful in many respects, are insufficient for explaining human behavior. Social actors, they suggest, have a larger behavioral repertoire that includes responsiveness to norms.

Theories of norm-driven behavior have two essential characteristics. First, they are not outcome oriented by design, meaning that norms do not in themselves point to actions producing results that an agent always prefers. I may or may not, for example, enjoy the consequences of having to remove my hat in a church. Norms can be distinguished, then, from consequentialist principles of action, such as instrumental rationality, whereby an agent acts so as to best satisfy her preferences. Norm-driven behavior need not, however, be beneficent or altruistic.[11] The decision to comply with a norm can be informed by instrumental, means–ends calculations. Fear of public reprimand may motivate me to remove my hat before entering a church. However, the desirability of the action to the agent is independent of the norm itself. Second, norms do more than describe patterns of behavior. They prescribe how people *ought* to behave. I may choose to remove my hat in church for reasons unrelated to a norm, if, say, the building has poor ventilation and removing the hat brings me comfort. By influencing how alternative actions are perceived and weighed, norms advise a course of appropriate action. Norms also serve as a yardstick for evaluating the conduct of others. These considerations do not imply that individuals always accept normative prescriptions or internalize them as part of their personal moral beliefs. To presume so would run afoul of Granovetter's (1985) critique of "oversocialized" conceptions of the individual. Granovetter distinguishes between norms and beliefs, suggesting that norm-driven behavior is neither mechanical nor deterministic, but *contingent* on expectations of others and grounded in concrete social relations.

This book is concerned with a special class of norms, namely, those regulating public bureaucracies. Although norms are widely observed within private sector organizations as well, public bureaucracies have characteristics that merit special attention.[12] Public agencies have policy mandates that are often vague, conflicting and difficult to measure (Wilson 1989).

[11] On the connections between norm-driven behavior, beneficence and altruism, see Bicchieri (2016).

[12] Gouldner's (1954) classic study of industrial bureaucracy in a gypsum plant shows how norms of reciprocity between supervisors and subordinates emerged and eroded over time. See also the seminal treatises on corporate culture in private firms (Kotter 1992).

Policy rules can be ambiguous or incomplete, often as a consequence of the policymaking process (Baier, March and Saetren 1986). For example, India's RTE Act fixes a legal duty on the state to provide free and compulsory primary education, but leaves unspecified who within the state (e.g., legislators, administrators and teachers) bears final responsibility for violations of the law. Even when policies are clearly written, residual uncertainty arises over when and how to apply rules in particular instances, creating the need for bureaucratic discretion. Managing discretion is central to the work of street-level bureaucrats (Lipsky 1980; Maynard-Moody and Musheno 2003; Piore 2011). These officials interact frequently with citizens and have to make complicated policy judgments when responding to individual cases.

I define bureaucratic norms as the informal rules that influence how bureaucrats relate to one another and understand an agency's collective purpose. Bureaucratic norms have two important features: (1) they are broadly understood and shared by an agency's members and (2) they are sustained in interactions that signal the approval (or reward) and disapproval (or sanction) of behaviors by fellow members.[13] Bureaucratic norms help orient state officials and align their behavior with collective goals, motivating them to act beyond narrow self-interest. To illustrate, Kaufman's (1967) landmark study of the United States Forest Service identified the normative "glue" that held the agency together, helping to steer geographically dispersed Forest Rangers toward a common purpose. Bureaucratic norms provide standards for behavior that is considered mandatory, permissible, prohibited and exemplary within an agency.[14] Exemplary behavior is important because, as Levi and Sherman argue, "[a] highly effective bureaucracy is one that evokes not only competence and honesty among its employees but also sustained extra effort and initiative" (1997, 332). Accordingly, research on the developmental state suggests the importance of bureaucratic norms for industrial transformation in late-developing countries (Woo-Cumings 1999; Haggard 2018). Autonomous, high-powered Weberian agencies in charge of industrial policy are shown to have facilitated rapid economic growth in East

[13] March and Olsen (2013) refer to these norm-driven dynamics as institutional "logics of appropriateness."

[14] Brinks (2006) enumerates norms that require, permit or prohibit actions by officials. To this I add norms for exemplary action. Supererogation, action that goes above and beyond the call of duty, commands special moral recognition. J.S. Mill (1969 [1865]) hailed the distinct value of non-obligatory meritorious action.

Asia (Johnson 1982; Amsden 1989; Wade 1990). Along with Weberian structures, Evans has called attention to "bureaucratic norms and relations within the state apparatus," which reinforce commitment to high performance (1995, 71). Studies of public service delivery in developing countries likewise suggest the importance of bureaucratic norms and cultures. Tendler's (1997) pathbreaking study of the health bureaucracy in the Brazilian province of Ceará reveals how, against expectations of patronage and corruption, bureaucratic norms instilled commitment among frontline health workers, supporting high quality services. Related findings emerge from research on "pockets of effectiveness" in developing countries, institutional enclaves of high performance in otherwise unfavorable political contexts (Geddes 1990; Grindle 1997; Leonard 2010; Roll 2014; McDonnell 2020).

Before I explore the mechanisms of my argument, it would help to differentiate a theory centered on bureaucratic norms with a principal–agent approach to bureaucracy. Scholars have modelled bureaucratic relationships and the dilemma of task delegation as a series of contracts between political principals and bureaucratic agents (or between supervisory and subordinate agents), to analyze the ways that hierarchical control may align the interests of principals and agents (McCubbins, Noll and Weingast 1987; Moe 1989; Huber and Shipan 2002).[15] This literature powerfully demonstrates the importance of formal institutional design and authority relations. It also has limitations, which become more apparent in the domain of frontline public services.[16] Public service bureaucracies exhibit what Dixit (2012) calls "multidimensional complexity," that is, they are responsible for multiple tasks, have multiple levels of hierarchy and are accountable to multiple principals, including supervisory officials, elected leaders and nongovernmental stakeholders. Designing explicit contracts and incentive schemes to encourage high performance on complex tasks, such as teaching, is inherently difficult.[17] Teachers may be induced to work toward measurable goals, resulting in distorted efforts (Holmstrom and Milgrom 1991).

[15] See the review by Gailmard and Patty (2012). These approaches build on the economics of organization literature, which treat principal–agent relations in a manner akin to the conflicts of interest between the owners and managers of firms (Moe 1984; Williamson 2000).

[16] The principal–agent literature's neglect of bureaucratic norms and culture has been critiqued. See DiIulio (1994), Meier and O'Toole (2006) and Fukuyama (2013). Also see the discussion in Pepinsky, Pierskalla and Sacks (2017, 253–257).

[17] Dixit (2002, 718–721) illustrates these arguments with the example of education.

Principal–agent approaches are also confounded by the institutional context in developing countries. Laws in developing countries often far exceed what bureaucracies can practically deliver and the pervasiveness of informal rules limits the purchase of formal contracts (Helmke and Levitsky 2004). While discretion is a common feature of street-level bureaucracies, the *de facto* discretion of local officials in developing countries is possibly greater. In rural China, Tsai observes, "[l]ocal officials have so much discretion in policy implementation that both citizens and researchers often refer to policy making by local officials rather than policy implementation" (2007, 7). The notion that politicians, higher-level bureaucrats and other principals control frontline officials is also questionable. In India, local agencies are entrusted to deliver a wide array of development programs. The proliferation of policy rules has placed extraordinary demands on frontline officials, amplifying the need for them to exercise discretion and jointly define priorities (Kapur and Mukhopadhyay 2007; Dasgupta and Kapur 2020).

Recognizing that norms are collectively instituted, my analytical framework identifies public agencies as organizational sites of collective action (March and Olsen 1989; Ostrom 2000). This approach is consistent with "relational" understandings of bureaucracy, which emphasize repeated interactions that evolve dynamically across time (Carpenter and Krause 2014). Research on relational contracting explores how market exchange and coordination is underwritten by recurring social interactions and norms of cooperation, what Durkheim called the "non-contractual elements of contract." Relational approaches to bureaucracy point to the recurrent exchanges among state agents and between them and societal actors (Bertelli and Smith 2010).[18] Accordingly, in what follows, I develop a typology of bureaucratic norms that highlights the alternative ways that officials understand their collective duties and relate to citizens on the ground.

2.3.2 Mechanisms of the Argument

I have so far described the theoretical contours of bureaucratic norms and their importance for public service delivery in developing countries. I now outline the causal mechanisms through which bureaucratic norms influence policy implementation. Summarized in Figure 2.3, the first

[18] See also the related work on governance and trust-based relations (Braithwaite and Levi 2003).

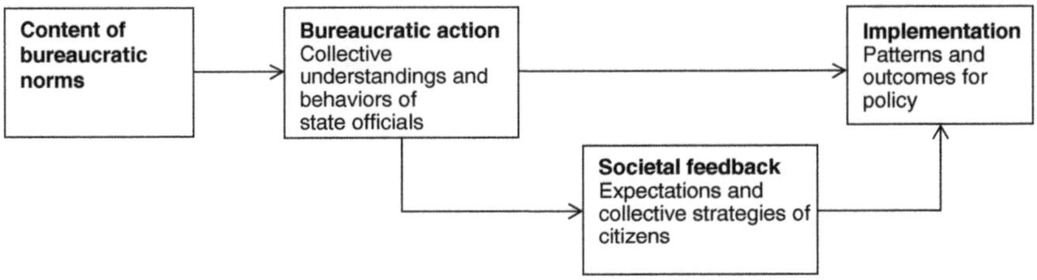

FIGURE 2.3 Summary of the argument

causal mechanism operates through bureaucratic action. I argue that bureaucratic norms drive implementation by influencing the *collective understandings and behaviors* of state officials. Before they can apply the law, bureaucrats need to interpret the law and what it demands of them (Yanow 1996). In agencies tasked with social service provision, street-level bureaucrats have to make fine-grained judgments over the meaning of policy rules. Given rule ambiguity and resource constraints, they must find ways to make practical sense of their duties. Bureaucratic norms provide the "framework of a set of tacit rules and procedures" that allow frontline agents to reach collective judgements over the use of discretion (Piore 2011, 150). Officials invoke norms when interpreting policies in specific cases and deciding on a course of action. These actions have material consequences for citizens and create moral dilemmas on the job (Brodkin 1997; Zacka 2017). Bureaucratic norms provide a way for officials to make sense of moral quandaries emanating from their work.

Bureaucratic action is necessary for implementing public services, but it is insufficient on its own. For services to function well, societal input is also needed, as the research on coproduction and local collective action demonstrates (Ostrom 1996; Banerjee, Iyer and Somanathan 2007). The second causal mechanism through which bureaucratic norms operate is *societal feedback*. Bureaucratic norms influence how frontline officials handle routine complaints and conflicts, such as those between service providers and households. The mechanism of societal feedback underscores the iterative process of public service delivery, involving repeated state–society interactions. In seeking services, citizens gain exposure to the local state and learn about its operations.[19] Learning occurs through direct experiences, say, when a mother drops her child off at school and

[19] On how exposure to local agencies influences citizenship practices, see Mettler (2002), Soss (2005) and Kruks-Wisner (2018).

is greeted by teachers. Learning also happens indirectly, through conversations with neighbors and the narratives about local agencies that circulate within an extended social network. Through these exchanges, citizens come to "see the state" and anticipate how local bureaucracy may behave (Corbridge et al. 2005). Experiences with the local state accumulate over time, leading citizens to form expectations and collective strategies for monitoring public services.

2.3.3 Legalistic versus Deliberative Bureaucracy: A Typology of Bureaucratic Norms

Having sketched the mechanisms linking bureaucratic norms to policy implementation, I now propose an analytical typology of bureaucratic norms, centered on the concepts of *legalism* and *deliberation*, and trace the mechanisms by which they impact on the implementation of public services. Where legalistic bureaucracy urges fidelity to administrative rules and procedures, deliberative bureaucracy promotes flexibility and problem-solving.[20] These two ideal types of bureaucracy have distinct normative underpinnings and sustain different organizational commitments, as I demonstrate based on disciplinarily diverse literatures in normative political philosophy, organizational theory and public administration. In Table 2.4, I summarize the theoretical differences between legalistic and deliberative bureaucracies on multiple dimensions of organizational behavior.

Legalistic Bureaucracy

A powerful line of argument from the philosophy of law's liberal tradition recommends legalism as an ethic for governance. In a seminal essay, Shklar identifies legalism as the "ethical attitude that holds moral conduct to be a matter of rule following, and moral relationships to consist of duties and rights determined by rules." (1964, 1). The legal profession and institutions occupy Shklar's inquiry, but the normative commitment to rule-following applies to various organizations, including public bureaucracies. For those in public office, legalism prescribes impartiality and consistency in the application of rules. Legalism also urges fidelity to procedure, as elaborated in the classical liberal notion of "rule of law," defined as a system of rules that are public, general in formulation, clear in meaning and applicable to all members of a polity (Hayek 1944, 54). Legalism imposes limits

[20] To ensure clarity, I use the adjectives "legalistic" and "deliberative" when referring to bureaucracies that exhibit these divergent types of bureaucratic norms.

TABLE 2.4 *Typology of bureaucratic norms*

Dimensions	Legalistic bureaucracy	Deliberative bureaucracy
Normative orientation	Rule based	Problem based
Organizational dynamics	Officials protect hierarchical boundaries and procedures	Officials participate across boundaries and modify procedures
Communication	Vertical lines of communication, primarily through formal channels	Vertical and horizontal lines of communication, through formal and informal channels
Information	Prioritize official knowledge, written documents and governmental data sources	Allow both official and colloquial knowledge, written and oral accounts and diverse data sources
Frontline agent discretion	Select among existing policy rules in response to particular cases	Modify policy rules or create unofficial rules in response to problems arising in particular cases

on state power by regulating administrative processes "in accordance with predetermined rules of considerable generality and clarity" (MacCormick 1989, 184). These precepts prevent states from exceeding their authority and help protect individual liberties.

As a norm of public administration, legalism is articulated most fully in the writings of Max Weber (1947).[21] In his studies of Europe's economic modernization, Weber observed the transition from patrimonial rule to a bureaucratic order that was rule-bound, hierarchical and meritocratic. The ideal-typical Weberian state was envisioned to motivate bureaucrats to set aside their private interests and advance the public good (Du Gay 2000, 2005). It did so by insulating bureaucrats from political pressures and instilling a commitment to rational-legal norms. Du Gay enumerates the ethical attributes of the Weberian bureaucrat to include "strict adherence to procedures, acceptance of sub- and superordination, *esprit de corps*, abnegation of personal moral enthusiasms,

[21] Benhabib and Linden-Retek (2018) connect Shklar's account of legalism thesis with Weberian rational-legal norms. On the links between liberty and Weberian bureaucracy, see also Du Gay (2005).

commitment to the purposes of office," which allows the state to maintain impartiality (2005, 54).[22] Moving from the individual bureaucrat to the collective agency, legalistic bureaucracy instills a *protective* organizational dynamic, urging deference to rules, procedures and hierarchical boundaries.[23] Supervisory officials use hierarchical authority to communicate goals and monitor subordinates, who in turn seek direction and upward accountability from superiors. Through the everyday enactment of hierarchy, bureaucratic authority gets preserved.

While hierarchical boundaries protect bureaucratic authority, fidelity to procedure restrains bureaucratic action. State officials committed to universal rules are expected to be more accountable and less prone to abusing their authority. In that way, bureaucrats are held "responsible for following rules with regard to their office with dedication and integrity and for avoiding arbitrary action and action based on personal likes and dislikes" (Olsen 2006, 5). Importantly, legalism encourages rule-based accountability, whereby bureaucrats are judged for following rules and *not* for the consequences that emanate from their actions (Kassel 2008). These Weberian precepts are supported by scholarship on bureaucracy and rule of law in developing countries. Cross-national studies find that the formal structures of Weberian bureaucracy – these include meritocratic selection, full-time employment, long-term careers and high salaries – contribute to economic growth and other outcomes (Rauch and Evans 2000; Dahlström and Lapuente 2017). Rational-legal norms, informal features of Weberian bureaucracy, are thought to be equally important (Evans 1995, 21–42; Lange 2005). Where rule of law is comparatively weak, bureaucratic commitment to abstract rules is seen as a bulwark against corruption and personalistic rule (Rothstein and Teorell 2008). Through fealty to explicit rules and written records, legalistic bureaucracy protects the state from the incursions of society and traditional forms of authority.

Deliberative Bureaucracy

An alternative school of thought recommends deliberation as an ideal for public administration. Deliberation involves the mutual exchange of ideas and reasons for the resolution of collective problems. The idea of deliberation has seen a resurgence in recent decades, in part because electoral democracy, a system of aggregating societal preferences through

[22] On impartiality as a principle of governance, see also Rothstein (2011).

[23] Meyer et al. (2014) enumerate other features of legalistic bureaucracy.

votes, has proven wanting for addressing many of society's complex challenges (Keane 2009). Noting the limits of pure "procedural" democracy, deliberative theorists suggest that the mutual give and take of reasons makes democratic governance more substantive, robust, legitimate and fair (Elster 1998). Political philosophers, such as Habermas (1994, 1998) and Cohen (1996), have grounded democracy in public reason, a standard of communication in a political community that asks its members to justify decisions publicly and, thereby, orients them toward the common good.[24] While social scientists have studied deliberative governance institutions, such as public juries, citizen assemblies and deliberative opinion polls, deliberation inside bureaucracy has received less attention. Likewise, the bureaucratic norms that sustain deliberative governance are undertheorized.

Drawing on deliberative democratic theory as well as pragmatist philosophy, I conceptualize deliberative bureaucracy as a distinct ideal type. Deliberation, according to Bohman, is a "dialogical process of exchanging reasons for the purposes of resolving problematic situations that cannot be settled without interpersonal coordination and cooperation" (1996, 27). This definition underscores the need for *dialogue*, the give and take of reasons and arguments, to achieve mutual understanding. The discursive process makes public policy meaningful, legitimate and binding.[25] Deliberative bureaucracy induces very different orientations and organizational dynamics in comparison to legalism (see Table 2.4). At its core, deliberative bureaucracy induces a *participatory* dynamic that urges officials to negotiate policy problems through discussion and adjust their outlooks to shifting circumstances. Whereas legalistic bureaucracy strives for consistency with policy rules, deliberative bureaucracy encourages a more expansive interpretation of policy. Bureaucrats maintain a more flexible disposition, which reflects a willingness to entertain alternative viewpoints.[26]

Further, deliberation as understood here is *problem*-driven, encouraging discussion around the resolution of practical dilemmas. The problem-driven ideal of deliberation is developed in John Dewey's (1927) pragmatic political philosophy. In his conception of democracy, public institutions

[24] Public reason, as a normative standard for the justification of democracy and its institutions, is elaborated in the political theory of John Rawls (1996).

[25] See Schmidt's (2008) account of "discursive" institutionalism as well as literature on deliberative policy analysis (Hajer and Wagenaar 2003).

[26] Gutmann and Thompson (1990, 80) discuss the value of flexibility in deliberation.

are designed to inspire problem-driven collective action by state and societal actors. Because problems are indeterminate and actions yield unforeseen consequences, Dewey recommends that institutions maintain a provisional stance toward policy. Implicit from Dewey's writings is the idea that public officials should have a problem-oriented disposition that questions assumptions, treats policy solutions as provisional and readjusts in light of feedback. Deliberation encourages officials to interpret policy mandates in broad terms, respond pragmatically to challenges and subject their decisions to revision.[27] Along with formal, written channels, deliberation supports informal communication. Norms for information exchange support oral and written accounts, colloquial knowledge and multiple forms of evidence.

Mechanism 1: Bureaucratic Understandings and Behaviors

Turning to the first mechanism behind implementation, legalistic and deliberative bureaucracies stimulate divergent bureaucratic understandings, which lead state officials to interpret and enact policy rules in very different ways (see Figure 2.4). Legalistic bureaucracy motivates officials to adopt a rule-based interpretation of policy, giving precedence to written rules and procedures. Bureaucrats will seek clarity in determining policy problems and adhere to hierarchical prescriptions. They will tend to favor narrow, well-defined goals that can be standardized and measured, working to minimize the vagueness of policy rules. Illustrating the behavioral dynamics of legalism, a study of microfinance loan officers in Mexico finds that agents adhering to the "letter of the law" understand policies as binding constraints that narrow the set of prescribed actions (Canales 2011). When differences arise, they will tend to search for (preferably written) rules and clarifications from supervisory officials before crafting a response. Doing so allows bureaucracy to assign responsibility and "forge subsequent links in the causal chain" of implementation (Pressman and Wildavsky 1984, xxiii). To be sure, the multiplicity and ambiguity of policy rules leaves room for frontline discretion. Officials must select which rule to prioritize and what standards to apply when monitoring services. However, they will tend to avoid actions that go beyond written policy stipulations.

[27] Ansell associates pragmatism with "evolutionary learning" processes, which generate "problem-solving capacity over time through continuous inquiry, reflection, deliberation and experimentation" (2011, 5).

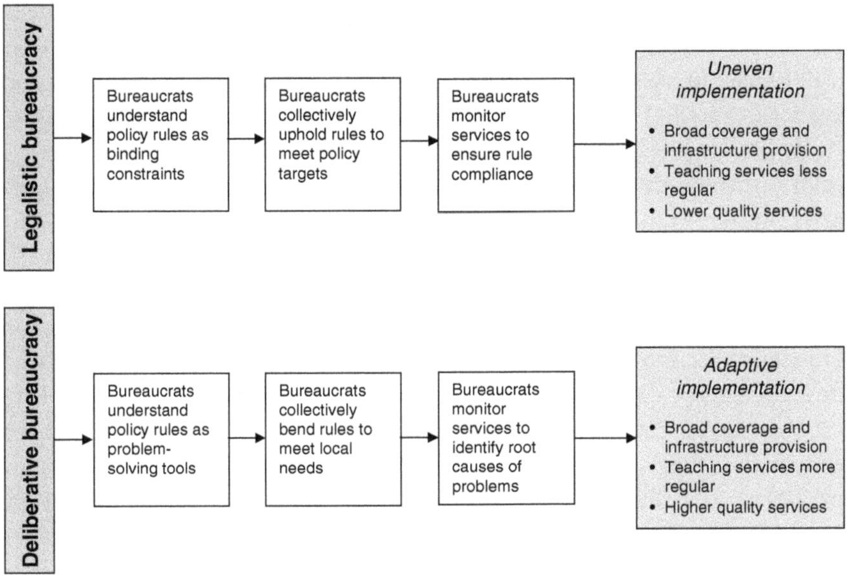

FIGURE 2.4 Mechanism 1: Bureaucratic understandings and behaviors

The commitment to a narrow interpretation of policy rules, I argue, enables officials to undertake codifiable tasks effectively. In the primary education sphere, these tasks include the enrollment of students, and provision of infrastructure and other schooling inputs. Legalism motivates officials to work collectively toward well-defined goals, while the preservation of hierarchical boundaries enables them to collectively withstand political pressures, leading to more consistent delivery of inputs. Legalistic bureaucracy is thus expected to generate broad coverage of the school as well as provision of school infrastructure.[28] Local monitoring practices will tend to support input provision as well. Frontline officials are likely to conduct school monitoring as an audit, inspecting for compliance with rules, which aids in the achievement of measurable policy targets, such as infrastructure and teaching inputs.[29] On the other hand, I expect legalistic bureaucracy to falter when undertaking intensive or complex tasks. The latter set of tasks call for fine-grained judgments and intensive coordination across organizational boundaries. At the higher

[28] Sinha (2010) shows how tight adherence to bureaucratic rules facilitated school enrollments in Gujarat.

[29] Honig (2018, 22–24) elaborates on the conditions when top-down monitoring works in foreign aid interventions.

levels of bureaucracy, the search for consistency through the application of common rules can lead state planners to overlook important differences in the local context of primary schooling. Intensive tasks, such as remedial education and specialized services for disadvantaged students, require officials from across administrative sub-divisions to pool information and resources. The observance of hierarchical boundaries and internal procedures can limit coordination between officials in different agencies.[30]

At the school level, inspections aimed at ensuring compliance help achieve measurable targets and may improve teacher attendance.[31] However, the motivation to secure compliance can also lead officials to downplay root causes behind low quality services. Honig and Pritchett (2019) suggest the limits of audit-based monitoring in education, which generates "thin accountability" within school systems. Downstream pressures to demonstrate compliance can interfere with the provision of academic support, leading to the demotivation of teachers. A parallel set of expectations about legalistic bureaucracy is suggested by research on regulation, which identifies the possibilities and limits of audit-based monitoring practices.[32] At the extreme, frontline officials will tend to reduce complex tasks to "compliance with formal policies and procedures," counteracting policies designed to enhance the quality of services (Andrews, Pritchett and Woolcock 2017, 32). In sum, legalistic bureaucracy generates a pattern of uneven policy implementation, marked by broad school coverage and input provision, but with significant shortfalls in the quality of services.

A very different dynamic is set in motion by deliberative bureaucracy. Deliberation leads officials to hold a flexible interpretation of policy and work collectively to solve problems rather than adhere to written rules. When confronted with competing policy interpretations, frontline agents will tend to discuss alternative viewpoints with senior officials and apply

30 As Chibber (2002) finds, bureaucratic adherence to administrative boundaries stifled interagency coordination around economic planning in India.

31 Experimental evidence from India suggests the benefits of school inspections for addressing teacher absenteeism (Duflo, Hanna and Ryan 2012; Muralidharan et al. 2017).

32 Bardach and Kagan (1982) argue that auditing can lead to excessive attention to rule compliance. Ayres and Braithwaite (1995) propose an alternative model of "responsive regulation," which allows for flexibility and negotiation of standards. Alternative approaches have been studied in the context of enforcing labor standards in developing countries, suggesting the advantages of flexibility and joint problem-solving by auditors and factories (Piore and Schrank 2008; Locke, Amengual and Mangla 2009).

collective judgment to negotiate a course of action. Through routine discussions, senior officials engage the perspectives of frontline agents, and in doing so, gain appreciation for what Scott calls *mētis*, "knowledge that can only come from practical experience" (1998, 6). As they learn about the practical realities of service delivery, state planners reinterpret policies in response to local needs. Likewise, they motivate frontline agents to think, plan and act beyond written rules, enabling them "to make policy in the course of implementation" (Moffitt 2014, 7). Frontline agents will tend to embrace policy ambiguities and modify rules in response to practical conditions since they can adapt policies to suit local contextual differences and better the needs of disadvantaged communities.

I argue that deliberative bureaucracy leads to more effective implementation of education services. The understanding of policy as a problem-solving tool allows frontline officials to perform a wider range of administrative tasks well. Along with student enrollment and infrastructure provision, deliberative bureaucracy outperforms legalistic bureaucracy on intensive and complex tasks. State planners will tend to discuss policy problems with colleagues in other offices and geographic locations, enabling more robust coordination. The participation of frontline officials in routine discussions increases the diversity of viewpoints, improving the bureaucracy's ability to address complex problems.[33] For the complex task of monitoring, school administrators will tend to work jointly with teachers to identify underlying problems affecting services. Rather than monitoring for strict compliance with rules, deliberative bureaucracy encourages frontline administrators to engage in what Sabel (1994) has called "learning by monitoring," a mode of continual discussion and collective problem-solving that maintains interpretive flexibility over the rules.[34] Frontline officials will tend to experience greater institutional support for local experimentation, enabling them to adapt policies according to local needs.

Notwithstanding its advantages, deliberative bureaucracy also has downsides, which may be more apparent in settings of low administrative capacity. Deliberation places considerable demands on officials to maintain regular communication. In an ideal scenario, street-level bureaucrats probe one another's decision-making and instill peer-based discipline in

[33] On the epistemic benefits of diversity for decision-making in organizations, see Page (2008).

[34] Noonan, Sabel and Simon (2009) apply the "learning by monitoring" framework to child welfare policies in the United States.

furtherance of agency goals (Zacka 2017; Møller 2021). However, this presumes the presence of professional norms and competencies among frontline workers, which are in shorter supply in developing countries such as India (Das, Hammer and Leonard 2008; Ramachandran et al. 2018).[35] Frontline officials would still need to justify their decisions with colleagues, but the absence of professional competencies raises the risk of deliberation becoming untethered from programmatic policy ends. Where horizontal mechanisms of professional accountability are weak, vertical communication between supervisory officials and frontline agents becomes even more critical for maintaining deliberation's constructive focus. Through vertical communication, senior officials help steer problem-solving toward programmatic ends, which sets constraints on local rule-bending. The need for vertical communication also suggests that deliberative bureaucracy can lead to delays in collective decision-making. The intensive communication requirements suggest, furthermore, that deliberation is likely to be more effective when agencies are smaller in size, enabling more frequent interaction.[36] Where administrative personnel are in short supply and have to manage large jurisdictions, legalistic bureaucracy has the advantage of undertaking codifiable tasks with greater efficiency. On the whole, however, these downsides of deliberation are counteracted by the gains it provides in terms of facilitating the execution of complex tasks.

Mechanism 2: Societal Feedback

Legalistic and deliberative bureaucratic norms stimulate varied mechanisms of societal feedback, in turn shaping citizen expectations and collective strategies in different ways, which impacts routine functioning and quality of services. My theorization of societal feedback draws on two separate branches of scholarship connecting state institutions with societal participation. First, the policy feedback literature directs us to the downstream political dynamics that social policies induce (Pierson 1993). Depending on their design, policies can shape citizen interests and political mobilization in different ways. Studies of the welfare state in the United States and Europe find that different social policy regimes have

[35] Studies of bureaucratic deliberation in Brazil's labor inspectorate (Pires 2011) and prosecutor's office (Coslovsky 2011) likewise identify the importance of professional norms and competencies.

[36] Karpowitz and Raphael (2014) suggest the advantages of deliberation within smaller-sized groups.

varied effects on civic engagement and trust in the state (Mettler 2002; Campbell 2005; Kumlin and Rothstein 2005).[37] Policy feedback research examining local state–society interactions demonstrates further how everyday engagement with school systems, the police and social welfare agencies shapes citizens' perceptions of the state and their own standing in relation to it (Soss 1999; Lawless and Fox 2001; Lerman and Weaver 2014). Related work on trust in government investigates how citizens' experiences with public agencies influence their expectations about institutional fairness and legitimacy, which in turn conditions their willingness to comply with laws (Tyler 1990; Soss 2005; Levi and Sacks 2009).

Another line of research examines participatory and deliberative institutions designed to harness citizen input into public policy. Participatory governance has been studied in a multitude of contexts, from community policing in Chicago, Illinois, to participatory budgeting in Porto Alegre, Brazil, to village assemblies in India (Fung and Wright 2003; Fung 2006; Baiocchi, Heller and Silva 2011; Karpowitz and Raphael 2014; Sanyal and Rao 2018). This work is largely optimistic about what societal participation can achieve. At the same time, research from developing countries underscores the difficulties of securing substantive participation from marginalized citizens, especially in light of power imbalances in society (Mansuri and Rao 2013; Hickey, Sen and Bukenya 2015; Fox 2020). Much depends on how participatory institutions address the practical roadblocks to societal engagement in service delivery.

Combining the insights of these literatures, I argue that the *same* policy programs and formal institutions of service delivery can induce very *different* societal responses during implementation depending on the bureaucratic norms that guide local state–society interactions. Figure 2.5 illustrates how legalistic and deliberative norms of bureaucracy each stimulates divergent forms of societal feedback. Maintaining a *protective* stance toward society, officials in a legalistic bureaucracy are likely to seek input from state-sanctioned agencies, avoiding informal associations (in Indian administrative parlance, "unregistered societies") that lack state recognition. They will tend to use rule-based protocols, such as administrative grievance procedures, to record citizen complaints and resolve conflicts. For example, India's universal primary education program assigns a prominent role to Village Education Committees (VECs),

37 Also see the important study by MacLean (2010) of policy feedback and citizenship practices in Africa.

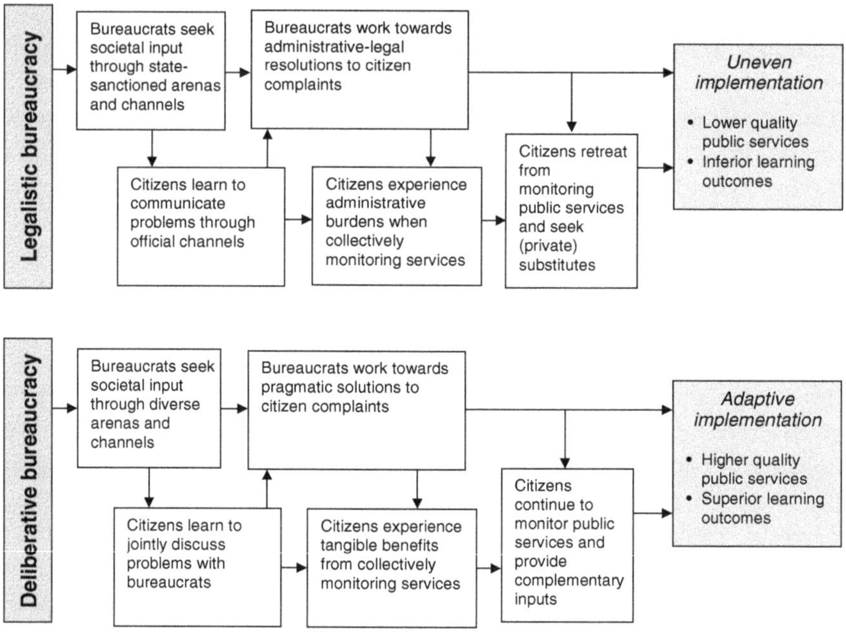

FIGURE 2.5 Mechanism 2: Societal feedback

comprising parents, teachers and village officials, to monitor government schools and lodge complaints with local administration.[38]

I argue that legalistic bureaucracy helps stimulate societal monitoring of services through official channels, but these channels also narrow the scope of participation and amplify administrative burdens for marginalized groups. Administrative burdens, Herd and Moynihan (2018) suggest, include the economic costs of learning how to monitor and comply with rules, as well as psychological frustrations and stigmas associated with cumbersome administrative processes. In India, Gupta (2012) shows how bureaucratic "red tape," the myriad rules and procedures of district administration, exacts a toll on marginalized groups when they seek services.[39] Beyond economic and psychological costs, marginalized groups can face backlash for registering official complaints against service providers. In rural India, women and lower castes risk violence

[38] Studies show that VECs have produced mixed effects on service delivery and education outcomes (Drèze and Kingdon 2001; Banerjee et al. 2007).

[39] Also see Goetz and Jenkins (2005) and Auyero (2011).

and ostracism for speaking out against powerful groups.[40] In the course of my field research, Dalit parents apprised me of these risks, including physical harm to their children, if they registered complaints against (often upper-caste) schoolteachers.

In view of the burdens and risks involved, marginalized groups will tend to follow through with complaints when they can expect concrete benefits and support from the state. Yet, the official channels of grievance redressal are often ill-suited for extending such support. As Goetz and Jenkins point out, "[p]rocedures for filing complaints about poor quality services may be insensitive to the special conditions facing the poor, or access points to officialdom too remote from the sites of injustice that require remedy" (2005, 48).[41] Local elites are often better placed to use these channels, given their political connections, resources and confidence in navigating public administration.[42] Furthermore, when applied to complex service-based tasks such as teaching, formal grievance procedures generate uncertainties, since it is inherently more difficult to assign responsibility for underperformance in these tasks.[43] These challenges get magnified in settings of low state capacity, given the likelihood of procedural delays and elite interference. Yet, similar dynamics are observed in high capacity, "strong rule of law" environments, such as the United States. Based on a study of welfare programs in Chicago, Illinois, Brodkin (1997) concludes, "[l]egal remedies offer only limited accountability, in part, because problems occurring in the 'gray areas' of quality and agency inaction are hard to challenge and because lawsuits are extremely difficult to pursue, especially for the poor" (1997, 25).[44]

In sum, I expect legalistic bureaucracy to stimulate societal monitoring of public services, but participation will tend to be episodic and fragmented. Citizens learn to communicate problems through official channels and grievance procedures, but they are likely to experience administrative burdens. Over time, these burdens dampen their expectations of what participation can accomplish. Some citizens may retreat from monitoring services. Households with the economic means will be

[40] Brulé (2020, 38–46) analyzes societal backlash in the context of enforcing women's property rights in India.

[41] For an illustration of these dynamics in Mexico, see Fox (2007).

[42] For example, Krishna (2011) finds that wealthier residents in rural India are more likely to utilize official channels, such as elected village councils, to access state services.

[43] During fieldwork, teachers often remarked that parental neglect was to blame for poor quality education.

[44] Also see the large literature on formal grievance procedures within firms.

more inclined to seek private substitutes, weakening the collective voice around public services. Consequently, I expect primary education services to be less functional and of lower quality.

To be clear, I do not claim that legalistic bureaucracy leads citizens to withdraw entirely from state services. Given the need for primary education and other services, few can afford to do so. Nor do I suggest that societal feedback under legalistic bureaucracy has no constructive effect on service delivery. The presence of official channels helps stimulate citizens' demands and grievances, which can, in some instances, lead to improvements in education services. All else equal, a legalistic bureaucracy that has institutional avenues for societal input is expected to yield superior outcomes for education compared to an agency closed off from society.[45] Legalistic bureaucracy may also induce the search for informal remedies. Some citizens may try to circumnavigate administrative rules, seeking political intermediaries and informal networks to influence bureaucratic decisions.[46] Others may publicly complain, using "rude accountability" to pressure service providers (Hossain 2010). Complaining is a political act, an expression of citizenship valuable in itself, separate from the outcomes it produces.[47] However, for the least advantaged, the tangible results of complaining also matter. For services like primary education, which involve repeated interactions between households and service providers, complaining is at best a partial remedy.

Societal feedback under a deliberative bureaucracy unfolds differently. The problem-based orientation of officials leads them to draw input from a more diverse set of societal actors. Also, arenas of participation will tend to be more inclusive as well, since officials work with state-sanctioned groups as well as informal associations, permitting a wider set of citizen perspectives to enter discussions. Through their participation, citizens learn how to address service delivery problems jointly with state actors, improving the chances of identifying locally appropriate solutions. Instead of administrative grievance procedures, state officials tend to manage conflicts by promoting dialogue between contesting parties. For instance, they will urge teachers and parents to discuss and resolve tensions

45 My conception of legalistic bureaucracy can thus be distinguished from the notion of a "closed" Weberian bureaucracy, insulated completely from society (Dahlström and Lapuente 2017, 54–59).

46 Several studies suggest the importance of political brokers in India, for example, Manor (2000), Krishna (2003), Jha, Rao and Woolcock (2007) and Auerbach (2019).

47 On the constructive politics of complaining, see also Corbridge (2007) and Kruks-Wisner (2021).

pragmatically. By urging citizens to deliberate with service providers, state officials help steer societal participation toward productive ends. Citizens will tend to experience tangible benefits from participation, which in turn would encourage them to continue monitoring services and provide complementary inputs that help achieve higher quality education outcomes. For example, Collins (2021) finds that deliberative school board meetings in the United States improve parental trust in local officials and their willingness to engage in future meetings. Similar dynamics are found in research on participatory governance institutions in developing countries. In their study of village assemblies (*gram sabhas*) in southern India, Rao and Sanyal (2018) observe that state officials effectively "school citizens" on how to participate and in public fora. Likewise, Baiocchi (2003) demonstrates how state-sponsored assemblies for participatory budgeting in Porto Alegre, Brazil, enable citizens to communicate needs as "public problems" and work toward collective answers.

Yet, participation in public fora does not guarantee that citizens are fully heard or that their demands for better services are met. Deliberative spaces can also marginalize the voices of women, lower castes and ethnic minorities (Heller and Rao 2015; Parthasarathy, Rao and Palaniswamy 2019). The adverse conditions of social inequality, Appadurai (2015, 69) notes, "have produced many deliberative failures and disappointments." He also suggests that the practice of deliberation can build on itself incrementally to strengthen the collective voice of marginalized groups, unleashing a "chain of participation." I argue that deliberative bureaucracy is a crucial link in the chain of participation, which helps strengthen citizen voice in service delivery. By actively encouraging marginalized citizens to voice concerns, state officials make policy problems *public* (Moffitt 2014). The arenas of participation may include official settings such as town halls and village assemblies, but importantly, informal spaces as well, such as impromptu meetings between residents and frontline service providers. Through deliberation, marginalized citizens learn to communicate material needs and aspirations, revealing their "hidden transcripts" of inequality (Scott 1990). When grievances are aired collectively, face-to-face in public, privileged groups are subject to the constraints of public reason and fairness, which can counteract elite domination. To illustrate, in their study of development projects in rural Indonesia, Gibson and Woolcock (2008) show how public discussion helps dislodge unequal power relations, particularly when state officials make deliberative spaces available to women, manual laborers and other subordinate groups.

Deliberative bureaucracy can also present downsides for societal participation, which should be noted. Encouraging marginalized groups to monitor and publicly voice complaints about public services can spark social conflict and elite backlash. In these scenarios, street-level bureaucrats may be needed to mediate conflicts, presenting a source of countervailing pressure, which signals the state's support for subordinate groups.[48] Alternatively, the bureaucracy's incorporation of informal associations and unofficial spaces may inadvertently dampen the critical edge of deliberation (Baccaro and Papadakis 2009). State control of deliberative spaces may also lead to greater dependency or cooptation of non-state actors (Brysk 2000). While recognizing these risks, I expect deliberative bureaucracy to strengthen societal monitoring of services. Through public discussions, supported by frontline officials, citizens learn how to solve problems and experience tangible benefits from participation. They will be more inclined to allocate time and resources toward monitoring services and make collective investments that complement governmental inputs, yielding services of higher quality and superior education outcomes.

My theoretical framework has fleshed out the ideal types of bureaucracy, namely, legalistic and deliberative, as well as the mechanisms through which they produce variations in the implementation of public services. Section 2.4 theorizes the political origins of bureaucratic norms. Before proceeding with that task, some clarifications are necessary. First, while I have drawn sharp distinctions between the two sets of bureaucratic norms, my theory should not be read as arguing for a simple binary. Legalistic and deliberative bureaucracies are better understood as being located on a continuum, with other variations of bureaucracy operating between them. Their many important differences aside, moreover, the two models of bureaucracy also share common properties. Deliberative bureaucracy must pay some obeisance to rules and hierarchies, without which it could scarcely function as a bureaucracy.[49] Likewise, legalistic bureaucracy cannot operate without some discussion between officials over what the rules are and how they ought to be followed.

Second, one should not expect perfect resemblance between my theoretical ideal types and the actual bureaucracies studied in this book.

[48] For example, Heller, Harilal and Chaudhuri (2007) show how state officials in Kerala supported the inclusion of women and lower castes in village council decision-making.

[49] My conception of deliberative bureaucracy can be contrasted with "network" or "open" governance, ideas that challenge conventional bureaucratic authority (Provan and Kenis 2008; Kornberger et al. 2017).

The typology identifies the central tendencies of each form of bureaucracy and the channels whereby they impact policy implementation. Typologies are designed to accentuate certain theoretical features, which aids in the comparison of empirical cases (Giddens 1973, 141–143). While such abstraction can be useful, the temptation to overstate resemblances between abstract models and observed behaviors should be resisted. Finally, the theoretical argument suggests the advantages of deliberative bureaucracy for implementing public services, but I should emphasize that deliberation need not always lead to better implementation. As noted earlier, there are downsides to deliberative bureaucracy, such as the human resource intensity and time it requires for decision-making. Given resource constraints, legalistic bureaucracy is theorized to undertake codifiable tasks effectively and perform well on some intensive tasks. However, as the complexity of tasks increases, I expect deliberative bureaucracy to perform better, producing services of higher quality.

2.4 THE POLITICAL ORIGINS OF BUREAUCRATIC NORMS

Having theorized the impact of bureaucratic norms, this section turns to the prior set of questions regarding the origins and propagation of bureaucratic norms. The historical emergence of bureaucratic norms has theoretical significance for a few reasons. Bureaucratic norms are difficult to establish, and like other features of public institutions, they can be resistant to change (Pierson 2005). Bureaucratic norms can also have unintended consequences, for example, encouraging vested interests to form around policies, thus limiting the control of state actors (Moe 2015). Given the costs of establishing bureaucratic norms, governing elites are likely to invest in them only under exceptional circumstances. The literature on state-building in Europe associates modern bureaucracy's development with the extraordinary conditions of war (Tilly 1992; Ertman 1997). The threat of military conflict pushed Europe's governing elites to create bureaucratic machineries capable of ordering society and amassing fiscal resources. Studies of state-building in developing countries suggest alternative paths and historical contingencies, including the colonial legacies of institutions (Acemoglu, Johnson and Robinson 2001; Kohli 2004, 2019).

Existing perspectives on state-building help illuminate the Indian case, but only partially so. As I argue in Chapter 4, colonial administration was crucial to the genesis of legalistic bureaucracy in UP. Kohli (2019) observes that the British Raj promulgated the idea of a "law and order" state in India, whose chief purpose was to preserve public order and further the crown's economic exploits. Legalistic bureaucracy was also seen as an institutional bulwark against Hindu–Muslim communal violence and caste conflict. Acknowledging India's colonial inheritance, an account is needed of how legalistic bureaucracy persisted after independence and evolved alongside democratic politics and clientelistic subversion of the state. Why other Indian states under British colonial rule, such as HP, diverged from legalism to forge a deliberative bureaucracy also merits explanation.

My argument for the origins and propagation of bureaucratic norms at the subnational state level highlights the strategic objectives of governing elites during historical periods of state-building and the relationships that evolved between them and bureaucratic leadership. Subnational state elites have a vision for the state, but their state-building strategies are not deployed in an institutional vacuum. In India's federal system, the balance of power between the central and subnational state governments created opportunities and constraints for regional politicians. Where the subnational state was politically powerful in relation to the central government, state leaders could influence national politics and public administration. Politicians in these states sought to preserve their power and directed officials to maintain order and stability, a strategy best achieved by promoting legalism. Bureaucratic leadership in these states learned to embrace legalism as well, as it helped enlarge their own authority. Despite a common interest in maintaining legalism, the relationships that emerged were conflictual, since bureaucrats and regional politicians had different objectives for the state. At cross-purposes, each sought to limit the other's influence over public administration, which reinforced hierarchical rule-following.

By contrast, where the subnational state was politically marginal vis-à-vis the central government, subnational political leaders were more constrained. Politicians in such states had strong incentives to cooperate with bureaucrats to identify collective goals and find common strategies for state-building. By joining hands, bureaucrats and politicians strengthened their collective bargaining position with central agencies, which improved the chances of obtaining resources and agreeable terms from the central government. Bureaucrats learned to work intensively with politicians for state-building, which reinforced their interdependencies. The collective behavior of governing elites sent a strong signal to subordinate officials, who were routinely called upon to communicate local concerns across hierarchical boundaries and identify solutions with their peers. Deliberation was thus reinforced by the cooperative relationship between political leaders and bureaucrats.

My argument for the emergence and consolidation of bureaucratic norms builds on scholarship on the politics of state formation. Challenging the traditional emphasis on economic modernization and external threats, studies have shown the importance of domestic elite politics for state-building (Geddes 1994; Slater 2010; Soifer 2015). Elite decisions can have far-reaching institutional consequences, especially in critical moments of state formation, when the rules of the game are more elastic. Nonetheless, as Slater (2010) argues, the choices available to elites are contingent on prior historical circumstances, which in the case of Southeast Asia, he finds, depended on the threat posed by subaltern groups. The evidence from northern India points to an alternative set of mechanisms. The development of bureaucratic norms was driven not by subaltern threats to security, but the subnational state's political and fiscal relationship to the central government. This portion of my theoretical argument takes a multilevel institutional perspective on the state-building process (Sheingate 2014). In particular, I build on the work of Sinha (2005), who demonstrates that distinct subnational models of development in India arose based on the strategic responses of state governments to central government policy rules. Likewise, I argue that the strategic objectives of regional politicians depended on the need for external resources and political support from the central government. These conditions help explain why, in the absence of external threats or subaltern social movements, politicians in HP cooperated with bureaucrats, and together they supported deliberation inside the state. Yet, the persistence of bureaucratic norms does not spring mechanically from elite decisions, but depends on the dynamic interactions between subnational state politicians and bureaucrats. In UP, where politicians routinely attempted to subvert policy rules for political purposes, bureaucrats worked to resist subversion by appealing to rules established by the central government, thereby maintaining bureaucratic authority.

2.5 VARIETIES OF BUREAUCRACY

My theoretical argument underscores bureaucracy's role in promoting social welfare and human development. It brings developmental state scholarship into conversation with research on public administration and policy feedback. Studies of the developmental state have shown how high-powered, Weberian bureaucracies, exemplified by MITI in Japan, supported industrial transformation and growth in East Asia (Johnson 1982). Along with autonomy, Evans (1995) demonstrates that developmental states are embedded in networks with industrial capitalists, facilitating robust coordination around policy goals. More recently, the developmental state's purview has been expanded to incorporate education, health and other human capability-enhancing services (Evans and Heller 2015).

My argument draws inspiration from this research, though it can be distinguished from existing approaches in several ways. First, the theorization of bureaucratic norms calls attention to *informal* features of the state, which are relatively underexplored. Developmental state scholarship pays homage to the Weberian state, a composite of bureaucratic structures and rational-legal norms, which together ensure administrative coherence and commitment (Evans 1995; Lange 2005). While much scholarly effort has gone into unpacking the formal structures of Weberianness, the informal norms operating inside bureaucracies have gained less attention.[50] There may be good reasons for this. Formal Weberian structures, such as meritocratic recruitment, mark critical differences between predatory and developmental states (Evans 1989). These structures are associated with economic growth, a reduction in poverty and less corruption (Evans and Rauch 1999; Rauch and Evans 2000; Henderson et al. 2007; Dahlström and Lapuente 2017). Where patronage is prevalent, Weberian structures offer safeguards against whimsical and personalistic rule, protecting against state failure (Kohli 2004; Grindle 2012). Moreover, bureaucratic norms can be challenging to study and quantify (like other informal institutions), making cross-national comparisons more difficult (Helmke and Levitsky 2004, 733–734).

Yet, formal Weberian structures are insufficient for encouraging high bureaucratic performance on the complex tasks of public service delivery. Bureaucratic norms, and other qualitative features of bureaucracy, are critical in this regard and can help us understand "intermediate" cases, such as India. Hardly a failed state, India is governed by a complicated admixture of formal (Weberian) and informal (non-Weberian) elements that eludes easy categorization (e.g., Fukuyama 2013, 362–363).[51] To

50 It is noteworthy that Haggard's (2018) comprehensive review of empirical research on developmental states discusses formal procedural aspects of Weberian bureaucracy but makes no mention of bureaucratic norms, culture or *esprit de corps*.

51 The presence of formal Weberian structures may also give the false impression of bureaucratic coherence (Pritchett and Woolcock 2004).

make sense of such cases, we need to penetrate "beneath the veneer of formal institutions and apparently clear goals, down to the relational substratum of people's actual lives" (Padgett and Ansell 1993, 1310). As I elaborate in subsequent empirical chapters, India's education bureaucracies may be described as semi-Weberian, with meritocratic selection and civil service rules, especially at the higher levels, but pervasive politicization on the front lines. Pritchett (2009) describes this duality, of highly capable elite agencies detached from the "limbs" of street-level bureaucracy as a "flailing state." This depiction of Indian bureaucracy raises questions. Why, for one, does a flailing state succeed in some tasks but fail in others (Kapur 2020)? How does the same formal bureaucratic structure yield such vast regional variations in the implementation of primary schooling?

My framework addresses these puzzles by penetrating the bureaucratic edifice, to reveal the ethos of bureaucracy. My approach is further distinct in that it integrates *street*-level bureaucracy into the theoretical fold (Lipsky 1980). Research on street-level bureaucracy, including recent work from developing countries, suggests that norms and other informal features of organization are as important for implementation as formal Weberian structures (Schrank 2009; Piore 2011; Canales 2014).[52] My argument points to the divergent normative commitments that motivate frontline officials and guide their behavior around administrative tasks. While primary education is ultimately a local-level service, I suggest that frontline officials respond to norms established upstream by higher-level officials. The empirical analysis in Chapters 4–7 is designed to mirror India's multilevel governance structure, examining the interrelationships between tiers of the state (Sinha 2005). Legalistic bureaucracy encourages a narrow interpretation of policy rules, enabling street-level bureaucrats to collectively resist political interferences, but at the same time weakening their ability to monitor routine services for quality.[53] Deliberative bureaucracy, meanwhile, encourages street-level bureaucrats to apply rules in a flexible manner, based on the collective discussion of problems across tiers of the state. My theory thus answers Evans' (2015) call for "bringing deliberation into the developmental state."

[52] A related set of findings emerge from research on experimental and pragmatist governance (Sabel and Zeitlin 2008; Ansell 2011).

[53] This portion of my argument resonates with Chibber (2002, 2003), who suggests the limitations of "bureaucratic-rationality" in India's elite economic agencies.

I recognize, however, that deliberative bureaucracy is not a panacea. Nor does it automatically trigger substantive participation by society. My argument about societal feedback acknowledges the real difficulties of sustaining societal participation around public services, especially among the least advantaged. Drawing on Evans' (1995, 1996) insight that state embeddedness in society is vital for implementation, the mechanism of societal feedback goes into the mundane politics of coproduction. I foreground the obstacles that marginalized groups experience when attempting to monitor services, highlighting how the local state influences citizen participation. Instead of depending on preexisting village networks, embeddedness in this context requires street-level bureaucrats to actively build and maintain connections with marginalized groups. Legalistic bureaucracy helps stimulate community monitoring of services, but the administrative burdens it places on marginalized citizens weakens their participation over time. Deliberative bureaucracy offers more capacious openings for citizens to discuss and communicate collective grievances to the state, which helps to sustain their participation.

The societal feedback mechanism that I have theorized can be contrasted with previous accounts, including Tsai's (2007) argument about state embeddedness and public goods provision in rural China.[54] Tsai demonstrates that when local officials are embedded in encompassing and solidaristic village associations, they submit to community pressures to provide schools and roads. Meanwhile, rural society in northern India is more unequal and socially divided, albeit with important regional variations. Even where village social ties are relatively encompassing, as I observe in the case of women's associations in the Himalayan region, registering claims with the local state remains a struggle. Bureaucratic norms are crucial within such contexts for sustaining collective action around governmental services, as I demonstrate through the comparison between HP and Uttarakhand. My argument about societal feedback also diverges from Heller's (1999) account of state embeddedness in Kerala, which was built on decades of social movement politics, led by lower castes and classes, followed by robust civil society networks. No comparable movements have obtained in the Hindi belt.[55] And yet, I find that norms of deliberation, established through the historical politics of state-building,

[54] Whereas Tsai examines the puzzle of state accountability in democracy's absence, my argument is concerned with the puzzle of varying state *capacity* in settings of weak institutions.

[55] See Ahuja's (2019) subnational comparative study of Dalit social movements across India.

condition how citizens pursue and engage with the local state. In the absence of social movements, rural women, Dalits and other subaltern groups in northern India face an uphill battle when seeking state assistance. On the long arc of human development, Heller's insight, about the need for social movement politics to underwrite bureaucratic initiatives in education and health, may well be correct. Nevertheless, I submit that bureaucracy can still make an independent and significant contribution toward the implementation of public services.[56] In that regard, my theory offers some hope for human development in places like the Hindi belt, where inequalities are entrenched and subaltern social movements are limited in their reach.

2.6 SCOPE CONDITIONS

This section clarifies the scope conditions for my theory. First, my theory applies to settings where a modicum of institutional stability and resources obtain, a condition that is satisfied by the majority of the world's countries. However, this condition eliminates failed states or those on the brink of institutional collapse. In a failed state, instability and internecine conflict renders it impossible for public officials to formulate policy goals, let alone implement long-term projects such as mass education. Likewise, where no administrative resources exist, implementation is very unlikely. Second, I anticipate that bureaucratic norms will have the greatest influence over implementation where formal bureaucratic institutions are comparatively weak and vulnerable to societal interferences (Helmke and Levitsky 2004). In strong institutional environments, with more autonomous Weberian bureaucracies, informal relations and societal influence over rules are less likely (Dahlström and Lapuente 2017). Where bureaucracy lacks Weberian autonomy, informal norms and relationships can play a larger role, widening the scope for bureaucratic norms to drive implementation. This second condition eliminates the few countries and political subdivisions in the world whose bureaucracies truly approximate the Weberian ideal, such as Denmark. My theory can, however, still apply to advanced economies where bureaucracy is less Weberian.[57]

56 Chapter 8 revisits the Kerala case from the lens of my theory, suggesting the importance of the historical state-building process in the context of social movements and private provisioning of education.

57 King and Lieberman (2009) describe how bureaucracy in the United States departs from the Weberian ideal.

Chapter 8 extends my arguments beyond developing countries, through a comparison of education in Finland and France, offering evidence (albeit suggestive) of the importance of bureaucratic norms within relatively strong institutional environments.

Third, although the study's policy domain is primary education, I expect my theory to apply to a wide range of policy areas in which bureaucrats have discretion, make frequent contact with societal groups and undertake complex "transaction-intensive" tasks (Andrews, Pritchett and Woolcock 2017). Along with higher education and vocational training, these include social services such as health and nutrition, housing, sanitation, employment and anti-poverty programs. My theory can also apply to the state's internal security and regulatory functions, such as policing, labor regulation and natural resource management. Beyond public bureaucracies, my theory is portable to nongovernmental organizations and private agencies, which are important providers of social services in many countries (Cammett and MacLean 2014). Likewise, it may apply to international aid agencies and hybrid organizations, such as those involved in microfinance and other social impact work[58] These agencies often have multiple objectives and complex relationships with government institutions, creating the need for norms to resolve conflicts. Lastly, I expect my theory to apply to the implementation of institutional reforms, such as democratic decentralization, participatory government and community-based development (Fung and Wright 2001; Mansuri and Rao 2004). These various policy contexts also differ from primary education in important ways, and the theory's suitability will therefore depend on the nature of administrative tasks at hand. With appropriate modifications, I expect the theory to have purchase across these different fields.

Fourth, the mechanism of societal feedback operates on the presumption that society has basic freedoms to organize collectively and express demands on the state. Legalistic and deliberative bureaucracies each stimulate different modes of societal feedback. Deliberative bureaucracy is expected to enhance the quality of services by sustaining more inclusive forms of community monitoring. For either mode of societal feedback to operate, the political freedom to associate and express disagreement is a necessary condition. These condition would appear to obtain most

[58] Studies from across these domains identify the importance of organizational norms. See, for example, Piore and Schrank (2008), Honig (2018), Canales (2011) and Battilana and Dorado (2010).

securely under democratic government. Deliberation in particular, as a normative ideal and political practice, is closely tied to conceptions of democracy. However, democracy, in its minimal form, need not inspire substantive citizen engagement in public services. Moreover, deliberative governance can exist in non-democracies as well, as research on East Asian developmental states has shown.[59] Chapter 8 considers my argument's applicability to China, a setting with non-democratic institutions that have some deliberative features (He and Warren 2011). I suggest that deliberative bureaucracy can, within limits, support public service delivery in a non-democratic context, provided that citizens have room to voice collective demands.

Bearing in mind that different policies induce different forms of politics (Pierson 1993), a closing thought on the politics of primary education is warranted. Political scientists treat education as a valence issue, something that voters normally want and politicians often declare a priority (Gift and Wibbels 2014). If the public favors an expansive education policy, this arguably makes it easier for bureaucracy to deliberate with citizens during service delivery. Compared to other redistributive programs, such as land reforms, which visibly penalize economic elites, primary education may occasion less societal resistance and conflict. That said, education is among the most fiscally progressive social policies, especially when resources are directed at the primary level of schooling (Hanushek 2002). Assumptions about a political consensus for universal primary education are questionable. In developing countries, politicians wax eloquent about their commitment to mass education, while public spending exhibits a fiscally regressive "tertiary tilt" favoring elite higher education (Kosack 2012). In India, teachers' unions show support for expanding education but resist proposals requiring them to work in distant, rural schools (Kingdon and Muzammil 2012). Turning to European history, education was among "the most fiercely debated of all institutions of the nineteenth century" (Ansell and Lindvall 2021, 146). Europe's experience of educational expansion was braided with conflicts over, *inter alia*, public versus private provision, religious versus secular schooling and centralized control versus local authority. Primary education remains a formidable site of contentious politics. The teaching of racial history in

[59] Kohli (2004) observes that South Korea's developmental state encouraged deliberation between policymakers and industrial elites, yet remained "repressive and authoritarian" in its dealings with labor. Cf. Sandbrook et al. (2007), who argue that *democratic* developmental states are better at promoting citizen participation and social equity.

schools in the United States or laws supporting the education of girls in parts of South Asia are but two contemporary examples.[60] These and other cases, from across countries and historical periods, suggest that the espousal of education in the abstract need not translate into political support during moments of implementation.

2.7 ALTERNATIVE POLITICAL EXPLANATIONS

This section situates my theory against alternative explanations for implementation. Chapter 1 noted some of these explanations, including levels of economic development, geography, the design of formal institutions, the education policy framework and, importantly, sociocultural norms, which are accounted for in my research design. Below, I consider political explanations for differences in the delivery of primary education in northern India.

2.7.1 Clientelism

An influential line of scholarship on distributive politics in developing countries observes that clientelist states provide public services selectively for electoral reasons. Clientelism, defined as the *quid pro quo* trading of material benefits for political support, can manifest in different forms, from direct "vote-buying" and patronage-based hiring, to the targeting of particular geographies or ethnic groups (Kitschelt and Wilkinson 2007; Stokes et al. 2013; Khemani 2015). Policy implementation under clientelism is seen as informal, discretionary and contingent on political support, in contrast to programmatic delivery through well-defined rules (Hicken 2011, 291). Yet, social programs do sometimes reach citizens in clientelist systems, suggesting possible avenues for implementation (Brun and Diamond 2014; Weitz-Shapiro 2014). As Hicken advises, "our standard for comparison should be not only programmatic political systems but also predatory or exploitative systems" (2011, 302). Accordingly, Table 2.5 summarizes the clientelism literature's expectations alongside those of my theory.

At one end of the spectrum are predatory bureaucracies, which have *de jure* rules but operate mainly through personal ties. These "neo-patrimonial" systems bend bureaucratic rules to the will of powerful

[60] Chapter 7 examines girls' education reforms in UP, highlighting the conflicts induced by policies that counter patriarchy and caste-based exclusion.

TABLE 2.5 *Varieties of bureaucratic norms and their predicted effects on policy implementation*

Bureaucratic norms	Observable implications for bureaucratic behavior	Predicted effects on implementation of primary education
Predatory	Bureaucrats bend rules to extract private rents; grant access to the state based on personal ties	*Extractive non-implementation* • Little to no implementation • Primary education policy captured by elites
Clientelistic	Bureaucrats bend rules to target politically preferred societal groups; grant access to the state based on political connections	*Selective implementation* • Primary education delivered with sparse coverage and lower quality services • Some (e.g., politically visible) codifiable tasks performed
Legalistic	Bureaucrats adhere to rules and procedures; grant access to the state through official administrative channels	*Uneven implementation* • Primary education delivered with broad societal coverage and lower quality services • Most codifiable tasks performed • Some intensive tasks performed
Deliberative	Bureaucrats apply rules flexibly based on local needs; grant access to the state through collective discussions	*Adaptive implementation* • Primary education delivered with broad societal coverage and higher quality services • Most codifiable and intensive tasks performed • Some complex tasks performed

interests, what Khan (2018) aptly describes as "rule by law" rather than rule of law. In predatory bureaucracy, mass public services like primary education are either unimplemented or fully captured by elites. Compared to predatory bureaucracy, the avenues for implementation are wider under clientelism. In India's "patronage-democracy," Chandra (2004) argues, voting is an instrument for procuring state resources, and politicians exert control over policy implementation to favor particular ethnic groups.[61] Clientelism is expected to lead to selective implementation of

[61] These expectations are borne out in research on public goods provision in India (Keefer and Khemani 2005). Posner (2005) makes a similar argument in the African context. Cf. Hicken and Simmons (2008), who suggest that clientelism may generate efficiency gains through localized targeting.

primary education. The provision of inputs will be sparse or geographically uneven, biased toward particular regions and ethnic groups, while education services will be of inferior quality.

Although it accounts well for poor implementation overall, clientelism is less helpful in explaining variation in the quality of services. The state of UP is seen as an exemplar of clientelism in India. The data presented earlier shows, however, that UP's primary school system has achieved near-universal coverage, broad provision of school infrastructure and other inputs, largely in compliance with standards set by the RTE Act, while simultaneously exhibiting service irregularities and low quality education. One might answer that clientelistic states tend to deliver policies that are "visible" to voters, which allow politicians to claim credit for implementation (Mani and Mukand 2007). Along these lines, Harding and Stasavage (2014) observe that African governments subject to political competition tend to implement visible education policies, such as the abolition of school fees, thereby improving enrollments. They also find no impact of democratic competition on infrastructure provision or education quality. Although plausible, the visibility thesis has difficulty accounting for why some clientelistic states implement less visible, quality--enhancing services. In India, the state of HP delivers comparatively high quality primary education services, even as close observers report a "culture of informality" as well as "expectations of patronage and favoritism" within the bureaucracy (Sharma 1999; Das et al. 2015). Bihar, which by many accounts has a clientelistic state, undertook massive efforts to institute quality-enhancing education reforms, albeit with limited success in transforming classroom practices.

Contra the predictions of clientelism, my theoretical framework expects that bureaucrats committed to legalism work collectively to uphold policy rules and resist political subversion. Societal access to the state is granted through official channels for administrative purposes, but which need not always accord with politicians' preferences. My study of implementation in UP (Chapter 4) subjects these expectations to a strong test, examining how local bureaucrats respond to politically motivated ethnic targeting of primary education policies.[62] I find evidence consistent with Chandra's (2004) ethnic particularism thesis, but I also find that bureaucrats resist interference and work toward programmatic

[62] Chapter 4 examines the Ambedkar Village Program, which is often depicted as an example of ethnic targeting.

goals. Deliberative bureaucracy, meanwhile, is expected to implement primary education more effectively, owing to its ability to adapt policies to local needs. The empirical study of HP (Chapter 5) reveals that bureaucrats perceive local politicians as "contractors" (*thekedars*), who extract rents from school construction and other activities. Yet, these same officials also find ways to coordinate with society to deliver relatively high quality services.

To clarify, I do not discount the presence of clientelistic dynamics in northern India. Informal networks of caste, subcaste (*jati*) and clan (*biradari*) were active in my field research sites. Village residents that I interviewed often reported that access to the state depends on who one knows (*jan pehchan*).[63] Schoolteachers in all four case study states described the "market" for postings and transfers.[64] However, I challenge the premise that bureaucracy lacks independent authority under clientelism. By unpacking the institutional side of distributive politics, my argument joins recent studies that complicate our understanding of how clientelism operates in northern India (Thachil 2014; Auerbach 2019; Bussell 2019; Auerbach and Thachil 2019). Although bureaucracy features less prominently in these studies, it is plausible that bureaucratic agencies assist (or counter) political efforts to make public services visible to voters, for example, by forging an independent reputation among citizens.

2.7.2 Political Mobilization

If clientelism is an impediment to programmatic service delivery, political mobilization by disadvantaged groups may act as a counterweight. As electoral participation by the poor increases, the state is expected to redistribute more resources to the poor (Meltzer and Richard 1981). Kosack's (2012) comparative study of education in Taiwan, Ghana and Brazil demonstrates that public spending tilts more toward mass education when poor constituencies are politically organized. Compared to other disadvantaged groups in India, Dalits, Banerjee and Somanathan (2007) find, have experienced larger gains in literacy, which is connected to their higher levels of voter turnout. Likewise, Nooruddin and Simmons (2015) associate higher turnout among the poor in state elections with increased education spending. They also show that state-level party systems

63 As described in the Appendix, I was routinely asked my *jati* by bureaucrats, teachers and village residents during fieldwork.

64 See also Ramachandran et al. (2018).

influence budgetary allocations. Indian states with two-party competition spend more on broad public goods, consistent with the findings of Chhibber and Nooruddin (2004). In line with these arguments, I observe that states with two-party systems (HP and Uttarakhand) implement primary education more effectively relative to states with more fragmented, multiparty systems (UP and Bihar). Political parties in the latter context target a narrower set of voters, lessening the incentive for governments to spend on inclusive social programs (Thachil and Teitelbaum 2015).

Still, it is plausible that heightened electoral participation by Dalits in the 1990s contributed to the growth of primary education in UP and Bihar. Under a majority government led by Mayawati, the head of the Bahujan Samaj Party (BSP), bureaucrats I interviewed reported experiencing heightened political pressure to monitor schools. This pressure sometimes came in the form of ethnic targeting of school infrastructure projects. In Bihar, the state government under Nitish Kumar put bureaucratic discipline high on the agenda and sought to institute quality-enhancing education reforms. Notwithstanding political commitment at the apex of the state, however, I show that implementation of education reforms suffered due to the legalistic commitments of local administration.

Political mobilization of Dalits and other marginalized groups may also support the mechanism of societal feedback. In rural UP, Dalit households spoke of their growing confidence and "recognition" (*pehchan*) in society following Mayawati's ascendance as chief minister. Village collective action for public services, by Dalit women in particular, may have been connected to these political changes. The confidence that Dalit children displayed in school was suggestive of a broader political awareness. Yet, my fieldwork also revealed an abiding disappointment with electoral politics. Few households expected that elections would lead to better quality education services. And while efforts by Dalit parents to monitor primary schools were supported at times by elected officials, their involvement was relatively limited.

2.7.3 Social Capital

Another set of arguments suggests that bureaucratic performance is enhanced when communities are well endowed with social capital, norms and networks of trust and reciprocity that facilitate mutually beneficial cooperation (Woolcock 1998, 155). Coleman's (1988) seminal work on social capital and education links the performance of school systems to neighborhood social networks. Based on the Tocquevillian insight that a robust civil society supports democracy, Putnam (1994) broadens social capital's purview beyond neighborhoods to argue that the density of civic associations improves democratic governance. Studies positively associate social capital with wide-ranging outcomes, from poverty reduction and public goods provision to interethnic cooperation and communal peace (Narayan and Pritchett 1999). These ideas have helped spawn programs for participatory and community-based development, including institutional arrangements for village management of public services (Mansuri and Rao 2004).

Theories of social capital rest on uneasy empirical ground in India. Using survey evidence, Chhibber (2001) reports very low membership in formal civic associations in India. However, the density of formal associations may be an inappropriate indicator for social capital in rural India, where informal networks are more prevalent (Krishna 2003). Informal networks can also be exclusionary, restricting the participation of women, lower castes and other marginalized groups (Sanyal and Rao 2018).[65] In my field research sites, caste and gender relations diverged markedly from the horizontal ties posited by social capital theory. Notably, however, I observed multiple forms of social cooperation, including shared religious practices, which are an underexamined feature of Indian political life (Chhibber 2014). To ensure valid measurement, I studied village social capital in contextually appropriate ways, cataloging religious institutions, women's groups, caste associations and labor-sharing practices, along with the presence of NGOs and other formal organizations. I investigated how encompassing these organizations are of different social groups in my study areas and whether the underprivileged participate in them.

Social capital theory expects primary education to be implemented more effectively where local norms and networks facilitate collective action. The empirical evidence in this book lends partial support to this argument. Preexisting forms of village collective action are found to produce meaningful impacts on implementation. In particular, women's associations in all four states have played a constructive part in monitoring primary education services. The extent and robustness of collective action by rural women and other marginalized groups varied, however, depending on local structures of inequality.[66] In the Himalayan states of HP and Uttarakhand, the more

[65] On the negative features of social capital, see Portes (1998, 15–18).

[66] These observations reinforce the importance of social inequality for village collective action (Bardhan, Ghatak and Karaivanov 2007).

equitable distribution of agricultural land and relatively inclusive caste and gender norms improved the chances for village-wide collective action. Meanwhile, rural communities in the Gangetic plains of UP and Bihar were more fragmented economically and had more restrictive caste and gender norms, which weakened the prospects for village-wide collective action. Consistent with prior research, I find that women in the Gangetic plains experienced substantially greater roadblocks to participation in local governance (Agarwal 2010). Yet, even in this more challenging social environment, I find that disadvantaged households were far from apathetic and often attempted to mobilize collectively for primary education.

My comparative field research also shows that the durability of village collective action and its impact on the delivery of primary education varied across the four states, in ways that social capital theory cannot explain. Although HP and Uttarakhand have similar sociocultural norms and village associations – the latter state also had a robust women's environmental movement history – I find that disadvantaged households in HP are far more effective in monitoring government schools, which I argue is enabled by deliberative bureaucracy. By contrast, legalistic bureaucracy in Uttarakhand is shown to place administrative burdens on disadvantaged households, inducing them to seek private substitutes and *non*-state services. Furthermore, I observe that differences in bureaucratic norms within UP sustain very different dynamics around societal participation, with divergent effects on implementation. As I demonstrate in Chapter 4, legalistic bureaucracy in UP reinforces local power imbalances, impeding collective action by Dalit women and other marginalized groups. By contrast, a study of Mahila Samakhya's gender-oriented programming in UP (Chapter 7) shows how deliberative agencies work to counter hierarchical relations, enabling marginalized households to participate, thereby improving the integration of Dalit girls in school. In sum, the comparative analysis across states suggests that bureaucratic norms influence the efficacy of village collective action around public services. These findings lend support to Krishna's (2003, 2011) argument that frontline institutions are critical for converting "stocks" of village social capital into "flows" of material benefits.

2.7.4 Political Culture

My theoretical argument's emphasis on the collective understandings and behaviors of bureaucrats contrasts with cultural explanations. Seen as a system of values and symbols, culture shapes action by directing human beings toward some pursuits rather than others (Douglas 1966; Geertz 1973). As noted in this chapter's opening, Weiner's (1991) landmark study of child labor in India advances cultural arguments about bureaucratic neglect of education. Through interviews of state officials, social activists, trade unionists and educators, he identifies the consensus view that children from poor households need to work rather than attend school. Weiner connects this political consensus to "belief systems of the state bureaucracy," rooted in the caste system, that "there is a division of labor between people who work with their minds and rule and people who work with their hands and are ruled, and that education should reinforce rather than break down this division" (1991, 5–6). This account is plausible considering the gross inequities of India's caste system. Upper caste privilege was inscribed in colonial education policies, which as noted in Chapter 3, has persisted after independence.

However, Weiner's argument also has some deficiencies, shared by other cultural explanations for education policy.[67] In seeking to demonstrate political consensus around non-provision of education, his argument has trouble accounting for large subnational differences in primary education. Weiner attributes the exceptional performance of Kerala to Christian missionary education. However, in other high performing states, such as Tamil Nadu and HP, missionary presence was negligible and child labor was prevalent in the agrarian economy (Drèze and Sen 2002, 177–179). Weiner's cultural argument also has difficulty accounting for change. Subsequent to the publication of his study, India's central government introduced programmatic initiatives for primary schooling (Mangla 2018). Instead of consensus, the analysis from Chapter 3 reveals considerable disagreement within the state over the provision of mass education.

What about subnational state-level differences in political culture? State elites that I interviewed pointed often to such differences. Officials in HP referred to the hill region as "*dev bhumi*" (land of the gods) and emphasized its "god-fearing" culture, which, they proposed, is what motivated teachers to serve, even when no one was monitoring them. These interlocuters were hard-pressed to explain, however, why the "lower hills" of HP – districts annexed from Punjab with cultural affinity to the plains – led the state in literacy. Bureaucrats in Uttarakhand

[67] Kosack (2012, 8) discusses the limitations of cultural explanations, including arguments about low reverence for education in Africa or "Confucian values" supporting education in East Asia.

likewise described their land as *dev bhumi* and flagged the many differences between hill-based (*pahari*) and plains-based (*maidani*) culture.

An alternative approach conceives of culture not as a unified corpus of values, but a fountain of diverse meanings and repertoires. According to Swidler (1986, 2013), culture does not determine the ends we pursue, but offers a "toolkit" to make sense of the world and construct strategies of action.[68] Culture's internal contradictions and *dissensus* create openings for challenging status quo norms. Appadurai (2002) demonstrates how, for example, Mumbai's urban poor subvert cultural understandings of sanitation and claim political recognition from the state through the performance of toilet festivals. This agent-centered understanding of culture has much to recommend it. As I show in the empirical chapters, marginalized groups in northern India use various "weapons of the weak" to demand accountability from the local state as well as dignity from society (Scott 1985).[69] However, the state's response to such demands varies, I argue, depending on the content of bureaucratic norms. In the theoretical framework presented in this book, bureaucratic norms are *politically* constructed and maintained through the purposive actions of state actors. Bureaucracies are connected to society as well, but bureaucratic norms are not simply mirror images of sociocultural norms. Depending on the historical politics of state-building, the same cultural fabric can spawn vastly different types of bureaucracies.

2.8 CONCLUSION

I have argued that bureaucratic norms are an important catalyst for the implementation of public services like primary education. Subject to the same policy framework and formal administrative structures, differences in the informal norms of bureaucracy lead officials to interpret their policy mandates and relate to citizens in very different ways. Drawing on disciplinarily diverse bodies of scholarship, I advanced the analytical typology of legalistic bureaucracy and deliberative bureaucracy and delineated the causal mechanisms leading to varied implementation patterns and outcomes. Further, I connected the divergence in bureaucratic norms to the historical process of state-building, highlighting the political relationship between subnational states and central administration.

[68] For applications of this cultural approach to questions of development and public health, see Rao and Walton (2004) and Hall and Lamont (2009).

[69] The empirical chapters illustrate these attempts with examples from my fieldwork.

The theory advanced in this chapter is premised on the understanding that policy implementation is a political process. Comparative indicators revealed significant differences in the coverage, routine functioning and quality of primary education services in northern India, the empirical puzzle motivating my study. It is important to note that these comparative statistics, while important, do not fully capture the political meanings attached to education in rural India. For Dalits, rural women and other historically excluded social groups, participation in schooling and the delivery of public services are political acts, which can also spawn conflict and backlash from society. The empirical investigation (Chapters 4–7) brings these political moments to life.

My comparative field research in northern India builds and tests the foregoing theoretical argument, opening up the institutional black box of bureaucracy to study its internal dynamics and external relations with society. Against overwhelmingly pessimistic expectations of what bureaucracy can accomplish in developing country settings, I catalog striking cases of bureaucratic effectiveness as well as variation therein. Policy implementation is a causally complex process that depends on multiple factors. Accordingly, this chapter weighed the merits of alternative explanations and their expectations in relation to my theory. As the empirical analysis will demonstrate, some of these factors, including political mobilization, social capital and, in particular, caste and gender norms, are found to influence the implementation of primary schooling. However, they do not account fully for the varied outcomes analyzed in this book.

Chapter 3 sets the empirical backdrop for the book's comparative inquiry. I trace the historical political economy of the Indian state's shifting involvement in primary education since independence, with a focus on the expansion of national programming for primary education in the post-liberalization period. These policy changes have also sparked societal demands for quality services, raising the political salience of implementation.

3

The State and Primary Education in India

> The State shall endeavour to provide, within a period of ten years from the commencement of this Constitution, for free and compulsory education for all children until they complete the age of fourteen years.
>
> – Article 45, Directive Principles of State Policy, Constitution of India, January 26, 1950

> Today, our Government comes before you to redeem the pledge of giving all our children the right to elementary education. The Right of Children to Free and Compulsory Education Act, enacted by Parliament in August 2009, has come into force today.
>
> – Prime Minister Manmohan Singh, Address to the Nation, April 1, 2010

3.1 INTRODUCTION

This chapter investigates the development of primary education in India and the political economy forces behind policy expansion.[1] It also presents the institutional context for my analysis of policy implementation. I focus on relatively recent policy developments, since the period of economic liberalization up to passage of the 2010 Right to Education [RTE] Act. An exploration of the past also raises questions about the state's colossal neglect of primary education in the first three decades

[1] Some parts of this chapter were previously published in my article, "Elite Strategies and Incremental Policy Change: The Expansion of Primary Education in India," *Governance*, 31.2 (2018): 381–399. I reproduce them here with permission from John Wiley & Sons.

after independence. Although these questions go beyond the scope of this book, I note some important threads in this chapter.

Political scientists often treat education as a valence issue (Gift and Wibbels 2014, 303). In India, public provision of mass education was highly contentious and triggered debates over whether the rural poor needed formal schooling and if so, in what form. Education policy was tied to questions about the federal separation of powers as well as political conflicts around language and religion, issues that became amplified in India's multiethnic federal system. The configuration of rural society and politics in much of the country also posed challenges for primary education programming. The Indian National Congress (INC) depended on patronage networks to secure votes, a political machine that operated through unequal agrarian social structures (Kothari 1974). In regions where patriarchy and caste exclusion were more entrenched, the education of underprivileged groups was perceived as a threat to the status quo. Together, these factors likely dampened the political incentive for states to undertake transformative social projects like mass education.[2]

Despite these obstacles, central government investment in primary education has expanded significantly in recent decades. Public expenditure on education grew from 1 percent of GDP in the 1950s to 4 percent in the late-1990s. Sarva Shiksha Abhiyan (SSA), India's flagship "Education for All" program, launched in 2000, led to a dramatic rise in enrollments and infrastructure provision. The national Midday Meal [MDM] Programme scheme, the world's largest school lunch program, has provided a free meal daily in government primary schools, improving child nutrition and attendance (Afridi 2011). The 2010 RTE Act placed a justiciable duty on the state to guarantee an education for all children.

What accounts for these significant policy shifts favoring universal primary schooling? Conventional wisdom suggests that social policy is a function of economic modernization. A growing economy raises the demand for education as well as the state's fiscal capacity to provide it. A second line of thinking maintains that mechanisms of democratic accountability, such as competitive elections, incentivize states to provide mass education. The findings presented in this chapter diverge from these arguments. Central government programming for primary education did not

[2] Kohli (1987) investigates the sociopolitical resistance to policy implementation in the context of India's land reforms.

mechanically emerge from a liberalized economy or income growth. Nor was it spawned by electoral demands from underprivileged groups. While these factors are important, they do not explain the timing, pace and process of policy development. As I demonstrate, universal primary education policies grew incrementally, beginning in the 1980s, a full decade prior to India's liberalization. Education policies were forged outside of the electoral arena, with limited input from Parliament.

Instead, I argue that the development of universal primary education policies was a slow-moving political process that followed a model of endogenous institutional change (Thelen 2004; Pierson 2005; Mahoney and Thelen 2010). Drawing on historical materials and interviews with policymakers and non-state actors, I find that a coalition of committed national bureaucrats spearheaded reforms with support from subnational policy elites, domestic civil society and international agencies. The critical antecedent for change, India's constitutional amendments and administrative shifts in the late 1970s, granted central government agencies significantly greater authority over primary education. Subnational policy initiatives led by reform-minded bureaucrats started gaining national attention in the 1980s. Through international collaborations, subnational policies were tested on a national scale through a process of "layering," whereby new reforms were incrementally added on top of the preexisting education systems (Hacker 2004). These incremental policy enhancements were accelerated after India opened up to the international economy in the 1990s, which also raised societal demand for education (Ansell 2010). India's collaborations with international agencies, particularly the World Bank, provided bureaucratic reformers a national platform to experiment and scale up programs, which culminated in the formulation of SSA and related policies.

This chapter begins by exploring the political factors behind governmental inertia in primary education. I then describe the political and legal shifts that spurred central government activity in primary education, highlighting administrative centralization as a critical antecedent of policy expansion. Next, I examine the gradual shift in primary education in the period of economic liberalization, detailing the expansion of policies and institutions of service delivery. I also discuss the most recent period of reform, characterized by greater involvement of Indian civil society and judicial action. Finally, I describe the subnational administrative architecture for primary education, which sets the backdrop for the analysis of implementation in Part II of the book.

3.2 FEDERALISM, LANGUAGE POLITICS AND POLICY INERTIA

Independent India emerged from a colonial legacy of educational neglect. Under British rule, the vast majority of Indians received little formal schooling. The first decadal census, taken in 1901, reported a literacy rate of 5 percent, rising to a meager 10 percent in 1941. British colonial education first arrived on Indian shores in the 1860s through the work of Christian missionaries. The 1882 Hunter Commission, which considered the importance of mass education policies, settled on a market-based approach to schooling provision. Private missionary schools expanded with government financial support, but public spending was limited. For colonial administrators, the purpose of schooling was to groom a narrow cohort of anglicized elites who could help govern the subcontinent. In his 1835 *Minute on Indian Education*, Lord Macaulay opined that Indians trained in English language and customs were needed "to form a class who may be interpreters between us and the millions whom we govern; a class of persons, Indian in blood and colour, but English in tastes, in opinions, in morals, and in intellect" (Harlow and Carter 2004, 237). The education system was thus designed to produce Indian clerks, inspectors and translators, who could occupy the state's lower echelons. The exclusive system of colonial schooling was established on top of India's highly stratified caste order, dividing society into those with "English-medium" education and the uneducated masses.[3] This bifurcation of society had lasting consequences for India's educational development. The first census after independence, taken in 1951, reported a literacy rate of 18 percent. Marginalized social groups, including Scheduled Castes (SCs), Scheduled Tribes (STs) and women, had much lower literacy, though the gap narrowed over time (see Figures 3.1 and 3.2).

The political circumstances at independence appeared promising for the development of primary education. The ruling Congress Party had unmatched political support and dominated national and state elections. Jawaharlal Nehru, India's popular first prime minister, led the country for fifteen years with an unrivaled following. Nehru's speeches conveyed a commitment to education, a key pillar in his vision for India's modernization and development (Raina 1993). Maulana Azad, a nationalist

[3] On colonial attitudes toward Indian education, see Fischer-Tiné and Mann (2004) and Sen (1997).

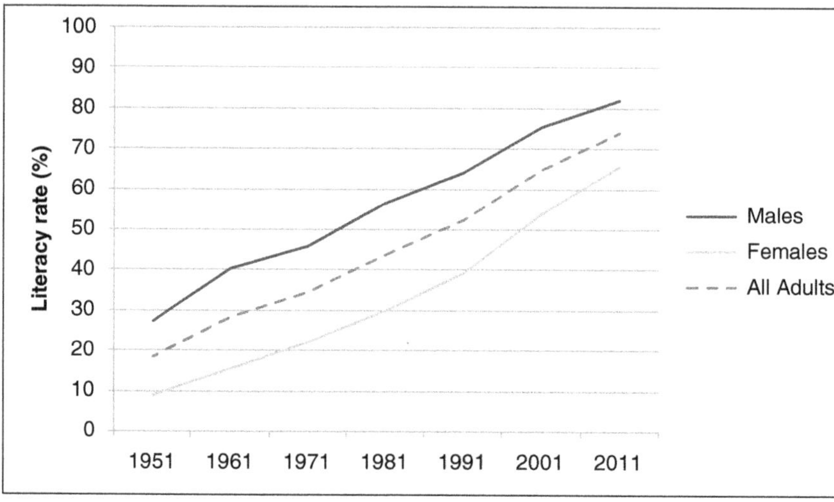

FIGURE 3.1 Adult literacy rate (%) for males and females in India (1951–2011)
Source: Census of India, multiple years.

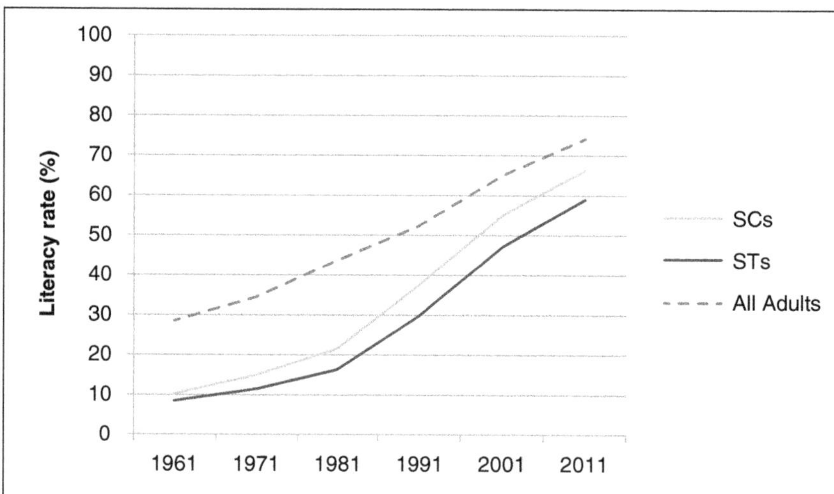

FIGURE 3.2 Adult literacy rate (%) for Scheduled Castes and Scheduled Tribes in India (1951–2011)
Source: Census of India, multiple years.

and India's first education minister, likewise waxed eloquent about the state's duty to educate the masses (Habib 2010). The normative ideal of universal education was also enshrined in the Constitution. However, like other social programs, primary education was not included in the Fundamental Rights enshrined in the Constitution, and this was not legally enforceable through the courts. Instead, education formed part of the Directive Principles of State Policy, unenforceable guidelines for the state to follow when making policy. Article 45 of the Constitution's Directive Principles assigned a goal of ten years for the state to provide free and compulsory education for all children under fourteen years of age. Fifty years later, the directive was unfulfilled, and by 1991, only 52 percent of Indians were literate. Behind lackluster gains in literacy were meager public investments in primary education. The state spent 0.6 percent of GDP on education in 1951, which grew to 2 percent in 1971. Moreover, state spending was biased in favor of higher education. In its Third Five Year Plan (1961–1966), the central government allocated 15 percent of education spending toward higher education. That figure rose to 25 percent in the Fourth Plan (1969–1974) and hovered at 22 percent in the Fifth Plan (1974–1979). The allocation for primary schooling lingered at 30 percent of the education budget, far below the norm of 50 percent in other developing countries (Tilak 2007).

India's federal structure and language politics constrained the central government's ability to promote a national primary education policy. In other large, multilingual polities, such as Indonesia and Malaysia, the postcolonial state pursued mass education as a means for establishing a dominant language and national identity (Horowitz 1989; Anderson 1991). The institutional space for Indian nationalists to act on similar motivations was limited. India's Constitution divided legislative authority between the central (or union) and state governments.[4] A "Union List" contained policy subjects of national importance, such as defense, foreign affairs and banking. A "State List" included local administrative functions, such as land, policing, health and other public services. Lastly, a "Concurrent List" enumerated items of joint central and state government responsibility, such as economic planning and criminal and civil law. Education policy was placed on the State List, which gave state

[4] Central government restraint in primary education had colonial origins. The Government of India Act of 1919 established the federal separation of powers, granting the central government authority over taxation and placing social policy under the purview of provincial governments.

governments full responsibility over it. State governments also controlled the recruitment and service conditions of schoolteachers, police officers and other frontline public employees, limiting central government influence over policy implementation.

India's education policies were also influenced by contentious language politics. Disagreements over the national language fomented societal conflicts that threatened to destabilize the country. In the Constituent Assembly, calls to make Hindi the national language provoked resistance from politicians representing non-Hindi-speaking regions. B.R. Ambedkar, who led the Constitution's Drafting Committee, noted, "There was no article which proved more controversial than article 115 which deals with the (Hindi) question. No article produced more opposition. No article, more heat" (Ambedkar 1989 [1955], 20). Although Hindi was widely used in north India, the majority of Indians spoke different languages. A compromise decision permitted state governments to adopt regional languages for official government business and allowed the central government to use English and Hindi as official languages. Linguistic divisions were institutionalized further through the States Reorganization Act of 1956, which redrew India's internal boundaries on the basis of language. The linguistic states proposal was adopted after much debate among nationalist leaders. M.K. Gandhi and Ambedkar supported linguistic states, since they believed that supporting regional languages and cultures could strengthen political cohesion (Mawdsley 2002). The States Reorganization Commission of 1953 likewise argued that preserving linguistic diversity was necessary for national unity. On the other hand, with the wounds of partition with Pakistan still fresh, Nehru and others feared that linguistic state divisions may balkanize the country and fuel separatist movements, thereby undercutting national unity and collective policy goals.

Despite compromises, the status of Hindi as a potential national language remained contentious. Politicians in south India suspected that central leadership in New Delhi would use education policy to spread Hindi and cement north India's political dominance (Das Gupta 1970, 234–242). After Uttar Pradesh (UP) and other northern states moved to adopt Hindi as their official administrative language, Indians in other regions feared that their access to positions in government and higher education could be compromised. Political leaders in Tamil Nadu organized protests, such as the Madras State Anti-Hindi Conference, and student demonstrations turned violent (Forrester 1966). Language politics was also contentious in the Hindi-speaking region. Gandhi and Nehru had advocated for "Hindustani," an inclusive version of Hindi written in both Urdu (Persian) and Devanagari (Sanskrit) scripts (Das Gupta 1970). Critical of the avowed "secularism" of the Congress, pro-Hindu parties like the Jan Sangh and Hindu Mahasabha promoted a Sanskritized version of Hindi in schools. Meanwhile, India's Muslim minority protested the downgrading of Urdu. Religious divisions in the education system gained political salience; for example, in UP universities were established by rival religious groups (Brass 1974).

3.2.1 The Kothari Commission

Forging a national education policy was contentious, but the large and growing number of out-of-school children could not be ignored. In 1964, the central government convened a National Commission on Education under the leadership of Daulat Singh Kothari, an eminent scientist. From 1964 to 1966, the Kothari Commission brought together academics, policy experts, state officials, along with representatives from domestic civil society and international agencies. The Commission made an explicit connection between public investment in education and India's social and economic development. Universal primary education was deemed "vital on grounds of social justice and to help the process of transformation of the national economy" (Tilak 2007, 877). A public spending target of 6 percent of national income on education was recommended, with the greatest share allotted toward primary education. As the Commission declared, "[w]e should strive to allocate the largest proportion of GNP possible to educational development" (Kothari Commission 1966, 889).

Based on the findings of the Commission, Prime Minister Indira Gandhi unveiled a National Policy on Education (NPE) in 1968, which called for a "radical reconstruction" of education to meet the economic and cultural development needs of the country.[5] Although short on concrete measures for financing primary education, the 1968 NPE was clear in one respect. It granted official recognition to India's "three language formula," a compromise granting state governments the option to use regional languages in schools, alongside Hindi and English. Non-Hindi-speaking states embraced their own languages as the medium of instruction, while Hindi-speaking states maintained instruction in

[5] National Policy on Education, Government of India, 1968. Available at: http://mhrd.gov.in/sites/upload_files/mhrd/files/document-reports/NPE-1968.pdf.

Hindi. The policy was not strictly enforced – Brass (2004) notes, for example, that Tamil Nadu banned the teaching of Hindi in schools – but it gave India's diverse linguistic communities a more equal footing. Importantly, both the Kothari Commission and the 1968 NPE endorsed existing constitutional arrangements granting states full control of education policy. A limited role for the central government was justified on the grounds that states needed autonomy and flexibility to create policies suited to their local conditions (Naik 1982, 150). The Kothari Commission took note of the country's wide regional disparities in education, but it opposed the expansion of central powers. J.P. Naik, member-secretary of the Kothari Commission, reflected on the Commission's report and the 1968 policy: "The implicit assumption of both documents was that while education should continue to be a *State subject*, it should also be looked upon as a topic of *national concern*" (Naik 1982, 150) (emphasis added). Against centralization was the argument that state governments should have autonomy to develop their own education policies. The central government's authority thus remained circumscribed and the Ministry of Education took on an advisory role to support state governments.

3.3 ADMINISTRATIVE CENTRALIZATION: THE GROUNDWORK FOR POLICY EXPANSION

To set national policy on primary education, the central government had to overcome challenges to its authority from states. Critical steps were taken in that direction by Prime Minister Indira Gandhi. Following confrontations with political rivals, Gandhi declared a state of National Emergency in 1975 (Chandra 2003). For twenty-one months, elections were suspended, opposition leaders imprisoned, civil liberties curtailed and the media censored (Frankel 2005, 633–638). Democracy was later restored, but the character of federalism was fundamentally altered. Gandhi took decisions away from regional politicians and reinvigorated central agencies, such as the Planning Commission. Breaking from earlier practice, she relied on loyal bureaucrats to administer policies rather than the Congress Party organization (Frankel 2005, 642). Central planners intervened increasingly in the economic affairs of states and used centrally sponsored programs and discretionary fiscal transfers to exert political influence (Chhibber 1995). Gandhi also enacted legislation enlarging the central government's powers, including far-reaching changes to the Constitution that transferred authority from states to the central

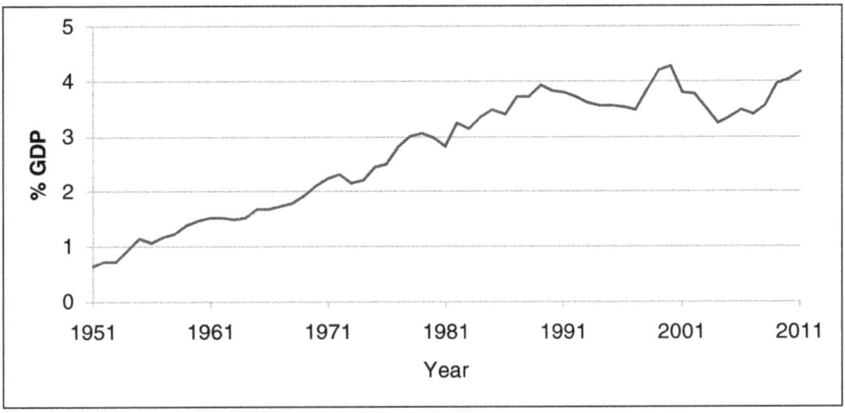

FIGURE 3.3 Public expenditure on education in India (1951–2011)
Note: Public expenditure includes total spending by central and state governments.
Source: Analysis of Budgeted Expenditure on Education, MHRD, Government of India (various years).

government (Das Gupta 1978). Among these was the 42nd Amendment, which moved education (along with family planning, forestry and other policies) out of exclusive state government control by placing it on the Concurrent List of policy subjects, granting central and state governments joint legislative authority. *De jure* centralization, however, did not automatically lead to an expansion of primary education policy. By 1976, a decade after the Kothari Commission had recommended an allocation of 6 percent of GDP for education, actual public spending by central and state governments was only 2.5 percent (Figure 3.3). It took yet another decade for Parliament to enact a national policy for primary education. Nevertheless, the 42nd Amendment provided the institutional opening for central government agencies to engage more in policymaking. Chief among these agencies was the Central Advisory Board of Education (CABE). Established in 1920, CABE acted beyond its advisory role to the central government, helping to draft legislation. Similarly, the National Council for Educational Research and Training (NCERT), created in 1961 for the training of teachers, broadened its mandate to include developing a national school curriculum.

Central government activity reached a critical turning point under Prime Minister Rajiv Gandhi, who took office in 1984. The Ministry of Education was renamed the Ministry of Human Resource Development (MHRD), signaling the agency's strategic importance for national development. The process leading to the enactment of the 1986 National Policy on Education (NPE) illustrates the growing influence of India's central administration in the formulation of policy. Union Secretary of Education Anand Sarup conducted a six-month policy review based on input from academics, bureaucrats, elected representatives, civil society and other stakeholders. The findings were released in a policy document, *Challenge of Education: A Policy Perspective* (Ministry of Education 1985). Candid in its critique of past failures, the document provoked a national debate on education. Other central agencies were engaged, including NCERT, which convened policy discussions and provided technical input. All in all, twenty-three task forces were organized to review various proposals (Little 2010). "A major decision which emerged from these discussions," Sarup reflected, "was that, as a follow up of policy formulation, a separate Action Plan for Policy Implementation would be prepared" (Sarup 1986, 130). The shift in focus to policy implementation was deemed essential for encouraging compliance by state governments. Central agencies also had newfound political support after Rajiv Gandhi appointed P.V. Narasimha Rao as HRD minister. A Congress Party stalwart, Rao held the education portfolio from 1985 to 1988, a crucial period in the development of India's primary education policy. Although Rao is widely known for presiding over India's economic liberalization as prime minister, his involvement in primary education was no less significant. Before entering national politics, Rao worked on education in his home state of Andhra Pradesh during his tenure as education minister (1968–1971) and chief minister (1971–1973). Rao also served as Chairman of the Telugu Academy in Andhra Pradesh (1968–1974), where he helped make Telugu the medium of instruction in schools. As HRD minister, Rao worked closely with Sarup and other bureaucrats to draft national policy, helping to steer policy discussions in CABE, the Planning Commission, the National Development Council (NDC) and other central bodies.

The prime minister and MHRD officials had differing views on what to prioritize in the 1986 NPE. Gandhi envisioned a top-tier school system in rural India modeled on elite boarding schools, which was realized through the Jawahar Navodaya Vidyalaya program.[6] The Navodaya program established tuition-free residential

[6] Interview with retired official that helped draft 1986 NPE, February 22, 2009.

secondary schools (grades 6–12) for gifted children in rural districts. However, MHRD officials feared that the Navodaya program would benefit rural elites and create inequalities in rural education (Deva 1985). The cost of administering 453 residential schools under the program threatened to divert scarce resources away from the mainstream school system, which was in disrepair.[7] Bureaucrats committed to broader school reforms offered different ideas. J.P. Naik, who served as member-secretary of the Kothari Commission, believed that schooling had to adapt to the economic realities of the poor. The traditional school system, in Naik's (1975) words, "offer[ed] neither help nor a second chance to those unfortunate children who miss its narrow doors of admission or who are compelled to step off it for social and economic reasons." Anil Bordia, a decorated Indian Administrative Service (IAS) officer and staunch advocate of education reform, likewise had faith in nonformal education. Bordia's prior experience in the labor ministry informed his view that integrating poor children would require a flexible approach to policy.[8]

Education reformers put these ideas into practice by "layering" new programs within existing education policies. Operation Blackboard, a central government program instituted in 1987, provided financial assistance to states to ensure that schools had a minimum of two classrooms, two teachers and instructional materials. In addition, a "nonformal" schooling program was created for working children, with an alternative curriculum and flexible timings. Public expenditure on education grew substantially in the 1980s, owing to central government spending. However, policy implementation by states was uneven (Chin 2005). To support implementation, MHRD officials drafted a 200-page Program of Action that detailed responsibilities and procedures, and also held frequent review meetings with state governments. Table 3.1 summarizes major policy and legal statutes for primary education in India since independence.

These policy initiatives were accompanied by growth in public spending on education, a significant break from the previous two decades. Around the time India adopted the 1968 NPE, public spending on education was

7 "Chalking a New Path: Navodaya Vidyalaya – Ambitious Educational Plan Faces Numerous Pitfalls," *India Today*, June 15, 1988.

8 Naik and Bordia offered views on nonformal education. See Naik (1977) and Bordia and Kaul (1992).

TABLE 3.1 *Timeline of central government policies and judicial action for primary education (1950–2010)*

Year	Policies and judicial action	Notes
1950	Article 45, Directive Principles, Constitution of India	• Free and compulsory education up to age 14
1968	National Policy on Education	• Built policies on the recommendations of the Kothari Commission (1964–1966) • Established the "three language formula" (Hindi, English and a non-Hindi regional language) • Regional languages used for instruction
1976	42nd Amendment to the Constitution	• Placed education on the Concurrent List of policy subjects, giving central and state governments joint legislative authority
1986	National Policy on Education	• Mandated free and compulsory education • Instituted a common school system with no tuition fees • Improved teacher pay, education and service conditions • Decentralized administration through District Boards of Education
1987	Operation Blackboard	• Provided basic school facilities (e.g., blackboards and books) and instructional materials for teachers • Additional teachers appointed in schools with enrollment of more than 100 students • Financing ratio: 60 percent central government and 40 percent state governments • Teacher salaries paid by central government for the first five years
1993	Supreme Court Decision: *Unni Krishnan* v. *State of Andhra Pradesh*	• Recognized the right to education as a legally enforceable fundamental right under the Constitution

(continued)

TABLE 3.1 *(continued)*

Year	Policies and judicial action	Notes
1994	District Primary Education Programme	• World Bank-funded program for primary schooling in underperforming districts • Program began in Bihar and UP and gradually covered 60 percent of the country, focusing on districts with low female literacy and high gender disparities in education • Focused on student enrollment, retention and achievement • Decentralized planning and administration at the district level • Created partnerships with state governments around technical training and administrative capacity-building
1995	National Programme of Nutritional Support to Primary Education (Midday Meal Programme)	• Mandated the provision of free meals in government primary and middle schools • Provided dry rations initially but progressed to cooked meals • Central government covered the cost of food grains • State governments covered conversion costs (e.g. salary of cooks, cooking fuel and utensils)
2000	Sarva Shiksha Abhiyan	• Central government "Education for All" program • Focused on access, enrollment, retention and achievement • Allocated resources to provide new schools, incentives for enrollment, teaching materials and school development grants • Financing ratio: 85 percent central government and 15 percent state governments • District Institutes for Education and Training created in each district to provide teacher training • Alternative Education programs for highly disadvantaged children • Kasturba Gandhi Balika Vidyalaya: residential schooling program for girls

(continued)

TABLE 3.1 *(continued)*

Year	Policies and judicial action	Notes
2001	Supreme Court decision: *People's Union for Civil Liberties* v. *Union of India & Others*	• Legally mandated state governments to provide cooked meals in school under the MDM Programme
2004	Free and Compulsory Education Bill	• Precursor to the RTE Act drafted by MHRD
2004	Education cess	• 2 percent tax earmarked for education, levied on central and state government sources of income
2010	The Children's Right to Free and Compulsory Education Act (Right to Education Act)	• Education declared a fundamental right enforceable by law • Guaranteed access to education to all children (ages 6–14 years) • Set minimum standards for provision of school infrastructure, facilities and teachers • Required rural habitation and urban neighborhood surveys to identify children out of school • Provided for special facilities and alternative education programs for out-of-school children • Mandated that 25 percent of seats in private schools be reserved for disadvantaged children (Scheduled Caste, Scheduled Tribe and Below Poverty Line)

a mere 1.7 percent of GDP. When the 1986 NPE was enacted, public spending had more than doubled to 3.5 percent of GDP (Tilak 2007). Operation Blackboard accounted for the major share of new public spending. Between 1987 and 1994, the central government spent ₹17.2 billion (more than $500 million in 1994 prices), making Operation Blackboard India's largest centrally sponsored program for education (Chin 2005). Most public spending was directed toward the construction of new schools and teacher recruitment, which supported gains in student enrollment, from 62 percent in 1971 to 79 percent in 1991 (see Table 3.2).

TABLE 3.2 *Gross enrollment ratios for grades 1–8 in India (1951–2011)*

Year	Boys	Girls	Total
1950–1951	46.4	17.7	32.1
1960–1961	65.2	30.9	48.7
1970–1971	75.5	44.4	61.9
1980–1981	82.2	52.1	67.5
1990–1991	90.3	65.9	78.6
2000–2001	90.3	72.4	81.6
2010–2011	104.5	103.3	103.9

Source: District Information System for Education MHRD, Government of India.
Note: Gross enrollment ratio is calculated as the total enrollment in a specific education level, regardless of age, expressed as a percentage of the official school-age population corresponding to that education level. The ratio may exceed 100 as it can include students older or younger than the official age group.

3.4 POLICY EXPANSION UNDER LIBERALIZATION

If administrative centralization laid the groundwork for education programming, India's embrace of globalization in the 1990s helped accelerate policy expansion. Ansell (2010) demonstrates that the opening of the Indian economy to global trade increased the demand for skills, which in turn helped raise aggregate education spending. In this section, I explore a different facet of globalization, namely, the *political* openings it created for bureaucratic reformers in India to expand central government programs for primary education. Following a balance of payments crisis, India sought a bailout and economic stabilization package from the International Monetary Fund (IMF). Under the terms of the agreement, which came with a structural adjustment plan, Prime Minister P.V. Narasimha Rao and Dr. Manmohan Singh, former finance minister, engineered far-reaching reforms to liberalize the economy. In 1991, the central government also reversed its earlier stance toward foreign aid by allowing international agencies to support education, and formulated guidelines for externally funded projects.[9] The World Bank's entry into the education sector provided committed bureaucrats a new platform to experiment with large-scale reforms.

[9] Drawn from the minutes of CABE meetings (Government of India 1992).

In July 1991, only a month after becoming prime minister, Rao appointed a committee to review the 1986 NPE. The Ramamurti Committee called for the expansion of Operation Blackboard and the Navodaya school program, changes that were enacted in 1992 (Ramamurti Committee 1990). Though the policy revisions were minor, Rao's swift action signaled his commitment to primary education, helping reformers overcome political resistance. Given tight fiscal conditions, expansion of primary schooling left lesser resources for higher education. Schoolteachers, who were protected by state civil service rules, resisted central government meddling in the terms of their employment.[10] An official helping to draft the policy explained:

> Rao brought together the key actors from different states to New Delhi. He worked out the details and handled the political opposition. The higher education lobby was not so happy. Then there were issues related to the autonomy of schoolteachers. Various bureaucratic agencies were having turf battles as well. Ultimately, the political buy-in came from Rao and his coterie of experts.[11]

Rao's leadership was more remarkable given the adverse political circumstances. Congress had a minority (220 out of 524 seats) in the Lok Sabha, requiring coalition partners to stay in power. Hindu–Muslim conflict was brewing after Hindu nationalists proposed tearing down the Babri mosque in the town of Ayodhya. India also faced double-digit inflation. The economy and religious tensions were, however, more salient issues for voters at the time (Varshney 2007, 251). Primary education was not high on the political agenda. Rao's interest in education had evolved over decades. He spearheaded education programs in his home state of Andhra Pradesh, first as education Minister (1968–1971) and later as chief minister (1971–1973). A scholar in his own right, Rao chaired the Telugu Academy (1968–1974), helping to make Telugu the language of school instruction in Andhra Pradesh. As the HRD minister (1985–1988) for India, Rao advanced the 1986 NPE, coordinating with central agencies like the Planning Commission and the NDC.[12] Rao supported other welfare programs as well, demonstrating his interest in the social sector (Manor 2011; Sitapati 2016).

[10] Interview with representatives of the teacher union, Lucknow, July 2010.

[11] Interview with retired IAS officer, New Delhi, June 2010.

[12] Interview with retired education official, New Delhi, November 2008.

In addition to central government prioritization of primary education, reform-minded bureaucrats harnessed a wave of global activism for child rights. UNESCO declared 1990 International Literacy Year, and the World Conference on Education for All was held that year in Jomtien, Thailand. Convened by UNESCO, the conference attracted 155 national governments, 20 intergovernmental bodies and 150 non-governmental organizations (NGOs) (Sadgopal 2006). MHRD officials and other Indian representatives participated, exchanging ideas with education experts and international aid agencies. India became a signatory to the "Education for All" goals for 2000. International agencies like the World Bank had previously sought to work in India but they had faced stiff political barriers. Rajiv Gandhi, who otherwise championed globalization, did not welcome international aid for education. According to a World Bank official, "*At the time of the [1986] new policy on education, there was big political resistance to external funding. Outside agencies were seen as a threat.*"[13] Following Jomtien, India opened the primary education sector to foreign assistance. In March 1991, CABE recognized foreign funding and set guidelines for externally aided projects. On the eve of the Jomtien conference, UNICEF had proposed a program in the state of Bihar. The Bihar Education Project began soon thereafter in underperforming districts. In 1992, the state government of Rajasthan initiated the Lok Jumbish Project with support from the Swedish International Development Agency (SIDA). A UNICEF official recounted: "*When the meeting happened in Jomtien, we committed ourselves to Education for All. New, innovative programs sprouted up across the country.*"[14]

An important source of external support for primary education, the World Bank expanded its partnerships with India's central and state governments. World Bank financial assistance for primary education, negligible in the 1980s, reached $2 billion by 2000. Education funding was part of the World Bank's "social safety net," designed to offset the fiscal tightening required under structural adjustment programs (Kumar, Priyam and Saxena 2001). The District Primary Education Programme (DPEP), the World Bank's flagship initiative in India, aimed to improve school access and local administrative capacity in underperforming regions. To administer DPEP and other central

[13] Interview with World Bank official, New Delhi, September 2008.

[14] Interview with UNICEF official, Lucknow, July 2009.

programs, the National Elementary Education Mission (NEEM) was established in 1995. Citing the persistence of "severe gender, regional and caste disparities in provision of elementary education," the central government called for NEEM to be "vested with full executive and financial powers" over primary education.[15] Beyond funding, DPEP provided technical assistance and a decentralized administrative design. Whereas education planning was conventionally performed by state-level agencies, DPEP devolved planning and oversight functions to district teams. An information management system monitored implementation and reported progress to state and central agencies. DPEP began with pilot programs in underperforming states. The UP Basic Education Project (UPBEP) was launched in 1993 in ten districts with low rates of female literacy. The Bihar Education Project (BEP) was initiated by UNICEF in 1990 and later taken over by the World Bank. A larger program was implemented in 42 districts of the country in 1994, expanding to 117 districts in 1997. By 2000, DPEP was operational in 240 districts across 16 states, covering 40 percent of India's territory.

It should be emphasized that primary education policies were not imposed on India by external agencies. India's primary education system was never subject to foreign diktat. As observers noted, DPEP was distinct from externally funded programs in other developing countries given the "marked Indianisation of the planning process" (Kumar, Priyam and Saxena 2001, 563). DPEP was instituted on top of various subnational policy initiatives, which were spearheaded by committed bureaucrats working in concert with Indian civil society. Some of these initiatives were funded by international agencies even before the central government officially allowed foreign aid in education. For example, the Andhra Pradesh Primary Education Program was implemented with UK government support in 1986. It operated in eleven districts of Andhra Pradesh to improve school access and teacher training. The Shiksha Karmi Project, introduced in Rajasthan in 1987 with funding from SIDA, sought to improve teacher motivation and mobilize participation from local communities. Likewise, Mahila Samakhya, a program for women's empowerment and education, commenced with Dutch assistance in 1988 in the states of UP, Gujarat and Karnataka.

[15] Report of the Committee for Re-constituting of NEEM, MHRD, Government of India, January 1998.

Subnational programs demonstrated the possibilities of implementing local reforms on a large scale. For example, Rajasthan's Shiksha Karmi Program recruited village youth to support enrollment campaigns and the running of primary schools. The idea of the *shiksha karmi* (education worker) arose from local initiatives of NGOs, such as the Social Work and Research Center and Seva Mandir. Anil Bordia, who served as Rajasthan's education secretary, had established ties with civic agencies and mobilized the state government to scale up local policy initiatives across Rajasthan (Clarke and Jha 2010).[16] Other Indian states adopted elements of the Shiksha Karmi program, particularly the hiring of para-teachers from within local communities. These subnational interventions also provided a blueprint for the central government to work with external agencies. MHRD officials in turn used the DPEP administrative platform to scale up various home-grown initiatives. For example, in 1995, the Rao government enacted the National Programme of Nutritional Support to Primary Education, popularly known as the MDM Programme. Pioneered in the state of Tamil Nadu in the 1980s, the program provided a free meal daily to schoolchildren (Harriss-White 1991). To expand the MDM Programme nationwide, MHRD officials first introduced it in DPEP districts, before extending it incrementally across the country.

For education reformers in the bureaucracy, the political opportunity for policy scale-up created by India's international engagement with agencies like the World Bank marked a crucial turning point. Traditionally, the primary education sector commanded little prestige within the Indian state. Primary education was not perceived as an attractive career path for IAS officers. Compared to high-status sectors such as finance, power and public works, education and health were seen as "*low-status portfolios*."[17] As noted by Weiner (1991, 200), the "low regard by officials and politicians for the education departments and ministry" continued well after central government involvement in education increased. With India's growing engagement in the international child rights agenda in the 1990s, the central government leaned on reform-minded officials in the MHRD. These officials had deep contextual knowledge of implementation at the subnational level as well as international exposure. They were called upon frequently to represent India at international

[16] Bordia negotiated a six-year joint venture for Shiksha Karmi between the central government, Rajasthan state government and SIDA (Methi and Jain 1994).

[17] These precise words occurred in multiple interviews with bureaucrats and elected officials.

conferences, and they led negotiations with international donor agencies regarding the administration of external programs, such as DPEP. The prestige associated with the primary education portfolio increased and the sector began to attract more officers from the IAS. An education official from UP explained:

> Primary education was never considered something we should talk about. It gained visibility within the government only when good IAS officers came to lead DPEP. In fact, the advantage of DPEP starting in Uttar Pradesh is that very good senior IAS officers became heads. They had status within the administration and could exert top-down pressure. That is how things happened. With these IAS officers in charge, the political will behind the program became apparent to everyone.[18]

The World Bank's evaluation of DPEP also found that "very competent officials" were placed in charge of the program. State commitment in India had "far exceed[ed] the levels usually seen in other low-income countries" (Abadzi 2002, 5). These positive external assessments helped raise the prestige of working in the primary education sector. India assumed a leadership position in the global Education for All movement. Following Jomtien, the MHRD held a summit with UNESCO in New Delhi. The 1993 Education for All Summit brought together the "E-9," nine high-population countries that faced major challenges in universalizing primary education.[19] The summit talks concluded with passage of the Delhi Declaration and Framework for Action. The declaration reaffirmed the Education for All goals laid out at Jomtien and created the E-9 Initiative, a forum for the nine countries to share best practices and monitor progress.

The central government also assumed greater fiscal responsibility for primary education. Although policymaking in the 1970s and 1980s had become more centralized, the share of education spending by the central government was still relatively small. More than 90 percent of education spending was borne by state governments. The fiscal pattern began shifting after Jomtien, as the central government's share increased to 25 percent (Figure 3.4). Foreign funding, which accounted for 9.5 percent of central government expenditure on primary education, grew to 30 percent by 2000. Alongside increased aggregate education spending, an

[18] Interview with MHRD official, New Delhi, 2008.

[19] The E-9 countries comprised India, China, Pakistan, Brazil, Bangladesh, Indonesia, Egypt, Nigeria and Mexico.

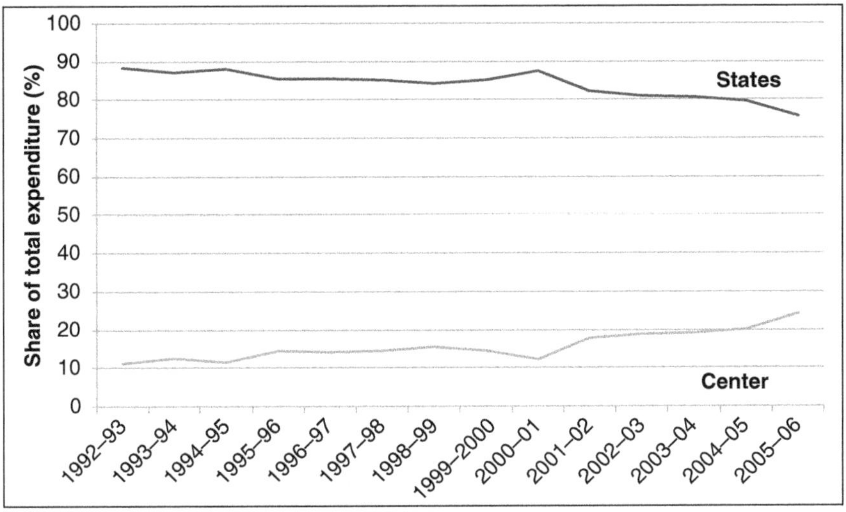

FIGURE 3.4 Indian central and state government shares (%) of total public expenditure on education (1992–2006)
Source: Analysis of Budgeted Expenditure on Education, MHRD, Government of India (various years).

increasing share was allocated toward primary education. Historically, education spending was tilted in favor of tertiary education, funding elite universities like the Indian Institutes of Technology (Figure 3.5). By the 1990s, the primary level of education accounted for more than 50 percent of education spending.

Following the committee's recommendations, NEEM was made an autonomous body within the MHRD and had the mandate to manage relations with the World Bank and other external partners. Complementary missions were constituted in each state and reported directly to New Delhi. These administrative changes were supported by the finance ministry and the Planning Commission as a way to consolidate externally aided programs (Colclough and De 2010). With the reconstitution of NEEM, the administrative authority to plan, execute, and monitor primary schooling, which previously had rested with state governments, was now extended to bureaucrats in New Delhi. As central government spending increased in the 1990s, India's education budget rose to a steady 4 percent of GDP, which brought notable improvements in the primary school system's coverage. As shown in Table 3.3, in 1992, almost 48 percent girls and 38 percent of boys in rural India were not attending school. By 1999, nonattendance had declined to 30 percent for girls and 19 percent for

TABLE 3.3 *Growth in primary school attendance and completion rates in India (1992–1999)*

	1992		1999	
	Female	Male	Female	Male
School attendance, age 6–14 years (%)				
Rural	52	72	70	81
Urban	79	85	86	89
Combined	59	75.5	74	83
Proportion of persons aged 15–19 years who have completed (%)				
Grade 5	51	73	61	77
Grade 8	36	54	43	56

Source: National Family Health Survey I (1992–1993) and II (1998–1999).

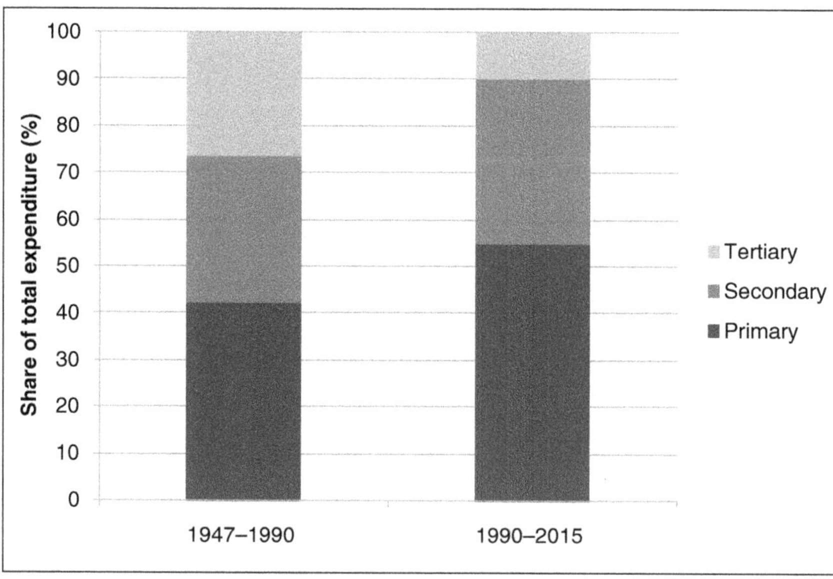

FIGURE 3.5 Allocation of public expenditure (%) on education in India by level of education
Source: Compiled by author based on reports of India's Planning Commission (multiple years).

boys. Still, India had a long way to go toward achieving universal enrollment. By 2000, India accounted for a quarter of the world's 104 million children out of school (UNESCO 2002). That year, the World Education Forum in Dakar aimed to review international progress in primary education since the Jomtien conference. Participating countries agreed to the Dakar Framework for Action, setting concrete steps to achieve the UN Millennium Development Goals (MDGs) for education by 2015, including MDG-2 (universal primary education) and MDG-3 (gender equality in education).

3.4.1 Scaling up Reforms: The "Education for All" Program

The discussion above sheds light on the process leading to the enactment of SSA[20] in 2001. Like the preceding Congress government, the Bharatiya Janata Party (BJP) was committed to liberalization, opening the economy to foreign direct investment, while also expanding central government programming in education. Education initiatives that started under Rao continued under Prime Minister Atal Bihari Vajpayee. Bureaucrats who had overseen DPEP established a reputation for administering large-scale education programs.[21] DPEP's success in school expansion and enrollment also lent credibility to the central government's involvement in policy implementation. DPEP offered a model to universalize education that worked within India's existing administrative architecture for school governance. A State Education Ministers' Conference led by HRD Minister Murali Manohar Joshi in October 1998 secured buy-in from state governments for a universal primary education program. In 2001, SSA was inaugurated with broad political support. SSA's principal objective was to provide free and universal primary schooling for all children of ages 6–14 years (see Table 3.4). SSA aimed to ensure that a primary school was available within a one-kilometer distance of every village along with the provision of teachers, learning materials and other inputs. Incentives were offered to support disadvantaged children, such as free textbooks, uniforms, schoolbags and scholarships conditional on enrollment. District Institutes of Education and Training (DIETs) were created within each district to give teachers comprehensive training and academic support. A computerized management system, the District Information System for Education (DISE), was developed to

[20] Sarva Shiksha Abhiyan is Hindi for the "Education for All Campaign."

[21] Multiple interviews with MHRD officials, 2008–2009.

TABLE 3.4 *Program components of Sarva Shiksha Abhiyan*

Program components	Notes
Infrastructure	• New primary school buildings and classrooms • Campus boundary walls, kitchen sheds and water pumps • Norms for the maximum school distance from villages: one kilometer for primary schools and three kilometers for middle schools
Incentives	• Scholarships provided on condition of enrollment • Free uniforms, schoolbags and textbooks for Below Poverty Line children, as well as SCs, STs and girls
Teaching and learning materials	• Subject-wise teaching guides and materials • Interactive wall hangings and posters
Teacher training	• District Institute for Education and Training established in every administrative district • Preservice training and biannual in-service training for all primary schoolteachers
Decentralized administration	• District Project Office created in each district to administer education programs • Decentralized planning at the district and habitation levels • Village Education Committees in charge of school management • School enrollment campaigns to identify and enroll out-of-school children • Information management system to track program inputs and monitor systems outputs

monitor input provision and track progress on program goals. The central government assumed 85 percent of SSA costs, with states covering the remainder. After Congress returned to power in 2004, it introduced an education cess, earmarking 2 percent of central government taxes for primary education.

Importantly, SSA adopted the institutional blueprints of previous reform programs administered by central and state agencies. The national SSA Mission, an autonomous body, was established under the MHRD, with corresponding missions created in each state. At the local level, SSA adopted a similar structure to DPEP by creating district-level teams in charge of planning, implementation and routine monitoring of primary schools. Having learned from prior initiatives, state officials sought to keep SSA "*insulated from political demands.*"[22] Technical rules and systems were created for the provision of infrastructure and other inputs. School expansion under SSA took place on a breathtaking scale. Within a decade, approximately 250,000 new schools and 1.3 million additional classrooms were built. Drinking water facilities were provided in 210,000 schools, and toilet facilities in 420,000 schools.[23] The program's greatest impact was on enrollment. In the target age group of 6–14 years, enrollment climbed from 160 million in 2002 to 193 million in 2011. State-level SSA project offices and district teams targeted disadvantaged communities and brought them into the school system at a rapid pace. In Gujarat, Sinha (2010) observes, SSA enrolled 75,847 out-of-school girls in 2003, and another 307,280 in 2006.

India's policy expansion, while significant, was not entirely conducive to effective service delivery. The institutional layering of multiple programs created problems of management and accountability. SSA state-level missions concentrated on infrastructure and enrollment, while state governments managed schoolteachers. These functions operated in parallel, often with little coordination.[24] The central government's strategy to pressure state governments through bureaucratic levers also revealed its limits. SSA could achieve only so much by layering on more policy rules and resources from above. In one official's words, "*Universal access has been achieved. The problem now is the retention of students and quality of education.*"[25] Deeper reforms were needed to address education quality, but these required greater initiative and cooperation by state governments.

Furthermore, political challenges to quality-enhancing reforms were posed by primary school teachers. As the MHRD introduced new programs, teachers and their unions mobilized to protect their interests. Individual teachers became enmeshed in systems of patronage to influence postings and other important decisions (Béteille 2015). Representation in state legislatures and through unions gave teachers disproportionate influence over school governance, undercutting community oversight within the school system (Béteille, Kingdon and Muzammil 2017). Along with seeking better pay scales, various

[22] Interview with former State Project Director of SSA, Lucknow, October 2009.

[23] World Bank, "Extending Education to the Millions of Out-of-School Children." Available at: http://go.worldbank.org/L7R3GZ7X10.

[24] Interview with MHRD official, New Delhi, December 2009.

[25] Interview with MHRD official, Dehradun, August 2009.

demands by teachers consumed already scarce time and administrative resources of the education bureaucracy, crowding out the concerns of underprivileged households. Problems related to teacher postings, attendance and accountability also went largely unaddressed (Ramachandran et al. 2018).

Nevertheless, policy changes altered the formal structure of the education administration. Civil servants in New Delhi saw their administrative authority and resources expand considerably. The MHRD exerted significant control over primary education through its links to SSA State Project Offices. States maintained a similar formal institutional structure, with the SSA program and MDM Authority operating under the Department of Education. Each district was overseen by a District Education Officer (DEO), who was also the head of the district-level SSA office. In line with decentralization, SSA brought planning functions down to districts and also established Village Education Committees (VECs) to manage schools. VECs were given charge of school management, monitoring the provision of infrastructure, SSA school development grants, the midday meal and other inputs. Along with representation from parents and head teachers of the schools, VECs included the elected head of the village council (*panchayat*), creating a mechanism for community oversight.[26] Under the 73rd and 74th Amendments to the Constitution, panchayats were granted authority over village public goods and services. However, as we shall see in subsequent empirical chapters, *de facto* control over school budgets and management decisions was retained by the state bureaucracies.

3.5 CIVIC-JUDICIAL ACTIVISM AND THE RIGHT TO EDUCATION

State elites drove the adoption of universal primary education, but the reform process did not end with state action. Over time, India's civil society and judiciary mobilized to cement policy changes into law and hold the state accountable for implementation. The adoption of the Right of Children to Free and Compulsory Education Act in 2009 was a culmination of civic and judicial initiatives. Known as the Right to Education [RTE] Act, this landmark legislation assigned a justiciable duty on the state to guarantee free and compulsory education for all children of ages 6–14.

[26] Following recent administrative changes, VECs in many Indian states have been converted into School Management Committees, which hold similar functions.

As noted earlier, the state's duty to provide education was not deemed a fundamental right, but instead was contained in the Constitution's unenforceable Directive Principles. The RTE Act thus marked an important shift in the legal status of education. The process leading to the adoption of the RTE Act was part of a broader set of political demands for socioeconomic entitlements that Ruparelia (2013) has called "India's new rights agenda." This ongoing process of reform reveals how the enactment of education policies has helped induce new forms of politics, generating new expectations and demands on the state (Pierson 1993).

Indian civil society has a rich history of engagement in the social sector. NGOs have long supported the implementation of public programs, at times blurring the boundaries between civil society and the state (Jenkins 2010). As India enacted new social welfare policies in the 1990s, in education, housing and employment, civic organizations adopted an activist stance, invoking the constitutional framework of rights to hold state agencies accountable for implementation (Jayal 2013). The Indian judiciary also began to aggressively pursue legal complaints brought against the state through public interest litigation, applying procedural innovations that allowed concerned parties to present cases on behalf of the aggrieved (Gauri 2009). Civic and judicial action spurred public debate regarding the right to education. The Supreme Court reconsidered the status of education in the 1989 case of *Mohini Jain* v. *State of Karnataka*. In its decision, the court stated that Article 21 of the Constitution, which mentions the right to life and personal liberty, implied other rights as well, including education. Later, in the 1993 case of *Unni Krishnan* v. *The State of Andhra Pradesh*, the Supreme Court declared that free education up to the age of 14 years was a fundamental right. In its judgment, the court decried the state's historic neglect of its constitutional duty to educate the masses.

Decisions by the courts helped galvanize civil society pressure for new legislation. The National Alliance for the Fundamental Right to Quality Education and Equity (NAFRE), consisting of 2,400 grassroots organizations from 15 states, demanded the central government enact a law recognizing the constitutional right to education. NAFRE members organized petitions, rallies, candlelight vigils and hunger strikes outside of Parliament.[27] They were joined by academicians, NGOs such as Child

[27] "NGOs rally to promote education for all," *Indian Express*, March 7, 2001. Available at: http://expressindia.indianexpress.com/fe/daily/20010307/faf04006.html.

Relief and You and Save the Children, and international agencies such as UNICEF. Responding to civic and judicial pressures, Parliament adopted the 86th Constitutional Amendment Act in December 2002, placing a legal duty on the state to provide free and compulsory education. To put the amendment into effect, the MHRD organized committees to draft new legislation. The RTE Bill's formulation involved "*several rounds of consultation*" between ministry officials, educationists, NGOs, teachers' unions and other civic bodies.[28] The bill that went before Parliament called for universal school enrollment and completion of grades one through five. It set national standards for school infrastructure, teacher appointments and curriculum. Prime Minister Manmohan Singh's cabinet approved the RTE Bill in July 2009 and it was passed swiftly by both houses of Parliament.[29]

With the passage of the RTE Act, policy discussions shifted from school expansion to thornier questions of service delivery and quality of education. To monitor the RTE Act's implementation, the National Commission for the Protection of Child Rights (NCPCR) was given a lead role. Established under the Ministry of Women and Child Development in 2007, NCPCR was mandated to ensure that public policy accorded with the rights of children, as expressed in the Indian Constitution and the UN Convention on the Rights of the Child. The Commission, which has included bureaucrats, academics and social activists with expertise in the domain of child rights, has worked with civic bodies to investigate violations of the RTE Act. Alongside legal action, globally recognized organizations, such as Pratham and the Azim Premji Foundation, have partnered with state governments to enhance teacher training and improve learning outcomes. The focus on quality and learning signals a new phase in the development of India's primary school system.[30]

Many stakeholders pointed out flaws in the RTE Act. Some criticized the exclusion of pre-primary education, noting the growing need for early child education. Others took issue with the onerous process for private schools to gain regulatory licenses and certifications, which

[28] Interview with civil society activist, Uttar Pradesh, August 2010.

[29] "Free and Compulsory Education for Children up to 14 Years," *Financial Express*, August 5, 2009. Available at: www.financialexpress.com/news/free-compulsory-education-for-children-up-to-14-yrs/498039.

[30] India enacted a "new" National Education Policy in 2020, with an express focus on learning outcomes. As the new NEP is yet to be fully implemented, I discuss it in the section on policy implications in Chapter 9.

burdened their operations. Teachers expressed concerns about the stipulation that children could not be held back for failing classes up to fifth grade. Perhaps the most controversial feature of the legislation, private schools were required to reserve 25 percent of seats for socioeconomically disadvantaged children. Funding shortfalls were identified as an obstacle as well, as state governments were required to bear 45 percent of implementation costs. A committee led by Anil Bordia conducted an assessment in 2010 to harmonize the RTE Act with SSA program rules. Cost-sharing between the central government and state governments was initially pegged at a ratio of 55:45. Following the committee's recommendation of 75:25, the central government agreed to cover 68 percent of implementation costs. Whereas two decades prior, primary education was perceived as a less important administrative portfolio, education officials were now accorded greater status and made responsible for overseeing negotiations between central and state governments. Implementation of the RTE Act rested on the joint efforts of bureaucrats, the judiciary and civil society actors.

3.6 CONCLUSION

This chapter has examined the gradual expansion of primary education policy in India. Under a multiethnic federal system, committed state officials pursued subnational reforms incrementally in the 1980s, using administrative levers to overcome political obstacles while scaling up reforms. Political openings in the 1990s, supported by the World Bank's engagement with India's education system, enabled reformers inside the bureaucracy to accelerate the expansion of primary education initiatives. These policy changes also sparked civic and judicial responses, which helped solidify programs into law, most notably the constitutionally recognized right to education, while instigating public demand for policy implementation. Societal mobilization for demanding the state to fulfill its obligations to guarantee quality education for all defines the most recent phase of policy development.

While suggesting how bureaucratic politics has shaped policy development, this chapter also signaled the limitations of reforms led by state elites. The growth of primary education reinforced power differences between state officials, teachers and disadvantaged households. Complicated questions around local institutional accountability and the quality of education services have largely gone unaddressed. Centralized bureaucratic control continues to influence service delivery, notwithstanding attempts to decentralize authority and promote local monitoring by communities (Béteille, Kingdon and Muzammil 2017). These and other matters of implementation are at the forefront of public debates on primary education. The central questions before the Indian state are no longer about *whether* it ought to provide an education for all children, but *how*. Part II will investigate how different state bureaucracies in northern India have addressed societal demands for education in vastly different ways.

PART II

IMPLEMENTING PRIMARY EDUCATION IN NORTHERN INDIA

4

How Legalistic Bureaucracy Generates Uneven Implementation

4.1 INTRODUCTION

Part II of the book analyzes subnational differences in primary education delivery in northern India. In each chapter, I first engage in historical process tracing to establish the political origins and propagation of bureaucratic norms. I then investigate the causal mechanisms behind implementation, drawing on multilevel comparative field research to demonstrate how bureaucratic norms impact the performance of key administrative tasks. This chapter examines the delivery of primary schooling in Uttar Pradesh (UP), a state that exemplifies the dynamic of legalistic bureaucracy theorized in Chapter 2. Located in the heartland of India's Hindi belt, UP is a least-likely case, a place where existing theories overwhelmingly expect public services to fail (see map in Figure 4.1). UP's lagging human development performance has been contrasted with the achievements of Kerala and Tamil Nadu, socially progressive states in southern India (Drèze and Gazdar 1996; World Bank 2003). To explain these stark regional differences, studies highlight societal cleavages and caste politics in UP, which encourage clientelism and weaken the incentives for delivering public services (Mehrotra 2006; Singh 2015).[1] The electoral mobilization of UP's underprivileged castes via "vote-bank" politics is contrasted with the programmatic politics built upon subaltern social movements in southern states (Ahuja 2019).

[1] The World Bank's *2004 World Development Report* attributes the dysfunction of public services in UP to the absence of political will along with societal collective action failures (World Bank 2003, 45).

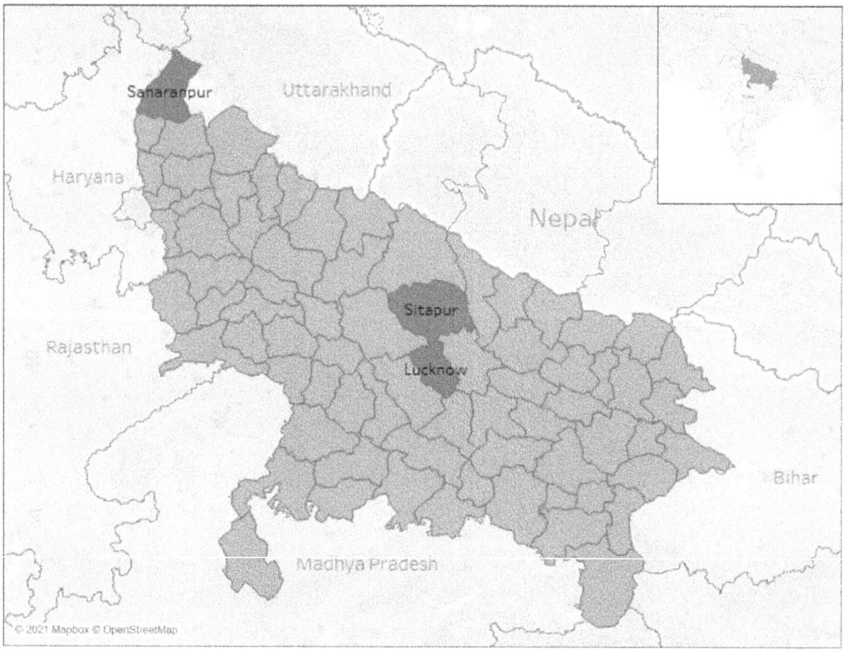

FIGURE 4.1 Study map of Uttar Pradesh
Note: Main study districts are highlighted.
Source: © Mapbox, © OpenStreetMap.

UP is also associated with growing "criminalization" of Indian politics, as legislators with criminal records float between parties, devoid of any commitment to programmatic causes (Vaishnav 2017).

Notwithstanding these adverse political conditions, UP recorded significant progress in primary schooling in recent decades, achieving near-universal coverage, broad infrastructure expansion and the provision of various teaching inputs. As discussed in Chapter 2, UP's enrollment rate is comparable to that of other states. On some indicators, particularly school infrastructure, UP performs as well if not better than other states. UP has been catching up with respect to literacy as well. In the 2011 Census, UP's literacy rate of 69.7 percent reflected a gain of 13.5 percent over the previous decade, higher than in neighboring Rajasthan, another Hindi belt state that has been lauded for its progress in primary education (Clarke and Jha 2010; Singh 2015). Nevertheless, UP's schooling system also displays egregious gaps in implementation, with low quality education services and weak learning outcomes.

What accounts for the lopsided nature of policy implementation and weak outcomes for primary education in UP? This chapter demonstrates the significance of bureaucratic norms in UP. I argue that uneven implementation, the gains with respect to provision of schooling inputs alongside gross deficiencies in the quality of services, is largely on account of legalistic bureaucratic norms, which promote deference to rules. My arguments proceed in the following order. First, I examine the historical origins and persistence of legalistic bureaucracy in UP, starting with colonial administration but focusing on more recent developments under multiparty competition. Second, I present empirical findings on implementation drawn from multilevel comparative field research. Through interviews with state officials, participant observation with local education bureaucracies, as well as interviews and focus group discussions with schoolteachers and citizens, I investigate how legalistic bureaucracy affects implementation processes across different administrative tasks, including school infrastructure provision, student enrollment and delivery of the Midday Meal [MDM] Programme. Bureaucratic commitment to rules has thus facilitated rapid school expansion, acting as a bulwark against political interference during implementation. Third, I bring the analysis down to the village, presenting a citizen-centric view of service delivery. I trace the evolution of village collective action around education over time, to demonstrate how bureaucratic norms interact with community monitoring primary schooling. Marginalized households in UP have mobilized to seek quality services from local administration, despite political divisions and socioeconomic inequalities. However, administrative burdens imposed by the local state have undermined societal efforts to monitor services, weakening the accountability and performance of government schools.

4.2 FORGING A LEGALISTIC BUREAUCRACY IN UTTAR PRADESH

This section examines the historical process of bureaucratic development in UP, connecting the emergence of legalistic bureaucracy to the political strategies of governing elites during critical periods of state-building. Legalism as a bureaucratic ideal had its origins in the British colonial state, though it gained greater purchase after independence. As the largest and most important state for national politics, UP has played an integral part in Indian politics and administration. I trace the emergence of legalism alongside shifting center–state political relations, from the colonial period to the post-independence era of democratic consolidation, up through the recent period marked by multiparty competition and lower-caste political mobilization. As governing elites in UP sought to enlarge their influence over the state, conflicts between political and bureaucratic leadership reinforced norms of hierarchy and rule-following. Along the way, I highlight important features of UP's sociopolitical context, including its economic and caste-based inequalities, which help to situate the chapter's analysis of implementation.

4.2.1 The Colonial "Law and Order" State

Located in the fertile Gangetic plains, UP was administratively pieced together by British conquest and annexation over a seventy-five–year period. An amalgam of diverse regions, the North-West Provinces were merged with the province of Oudh to form the United Provinces of Agra and Oudh in 1902, eventually renamed the United Provinces. Building a bureaucracy to maintain public order and extract revenues within this large, heterogeneous province was a conflict-ridden process. Colonial administration amassed revenues through the institution of *zamindari*, a feudal land tenure system that gave upper-caste landlords (*zamindars*) permanent, hereditary and transferable *de jure* rights over land and agricultural income (Hasan 1989). As Brown notes, "land revenue collection was the government's primary function and it molded the institutions and patterns of administration" (1994, 56). Zamindars forwarded tax payments to the crown, squeezing lower-caste peasant cultivators. While zamindari was widely instituted, land revenue systems varied throughout UP (Neale 1962).[2] In western UP, revenues were pooled by village upper-caste collectives in a system known as *bhaichara*. In central UP (Awadh) and the eastern belt (*purvanchal*), mega-landlords (*talukdars*) had a monopoly on revenue collection. Their powers extended to other institutional arenas, including policing and credit provision. Zamindari ensured the dominance of upper castes, who acted as intermediaries between lower-caste peasants and the state.

Along with revenue collection, the state's other primary function was to maintain law and order. To that end, the colonial government created the Indian Civil Service (ICS). Prior to the ICS, the British East India

[2] Banerjee and Iyer (2005) associate zamindari with lower long-term economic performance of districts. Iversen, Palmer-Jones and Sen (2013), who critique their classification of land tenure systems, arrive at different results.

Company had hired clerks on contracts. Underpaid, they amassed large deficits for the Company and extracted from local populations (Taub 1969, 7). To encourage discipline, ICS salaries were raised and gifts from "natives" were deemed impermissible.[3] ICS officers occupied the influential post of District Collector (DC), the highest-ranking local official. The DC oversaw revenue collection and simultaneously acted as the District Magistrate (DM), chief custodian of the law.[4] Vesting revenue and judicial functions in a single individual gave the DC immense authority. According to O'Malley, an official ICS historian, "One good test of an officer is his capacity for keeping things quiet" (1931, 164). The merging of bureaucratic and legal functions accentuated the importance of law and order activities, the dispensation of which was associated with administrative excellence.

A similar bureaucratic setup existed across most of British-administered India, but UP stood out for the extent that "law and order" became infused into routine public administration. In that regard, the 1857 rebellion was a defining moment in colonial UP. On May 10th of that year, Indian officers in the Company army held a mutiny in Meerut, a western UP garrison town. Peasant rebellions spread throughout northern and central India, though UP was home to the most sustained uprisings (Metcalf 1964; Stokes 1986). Having quashed the rebellions, the Government of India Act of 1858 transferred power officially to the British crown. Enforcement of "public order" became a chief objective of UP's government, a reason given to justify the further extension of state powers (Kudaisya 2006, 39).[5] Hindu–Muslim communal tensions added to the government's apprehensions about public order, and by the 1930s, police and army contingents were deployed to prevent communal violence across UP. Muslim aristocrats, who formed the dominant propertied class in Mughal India, saw their landholdings and political influence diminish under British rule (Robinson 1974). Hindu challenger elites seized the opportunity to claim a superior position, a process that deepened communal cleavages. The political project to make Hindi the dominant language of India also had its roots in UP's Hindu revivalist

3 Administrative reforms were initiated in the late-eighteenth century by Robert Clive, Warren Hastings and Lord Cornwallis, East India Company governors.

4 Hereafter, I use District Magistrate (DM) to refer to both posts, in line with common practice in UP public administration.

5 UP municipal centers were designed to be "riot-proof," with military cantonments and police stations placed strategically to control public gatherings (Kudaisya 2006, 50–58).

movement.[6] Debates over the use of Hindi versus Urdu in school curricula became a recurring source of Hindu–Muslim conflict.

4.2.2 Legalistic Bureaucracy in Postcolonial Uttar Pradesh (1950s–1970s)

The introduction of democracy in India substantially altered the aims and responsibilities of the UP state bureaucracy. Jawaharlal Nehru's Indian National Congress (INC) had two overarching national goals, namely, consolidation of democracy and economic planning for development. Both objectives were understood to require a bureaucracy committed to rule-following.[7] Despite holding conflicting views on the ICS, Nehru and Sardar Patel, another nationalist leader, agreed to maintain colonial-era administrative structures.[8] A disciplined organization with an all-India outlook, the ICS was credited with maintaining national unity and stability. Although an overhaul of the ICS was contemplated after independence to meet the fledgling country's needs, institutional reform was never pursued.[9] The Indian Administrative Service (IAS), which replaced the ICS, retained similar institutional structures.

Despite formal administrative continuities, the political goal to establish mass democracy placed bureaucrats in a new relationship with society. India adopted universal suffrage at the outset, a rare move in the history of democracy, and one that carried implications for bureaucracy as well. Shani's (2017) historical study of how a rule-oriented bureaucracy instituted India's early elections is instructive. State officials in charge of elections applied universalist principles of citizenship to enumerate voters, for example, by removing caste and religious identities from the earliest voter rolls. UP was an important site of such changes, as its population size, political significance and geographic proximity to New Delhi made the state pivotal to the Congress Party's national aims, including democratic consolidation. In the first three general elections

[6] Hindu "revivalism" swept northern India in the late-nineteenth century. Organizations like the Arya Samaj and Brahmo Samaj established themselves in UP and revitalized the study of Hindu scripture and traditions.

[7] Chibber (2003) demonstrates the political significance of bureaucratic rule-following within India's planned model of development. On bureaucratic rule-following and administration of Indian elections, see Shani (2017).

[8] Patel championed the ICS and its successor, the IAS (Goel 2013).

[9] Nehru lamented his inability to alter colonial administrative systems, which he conceded as his greatest failing as prime minister (Potter 1989, 128).

(1952, 1957 and 1962), Congress won almost 75 percent of seats in Parliament's Lok Sabha and dominated UP state assembly elections. Nehru and other nationalist leaders hailed from UP and the majority of Indian prime ministers were elected from UP constituencies.[10] UP's governing elites likewise comingled provincial politics with national issues.[11] The career of Govind Ballabh Pant, UP's first chief minister, illustrates these links. A Congress Party stalwart and independence movement leader, Pant served as chief minister for a decade and then moved to the central cabinet in 1955, serving as home minister until his death in 1961.[12] Pant's political assignments in the central government included mediating between rival organizational wings of the Congress Party (Brass 1965, 51).

The political significance of UP extended to public administration. The UP state bureaucracy's importance was visible within the formal structures and informal practices of the IAS. British rulers had considered UP to be "one of India's best governed states," a distinction that it maintained in the early decades after independence (Pai 2007, xvi).[13] Gifted public servants were most eager in UP, whose law and order bureaucracy was deemed a model for India as a whole. Notably, from the 1950s till present, fifteen of thirty-one cabinet secretaries of India–the highest-ranking civil service post–have been from UP, signaling the state's administrative importance (Table 4.1).

It is no surprise, then, that many IAS aspirants sought a position in the UP civil services, which was also seen as a stepping stone for reaching the central administration in New Delhi.[14] The prestige of the UP cadre was palpable early on in an IAS officer's career. India's elite training institute for the civil services was established in 1959 in the UP hill town of Mussoorie, later named the Lal Bahadur Shastri National Academy of Administration. The institute conducted the five-month Foundations Course for IAS "probationers." In addition to the essentials of public

10 Nehru was educated in Allahabad, a center of education in UP.

11 Singh (2015, 152–162) likewise observes that India's national politics comingled with state politics in UP.

12 Before independence, Pant served as premier (equivalent to chief minister) of the erstwhile United Provinces during 1937–1939 and 1946–1950.

13 A study of Block Development Officers from the 1960s found that UP bureaucrats performed better on development tasks compared to bureaucrats in Rajasthan (Mathur 1972).

14 Interviews with IAS officers in UP and New Delhi revealed a common assessment that a position in UP's IAS cadre offered advantages for one's career mobility in the civil service.

TABLE 4.1 *List of cabinet secretaries, Government of India (1950–2018)*

Year	Officer	Service	State cadre
1950–1953	**N.R. Pillai**	**ICS**	**United Provinces/Central Provinces**
1953–1957	Y.N. Sukthankar	ICS	Bombay
1957–1958	M.K. Vellodi	ICS	Madras
1958–1960	**Vishnu Sahay**	**ICS**	**United Provinces**
1960–1961	**B.N. Jha**	**ICS**	**United Provinces**
1961–1962	**Vishnu Sahay**	**ICS**	**United Provinces**
1962–1964	**S.S. Khera**	**ICS**	**United Provinces**
1964–1966	**Dharma Vira**	**ICS**	**United Provinces**
1966–1968	D.S. Joshi	ICS	Bombay/Maharashtra
1969–1970	B. Sivaraman	ICS	Orissa
1970–1972	**T. Swaminathan**	**ICS**	**United Provinces**
1972–1977	B.D. Pande	ICS	Bihar
1977–1980	N.K. Mukarji	ICS	Punjab
1980–1981	S.S. Grewal	IAS	Punjab
1981–1985	C.R. Krishnaswamy Rao Sahib	IAS	Andhra Pradesh
1985–1986	**P.K. Kaul**	**IAS**	**Uttar Pradesh**
1986–1989	B.G. Deshmukh	IAS	Maharashtra
1989	T.N. Seshan	IAS	Tamil Nadu
1989–1990	V.C. Pande	IAS	Rajasthan
1990–1992	Naresh Chandra	IAS	Rajasthan
1992–1993	S. Rajagopal	IAS	Maharashtra
1993–1994	Zafar Saifullah	IAS	Karnataka
1995–1996	**Surendra Singh**	**IAS**	**Uttar Pradesh**
1996–1998	**T.S.R. Subramanian**	**IAS**	**Uttar Pradesh**
1998–2000	**Prabhat Kumar**	**IAS**	**Uttar Pradesh**
2000–2002	T.R. Prasad	IAS	Andhra Pradesh
2002–2004	**Kamal Pande**	**IAS**	**Uttarakhand (formerly part of Uttar Pradesh)**
2004–2007	**B.K. Chaturvedi**	**IAS**	**Uttar Pradesh**
2007–2011	K.M. Chandrasekhar	IAS	Kerala
2011–2015	**Ajit Seth**	**IAS**	**Uttar Pradesh**
2015–2019	**P.K. Sinha**	**IAS**	**Uttar Pradesh**
2019–	Raijv Gauba	IAS	Jharkhand

Notes:
Lines in bold indicate officers from the Uttar Pradesh cadre ICS officers (unlike IAS) could be assigned to more than one province.
Sources: List of names compiled from "Cabinet Secretaries," *Cabinet Secretariat*, Government of India, available at: https://cabsec.gov.in/content.php?page=14 (accessed February 12, 2017). State cadres compiled from personnel records and author interviews with retired IAS officers.

administration and India's constitutional-legal framework, the academy cultivated *esprit de corps* among IAS officers.[15] To acquaint probationers with rural socioeconomic realities, they were sent for two weeks to a "backward" UP district and asked to report on their field observations. Training in UP gave IAS probationers their first experiences of the weighty responsibilities of district administration.

Beneath the UP bureaucracy's illustrious veneer, the actual conditions of local public administration were daunting. The UP Congress filled its organizational ranks with landowning Brahmins and Thakurs, local strongmen who found novel ways to use (and misuse) administrative rules to their advantage. The DM's office was frequently pressurized by upper-caste landlords, who held *de facto* authority in the rural hinterlands, where 80 percent of UP's electorate lived. The Congress electoral machine all but ensured that local bureaucracy served upper-caste interests, as demonstrated by the poor implementation of land reforms (Herring 1983).[16] Anti-zamindari laws imposed ceilings on the size of landholdings and called for the redistribution of surplus land, but enforcement was feeble (Kohli 1987, 214). The Congress Party adapted to local power structures, building its patronage network on the remnants of zamindari (Weiner 1967). The "Congress system" used patronage to cultivate support from landlords, who secured votes from economically dependent peasants (Kothari 1964). Local "link men" connected voters to the party and state, mediating their access to district administration. District Congress Committees were created to mirror the bureaucratic organization, facilitating patronage-based distribution of public resources.

4.2.3 Lower-Caste Mobilization and Administrative Turmoil (1980–2000s)

The political mobilization of lower castes, a process that accelerated in the 1980s, fundamentally altered state politics. A decade prior, regional and local formations representing subordinate groups started challenging

[15] Potter (1996, 180–211) discusses the evolution of the National Academy and shifting priorities for training and professional development.

[16] The Planning Commission's 1973 Task Force on Agrarian Relations noted: "In no sphere of public activity in our country since Independence has the hiatus between precept and practice, between policy pronouncements and actual execution, been as great as in the domain of land reform" (Herring 1983, 126).

Congress Party dominance. The first challenge came from agriculturalists belonging to middle and backward caste. A diverse assortment of upwardly mobile farmers, the Other Backward Classes (OBCs) benefited from technological changes under India's Green Revolution, generating gains in farm productivity.[17] Charan Singh, who hailed from the community of Jats, middle-caste cultivators, led the farmer movement and won UP state elections in 1967 (Jaffrelot 2000, 92). Subsequently, UP had unstable coalition governments whose tenure became increasingly short-lived. The first fifteen years of UP's statehood were comparatively stable and chief ministers completed their five-year terms. In subsequent years, the Congress Party held on to power and limited partisan competition, but UP chief ministers rarely completed their full terms (Table 4.2). As the time horizon for political office shortened, state governments became preoccupied simply with holding on to power, impeding the bureaucracy's ability to undertake transformative social projects (Kohli 1987, 189–222). The fragility of Congress-led governments reinforced New Delhi's political presence in UP. The invocation of President's rule, which became more frequent under Indira Gandhi's premiership, was also disruptive for the state bureaucracy.

The 1980s were years of political tumult that instigated changes in the ordinary relations between bureaucracy and rural society. Middle caste and OBC peasants mobilized politically for agricultural price subsidies from the state (Lerche 1999, 185–186). In western UP (and adjoining states), a region of mixed owner and tenant cultivation, farmer agitations became frequent. Western UP also saw faster agricultural growth, outpacing economic development in other parts of the state.[18] Varshney observes that small farmers from western UP learned "to deal with the bureaucracy more effectively" in this period, exhibited, for example, in their demands for more reliable electricity and water supply from public providers (1998, 132). However, farmer associations catered to middle castes and OBCs, leaving landless laborers, mostly Dalits, behind. The latter group lacked access to public resources and therefore became indebted to private moneylenders.

Backward castes coalesced around the Janata Dal party of V.P. Singh, who became UP's chief minister in 1980. Singh led a coalition defeating Congress in the 1989 general elections. In his brief stint as prime minister,

[17] On the Green Revolution's democratizing effects, see Dasgupta (2018).

[18] See Varshney's (1998) study of agrarian politics in this period. On the political mobilization of middle castes and OBCs, see Jaffrelot and Kumar (2012).

TABLE 4.2 *Uttar Pradesh state government leadership (1952–2022)*

Ruling party	Term in office	Chief Minister
INC	1950–1954	Govind Ballabh Pant
INC	1954–1960	Sampurnanand
INC	1960–1963	Chandra Bhanu Gupta
INC	1963–1967	S.K. Mendhwal
INC	1967	Chandra Bhanu Gupta
BKD	1967–1968	Charan Singh
President's rule	1968–1969	–
INC	1969–1970	Chandra Bhanu Gupta
BKD	1970	Charan Singh
INC(O)	1970–1971	T.N. Singh
INC	1971–1973	Kamlapati Tripathi
President's rule	1973	–
INC	1973–1975	H.N. Bahuguna
President's rule	1975–1976	–
INC	1976–1977	N.D. Tiwari
President's rule	1977	–
Janata Party	1977–1979	Ram Naresh Yadav
Janata Party	1979–1980	Banarsi Das
President's rule	1980	–
INC	1980–1982	V.P. Singh
INC	1982–1984	Sripati Mishra
INC	1984–1985	N.D. Tiwari
INC	1985–1988	Vir Bahadur Singh
INC	1988–1989	N.D. Tiwari
Janata Dal-led coalition	1989–1991	Mulayam Singh Yadav
BJP	1991–1993	Kalyan Singh
President's rule	1992–1993	–
SP-led coalition	1993–1995	Mulayam Singh Yadav
BSP-led coalition	1995	Mayawati
President's rule	1995–1997	–
BSP	1997	Mayawati
BJP	1997–1999	Kalyan Singh
BJP	1999–2000	Ram Prakash Gupta
BJP	2000–2002	Rajnath Singh
President's rule	2002	–
BSP-led coalition	2002–2003	Mayawati
SP	2003–2007	Mulayam Singh Yadav
BSP	2007–2012	Mayawati
SP	2012–2017	Akhilesh Yadav
BJP	2017–2022	Yogi Adityanath

Note: BSP: Bahujan Samaj Party; BJP: Bharatiya Janata Party; BKD: Bharatiya Kranti Dal; INC: Indian National Congress; INC(O): Indian National Congress Organisation; SP: Samajwadi Party

Source: Election Commission of India.

Singh promoted reservations (or quotas) to ensure OBCs preferential access to government jobs (Hasan 2002, 148–149). Till then, the constitution had provided reservations in public employment for SCs and STs, which were capped at 23 percent of posts. The National Commission on Backward Castes, led by B.P. Mandal, submitted its recommendations in 1983 calling for a separate OBC quota of 27 percent.[19] The central government under Singh implemented the Mandal Commission's recommendations in 1990. Cumulatively, the share of reserved posts increased to 50 percent.[20] Reservation policies helped unite OBCs but polarized UP's electorate, setting off protests by upper castes. Reservations also resonated with among lower-caste politicians, who framed debates on bureaucratic reform in terms of caste-based representation. Mulayam Singh Yadav, the head of the Samajwadi Party (SP), became UP's chief minister in 1989. His party, which embraced the cause of reservation, drew support from OBCs along with Muslims.

In the 1990s, farmer politics gave way to the "second democratic upsurge," as electoral mobilization by lower castes swept northern India (Yadav 2002). The Bahujan Samaj Party (BSP) became a formidable force, catalyzing a "silent revolution" of Dalit mobilization in UP (Jaffrelot 2003). The BSP was created in 1984 by Kanshi Ram, who founded the Backward and Minority Communities Employees Federation Union in 1978, a union representing lower-caste public employees. Kanshi Ram and Mayawati, his successor, belonged to the Chamar (or Jatav) subcaste, the BSP's core support base. In 1995, Mayawati made political history, becoming the first Dalit (and female) chief minister of UP. She assumed the mantle as BSP president in 2001 and forged a broader coalition of marginalized castes, Muslims and tribal groups, who formed the "Bahujan," or majority of the people.

Dalit political mobilization was a major development, especially in the context of UP's highly unequal caste structure. Upper divisions of the caste (*varna*) system – these include Brahmin, Kshatriya and Vaisya – account for approximately 20 percent of state's population.[21] Castes in UP are divided into finer segments, including subcaste (*jati*), brotherhood (*biradari*) and clan (*khandan*). In village society, jati has long inscribed

[19] Ahead of the central government's announcement on reservations, the UP government issued an ordinance granting a 15 percent quota to OBCs in the bureaucracy (Hasan 1998).

[20] Mandal was the first OBC chief minister of Bihar.

[21] Upper-caste and OBC population shares are based on India's 1931 Census, the last time the government reported comprehensive caste data.

social practices, from ordinary greetings and sharing meals to marriage customs. Hierarchies have even existed among jatis of the same caste. Shudras occupy the fourth rung of the varna ladder. Recognized administratively as OBCs, they comprise approximately 40 percent of UP's population. SCs or Dalits, account for 21 percent of the population. Pariahs of the caste system, Dalits were customarily deemed polluted and untouchable. Historically, the main occupational categories and agrarian labor relations in UP were closely tied to caste.[22] Zamindari abolition in UP hastened the decline of patron–client relations, but various forms of caste discrimination endured, as evidenced by caste-based segregation in villages (Lerche 1999). For example, by the late-1990s, only 30 percent of UP villages had access to a primary school, yet a disproportionate share were located in upper-caste habitations (PROBE 1999, 10).

In a context of entrenched caste inequality and discrimination, Dalit mobilization in UP has been a noteworthy political achievement. Participation by Dalits in local government and their growing presence in leadership roles is found to shape social attitudes towards the inclusion of lower castes (Jensenius 2017). However, the extent to which these changes have impacted ordinary caste relations in UP remains open to debate. Evidence that the BSP and SP have directly challenged village power structures is limited (Jeffrey and Lerche 2000; Pai 2002;). Nevertheless, as Dalit political clout and economic participation has increased, improvements in their social status are visible. Kapur et al. (2010) report changes in the occupations that Dalits perform, their increased participation in social functions, as well as new consumption habits traditionally associated with upper castes. In my own fieldwork, interviews with Dalits, OBCs and upper castes revealed the growing questioning of caste boundaries across the social spectrum, particularly among younger cohorts. Village-level fieldwork, reported later in this chapter, also demonstrates the growing collective mobilization by Dalit women and households around primary education and other public goods, which marks a major shift considering their historical exclusion from local governance. On the other hand, caste discrimination and untouchability have persisted in rural UP. As I observed, Dalits were barred from accessing upper-caste temples, public meeting spaces and water sources (e.g. wells and handpumps). Village residential hamlets and public facilities have also continued to be segregated by caste.

22 According to *jajmani*, a system of patron–client ties, occupational lower castes (*kamins*) provided labor to patrons (*jajmans*) in exchange for subsistence (Raheja 1988, 24–31).

If the broader impacts of Dalit electoral mobilization are subject to debate, many observers agree that clientelism and caste politics have sharpened UP's political cleavages, making it more difficult for the state to provide public goods. Political parties in UP have supported targeted policies rather than universal social programs (Keefer and Khemani 2004). Whereas in states like Tamil Nadu and Maharashtra Dalit social movements pressured political parties to promote social rights, the absence of such movements in UP has rendered parties less accountable for services like health and education (Ahuja 2019). UP also exemplifies what Chandra has coined "patronage-democracy," where elections are premised on the "ability of those who control the state to exercise discretion in the *implementation* of state policy" (2004, 116).[23] From land records and birth registration to anti-poverty programs, politicians often interfere in the distribution of state resources. Instead of advancing policy platforms, UP politicians make identity-based appeals to win votes. Citizen–state relations are thus depicted as transactional and corrupt.

Lower-caste political mobilization has also influenced UP's bureaucratic development, in rather complex ways. The SP and the BSP have exerted political control over the state, redirecting programs to benefit target constituencies. They have also supported caste-based reservations. As chief minister, Mulayam Singh Yadav pressed for lower-caste representation in the bureaucracy, expediting recruitment of OBCs (particularly Yadavs) into teaching, police and other frontline positions. Of the 900 teachers recruited under his government, 720 were Yadavs, as were 1,223 of 3,151 newly appointed police officers (Jaffrelot 2000, 103). At higher levels of administration, Yadav transferred upper-caste bureaucrats and assigned OBCs to influential posts, changes that were widely publicized by his government. Mayawati was equally known for enacting bureaucratic reshuffles. In one fell swoop, she transferred more than a hundred senior bureaucrats (Kumar 1999, 824). She gave powerful portfolios to loyal civil servants, while demoting those who challenged her government's directives.[24] These pressures have exacted a toll on bureaucratic morale.[25] During the first two years of fieldwork for this book,

[23] Emphasis in original. See also Chandra (2014).

[24] "Mayawati suspends two senior bureaucrats; transfers 100," *Hindustan Times*, May 13, 2007. Available at: www.hindustantimes.com/lucknow/mayawati-suspends-two-senior-bureaucrats-transfers-100/story-EzysaJzQWAoN4HpoLYMz3M.html.

[25] Interviews of current and retired IAS Officers suggest the negative impact of transfers on bureaucratic morale. Also see local media coverage, for example, "Transfer raj in Uttar Pradesh: Shifting of officers upsets bureaucracy," *Hindustan Times*, October 3, 2012.

UP's education secretary changed five times. In one local official's words, "*Forget years, now we count days and months that the Secretary holds office.*"[26] Yet, the prevalence of bureaucratic transfers is not a recent phenomenon, nor one that is unique to UP.[27] In Himachal Pradesh, for example, the post of Sarva Shiksha Abhiyan (SSA) State Project Director also lay vacant for more than two years of my field research.

Notwithstanding these political disruptions, bureaucrats have used rules to reinforce their authority and status. The continued emphasis on written documentation, including official orders, advisories and circulars, offers a case in point. As Gupta observes, the proliferation of written records in UP has helped maintain bureaucratic hierarchy by ensuring that communication "traveled easily from higher levels of authority to lower ones" (2012, 207). The political incorporation of lower castes has also bolstered the importance of bureaucratic documents and rules in shaping citizens' lives.[28] While privileged castes have often used social connections (*jan pehchan*) to access state agencies, Dalits and other marginalized groups have long struggled to gain state support (Jeffrey and Lerche 2000, 866; Ahuja and Chhibber 2012). There are well-documented cases of mistreatment of Dalits by frontline functionaries, most notably the police (Jaffrelot 1998). Responding to such violations, a signature effort by Mayawati's government was to strengthen law and order through the implementation of the SC-ST Prevention of Atrocities Act, legislation protecting Dalits from discrimination and caste-related violence. . By encouraging registration of cases with local administration, along with swift police and judicial action, the BSP government has "had a profound impact on the Dalit's relationship with the law," Jaoul observes, helping to spawn "[a]n informal culture of legal activism" (2015, 175).[29] Lower-caste political mobilization in UP appears, then, to have helped reinforce bureaucratic legalism from below.

Available at: https://economictimes.indiatimes.com/news/politics-and-nation/transfer-raj-in-uttar-pradesh-shifting-of-officers-eupsets-bureaucracy/articleshow/16647502.cms.

[26] Interview with local official, Mathura district, February 2009.

[27] Potter (1996) reports that two-thirds of UP district officers in 1936 held their posts for less than one year. Iyer and Mani (2011) find that the probability of an IAS officer being transferred is 53 percent, with the rate in UP being slightly higher.

[28] Elsewhere, Chandra argues (2014) that "patronage-democracy" in UP has helped bind underprivileged citizens to the state and may have helped strengthen the legitimacy of bureaucratic rules, particularly rules surrounding the democratic process.

[29] Citing Jaffrelot (1998), Jaoul notes a fifteen-fold increase in First Information Reports (FIRs) filed by Dalits in UP police stations between 1990 and 1995, partially due to "local administrators' newly receptive attitudes to Dalit complaints under the first BSP government" (2015, 174).

During her subsequent term as chief minister, Mayawati bolstered her reputation for disciplining the police and promoting law and order.[30] After a decisive victory in 2007, her party formed the first majority government in UP after twenty-six years. In an election causing political ripples, the BSP stitched a cross-caste coalition between Dalits and upper castes, a strategic shift to represent "*sarva samaj*" (all of society). Political attention to law and order influenced how frontline officials interacted with underprivileged groups. Personal security and dignified treatment by the police have remained core concerns for Dalits in UP. As I demonstrate in subsequent sections, governmental pressure on DMs and other local officials to follow through with administrative and judicial processes has also encouraged Dalits to voice complaints and activate formal grievance procedures within the state.

The preceding discussion has outlined the political process whereby legalistic bureaucracy in UP emerged and propagated across time. While originating in the colonial ideal of a "law and order" state, UP's political centrality to Indian national politics after independence supported bureaucratic rule-following. State officials used rules to expand their authority in the face of political interferences. And while the rise of multiparty competition and lower-caste political mobilization has challenged bureaucratic authority, these political changes have also reinforced legalism from below, encouraging subaltern claim-making through administrative and legal processes. In the rest of this chapter, I offer field-based evidence to demonstrate how legalistic bureaucracy in UP has carried out the mandate for universal primary education.

4.3 HOW LEGALISTIC BUREAUCRACY PROMOTES ENROLLMENT AND SCHOOL INFRASTRUCTURE PROVISION

This section investigates how legalistic bureaucracy in UP has promoted gains in primary school enrollment and infrastructure, which has improved considerably since the late 1990s, notwithstanding the state government's weak political commitment to primary education. Evidence from state-, district- and village-level fieldwork reveals the mechanisms by which legalistic bureaucracy has contributed to these improvements. I first examine the SSA program in UP and its organizational links to the wider state bureaucracy. I then turn to local implementation in rural

[30] Interviews with senior bureaucrats and police officers, Lucknow, June 2009.

districts, showcasing how bureaucratic commitment to rules has percolated down the administrative hierarchy, motivating frontline officials to adopt a narrow interpretation of rules and resist political interferences while providing schooling inputs in underserved villages.

4.3.1 The Education for All Program

The SSA program became operational in UP in 2002. The State Project Office in Lucknow was mandated to administer the expansion of schooling. How did senior bureaucrats understand the policy mandate for universal primary education? How, moreover, did they address political interferences amid school expansion? Historically, upper castes had vested interests in the location of schools and held political sway over decisions. Primary schools were often located in upper-caste hamlets, making it difficult for lower-caste children to access schooling. Primary school buildings also served as voting booths, a political dimension to school development in India that has persisted (see Figure 4.2). A senior education official described these dynamics: "*Providing socially disadvantaged groups access ... that was always a tough issue. The fact is that the elementary school is not only a place of learning, but also the election booth.*"[31] Placing schools closer to their hamlets, upper castes could influence elections, while also excluding lower castes from participating in education. Furthermore, the contentious politics of schoolteachers crowded out other pressing issues facing schools and stymied implementation (Kingdon and Muzammil 2003).

To counter these tendencies, the SSA program provided school resources and teaching inputs, but importantly, it also gave bureaucrats institutional space to circumvent the contentious politics of education. UP's Department of Education held managerial charge of the school system and its human resources, overseeing teacher postings, pay and promotions. As a retired official noted, the two subdivisions "*respected one another's boundaries,*" working within their respective mandates.[32] Maintaining clear separation administrative boundaries, the bureaucracy upheld a division of *political* labor between SSA's State Project Office and the Department of Education. A former SSA State Project Director described the arrangement:

[31] Interview with senior education official, Lucknow, June 2009.

[32] Interview with former Director of Education, Lucknow, December 2009.

FIGURE 4.2 Voting for national elections underway in a government primary school (Saharanpur, Uttar Pradesh)
Note: Author photograph (2009).

> Planning under SSA has taken a project mode, almost like an autonomous organization. That organizational divide has protected us from the routine politics in the Department of Basic Education. The Directorate [of Basic Education] has kept up that [political] part of the routine, allowing us to focus on the school development side. And to our benefit, we have been insulated from various political demands. That space has been critical for planning. We could stay busy expanding infrastructure without being bogged down by systemic political issues.[33]

Likewise, another official noted that "*organizational autonomy*" allowed SSA to concentrate on enrollment campaigns and infrastructure expansion.[34] Collective adherence to administrative boundaries shielded SSA officials from the political pressures of schoolteachers. Given prior experiences of elite interference, bureaucrats sought clear and enforceable standards for school infrastructure provision. SSA guidelines required that all habitations should be provided a primary school within a one-kilometer walking distance. Education officials adopted a strict interpretation of this guideline, which became the chief criterion for prioritizing school construction. An official explained:

[33] Interview with former State Project Director, SSA, Lucknow, December 2009.
[34] Interview with senior education official, Lucknow, January 2010.

From the point of view of SSA, providing access to education is the only relevant issue, and as long as we can show that a habitation has the need for a new school building, then our requirements for planning are met … At the grassroots level, politics still plays a very important role. But we have avoided that at the planning stage by sticking to our needs-based assessment.[35]

State planners also found it advantageous to apply rules uniformly throughout the state, instead of planning separately for each region. Common rules were seen as the "*first line of defense*" against meddling by politicians.[36]

Strict interpretation of program rules by senior officials motivated local school officials to adhere to targets and combat interference. SSA devolved authority locally to District Project Offices, where local officials formulated annual plans, monitored services and reported progress to state officials. District Coordinators were appointed to manage different policy components, such as enrollment, school construction, girls' education and specialized programming for out-of-school children. In UP, the District Education Officer, or Basic Shiksha Adhikari (BSA), oversaw local school administration. Frontline officials monitored progress on goals, such as universal coverage and enrollment of out-of-school children. Instead of adjusting evaluation targets according to the diverse socioeconomic conditions across UP, they applied a common formula for government primary schools in all seventy-one districts. A uniform framework helped maintain what officials called a "*rational*" system, which sent a clear signal down the hierarchy that "*objective*" and "*fair*" methods were employed to monitor district administration.[37] Senior officials performed painstakingly detailed documentation for performance reviews, pressuring districts to report enrollment figures and document provision of schooling inputs, such as uniforms, textbooks and financial incentives. An official described the bureaucracy's approach to monitoring:

We try to make the evaluation objective. We have made a target for the BSA [District Education Officer] and ABSA [Block Education Officer] to visit forty schools per month. Twelve officers multiplied over forty schools means four hundred and eighty school visits per month in each district. And the outcomes need to be appropriately documented.[38]

Establishing "*discipline*" through monitoring was deemed necessary given external political pressures. A senior official involved in district

35 Interview with senior official, SSA, Lucknow, March 2009

36 Interview with local education official, Mathura, April 2009.

37 Interviews with several SSA program officials, Lucknow, February 2009.

38 Interview with senior official, SSA, Lucknow, March 2009.

monitoring made the point succinctly, "*If policy targets can be changed, they can also be manipulated.*"[39] Other officials expressed misgivings about applying common targets and planning formulae throughout the state. For example, they highlighted the particular difficulties of working in economically deprived districts of eastern UP, where schools catered to first-generation learners. However, these concerns about regional differences were outweighed by bureaucratic commitment to ensuring uniformity of rules.

4.3.2 Policy Implementation in Rural Districts

Interviews of senior education officials suggested that a commitment to legalism shaped planning and monitoring activities, supporting the expansion of school coverage. They also raised questions as to whether a rule-based orientation percolated down to district administration. How did officials at this level cope with pressures to follow rules amid political interferences and caste conflict? I present local-level findings from comparative fieldwork in Saharanpur and Sitapur, two very different administrative districts (see the map in Figure 4.1). Saharanpur is relatively urbanized, located in the high-growth agricultural belt of western UP, while Sitapur is a poorer district in central UP, with weaker socioeconomic indicators (Table 4.3). Electoral politics also differs between the districts. Saharanpur has been a political mainstay of the BSP, which ruled UP with a majority government during my fieldwork. The party had organizational roots near Saharanpur and Dalits living there had higher literacy than in other parts of UP (Pai 2002). After the 2007 state elections, the BSP held four of five Saharanpur assembly seats. In Sitapur, assembly seats were split between the BSP and its main rival, the SP. Among Dalits, Chamars in Western UP formed the backbone of the BSP's electoral support.[40] Sitapur, by contrast, has a high proportion of Pasis, another Dalit jati. Pasis supported the BSP, albeit with less enthusiasm since the party was perceived to be more dedicated to working for Chamars (Duncan 1999). The political importance of Saharanpur for the BSP was evident from Mayawati's decision to appoint Dharam Singh Saini, a Member of the Legislative Assembly (MLA) from Saharanpur, as education minister.[41]

[39] Interview with senior education official, Lucknow, March 2009.

[40] Former Chief Minister Mayawati, who belongs to the Chamar caste, was raised in western UP's Meerut district.

[41] Saini was elected from the Sarsawa assembly constituency in Saharanpur.

TABLE 4.3 *Comparative socioeconomic indicators for Uttar Pradesh study districts (2011)*

	Saharanpur	Sitapur	Uttar Pradesh
Population	3,466,382	4,483,992	199,812,341
Urban (%)	30.8	11.8	22.3
Scheduled caste (%)	22.1	32.3	20.7
Muslim (%)	42.0	19.9	19.3
Adult literacy rate (%)	70.5	61.1	67.7
Gender gap in literacy (%)	16.5	19.6	20.1
Child sex ratio (females per 1,000 males, ages 0–6)	887	930	902
Income per capita (₹ at 2011 prices)	38,851	25,182	32,002
Poverty headcount ratio (%)	26.7	53.3	43.2
Deprivation index	37.77	70.55	54.53

Sources:
Demographic and social indicators from the 2011 Census of India.
Income per capita from Uttar Pradesh Economic Survey, 2011–2012, using 2011 prices.
Poverty headcount ratio from National Sample Survey (2011).

Local officials in Saharanpur had direct access to the state education establishment, improving the prospects for policy implementation.

Given stark differences between the two districts, the similarities I observed in how their local education bureaucracies operated were surprising. Local officials understood their policy mandates in very similar ways, as evidenced in monthly review meetings held by the BSA in each district. The meetings began with the BSA combing through district annual work plans and assessing the fulfillment of SSA targets. Junior functionaries were asked to explain whether programs were on track or lagging. In a meeting in Saharanpur, I observed the BSA scrutinize a table containing "physical targets" (*bhautik lakshya*) for school infrastructure. During the review, a case emerged about a school in Gangoh block. An inspection revealed that construction at the school had failed to meet prescribed standards. Iron rods supporting the edifice were incorrectly installed, creating the risk of a building collapse. The BSA asked his subordinates what "follow-up action" (*karyavahi*) had been undertaken. They handed him a notice sent to the contractor ordering a halt to construction. The contractor had flouted the warning and continued building. Studying the letter, the BSA summoned the contractor to his office, where he was castigated. The BSA's office drafted a circular for SSA building standards, which was issued to all local contractors involved in school construction in Saharanpur.

The importance given to SSA rules was shared by local administration in Sitapur. In Sitapur's district education office, officials were eager to show me the district annual work plan and progress reports. We discussed a table showing that the enrollment of girls and lower-caste children had increased over the previous year. The table relied on a chain of data from enrollment registers maintained by teachers to "cluster" registers of Nyaya Panchayat Resource Coordinators, to Block Resource Coordinators (BRCs), who compiled block-level data. Data gathering and reporting at each level was a painstaking process. Figures needed to be cross-checked and discrepancies accounted for with the higher-ups. These bureaucrats understood SSA reporting as their paramount responsibility and assigned high importance to maintaining official "government documents" (*sarkari kaghaz*). Sitapur's BSA, for example, saw documentation as a means for "*disciplining*" subordinates, who maintained tidy records to signal their observance of rules.[42] A BRC, whose duty it was to maintain records, discussed the importance of documenting SSA enrollment figures:

> We [BRCs] have to keep enrollment statistics (*aankde*) on our fingertips. At any moment, Sahib (senior officer) can call us to inquire about why the number has gone down in one school or why, in another school, it has suddenly increased ... Sitting here [at the BRC office] I can come up with any story, but what I say has to corroborate with the enrollment register at the school ... I have seen other BRC's get reprimanded for not having the correct figures. One doesn't want to be made a donkey (*gadha*) in front of others.[43]

The burden of documentation also drew criticism from officials. Some referred to SSA reporting as a "statistical play" (*aankdebazi*), which the bureaucracy performed at the World Bank's behest.[44] Yet, these same officials showed appreciation for the discipline produced by reporting, which was seen to prevent bureaucratic "laxity" (*dhilapan*).[45] In one official's words: "*Without the requirement to report, how could we know the [school] system's performance? Were it not for our rules, the whole system would collapse.*"[46]

42 Interview with local education official, Sitapur, May 2009.
43 Ibid.
44 A similar complaint was made by teachers in Sitapur, who noted that pressures to fulfill administrative duties overshadowed teaching.
45 Focus group discussion with block-level officials, Sitapur, April 2009.
46 Ibid.

FIGURE 4.3 New government primary school building (Saharanpur, Uttar Pradesh)
Note: Author photograph (2009).

Bureaucratic pressures to abide by program rules also helped safeguard infrastructure provision from political interference. In both study districts, officials recounted several cases of local elites attempting to subvert or capture school construction (see Figures 4.3 and 4.4). Consider the example of Mr. Rana, a BEO in Saharanpur with twenty years of experience. When visiting Mr. Rana's office, I observed routine interactions between education officials, building contractors and village leaders. On a typical day, Mr. Rana received eight to ten visits from contractors and village representatives, often seeking assistance with construction work. On one occasion, a contractor informed Mr. Rana that his cement delivery had been delayed due to a road accident. Mr. Rana called a village official to make further inquiries. After the call ended, he abruptly asked the contractor to leave the room. Gazing at his desk, Mr. Rana said to me, "*Look at what we have to deal with. I just learned that this guy [the contractor] hired a truck that was in a cement robbery. The truck was being held by the police ... This is the third time we have seen this happen in a week.*" He reviewed the invoice for the cement purchase, which he suspected was fraudulent. In situations like this, he noted, village representatives sometimes kept a check on contractors. More often, he found that the two parties operated in collusion to "*eat*"

FIGURE 4.4 Government primary school classroom (Sitapur, Uttar Pradesh)
Note: AUTHOR PHOTOGRAPH (2009).

government contracts. He preferred all school infrastructure work to be documented in writing, with photographs attached.

Commitment to rules was also evident when village elites tried to influence construction of new primary schools. Ms. Bansal, an official working alongside Mr. Rana, described how village leaders tried controlling the location of schools. She received phone calls the previous week from local politicians, including an MLA, requesting to have three primary schools built in his constituency. She reviewed the request with Mr. Rana and learned that two of the three villages already had a school within walking distance. The third village, a smaller hamlet, was ineligible since a school had been sanctioned in the more populous adjoining hamlet. Ms. Bansal declined the MLA's request and clarified that local administration was bound by "rules" (*niyam*) for eligibility. During the next few days, I observed village leaders visit Mr. Rana's office, demanding an explanation for why the schools were not sanctioned. The conversation became heated as Ms. Bansal argued with Pratap Singh, a village leader, who demanded a new school in his hamlet. Ms. Bansal tried to reason with him, noting that the hamlet had access to a school half a kilometer away in the next village. Pratap Singh was not satisfied, noting that other villages in the area had more than one primary school. "*That is because those villages have large numbers of children*," Ms. Bansal retorted. She pulled out a booklet summarizing SSA program rules. Pratap Singh accused Ms. Bansal of showing favoritism and threatened to use his "*approach*" (with politicians) to get her transferred. In a stern voice, Ms. Bansal responded: "*bullying* (dadagiri) *will get you nowhere*." She suggested that he go file complaints against her, but she was not budging. Incidents like this occurred frequently in Saharanpur. According to Ms. Bansal, the bureaucracy's close adherence to program rules occasioned conflicts, but it also enabled her to challenge societal demands without hesitation. If she worked by the rules and kept written records, she expected senior officials to support her. In the contentious arena of local politics, rule-following gave frontline officials a sense of stability and confidence.

4.3.3 Coping with Political Clientelism

I have shown so far how legalism shapes bureaucratic behaviors for tasks such as student enrollment and school infrastructure provision. This section examines how local education officials cope with particularistic pressures during implementation. The Ambedkar Village Program (AVP) distributes public programs and infrastructure to Dalit villages. Initiated by Mulayam Singh Yadav's government in 1991, the AVP scheme initially provided development assistance, for example, for footpaths and water pumps, in villages with a majority of Dalits. AVP has been interpreted by scholars as a form of caste-based favoritism, since it targets public resources toward a subsection of rural society. Pai (2002) finds that a narrow slice of Dalits have benefited from the program, creating resentment among other disadvantaged groups. Likewise, Singh critiques the AVP for "siphoning of funds away from development schemes meant for the entire state and concentrating them in small Dalit enclaves" (Singh 2015, 166). Village development projects are allocated based on caste considerations rather than demonstrated need. After the BSP assumed power in the mid-1990s, Chief Minister Mayawati enthusiastically took up the program. Mayawati brought down the Dalit population threshold for villages to qualify for AVP, reducing it to 22–30 percent of residents, while also expanding the scheme's territorial reach (Pai 2002, 130). Her government also expanded the list of approved projects in 1997 to include village electrification, drainage, irrigation, housing and education.

At the time of my fieldwork, the Mayawati government issued directives for all districts to prioritize Ambedkar Villages for school infrastructure projects. Interestingly, I found that local education officials used *programmatic* SSA rules to work around the government's directive. To understand how bureaucrats combated particularism, we need to unpack the practical mechanics of administering the AVP. Villages included in the AVP list were revenue villages, whose administrative boundaries are maintained by the *patwari*, an official in charge of village land records, as well as the Panchayat Secretary. A revenue village has multiple hamlets (*bastis*) for different caste groups. The administrative unit used for local development planning is the habitation, comprised of multiple bastis. The Department of Education performed habitation-level planning to identify where schools needed to be built. After a revenue village was selected for the AVP list, the choice of habitation to target for infrastructure provision was left to the discretion of local bureaucrats. An example from my fieldwork helps to illustrate the discretionary process. In Saharanpur, I obtained the AVP list for 2008–2011 from district administration. The list contained 213 revenue villages (out of 1,264 in total) within the district. In focus group discussions, district officials compared the AVP list with their village database and habitation maps. An official summarized how they interpreted the AVP rules to achieve infrastructure goals:

> For school building improvements, we generate our own list of villages to inspect first. This includes the Ambedkar Villages. We receive proposals from the *gram pradhan* as well … However, we only take the decision to move ahead with a project once we are satisfied that our conditions are met. In the end, the work has to be done according to our norms. On this we don't budge.[47]

Other officials chimed in, explaining how "*need*" was interpreted in accordance with SSA rules, which allowed them to target schools requiring new infrastructure.[48] Some were critical of AVP, referring to it as a "*show*" (*dikhava*), a cosmetic undertaking. Politicians used the program to target work in their preferred villages, a means for scoring political points. Political involvement in the AVP also created community tensions. A district official narrated an instance where the *pradhan* of an Ambedkar Village kept showing up at his office to demand construction of a new classroom, even though the school's infrastructure had already

[47] Focus group discussion with BEOs, Saharanpur, Participant 1, March 2009.
[48] Focus group discussion with BEOs, Saharanpur, Participants 3, 5 and 6, March 2009.

been upgraded.[49] The pradhan organized a meeting (*baithak*) with village leaders and residents, where they accused district officials of failing to perform their duties. "*Because of these situations*," the official remarked with frustration, "*I have to personally visit the proposed village and document all the work that has already been completed.*"[50]

To further investigate how AVP impacted implementation of schooling, I conducted participant observation of primary schools in three Ambedkar Villages in Saharanpur.[51] In all three villages, schools were targeted with new infrastructure under AVP. However, village residents I spoke with praised the local education bureaucracy for making improvements, even though local politicians claimed the credit.[52] Take the case of Rangpura, an Ambedkar Village located sixteen miles from Saharanpur's district center. During my field visit, infrastructure upgrades through AVP, including cemented footpaths and new shauchalay electricity lines, had been completed. Primary and middle schools in the village also had new infrastructure, including three large, freshly painted classrooms, a kitchen shed, boundary wall and new water supply. The latest addition, a girls' bathroom (*balika shauchalay*) had been completed the previous week. Teachers and parents I interviewed saw the bathroom as a welcome addition that would help improve the regularity of attendance by girls. Parents credited BEOs for installing the bathroom. They also praised a retired teacher from Rangpura for helping to monitor its construction.

AVP had an impact over and above infrastructure provision. As teachers noted in interviews, inspections by local administration made them more conscious of their schools' physical conditions and how this impacted students. For instance, they took greater care to ensure that girls' bathrooms were well maintained. Teachers also had explicit instructions from the education bureaucracy to monitor child attendance, especially during the harvest season, when many adolescent boys and girls missed school to perform agricultural labor with their families. Rangpura's headmaster described the process of monitoring:

> We receive monitoring visits from officials about once a month. Mostly it is from the Education Department, but it can be officials from other departments as well ... Anyone can come at any time to inspect us ... They [inspections]

49 Focus group discussion with BEOs, Saharanpur, Participant 2, March 2009.

50 Ibid.

51 I selected three villages from the AVP village list based on their distance from major roads, allowing variation in accessibility and likelihood of monitoring by local administration.

52 Local politicians I met in Saharanpur often took credit for development projects.

are time-consuming, and take us away from our teaching, but they also keep us alert ... The school boundary wall and girls' bathroom were constructed under the Ambedkar Village Scheme only after the inspections ... Now they [the monitors] are especially concerned to know if the girls' bathroom is working.[53]

The impact of monitoring was not confined to schools located in Ambedkar Villages. Teachers interviewed from three different administrative blocks of Saharanpur reported that AVP had instilled a "*fear of inspection*" (*nirikshan ka dar*) throughout the district. Local bureaucrats paid multiple visits to ensure that enrollment and infrastructure standards were met. Participant observation with local officials during monitoring visits, along with my observations of schools in non-Ambedkar villages away from Rangpura, suggested that school inspections were extensive and took place regularly.

Implementation of AVP may arguably have been more effective in Saharanpur given the BSP's political standing in the district. To probe further, I sought comparative evidence from Sitapur, where the BSP and SP competed for influence over district administration. Traveling from Sitapur's central market out to villages, I observed community centers with Ambedkar's name and photograph displayed outside. These community buildings, provided by Mayawati's government, were visible markers of AVP program but also signified the presence of new political spaces for Dalits. Compared to Saharanpur, local bureaucracy in Sitapur operated in a more contentious political environment due to conflicting demands between rival parties catering to Dalits and OBCs. The education bureaucracy in Sitapur was directed to construct new boundary walls to schools in Ambedkar Villages on a priority basis, but local officials were caught in the crossfire of competing political claims.[54] In a focus group discussion, officials described the myriad ways that AVP had made their lives difficult. An official recounted an incident in Shahpur, an Ambedkar Village, where a new primary school boundary wall had been sanctioned:

The pradhan [of Shahpur] caught hold of us as we were approaching the school to assess the building for installing the boundary wall. He started making demands for a hand pump and an additional classroom. But the school already had the full facilities given by SSA. I explained [to him] that we have strict guidelines for school infrastructure. I told him that even the boundary wall was only being provided after an assessment by the [Education] Department.[55]

[53] Interview with teacher, Saharanpur, March 2009.
[54] Interviews with local officials, Sitapur, May 2009.
[55] Interview with local education official, Sitapur, June 2009.

Reinforcing her colleague's point, another official suggested that village leaders created confusion among residents by making unreasonable demands. For example, she noted that another village leader from Shahpur called her office to complain that the school had not received a new hand pump, even though he had learned that hand pumps were installed in non-Ambedkar villages nearby. She tried clarifying that support from AVP pertained to school boundary walls and did not include the provision of hand pumps. Unconvinced, he threatened to escalate the matter to the local MLA.

Education officials in Sitapur experienced AVP as a source of political tension and unreasonable demands. At the same time, the program enabled them to pursue education goals under SSA. BEOs had strict orders to provide boundary walls to schools located in Ambedkar Villages, but the orders were ambiguous about other infrastructure, such as bathrooms and kitchen sheds. Local officials used the ambiguity in rules to meet school infrastructure targets in non-Ambedkar villages as well.[56] That way, they could achieve "*balance*" (*santulan*) between rival parties and demonstrate that no particular group was being favored.[57] The strategy also allowed them to provide school infrastructure more efficiently. By the time bathrooms were completed in non-Ambedkar villages, boundary walls for schools in Ambedkar Villages were also completed, helping local administration achieve SSA infrastructure targets simultaneously in multiple locations.

The preceding discussion has shown how legalistic bureaucracy in UP has worked to improve school coverage and infrastructure provision. At the upper tiers of the education bureaucracy, state planners adhered closely to SSA rules and administrative boundaries circumventing political pressures to meet program goals. A rule-based orientation percolated down to lower-level bureaucrats as well, stimulating shared understandings and behaviors among officials based in very different sociopolitical regions of UP. District officials collectively reinterpreted political directives to accord with programmatic rules, countering interference in school infrastructure provision. The findings also suggested that caste politics presented significant challenges for implementation. In Section 4.4, I explore how legalistic bureaucracy deals with societal divisions and inequalities, particularly while engaging marginalized castes in service delivery.

56 For example, in Pisawan block, local officials oversaw construction of bathrooms and other facilities in non-Ambedkar villages.

57 Interview with local education official, Sitapur, June 2009.

4.4 THE MIDDAY MEAL PROGRAMME: ACCOUNTING FOR SERVICE DELIVERY

This section examines implementation of the MDM Programme in UP. The world's largest child nutrition intervention, the scheme aims to tackle malnutrition and improve student attendance. Through multilevel field research, I show that legalistic bureaucratic norms facilitated broad coverage by the MDM Programme but weakened routine monitoring of services, leading to lower quality provision of school meals. Through administrative grievance procedures, the MDM Programme in UP sought to improve service delivery by encouraging participation from local communities. However, the rule-based approach to grievance redressal has imposed administrative burdens on citizens, while reproducing social inequalities and caste stigmas, which in turn has weakened community oversight of the program.

4.4.1 The MDM Authority in Lucknow

The MDM Program in UP covers 168,000 primary and middle schools, providing a free midday meal daily to an estimated 17 million children. The program has achieved broad coverage, as indicated in Chapter 2, but the quality of services is found wanting.[58] Senior MDM officials were forthcoming in interviews about implementation defects – the use of low-quality grains, children falling sick with food poisoning, untouchability and discrimination against lower-caste children – which made frequent newspaper headlines.[59] "*The media has shown no mercy*," an official remarked.[60] Along with intense public scrutiny of the scheme, the Mayawati government also came under heavy media criticism. In response, Mayawati wrote a letter to Prime Minister Manmohan Singh, urging that the central government reconsider the program's design, since the system of providing cooked meals seemed to be floundering.[61] Several

[58] See the Accountability Initiative (2013) PAISA Survey. The Comptroller and Auditor General of India reported disruptions in cooked meal provision in UP schools for thirty-two days on average in a school year (CAG 2015, 112).

[59] "125 children taken ill after consuming mid-day meal in Uttar Pradesh," *Indian Express*, March 19, 2016. Available at: http://indianexpress.com/article/india/india-news-india/125-children-taken-ill-after-consuming-mid-day-meal-in-uttar-pradesh.

[60] Interview with senior official, MDM Authority, Lucknow, February 2009.

[61] "Mid-day meal scheme defective: Mayawati," *The Hindu*, October 24, 2007. Available at: www.thehindu.com/todays-paper/tp-national/tp-otherstates/Mid-day-meal-scheme-defective-Mayawati/article14862915.ece.

bureaucrats that I interviewed agreed with the Mayawati government's prognosis. In place of cooked meals, they recommended that the UP government reinstate an earlier system of distributing dry rations for students to take home. This option was blocked, however, by a 2001 Supreme Court ruling requiring the provision of cooked meals (Drèze and Goyal 2003).

Headquartered in Lucknow, the MDM Authority oversaw program administration. The MDM Director was supported by a team of assistant directors, finance officers, computer specialists and support staff. The MDM Authority was supervised by a management committee of senior bureaucrats, including the Principal Secretaries of education, finance, planning, rural development and panchayati raj, and chaired by the chief secretary. The administrative structure was designed to encourage collaboration between departments, but in practice, the MDM Authority operated independently. Engagement from other departments was limited, except for the public distribution system, which supplied food grains. In interviews, state officials expressed a rule-based understanding of the MDM scheme. Several of them referred to the MDM Program as an "*accounting scheme*," and described their primary duties to involve managing the flow of funds to district administration.[62] Summarizing these perspectives, an MDM official explained:

> The administration of the Midday Meal program … it is basically a financial management scheme. The state government (our office), gives the funds to the District Magistrate (DM), who is the nodal officer at the local level. Under the DM sits the District Education Officer (Basic Shiksha Adhikari), and he is the real person responsible for implementation.[63]

Other officials similarly described the MDM scheme as a means of "*fiscal decentralization*," allowing district administration greater authority to manage funds.[64] The, responsibilities of the BSA went far beyond fund management. The BSA oversaw local program implementation and monitoring, including construction of kitchen sheds and provision of inputs to schools. Along with disbursal of funds, the MDM Authority issued circulars to districts notifying program rules for appointing cooking staff, provision of physical inputs including grains and cooking supplies, as well as hygiene standards for meal preparation. With media portrayals

[62] Interviews with several officials, MDM Authority, Lucknow, February–April 2009.

[63] Interview with senior official, MDM Authority, Lucknow, February 2009.

[64] Interviews with several officials, MDM Authority, Lucknow, February–April 2009.

of children falling ill after consuming school meals, officials were under pressure to ensure cleanliness in schools. A senior MDM official explained:

> The Government of India has provided strict norms for the Midday Meal Programme. There has to be a kitchen shed, which is financed through a one-time grant of ₹60,000. Also, there must be containers for food, utensils, and such. Then cooks must also be hired at the local level. We don't need them to be full-time cooks, but we do require hygienic conditions … Things [in the MDM program] do not always run perfectly, but on hygiene we don't compromise.[65]

Concerns regarding "*hygiene*" were expressed by other senior officials as well. To enforce standards for food preparation, district authorities needed to work with teachers and community members, who were encouraged to monitor the program.

Community participation was built into the MDM Programme's design. SSA's administrative structure authorized Village Education Committees (VECs) to help manage schooling inputs, including meal preparation. VECs consisted of parents, the school head teacher and the elected head (pradhan) of the village council (*panchayat*). Program activities, such as selection of cooks, grain procurement and meal preparation, were managed by the VEC. However, community involvement also created risks of local elite capture, a concern expressed by several state and local officials.[66] The pradhan and head teacher, designated as VEC chairperson and secretary, respectively, managed MDM accounts together. *De jure* control over funds gave the pradhan and head teacher *de facto* control over implementation. Reports of collusion between the two were frequent. Some amount of "bungling" (*ghapla*) was to be expected, officials explained. An oft-cited scenario noted in my interviews, head teachers would inflate student attendance figures and pradhans would prepare invoices for higher amounts, siphoning away excess funds and foodgrains.

The MDM Authority's dependency on school attendance registers raised questions about the reliability of its monitoring systems. A "*solution*," recommended by some officials in Lucknow, was to create a digitized system for grain procurement, student attendance and the counting of meals. Having more accurate, up-to-date information it was thought would help curb "*chicanery*" (*hera pheri*) by the pradhan and head teacher.[67] Other officials were skeptical of how far technology could

65 Interview with accountant, MDM Program, Lucknow, March 2009.

66 Interviews with MDM officials, Lucknow, Saharanpur and Sitapur, February–April 2009.

67 Interview with official, MDM Authority, Lucknow, February 2009.

address collusion. If the head teacher and pradhan conspired to produce handwritten accounts, what prevented local actors from tampering with computerized records? Local authority over the program was vested in VECs for a reason. As an official elaborated: "*Unless the [Midday Meal] scheme is community owned, it can't run. The government can push only so far. The community has to take ownership for it to be successful.*"[68]

On the subject of community ownership, education officials in Lucknow articulated a rather narrow understanding of community. In interviews, discussion of "*community*" (*samuday*) did not prompt any observations about the plurality of social groups in rural UP or barriers to cooperation. Instead, community was equated with the VEC. An agency vested with official authority, the VEC was understood in rule-based terms. Although a committee by design, the term "VEC" was used by officials as shorthand to mean the head of the VEC, the panchayat pradhan. In the words of an MDM official:

> Wherever local participation is strong, by that I mean the pradhan, there the Midday Meal Scheme is running beautifully. Cooking utensils, high quality food grains, and other requirements are all there. If the pradhan is active, then it means a lot.[69]

"*Local participation*" was taken to mean the pradhan's oversight of the MDM scheme. To complicate matters, the pradhan and head teacher were often upper castes and wielded informal authority in villages. When I asked officials how lower castes and other disadvantaged groups were engaged in monitoring school meals, virtually all of them pointed me to administrative grievance procedures. An MDM official explained:

> If they [parents] have problems with the midday meal, they can call the District Coordinator and Basic Shiksha Adhikari. Each school has the contact numbers of these officials painted outside on the wall.[70]

The grievance procedures for the MDM Programme were highlighted in government reviews and official monitoring documents as well. For example, a review by the central government's Ministry of Human Resource Development (MHRD) noted the UP state government's grievance redressal system, highlighting the toll-free number for registering complaints, as well as the option given for, "sending a simple letter to MDM Authority at State level or other district level

68 Interview with senior official, SSA, Lucknow, January 2009.

69 Interview with senior official, MDM Authority, Lucknow, February 2009.

70 Interview with senior official, MDM Authority, Lucknow, March 2009.

authorities."[71] Observations from state-level fieldwork raised questions about how grievance procedures and community oversight of the scheme worked in practice. When problems surfaced during program delivery, how were complaints registered with local administration? What was the follow-up process for grievance redressal? I answer these questions in the next section, based on village-level fieldwork in Saharanpur district.

4.4.2 The Enforcement of "Hygiene" in Langra

Interviews with bureaucrats in Lucknow revealed the common understanding that likened monitoring of the MDM Programme to an "accounting" exercise, with community participation taken to mean involvement of village officials. In this section, I investigate how common understandings of the MDM program established by state–level officials operate further down the bureaucratic hierarchy to influence local implementation. The study site was Langra, a village in Saharanpur's administrative block of Rampur Maniharan. I selected Langra because it had characteristics associated with better-quality public services. The village had a large population of Gujjars (48 percent) and Chamars (28 percent), politically dominant castes in the region. Located on a major thoroughfare, Langra's primary school was accessible by bus or car. Teachers at the school informed me that inspections by district officials were common. Parents in Langra, I learned, were actively involved in the school, assisting teachers with enrollment campaigns. Further, a Self Help Group (SHG) consisting of Dalit women monitored the school, and assisted with distribution of uniforms and SSA incentives for disadvantaged children.

Nevertheless, the school meal program was in a problematic state. Education officials in Saharanpur reported receiving multiple complaints about the erratic supply of meals in the village.[72] Parents corroborated their accounts. According to a father whose children attended the school:

> Sometimes they [the children] come home from school and tell us that they did not receive any food or that it was much less [than expected] … And meanwhile

[71] "Report of the Fifth Joint Committee on Midday Meal Scheme, Uttar Pradesh," July 2013, MHRD, Government of India. Available at: http://mdm.nic.in/mdm_website/Files/Review/Fifth_Review/UP/Final_Report_JRM_UP.pdf.

[72] Interviews with local education officials, Saharanpur, April–May 2009.

we have come to know that Masterji [the headmaster] invites his friends to play cards and they all enjoy the food in his office.[73]

This father took the bold step of contacting district officials to complain, though his neighbors advised him against it. Another resident remarked, "*What is there to gain by upsetting Masterji? In the end, our kids would have to suffer the consequences.*"[74] The "*consequences*" (*parinam*) he was referring to could take different forms. Children could be ostracized by teachers and other students, receive lower grades, or, worse, suffer physical abuse from teachers. That these and other forms of discrimination existed throughout UP became apparent from fieldwork in the state. Parents I spoke with hesitated to lodge official complaints out of fear that their children may suffer as a result.

Undeterred, some courageous parents in Langra publicly censured the teachers for neglecting their duties. The most vocal critics were Dalit women, members of the village SHG, which became involved in school meal preparation (see photograph in Figure 4.5). In a focus group discussion, SHG members narrated in detail how the school headmaster would misrepresent student attendance figures and set the excess food aside for his personal visitors. MDM Programme rules required student attendance figures to match entries in the food grain register. The women depended on the headmaster's attendance count to determine the quantity of food to prepare. Sometimes, they noticed that the quantity of food they produced was much greater than the amount students had consumed. Excess food would be taken by the headmaster. Other times, the quantity produced was insufficient to feed all students. The SHG members were illiterate, but this did not prevent them from keeping an eye on student attendance. They enlisted help from their own children, having them tally the number of students, which they compared against the headmaster's attendance figures. When discrepancies arose, they questioned the headmaster, who dismissed their concerns. On one occasion, he threatened to have the women removed from the school premises for failing to cooperate. According to parents, the headmaster asked the women to prepare extra flatbreads (*chapatis*) for his guests visiting the school. SHG members had no official authority over the headmaster, but they refused to be party to his schemes. One day, they devised their own plan to retaliate. After providing the day's allotment of grains, the headmaster asked the

[73] Interview with a father, Langra, May 2009.

[74] Ibid.

FIGURE 4.5 Women's association members preparing the midday meal (Saharanpur, Uttar Pradesh)
Note: Author photograph (2009).

women to make extra chapatis for his guests. Instead, they used the grain allotment to make thicker chapatis for the students.

Mobilizing to improve the school meal program, Dalit women applied "weapons of the weak," challenging the headmaster, who was a Brahmin (Scott 1985). Their collective efforts did not always produce the desired results. One afternoon, I arrived at Langra's primary school to find the headmaster visibly irked. The women had locked up the cooking utensils and kept the key, scuttling his plans for morning tea. The SHG members, in his view, had overstepped their bounds: "*These illiterate women (anpadh mahilaen) ... what is their standing (aukat)? They have no place telling us how to run the midday meal (madhyan bhojan).*"[75] He gave examples of other schools near Langra, where teachers administered meals without parental interference. Lower-caste parents in Langra had very different experiences of participation at the school. In a focus group discussion with residents in Langra's Chamar hamlet, I learned that the headmaster and teachers routinely excluded parents from VEC meetings, which many referred to as the "*pradhan's meeting*" (*pradhanji*

[75] Interview with headmaster, Primary School, Langra, May 2009.

ki baithak).[76] Sometimes, parents were given the wrong meeting dates or locations. When parents did attend meetings and tried speaking up, they were reprimanded by the teachers for "*interfering*" (*dakhalandazi*) in the school's affairs.[77] The experiences reported by parents in Langra were not unique. In study villages across Saharanpur and other districts (Sitapur and Mathura), Dalit parents found it difficult to participate in VEC meetings and engage in the MDM Programme.[78] In many cases, when concerned parents tried to monitor services, their efforts were scuttled by administrative rules restricting participation to official VEC members and designated village authorities.

Taking matters a step further, the headmaster in Langra filed a complaint against the SHG for mismanaging the school meal program. The SHG members were accused of maintaining "*unhygienic*" conditions for meal preparation. When local officials arrived in Langra to inspect the school, the pradhan publicly extended his support for the headmaster. He also organized influential households to speak out against the SHG women. These parents had instructed their children not to eat the midday meal, citing absence of "*cleanliness*" (*saph-saphai*) in the kitchen shed. Given the salience of village caste norms, the accusation regarding cleanliness held a double meaning. The food prepared by Dalits was already deemed polluted by upper castes. Amid backlash from influential households in Langra, the Chamar women struggled to explain to local officials that the headmaster had inflated the attendance figures. Although no visible indication of uncleanliness existed, the headmaster's complaint was acknowledged by officials, and they issued the SHG members a warning. Langra's school meal program was placed on administrative watch. The headmaster responded further by lodging a legal case against the Chamar women for serving unhygienic food. In response, SHG members organized a group of households to visit district administrative headquarters in Saharanpur. For a full day, they sat outside the education bureaucracy's office to protest the handling of the case. Education officials advised the parents to file a legal case against the headmaster for caste discrimination, an option available under the SC-ST Prevention of Atrocities Act. Weighing their options, the parents decided against pursuing a legal case. Some feared the repercussions of a prolonged judicial process; others felt that an official complaint might further damage village social relations.

76 Interviews with parents, Langra, May 2009.

77 Interview with female resident, Langra, April 2009.

78 I visited nine additional villages in each of these districts.

The situation in Langra can, on the one hand, be read as a straightforward case of elite capture. However, lower-caste parents asserted themselves by using the administrative complaint system, taking an available avenue to make claims on the local state. Through their very participation in the school meal program, Chamar women challenged dominant caste norms. They also publicly questioned the headmaster and aired grievances before the district administration. Local officials did not appear to favor Langra's panchayat pradhan or schoolteachers. Nevertheless, bureaucracy's adherence to MDM rules worked to the advantage of the privileged castes. According to a local official who had knowledge of the situation in Langra:

> If you ask me, the Midday Meal Programme run by the *mahila sangha* [women's group] has gone well. The women have done a good job managing it. But now you see what happens ... Competing parties in the villages go against Dalit women, and they know we have strict rules covering the midday meal, so that becomes the locus of their political battles.[79]

By the official's account, the women's group in Langra mobilized against sizable odds to support the MDM Programme. In her estimation, the pradhan and the headmaster in Langra likely framed the issues around food hygiene, which raised their confidence in pursuing a case against the Chamar women. The same official narrated an occurrence from another village near Langra, where two cooks had been dismissed from school:

> One afternoon, I received a complaint [about the Midday Meal] at 3:30pm. I reached the school by 4pm. The lentils (dal) were sitting in a bucket filled with maggots. When I inspected more closely, it looked like someone had thrown the maggots on top ... I doubt they [the cooks] could have done that. But if the school headmaster and gram pradhan want to remove them from the school, they find ways to seize control ... As officers, our first aim (*uddeshya*) is to enforce the rules.[80]

A legalistic understanding, as this bureaucrat articulated it, demarcated the appropriate actions that she could undertake. Bureaucratic pressure to follow rules was palpable from my fieldwork across Saharanpur. Reports of unhygienic school meals were high on the political radar. The MDM administrative machinery was mobilized to avert negative media coverage. According to another district official:

[79] Interview with local education official, Saharanpur, March 2009.

[80] Ibid.

> It's as if the midday meal has become god (*bhagwan*). News of any mishap lands not just in Lucknow but goes straight to Delhi. We are instructed to taste the meal for quality and hygiene ... and we have to report when the quality of the food is bad.[81]

This account was substantiated in my observations of school inspections with other bureaucrats. They described monitoring the school meal program as the most urgent (and stressful) part of their work. Fear of children falling ill added to their accountability pressures.

In sum, administrative grievance procedures provided an opportunity for parents to register complaints regarding the school meal program with local administration. However, these mechanisms were ill-suited for addressing legitimate concerns of parents in places like Langra, where participation in service delivery was braided with caste and gender inequalities. Bound by procedures, local administration made it more difficult for disadvantaged households to participate. A state-commissioned review of the MDM Programme in UP observed that "In most instances, the community remained cut off from the process and was not aware of the quality and quantity that was being served to the children. They neither showed any specific interest in this regard."[82] On the contrary, field-based evidence from Langra, and other UP villages, suggests that parents were alert to problems with the school meal program and tried using the formal grievance system. However, this system created administrative burdens and offered little practical support to marginalized citizens when they voiced complaints.

4.5 LEGALISM AND EPISODIC COLLECTIVE ACTION: PRIMARY EDUCATION IN PANCHAL VILLAGE

The empirical analysis has shown how bureaucratic norms operate across the organizational hierarchy to influence the collective understandings and behaviors of officials. In this section, I examine implementation from the vantage point of citizens seeking state assistance. Through an ethnography of Panchal, a village in Saharanpur district, I examine the mechanism of societal feedback, tracing citizen interactions with local state agencies across time. Scholars have cited "public apathy" in UP

81 Interview with Block Education Officer, Saharanpur, April 2009.

82 "Report of the Fifth Joint Committee on Midday Meal Scheme, Uttar Pradesh," July 2013, MHRD, Government of India. Available at: http://mdm.nic.in/mdm_website/Files/Review/Fifth_Review/UP/Final_Report_JRM_UP.pdf

as a cause for poorly functioning rural education and health services (Drèze and Gazdar 1996). Others, likewise, report a lack of awareness and petitioning by UP residents about nonfunctional services, owing to an absence of solidaristic community ties (Singh 2015). Given Panchal's political divisions and socioeconomic inequalities, one would expect little community mobilization for primary education. On the contrary, I observe that residents in Panchal were highly aware of conditions in their primary school and mobilized collectively to improve services. However, the response of local administration was patchy and created administrative burdens, which gradually eroded community oversight of schooling, contributing to lower quality services.

4.5.1 Village Governance and Socioeconomic Characteristics

A remote village, Panchal (pop. 2,463) was an unlikely setting for primary education services to function well, as evident from village socioeconomic characteristics (Table 4.4). Set nearly seven kilometers inland from a road connecting Saharanpur to Muzaffarnagar district, the path leading to Panchal was unpaved (Figure 4.6). The nearest bus stand was two and a half hours by foot or forty-five minutes by a bullock cart (*bail gari*). Panchal had a majority of Dalits, or SCs (55 percent), along with OBCs (23 percent) and upper castes (22 percent). Chamars (leather workers) were the largest Dalit contingent, followed by Balmikis, a stigmatized group that traditionally removed excrement from village sewers. Social groups lived in spatially segregated hamlets, or "neighborhoods" (*mohallas*) as residents referred to them, each having its own distinct place of worship. The oldest village temple, the Shiv Mandir was where an informal council of upper castes held its meetings. Barred from entering the temple, Chamars and Balmikis had a separate religious site honoring the Dalit mystic, Sant Ravidas, a space they used for weddings and social events. Signaling its political importance, the site bore a photograph of Ambedkar on its front gate. A group of lower-caste Sikh (*sardar*) families had an encampment (*dera*) on Panchal's western edge, where they constructed a Sikh temple (gurdwara).[83]

Panchal's sociocultural diversity was interlaced with economic inequalities. The village produced wheat and sugarcane, supplying nearby mills

[83] Although they originated in Hinduism, caste-based norms and identity markers are observed within some Sikh communities as well (Jodhka 2004).

TABLE 4.4 *Panchal village: Socioeconomic indicators*

Village	Panchal
Administrative district (block)	Saharanpur (Balia Khedi)
Population	2,463
Number of households	316
Distance to motor road	6.8 kilometers
Caste composition	22% General (Brahmin, Baniya)
	23% OBC (Lohar, Kumhar, Saini, Nai)
	55% SC (Chamar, Balmiki)
Religious composition	95% Hindu (various castes)
	5% Sikh (OBCs and SCs)
House type	20% finished (*pucca*)
	65% semi-finished (*semi-pucca*)
	15% unfinished (*kaccha)*
Village economy	Agriculture (sugarcane, wheat)
	Local sugarcane mill
	Day labor (agriculture, construction)
	Mistri (mechanic) work
	Professionals (education, law and police)
Places of worship	Shiv Mandir (Hindu upper castes)
	Devta Mandir (Hindu OBCs)
	Sant Ravidas Mandir (Hindu and Sikh SCs)
	Gurdwara (Sikh OBCs and SCs)
Other associations	Informal caste panchayat (Brahmins)
	Women's Group (*Mahila Sangha*)
	Adolescent Group (*Kishore Sangathan*)

Source: Village data collected by the author.

in Saharanpur. My fieldwork coincided with the *rabi* season's harvest of sugarcane. Tyagi Brahmins owned most of the land. Upper castes were employed in professional services, working as government clerks, schoolteachers, lawyers and Ayurvedic doctors. Their wealth on display, upper castes lived in gated compounds with finished (*pucca*) houses made from brick. Several OBC and SC households had marginal landholdings and semi-finished houses made from mud and brick. Women performed agricultural labor, while most men worked as mechanics (*mistris*), specializing in making hand pumps. "*Our village is famous for its mistris*," one man stated with pride.[84] The most destitute group, Chamars were landless and performed wage labor (*mazduri*) on farms and construction sites, earning

[84] Interview with a male resident, Panchal, May 2009.

FIGURE 4.6 Unpaved path leading to village (Saharanpur, Uttar Pradesh)
Note: Author photograph (2009).

daily wages of ₹120 (US$ 1.75). Their homes were mud-based and unfinished (*kaccha*) with thatched roofs. A few Chamar families had members employed by the state, including two police constables. The recruitment of Chamar constables through caste-based reservation (*arakshan*) policies drew the ire of village upper castes, who felt that their children had greater difficulty obtaining government jobs.

Despite their socioeconomic differences, Chamars joined hands with *Tyagi Brahmins* to elect the BSP candidate for state assembly elections.[85] Similarly, in a recent panchayat election, they had voted across caste lines for Mr. Gupta, a *Baniya*. Mr. Gupta was an educated lawyer and perceived by most residents as capable and diligent. Some contrasted him with the previous pradhan, from the Chamar community, who ran a liquor store and had a reputation for abusing his position. In one resident's words:

As far as pradhans go, the Baniya pradhan is a good guy. The Chamar pradhan wasn't helping anyone except himself and his immediate family. He didn't do anything for the larger village. The new pradhan is better educated, and he's done

[85] The alliance was described as tenuous, resting on both groups benefitting from the BSP government.

more for the village. He had a *kharanja* (brick lane) built in our hamlet. He also got the *nalas* (sewage lines) cleared out and had new bathrooms built throughout the village.[86]

During his first year in office, Mr. Gupta installed footpaths and bathrooms and had village sewers cleaned of debris, improvements that earned Panchal the National Clean Village Prize (Rashtriya Nirmal Gram Puruskar) under the central government's Total Sanitation Campaign.

However, elections were perceived as having little constructive impact on public services. Rarely did the panchayat hold village assemblies (*gram sabhas*) to discuss collective issues. In the context of education services, one father lamented: "*Village elections have nothing to do with public services. They are about handing out booze and drinking. There is no value to our vote.*"[87] Residents were engaged politically, but they did not view voting as a mechanism for substantive accountability. Panchal also had several active BSP party workers, but most households felt that issues of health and education were not their priority. Nevertheless, Dalits in Panchal expressed pride in Mayawati's political ascent. According to one man, Mayawati gave Chamars like him "*recognition*" (*pehchan*) in the public sphere.[88] Mayawati's government, he pointed out, was also combatting an unequal social structure (*samajik dhancha*) inside the bureaucracy, akin to the inequalities his family confronted in society.

4.5.2 The State of Primary Education in Panchal

Panchal's social fragmentation was glaring, particularly in the domain of education. Three private schools had sprouted up, catering to different castes and classes. Wealthy households sent their children to private schools in Saharanpur and Roorkee, a town in neighboring Haridwar district. Each morning, their children stood at the village entrance, awaiting the makeshift vehicle (*jugaad*) that drove them to school. Other upper-caste children attended the private Saraswati Vidya Mandir, run by Sharmaji, a retired government teacher. A second private school catered to Chamar children. The Dr. B.R. Ambedkar Private-Aided Primary School, or "Ambedkar School," as residents called it, was established in

86 Interview with a male resident, Panchal, May 2009.

87 Focus group discussion with men, Panchal, May 2009. Ahead of the 2009 national elections, party workers ran liquor stands distributing *kaccha daru*, a country liquor extracted from the *mahuwa* tree.

88 Interview with a man, Panchal, April 2009.

1994, with government subsidies. Classes were held in a barnyard, with children seated on top of haystacks. Sharmaji's school was also crowded. Four classes were held in a single room, the spaces demarcated with masking tape. The cramped conditions were an indication of the growing enrollment in private schools.

Education was a chief marker of social differences in Panchal. An upper-caste father spoke of these differences bluntly: "*Children from here go to this school [pointing to Sharmaji's school], and children from that neighborhood go to that school.*"[89] Balmiki families refused to enroll their children in the Ambedkar School, which they called the "*school for the Chamars*" (*Chamaron ka school*).[90] The poorest families attended the government primary school. Established in 1955, the government school got a new building in 2003. It had a large playground, boundary wall, kitchen, and working bathrooms, infrastructure far superior to that of private schools. Two additional classrooms were constructed in 2006, along with a new water tank and hand pump. The walls were painted afresh each year. Despite these improvements, enrollment had fallen sharply. A dearth of teachers led some parents to remove their children from the government school. Others noted that private schools had one teacher per grade and English-medium instruction, which was seen as crucial for their economic progress.

My observations at the government school corroborated parents' concerns. The school had a headmaster, Pandeyji, and two contract-based teachers (*shiksha mitra*). All three teachers attended school daily during my field visits. Although the para-teachers worked diligently, Pandeyji arrived late each morning and spent most of his time in administrative tasks. As one resident remarked, "*The issue is that Pandeyji likes spending his days basking in the sun.*"[91] On one occasion Pandeyji asked me to sit with him for chai. He summoned two students (girls) to make tea. I declined the offer, but he insisted that we meet at his home that afternoon. He engaged me there in a conversation about the difficulties of teaching "lower-class children" (*niche varg ke bacche*).[92] By his account, the students often arrived late to school, forgetting their notebooks, their hair unkempt and uniforms soiled from playing outside. They received little parental guidance or support with homework. Learning levels at

[89] Interview with a father, Panchal, May 2009.

[90] Interviews with several Balmiki households, Panchal, May 2009.

[91] Interview with a father, Panchal, May 2009.

[92] Interview with a school headmaster, Panchal, May 2009.

the government school were inadequate. Many fifth-grade students could not perform basic arithmetic. Third graders had difficulty recognizing Hindi letters.

The contract teachers, Dhiraj and Seema, noted the difficulties of teaching first-generation learners. "*Some parents*," Seema noted, "*only send their children here for the free food (khana) and scholarship (vajipha). Education is not their top priority.*"[93] Showing me the fifth-grade textbook, Dhiraj remarked, "*The [Education] Department makes us teach this entire syllabus. But these students are not prepared to complete even half of it ... I try to explain this to our education officers (shiksha adhikaris), but they don't want to hear it.*"[94] Department of Education training provided little guidance on how to manage multigrade classrooms with students at different levels. School inspections, they found, were oriented toward compliance and unsupportive of teachers. According to Seema, "*So long as they see the enrollment and midday meal registers, the Vibhag [Department] thinks its job is done. What learning happens or doesn't happen, only God knows.*"[95]

It was tempting to infer that Panchal's residents lacked the collective interest or capacity to mobilize for quality education. However, the government school had a functioning VEC that held periodic meetings. Led by the pradhan, Mr. Gupta, the VEC had coordinated with local administration to upgrade the school's infrastructure. Parents were aware of the VEC and some attended its meetings. Yet, they had little faith in the VEC's ability to improve education services. As one father remarked:

> Just look at the condition (*halat*) of the government (*sarkari*) school. There is no education (*shiksha*) taking place there at all. We are sending our children there only out of compulsion. We have no land and we can't afford private school fees ... Anyone here who has a means (*jugaad*) will rely on private schooling.[96]

The father, who was Chamar, shared his aspirations for his children. He believed that quality education was critical to their future. "*Why should they get pushed around like me?*," he said.[97]

Apart from the VEC, parents informally monitored the school, including some mothers belonging to Panchal's women's association. Consisting of 22 Chamar women, the association was formed with support from

93 Focus group discussion with contract teachers, Panchal, May 2009.

94 Ibid.

95 Ibid.

96 Interview with father, Panchal, April 2009.

97 Ibid.

local administration in 1993 during the state's national literacy campaigns and immunization drives. The women mobilized successfully to seek abolition of school fees, which Pandeyji (and the headmaster before him) used to charge illegally. Group members also took turns checking whether teachers arrived on time and that school meals were well-provided. At times, their attempts to monitor services led to conflicts with teachers. In a focus group discussion, the women's association head (*adhyaksh*) recounted:

> The education at the primary school is next to nil (*nil ke barabar*). The headmaster [Pandeyji] shows up drunk. Sometimes he even drinks in the school ... We tried to reason with him, hoping he would understand that this was wrong. But we became fed up ... One morning, we locked the gate of the school and promised to keep it locked until he agreed to perform his duties properly ... We thought this would have an impact on him. But things didn't improve. Instead of changing his ways, he threatened to call the Department (*Vibhag*) and have us banned from the school campus.[98]

Their attempts to discipline Pandeyji backfired. He took action against the women's group for filing a complaint against him. The recent hiring of two Chamar women as cooks in the school school was a sticking point for upper-caste and OBC families, some of whose children attended the school. According to a father from the Nai (barber) caste, "*Kids belonging to higher castes would obviously not like the food cooked by them [the Dalit women].*"[99] Swallowing insults from upper castes, Chamar women continued to cook the midday meal. They even used their precious group savings to cover the cost of meal supplies for two months, coping with delayed payments from district administration.

4.5.3 Tracing the Decline of Community Mobilization

Deficiencies at the government primary school in Panchal persisted, despite the collective vigilance of parents. Still, one could argue that Panchal's caste inequalities made village-wide collective action difficult to sustain. In the parlance of social capital theory, Panchal exhibited strong "bonding" ties among Chamars and other jatis but lacked "bridging" ties between castes (Woolcock and Narayan 2000). Upper-caste households had exited for private schooling, weakening community oversight of government schools. However, privatization

98 Focus group discussion with women's association, Panchal, April 2009.
99 Interview with a father, Panchal, May 2009.

was a recent phenomenon and most adults in Panchal were educated in the government system.

To understand how village collective action evolved over time, I recorded oral histories of elderly residents in Panchal. I learned that households had previously mobilized across caste boundaries for education. Panchal's first primary school, built near the Shiv Mandir in 1939, came about through village-wide collective action. Parents had petitioned to gain accreditation for the school from the Department of Education. A new building was inaugurated by district administration in 1955, but operational resources for the school were provided by residents. Poor and affluent households alike made contributions of land, labor, and financial donations for the school's upkeep. The school catered mainly to upper castes, but lower castes helped to maintain the school. An elderly Chamar man recounted: "*The level of awareness was much less in those days. But we did what we could for the village school. It was a matter of pride for us.*"[100]

In the 1970s, Panchal's residents organized to establish a middle school. Raising private funds was difficult, but in 1976, a Chamar family received financial compensation from the state government following the untimely death of their daughter. The family donated the funds to Panchal's middle school in her memory. Inaugurated in 1979, the school ran informally for twenty years through private contributions and volunteer teachers. As enrollments increased in the 1990s, informal arrangements became insufficient. Parents wrote letters and met with district officials, requesting additional teachers and better infrastructure. Bauji, an elderly man who volunteered at the school, recounted:

> They [local administration] told us that the school was unrecognized and that administrative guidelines made it impossible to provide teachers ... They cautioned us as well that, because the school ran informally, it could be closed down if someone came for an inspection. Instead of help we were given advice to withdraw our requests.[101]

A retired government teacher himself, Bauji understood what school inspections meant in practice. Panchal's middle school failed to meet regulatory standards on several counts: The school building lacked appropriate clearances, volunteer teachers did not have the requisite qualifications and classes were conducted outside of school hours. If an inspection were to have been conducted, the school might have been shut down.

[100] Interview with a village elder, Panchal, May 2009.
[101] Interview with a village elder, Panchal, April 2009.

In 2006, the Department of Education officially recognized Panchal's middle school. By then, affluent households had switched to private schools. As a mother put it: "*If we had waited for the local administration to respond to our demands, our children's education would have gone to waste.*"[102] Nevertheless, some parents were encouraged by the state's recognition of the middle school. They worked with the VEC to improve the middle school's infrastructure, which was in good condition during my fieldwork. They demanded additional teachers as well. The school had two regular teachers, but none were qualified to teach math and science. Parents sought assistance from Mr. Gupta, the pradhan, who petitioned the local education bureaucracy. Seated with a group of residents outside his home, Mr. Gupta recounted:

> I personally wrote letters to officials, from the District Magistrate all the way up to the education minister ... They told us that there is no mandate that guarantees math and science teachers ... Now they have stopped responding to our letters.[103]

Pressing their demands further, women's association members visited the district education office in Saharanpur. Some parents whose children attended private school joined in the effort. They lamented having to pay fees for private education when their village had a government school with good infrastructure and trained teachers. However, the demands of parents went unheeded by local administration. As a women's association member expressed it, "*The [Education] Department doesn't recognize us. We have no standing in their eyes.*"[104]

My observations from Panchal suggested that societal collective action was episodic. Citizens attempted to access the local state at certain moments, but the administrative burdens they experienced at each juncture were onerous, and became too much to bear, leading to a sense of disempowerment. After completing fieldwork in Panchal, I met with local education officials to understand their perspective on community demands for services. "Government rules" (*sarkari niyam*), they explained, did not permit the allocation of math and science teachers to every school. A clear policy was needed, in their view, to allocate teachers for these subjects. Ms. Singh, a local education official, explained:

> When I visit schools, children come up to me saying, '*Ma'am please send us a math teacher!*' I always say that I will try my best, but we have no policy

[102] Interview with a mother, Panchal, May 2009.
[103] Interview with pradhan of village panchayat, Panchal, May 2009.
[104] Interview with a mother, Panchal, May 2009.

provision for that ... I cannot make an accommodation for just one school ... It is hard enough getting schools recognized when they have been running unofficially for so long.[105]

Ms. Singh described how her hands were tied by administrative rules. Furthermore, her previous experiences of attempting to work around administrative rules taught her to avoid questioning by supervisors. Ms. Singh narrated an occasion, etched in her memory, when she had attempted to improve the quality of teaching:

In my previous posting [in a different block], I took the most good-for-nothing (*nalayak*) teachers ... the ones who were most influenced by local politics ... and motivated them. We got the best work done together. We helped improve their schools ... But for all this work, the [Education] Department showed no appreciation. What matters are regular duties, the [school] building register, the attendance register, the "official process" for SSA. But this type of hard work ... it is seen as extra work (*anya kaam*). We get no recognition for doing it.[106]

In her view, attention to the quality of education was "*entirely missing*," while the pressure to follow rules was immense. Ms. Singh handed me an SSA circular that instructed district administration to ensure that schools were built within the prescribed one-kilometer distance from villages. "*I would say that this is a good step ... But the problem now is that the school is built in front of the kid's house and the kid isn't going to school ... And we are not able to face this fact.*"[107] Ms. Singh was referring to the declining status of government schools and corresponding rise of private schooling, which she believed weakened the state's ability to provide quality education.

The findings of this section run counter to prior studies suggesting that UP households are "apathetic" to the quality of public services. What may have initially appeared as "public apathy" was, on further inspection, the culmination of citizens' efforts to participate in public service delivery, the accumulated experiences of voicing demands to local administration. Residents attempting to improve conditions at Panchal's primary school were effectively sidelined by a legalistic bureaucracy that gave precedence to rules over the legitimate needs of marginalized groups. These observations are presented from one village, but research conducted in other UP field sites overwhelmingly corroborates the findings from Panchal. As a local education official from Sitapur district remarked, "*My phone never*

105 Interview with education official, Saharanpur, June 2009.
106 Ibid.
107 Ibid.

stops ringing in the morning with complaints from parents."[108] The official described how official grievance procedures worked, often making it difficult for marginalized households to challenge errant teachers and secure quality services.

4.6 CONCLUSION

This chapter has demonstrated how legalistic bureaucracy has facilitated the uneven implementation of primary schooling. In the backdrop of UP's fragmented party system and divisive caste politics, the state bureaucracy has faced growing demands from electorally mobilized lower castes. However, the delivery of primary schooling was not simply driven by caste politics. The historical development of legalism was critical as well. Spurred by the political and administrative centrality of UP's "law and order" state, legalistic bureaucracy was subsequently reinforced through the competition for authority between bureaucrats and politicians. Research performed at the state level, across two administrative districts and multiple villages, revealed how bureaucratic commitment to rules has impacted the provision of school infrastructure and growth in enrollments, enabling officials to resist political interferences when providing inputs to schools. By upholding a narrow, rule-based interpretation of AVP, a program exemplifying particularism and caste-based targeting of public goods, frontline officials maneuvered around particularistic interferences to utilize public resources for programmatic purposes. Legalistic bureaucratic norms were found to operate similarly in Saharanpur and Sitapur, districts with very different institutional histories and political economy conditions. Contrary to received wisdom, these findings suggest that bureaucracy in UP is not simply captured by political forces, but can exert independent authority over implementation. Having a centralized administrative structure for primary education, with relatively autonomous state-level agencies overseeing SSA and the MDM Programme, likely helped insulate the education bureaucracy from political pressures.[109] The decentralized features of these programs may have also created opportunities for political interference. Nevertheless, bureaucratic commitment to rules helped counteract particularism at the local level.

[108] Interview with education official, Sitapur, July 2009.

[109] In that regard, SSA's institutional design has some commonalities with effective social programs in Latin America, such as Mexico's *Progresa* and Brazil's *Bolsa Familia* (Sugiyama and Hunter 2013; Weitz-Shapiro 2014).

On the other hand, evidence from fieldwork also demonstrates that legalistic bureaucracy in UP is ill-equipped to undertake complex tasks requiring intensive and repeated interactions between the local state and society. The MDM Authority expanded the school meal program's reach throughout UP, but services remained erratic and of poor quality. As the case study of Langra showed, having a VEC and administrative grievance procedures available enabled the registration of complaints by parents. Furthermore, Dalit women used "weapons of the weak" to challenge village elites and make injustices visible to the state (Scott 1985). They applied "rude accountability" tactics, for instance by publicly shaming the head teacher and village officials for pilferage of foodgrains (Hossain 2010). These quotidian acts of collective resistance by Dalit women are important examples of "active citizenship" in rural UP (Kruks-Wisner 2018). In that sense, legalistic bureaucracy's embrace of administrative grievance mechanisms has helped stimulate programmatic participation by society, centered on collective needs (Davies and Falleti 2017).

Meanwhile, official channels of oversight imposed sizable administrative burdens on marginalized households. In Langra and other villages, households that depended on school meals put time and effort toward registering complaints, putting themselves at risk and suffering caste-based stigmas. For Dalit parents, the lack of institutional support from local administration was disempowering. Bureaucratic monitoring practices, which centered on ensuring the "hygiene" of midday meals, left Dalit citizens vulnerable to conflicts with with village elites and teachers. These findings accord with Gupta's (2012) analysis of local implementation of health and poverty alleviation programs in UP. "The emphasis on following the rules," he explains, "rather than on achieving results has the effect of preserving bureaucratic order, regardless of its consequences for the clients of those programs" (Gupta 2012, 50). He notes further that the seeming "arbitrariness" of bureaucracy "is not itself arbitrary; rather, it is systematically produced by the very mechanisms that are meant to ameliorate social suffering" (Gupta 2012, 22). I have shown, in a similar vein, that local officials tasked with monitoring education responded systematically to norms propagated by the MDM Authority in Lucknow. The narrow interpretation of the school meal program as an "accounting" scheme conditioned the behaviors of local officials, with little regard for community needs.

This chapter has highlighted the uneven outcomes that bureaucratic commitment to rules generates for primary education. The pitfalls of legalistic bureaucracy are most visible when it comes to providing education services, as demonstrated in the case of Panchal. On the one hand, bureaucratic adherence to rules helped stimulate collective demands from parents. At various moments, Panchal's residents were hopeful when seeking state support for education through administrative channels, including the panchayat. They mobilized across caste lines for school infrastructure and additional teachers. These societal efforts are noteworthy considering that Panchal's socioeconomic inequalities and political divisions presented obstacles for village-wide collective action. On the other hand, legalistic bureaucracy created hurdles for marginalized households seeking services from the state. Local administration's adherence to rules imposed administrative burdens on concerned parents which prolonged their waiting and suffering, and contributed to the fracturing of collective action over time. Privileged households in Panchal exited the government school system early on, while others soon followed suit with the mushrooming of low-fee private schools. The least advantaged households in Panchal, meanwhile, continued to bear the difficulties of monitoring the government primary school. Their motivation to co produce public services did not entirely disappear. However, their expectations of the state gradually diminished and village collective action became episodic. Cumulatively, these processes contributed to low quality education.

5

How Deliberative Bureaucracy Facilitates Adaptive Implementation

> Implementation of any development project is not possible without the active and widespread participation of the people. It becomes the responsibility of the administrative authority to spot active persons in the local population, awaken their interest and mobilise their initiative.
>
> – Himachal Pradesh State Development Report (GoI 2005; 255)

5.1 INTRODUCTION

Chapter 4 analyzed the uneven implementation of primary schooling in Uttar Pradesh (UP). In accordance with the theory presented in Chapter 2, I showed how legalistic bureaucracy overcomes political obstacles to support infrastructure expansion and enrollments, but at the same time, imposes administrative burdens on local communities attempting to monitor schools, leading to lower quality education services. This chapter considers the prospects for delivering high quality public services in northern India. It investigates how deliberative bureaucracy works to generate superior outcomes for primary education in Himachal Pradesh (HP). Landlocked by the western Himalayan mountain range, HP is an improbable setting for primary education to be well-implemented (see map in Figure 5.1).[1] The region's physical terrain, harsh winter climate and perennial landslides during monsoons make public goods and services extremely challenging to administer.

At independence, HP was among India's least literate states, with education indicators no better than in other Hindi belt states like Bihar and UP.

[1] "Himachal" derives from the Hindi words *him* (snow) and *aanchal* (lap), to mean "in the lap of snow."

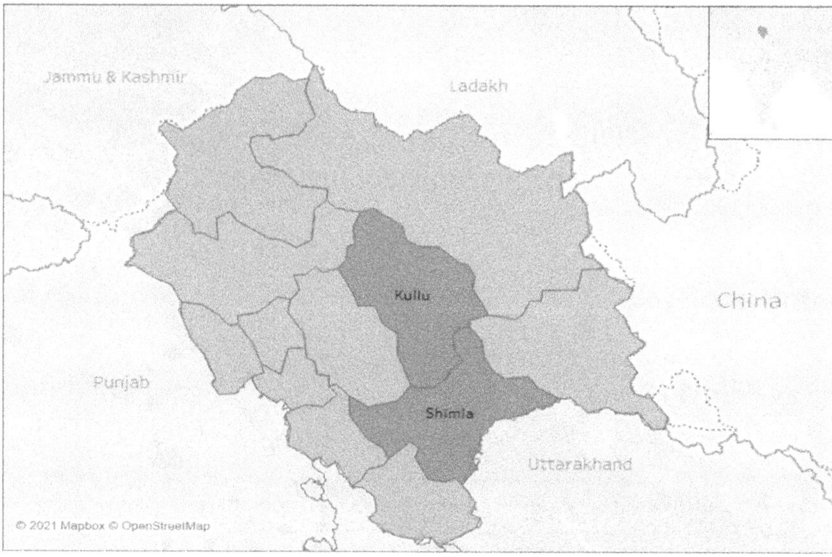

FIGURE 5.1 Study map of Himachal Pradesh
Note: Main study districts are highlighted.
Source: © Mapbox, © OpenStreetMap.

Not long after its founding, in 1971, HP began to record significant gains in primary schooling, outperforming wealthier, more industrialized states in the plains. At present, HP not only exhibits universal enrollment and attendance but delivers comparatively higher quality services as well. Government primary schools have responded effectively to the disparate needs of hard-to-reach communities, ensuring that educational gains are distributed more evenly across regions and social groups (Das et al. 2015).[2] HP is now among India's leading states with respect to literacy and primary education policy indicators, trailing only the southern coastal state of Kerala. Remarkably, HP embarked on its educational journey much later than Kerala, under more adverse conditions. In the first few decades after independence, HP had a weak industrial base and comparatively low per capita income (UNDP 2002, 10–15). In contrast to Kerala's high population density and coastal economy, HP has remained one of India's least urbanized states. More than 90 percent of Himachalis reside in geographically scattered villages, earning a living

[2] Das et al. (2015, 29–32) report that, by 2011, HP had the lowest share of individuals with no education in northern India, a pattern that has held across social groups.

from small-scale agriculture and animal husbandry. Income growth began to take off in the 1990s, as the economy diversified into horticulture (e.g. apple production) and other high-value crops, by which time HP had already made sizable gains in education (Drèze and Sen 2002, 177–185; World Bank 2007). Equally notable, these achievements were produced almost entirely by the government school system, in contrast to the relatively high rates of private schooling in Kerala and other parts of India.

What has allowed HP to effectively implement universal primary education? Why and how do education policies in HP translate into higher quality services? This chapter highlights the catalytic role of deliberative bureaucracy, analyzing the mechanisms by which it produces superior education outcomes. It demonstrates how deliberation operates inside the state bureaucracy, enabling frontline officials to perform complex tasks and encourage participation of marginalized groups in service delivery. Local deliberation between frontline officials and citizens has helped sustain community oversight of primary education, in particular, by empowering women's associations.

My arguments in this chapter are structured as follows. I first explore the emergence of bureaucratic deliberation in HP, drawing on historical sources and interviews with state officials to examine the politics of state formation in the 1970s and 1980s. I then present findings from qualitative field research conducted inside the state bureaucracy, with local administration and in select villages, showing how deliberation influences the performance of various administrative tasks. These include state planning to expand infrastructure and integrate disadvantaged children, as well as bureaucratic efforts to support women's participation in school monitoring and, finally, local agency initiatives to enable societal coproduction of village education services.

5.2 FORGING A DELIBERATIVE BUREAUCRACY IN HIMACHAL PRADESH

In the mid-nineteenth century, British viceroys and military brass escaped the summer heat of the plains for the erstwhile "Punjab Hills." However, the colonial government made little investment in mass education. After independence, HP was administered directly by India's central government, achieving statehood belatedly in 1971. This section traces the political origins and development of deliberative bureaucracy in HP. I argue that HP's political marginalization and unfavorable fiscal conditions spurred governing elites to cooperate for obtaining resources from the central government, encouraging deliberation between elected officials and bureaucrats. I first describe the nature of colonial administration and subsequent central government control of HP. I then examine the politics of state-building since 1971, highlighting the importance of elite cooperation. Drawing on interviews with active and retired state officials, I show how relations between governing elites and lower-level bureaucrats supported deliberation further down the administrative hierarchy. Finally, I discuss how electoral politics and socioeconomic conditions in HP have helped maintain of deliberative bureaucratic norms.

5.2.1 From British Summer Capital to Union Territory

Prior to British occupation, HP consisted of several hundred Rajput principalities.[3] Nepali Gorkhas seized control of the region but were expelled by the British in 1814 (Ahluwalia 1998, 24–28). The Rajput principalities were restored under British suzerainty, through the recognition of *sanads* (princely states), forming the Punjab Hills administrative division. Colonial administrators established hill stations in strategic locations, which "appeared best adapted for military positions" (Verma 1995, 37). Shimla became the summer residence of British Governors General and the official homestead of the Indian army's commander-in-chief. In 1863, John Lawrence, Viceroy of India, declared Shimla the summer capital of the British Raj.[4]

British colonial administration did little to alter feudal practices within Rajput principalities. The customary system of forced labor, known as *begar*, persisted under colonial rule (Negi 1995).[5] Tax settlements required princely rulers to furnish a quota of forced laborers (*begaris*) to the British in proportion to revenues generated from agricultural land. A related system of *beth*, or compulsory labor, was imposed by landlords (*zamindars*) on lower-caste peasantry. Land was leased out to local farmhands (*bethus*) for cultivation. Bethus had no land rights, but they received a share of the harvest as payment for labor (Alam 2007,

[3] Princely states included Kangra, Chamba, Kullu, Bushahr, Nurpur, Bilaspur, Suket, Mandi, Jubbal, Keonthal, Baghal, Baghat and Sirmaur.

[4] On the development of Shimla and other colonial hill stations, see Kanwar (2003) and Kennedy (1996).

[5] On Himalayan systems of feudalism and forced labor, see Negi (1995), Alam (2007) and Snehi (2016).

40–41). The Punjab government abolished beth in 1929, but labor exploitation continued in the hill region, along with caste discrimination and untouchability.

Mass education received little attention from the colonial regime, though it handsomely supported private education for the families of British officials. Lord Canning, Governor General of India, issued a Minute on Education in 1860 recommending the education of children of European descent, lest they become a "floating population of Indianized English, loosely brought up, and exhibiting most of the worst qualities of both races" (Kennedy 1996, 138). Grants were extended to Christian-denomination boarding schools, modeled after high-end private and missionary schools in England. The policy drew from the ideas of Bishop Cotton, an Anglican clergyman who served as Bishop of Calcutta. He founded the famous Bishop Cotton School in Shimla in 1859. Boarding schools were established across the hill region to provide English-style education to prepare students for careers in military and civil administration.[6] Shimla became a destination for elite education, and by 1905, it had approximately sixty schools catering to Europeans (Arnold 1979, 109).

In the 1920s, the Indian National Congress (INR) called on princely rulers to establish representative government. During the Praja Mandal movement, local political leaders organized to demand statehood for HP; many joined the Congress Party. In 1948, HP was made a Union Territory by India's central government, an amalgamation of thirty-one princely states. Four years later, HP was raised to a "Part C" state, a quasi-democratic arrangement that allowed for a Council of Ministers, albeit under Parliament's administrative control. Political leaders from HP rallied for full statehood in 1955, when the States Reorganisation Commission was appointed to reassess India's internal boundaries. The Commission recommended HP be merge with Punjab, citing the high fiscal burden of creating a separate hill state.

The creation of HP was also influenced by other political developments throughout India. Central government policies to establish linguistic states led to the reorganization of Punjab, based upon the claim that its languages and customs were sufficiently distinct from those of Hindi-speaking states. Following Punjab's reorganization, HP annexed four Hindi-speaking districts (Kangra, Kullu, Lahaul–Spiti and Shimla) in

[6] Elite boarding schools in HP included Bishop Cotton (established in 1859), Lawrence School (1847), Loreto Convent (1895) and Convent of Jesus and Mary (1866).

1966, a move that intensified the political agitation for statehood. The hill districts had distinct sociocultural identities. However, demands for statehood relied less on popular mobilization and more upon collective action by political elites. Unlike Punjab, HP did not claim separation based on a shared language or separate sociocultural identity.[7] Despite having the colloquial Pahari, an umbrella language consisting of thirty distinct dialects, the state's official language remained Hindi.[8] Due to trade links, migration and intermarriage, Punjabi was widely spoken in some areas of HP, particularly the "lower" districts bordering Punjab. The formation of HP also served the strategic objectives of central government leadership. Nehru in particular sought to contain linguistic separatism in his bid to uphold national unity (Das Gupta 1970). Political concerns in New Delhi about Punjab's separatist movement, as well as the hardening of regional identities elsewhere in India, led the central government to extend support for HP's recognition as a Hindi-speaking state.

5.2.2 State Formation and the Making of Deliberative Bureaucracy

On January 25, 1971, Parliament enacted a resolution granting statehood to HP. The challenges confronting the political leadership of HP were formidable. Limited industry and a subsistence-based agrarian economy provided brittle economic foundations for state-building. HP was the first Indian state to be deemed financially unviable, since public administration costs could not be met with internal resources. Only three other states or Union Territories (Bihar, Orissa and Manipur) had a lower per capita income at the moment of state formation (Bhattacharjee 2016, 323). HP thus remained financially dependent on the central government. Dr. Yashwant Singh Parmar, who led the demand for statehood, served as HP's first chief minister. Parmar had a strong political following within HP. However, despite being a recognized nationalist and Congress Party stalwart, his political clout within the Congress was limited.[9] The contrast with state political leadership in UP was stark. UP politicians, who were awarded cabinet berths, governorships and senior Congress posts, frequently ascended to the national political stage. The

[7] Elmore (2016) observes that the Himalayan region's distinctive religious practices were promoted politically after HP attained statehood.

[8] The Tankri script, used for writing Pahari languages, fell into disuse after independence. Migration from Punjab and Haryana diluted the use of Pahari in some regions of HP.

[9] Interviews with retired HP Congress Party officials, Shimla, August 2008.

central government and Congress Party national leadership kept a close eye on UP's political developments. Politics in HP, meanwhile, was of marginal significance to the Congress high command.

Fiscal dependency on New Delhi and a lack of influence within the Congress Party constrained the political opportunities for HP's governing elites. Yet these selfsame conditions provided strong incentives for governing elites to mobilize collectively for state-building. Parmar, who recognized the limitations of a subsistence economy, resolutely supported policies for road and bridge construction, with an aim to attract new industries and investment in manufacturing (Das et al. 2015). Due to prohibitive transportation costs and scattered habitations, physical "*connectivity*" was seen as a necessary step for economic growth in the hills.[10] Power generation was also high on the policy agenda. Parmar coordinated with state planners and senior Indian Administrative Service (IAS) officers in charge of major portfolios to ensure that line departments followed through on these priorities. Political commitment to public infrastructure development was unwavering. In a retired IAS officer's words, "*Parmar would himself review the progress of road construction. 'Roads, roads and roads,' he would say … the message was clear to us that without roads, no development would happen.*"[11]

Bureaucrats working in Parmar's government also played a crucial part in state-building. In particular, they sought to secure funding for infrastructure and other policy priorities, working closely with administrative counterparts in central government agencies. Economic relief came when the central government awarded HP "Special Category status," a designation given to states unable to amass internal resources for development.[12] Eleven states, mostly those in the Himalayan region, met the criteria for federal assistance, which made them eligible for loan waivers and tax concessions to attract industry.[13] Federal funds were made available through three central government mechanisms: (1) Planning Commission funds for planned development expenditures; (2) the Finance Commission, which distributed tax revenues and grants-in-aid based on state populations and other

[10] Interview with retired IAS officer, Shimla, April 2010.

[11] Interview with retired IAS officer, Shimla, August 2008.

[12] The criteria for Special Category status included: (1) hilly terrain, (2) low population density and/or a large tribal population, (3) strategic location (e.g. bordering other countries), (4) weak economic base and (5) nonviable state finances.

[13] In 2015, India had eleven Special Category states: Arunachal Pradesh, Assam, Himachal Pradesh, Jammu and Kashmir, Manipur, Meghalaya, Mizoram, Nagaland, Sikkim, Tripura and Uttarakhand.

factors; and (3) centrally sponsored schemes, fiscal transfers earmarked for federal programs. Of these mechanisms, the Finance Commission provided the lion's share of resources. The Planning Commission, meanwhile, had a major hand in establishing the state's administrative architecture and policy priorities. Bureaucrats in HP's Planning and Finance Departments coordinated with central agencies to fulfill the fiscal requirements of the central government.

Meetings between state planners from HP and central administrators took place on a recurring basis. In anticipation of these high stakes engagements, HP officials learned to strategize collectively, thereby improving their chances of obtaining central government funds. For example, HP Finance Department officials had to ensure that budgetary requests from planning and other departments were in compliance with central government policy mandates and associated targets. As a senior official noted, finance and planning worked closely together, ensuring that they were "*speaking in the same language*" when interacting with administrative counterparts from New Delhi.[14] Furthermore, HP's Planning Department brought line departments together to discuss the execution of public programs, helping to ensure that state planning, fund utilization and reporting processes met the stipulations set by central agencies.

The coordinating functions performed by the Planning and Finance Departments encouraged officials from line departments to also discuss plans jointly.[15] And while high-level policy discussions took place among elite agencies, pressures to obtain external resources filtered down to district administration as well. Central government assistance came with monitoring and reporting obligations, prompting senior officials to communicate regularly with subordinates. Fulfillment of targets, for fund utilization and policy outputs, was discussed among district administrations and shared with state-level agencies, which in turn reported progress to central agencies. A State Planning Department official explained, "*The expenditure of allotted funds was a key criterion for continued central funding.*"[16] Meeting targets consistently required the involvement of frontline officials tasked with policy implementation. These officials reported back to supervisors from line departments and gave regular updates on local public projects.[17]

[14] Interview with retired IAS officer, Shimla, February 2010.

[15] Interviews with several officials from HP's Planning Department and Finance Department, June–August 2010.

[16] Interview with retired HP state official, Shimla, August 2010.

[17] Interviews with retired district officials, Shimla, May 2010.

Through routinized communication, monitoring and reporting, HP's bureaucracy built a reputation for effectively managing externally funded programs. State officials diligently protected this reputation, which allowed them to negotiate for additional resources from central government agencies.[18] It should be noted that central funds were not only deployed for programmatic policies but enabled the dispensation of patronage as well. As state officials working in HP themselves have noted, Finance Department funds supported the growth of public sector employment, and political competition between the Congress Party and the Bharatiya Janata Party (BJP) stoked patronage demands (Sanan 2004). The public sector in HP became the primary source of formal employment, giving some households the chance to move beyond subsistence agriculture. In the primary education sector, the state's drive to expand teacher recruitment by granting village councils (*panchayats*) the power to hire assistant teachers (*vidya upasaks*) is but one example of how public employment was entangled with patronage politics.

If HP's fiscal and political conditions spurred elite cooperation for state-building, political leadership reinforced deliberation between state departments. Parmar's regime governed HP for the first ten years of statehood. Within this period, an informal practice emerged of politicians and bureaucrats meeting regularly to discuss local implementation challenges. Parmar took field expeditions on foot, traveling long distances to observe local conditions throughout the state. He frequently met district officials and sought their perspectives on local governance and community demands.[19] In an interview, a decorated IAS officer who previously served as Secretary of Education narrated his interactions with Chief Minister Parmar. During an early field posting to a district, he recalled:

> Parmar would come to my district once in a while. We would walk together for three to four days, visiting villages and moving from here to there … This gave me, as District Collector, the opportunity to interact with him on his views and vision for the state … Parmar had very great faith in ordinary people's judgment. He would say, "*These people have survived for thousands of years. They have the wisdom, knowledge and technology of survival, far better than you or I could bring to them from outside.*" … When the leadership reposes that much faith in people, it affects administration on every side. The message gets across. It made district officers like me think that we [the bureaucracy] must try harder to understand the needs of the public.

[18] Interviews with Planning Commission officials, New Delhi, September 2011.

[19] Dr. Parmar's travels throughout HP and interactions with local bureaucrats was a topic in multiple interviews with serving and retired state officials from HP.

Parmar's engagement with district administration and rural communities sent a strong signal to local officials about the value of deliberation. Another retired IAS officer who served as Principal Secretary of Social Welfare noted that Parmar brought ministers and senior bureaucrats together with lower-level officials. The latter were encouraged to share practical experiences from the field. "*The CM acted as a role model for lower bureaucrats,*" she recalled.[20]

One may suppose that deliberation was limited to IAS and other senior officials stationed in Shimla. Given their presence in the state secretariat and departmental headquarters, senior bureaucrats were in closer proximity to Parmar and senior political leadership. To investigate the salience of deliberation in other administrative districts, I used personnel records to identify officials who were posted for significant duration outside Shimla. Most bureaucrats, including those working in Shimla, had spent a good part of their careers in different districts. Local officials held their geographic posts for 2.4 years on average before being transferred elsewhere. District officials that I interviewed in Shimla had spent five to ten years elsewhere in the state. Narrating their experiences of working in different districts, they described Shimla as "normal" (*aam*) and "average" (*samanya*) when it came to local administrative practices. In Shimla district, field visits by senior bureaucrats were more frequent, to be sure, but deliberation was a common feature in other districts as well. Some officials even suggested that deliberation was more robust in the far-flung districts of Kinnaur and Lahaul-Spiti, owing perhaps to their physical isolation. District officials in these areas had even fewer resources and were cut off from state-level administration, motiving them to deliberate collectively.

The importance attached to local deliberation was evident from interviews with frontline officials in different departments. Consider the example of Mr. Dhiman, a Block Development Officer (BDO) who spent his career working on infrastructure projects all throughout the state. Some of his most formative professional experiences were when stationed in the tribal belt of Lahaul–Spiti. Winters in Lahaul-Spiti were unforgiving, he recounted, his office virtually cut off from the rest of HP. Apart from the District Magistrate (DM), few senior bureaucrats were available to monitor and support local administration. Local officials learned to discuss practical issues with their peers. As Mr. Dhiman described:

[20] Interview with retired IAS officer, Shimla, July 2008.

> When I was stationed in Lahaul Spiti, major government programs for infrastructure, employment and public services had been introduced. Large stakes were involved in these projects and issues of accountability came up ... I also could not overlook the concerns of block-level officers. I kept in constant touch with them and came to learn of the pressures they had to manage from the *gram pradhan* and other elected leaders, including the pressure to misutilize funds ... I realized that we had to work together, because public services are only effective when the needs of the officer sitting in the remotest corner of the district.[21]

By Mr. Dhiman's account, bureaucratic deliberation was a counterweight to local political pressures. If anything, physical distance from departmental headquarters motivated local officials to learn how to discuss and respond collectively to political and administrative challenges.

Deliberation inside HP's bureaucracy persisted after Parmar's government and percolated more widely across the state. It is important to note that electoral politics in HP may have supported the sustenance of deliberation. Table 5.1 illustrates the term of leadership by successive

TABLE 5.1 *Himachal Pradesh state government leadership (1971–2022)*

Ruling party	Term in office	Chief Minister
INC[1]	1967–1977	Yashwant Singh Parmar
INC	1977	Thakur Ram Lal
President's rule	1977	–
Janata Party	1977–1980	Shanta Kumar
INC	1980–1983	Thakur Ram Lal
INC	1983–1990	Virbhadra Singh
BJP	1990–1992	Shanta Kumar
President's rule	1992–1993	–
INC	1993–1998	Virbhadra Singh
BJP	1998–2003	Prem Kumar Dhumal
INC	2003–2007	Virbhadra Singh
BJP	2007–2012	Prem Kumar Dhumal
INC	2012–2017	Virbhadra Singh
BJP	2017–2022	Jai Ram Thakur

Note:
1. The first state assembly commenced in 1967, a few years before HP was officially granted statehood.
Source: Election Commission of India.

[21] Interview with local official, Shimla, September 2008.

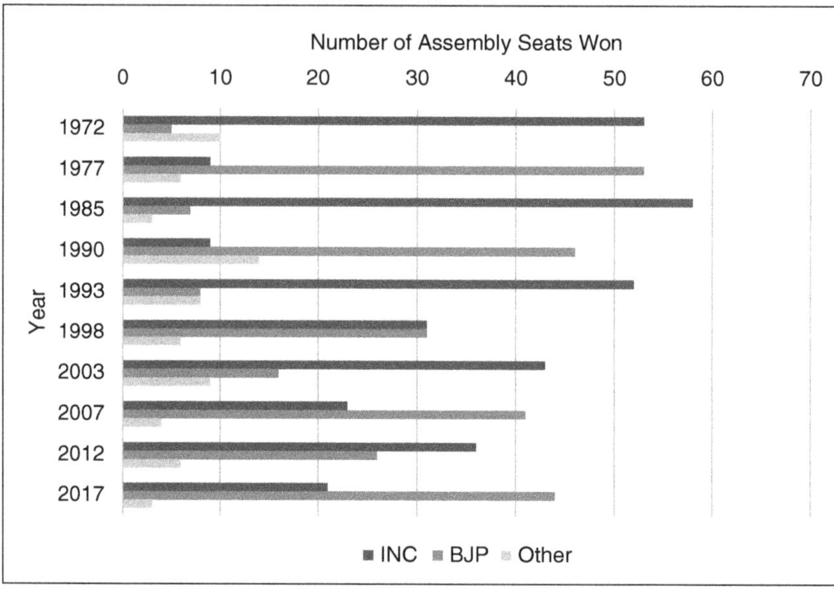

FIGURE 5.2 Himachal Pradesh state assembly election results (1972–2017)
Note: The opposition to the Indian National Congress (INC) in 1972 elections was the Bharatiya Jana Sangh, and in the 1977 elections, it was the Janata Party, both political predecessors of the Bharatiya Janata Party (BJP).
Source: Election Commission of India.

state governments, which tended to complete their full periods in office. Furthermore, decisive electoral victories allowed state governments to function with a clear mandate. Figure 5.2 shows the number of assembly seats won (out of sixty-eight seats in total) by competing parties in state elections from 1972 through 2017. In each election cycle, the winning party held a sizable majority of seats, allowing for stable, uncontested terms in office. Electoral politics also underwent a shift over time. After more than a decade of Congress Party domination, political competition intensified. By the 1990s, HP settled into a two-party system, with Congress and the BJP alternating in power (Sharma 2003). Relative stability allowed political leaders in HP to cultivate robust working relationships with bureaucrats, with whom they organized collectively to secure central government funds. Meanwhile, political competition maintained pressure on bureaucrats, ensuring that funds were utilized for development projects, irrespective of the party in power.

The electoral dynamics in HP can be contrasted with the pattern in UP, examined in Chapter 4. The Congress Party's steady decline in UP happened alongside the rise of regional parties and multiparty coalition governments. UP chief ministers often failed to complete their full terms, using precious time and political energy simply to hold on to power. Other sociopolitical contrasts are worth noting as well. Dalits are numerically significant in HP, comprising 25.2 percent of its population, the second highest share among Indian states. Unlike in the Gangetic plains, however, ethnic parties seeking to consolidate Dalit votes did not make major inroads in HP. Between 1990 and 2017, the Bahujan Samaj Party (BSP) garnered only one assembly seat in HP state elections. The Congress Party in HP drew support from disadvantaged groups, receiving 50 percent or more of Dalit votes according to post-election surveys (Kumar and Chauhan 2003). In the 2017 assembly elections, the BJP significantly outperformed the Congress in constituencies reserved for Dalit candidates (Attri and Bhattacharya 2019). Even today, however, few Dalits hold leadership positions within the state government or political party ranks. Neither party has fielded Dalit candidates in state elections except in constituencies officially reserved for Dalits. Electoral politics has thus remained dominated by upper castes, especially Rajputs, who account for five of the previous six chief ministers.

On the other hand, certain socioeconomic features of HP may have been conducive to the maintenance of deliberative bureaucracy. Rural society in HP has been less stratified economically than in the Gangetic plains and the distance between castes less pronounced (Singh 1998). The historical absence of *zamindari* allowed for more equitable distribution of land, lessening the economic disparities and occupational rigidities commonly associated with caste. HP's agrarian economy has consisted of peasant-cultivators, with a comparatively smaller share of landless laborers. The 2012–2013 National Sample Survey recorded 23.9 percent of households in HP as landless (against 43.8 percent nationally), with comparatively lesser inequality in landholdings across caste groups (Anand 2016). Most households own small plots of land, which provides an economic buffer, though it also limits surplus production.[22] Intercaste disparities in occupation are also lower in HP compared to other north Indian states (Das et al. 2015, 25–29). These economic conditions improve the prospects for social cooperation between castes and

[22] As per the 2011 Census, 88 percent of land in HP is held in small or marginal holdings (average plot size 1 hectare, or 2.5 acres). While two-thirds of the land is forest, only 17.2 percent is available for cultivation (Government of Himachal Pradesh 2018).

FIGURE 5.3 Temple for village deity (Theog, Himachal Pradesh)
Note: Author photograph (2010).

village-wide collective action for public goods, evidenced, for example, by community governance of forests and other natural resources (Agrawal and Chhatre 2006).

Anthropological studies have also revealed the importance of inter-caste cooperation in the domain of religion, supported by less austere Brahminical practices in the hill region (Berreman 1979). Village religious activities revolve around a local deity (*devta*), with dedicated temples and worship sites (*devta sthal*), as illustrated in Figure 5.3. The Deity Committee (devta Samiti) also serves as an informal institution for village governance and dispute resolution. In contrast to Vedic orthodoxies and rituals in the Gangetic plains, Hinduism in the western Himalayas has a wider pantheon of gods and confers certain religious responsibilities to lower castes and women. Dalits in HP can serve as designated "mediums," communicating between village leaders and deities (Chophy 2019). Religious pilgrimages call for women's participation (Sax 1991). Gender norms in HP are also more inclusive compared to the plains. Women in the hill region are not subject to seclusion (*purdah*) and have fewer restrictions on their physical movement. Ethnographic studies suggest that marriage practices, such as dowry, are less burdensome for women in HP (Sharma 1980; Snehi 2011). Relatively inclusive gender norms in HP may have helped the state achieve a much higher rate of female labor force participation than in other parts of India, driven by women's self-employment in agriculture.[23] Women's decision-making authority in the household may have also been enhanced by relatively high rates of male out-migration from the hill region. Women's participation extends to the public sphere as well. HP is known for its active women's associations (*mahila mandals*), involved in village governance, including the management of primary schools (Drèze and Kingdon 2001).

In taking note of HP's facilitative social environment, one must be careful not to understate the potency of caste divisions and gender discrimination within the state. Though the overall sex ratio in HP (1,040 females per 1,000 males) is higher than the national average (1,020), in a worrisome trend, the child sex ratio at birth (875) has been deteriorating and is now worse than the average for India (929) (NFHS-4 2015–16). Discrimination against lower castes is also common, exhibited by the caste-based segregation of rural settlements. Residential hamlets for different castes are physically separated, often by long distances, and they can have unequal access to public amenities (Vasan 2001). Likewise, mahila mandals in HP are found to be divided sometimes on caste lines, rather than fully encompassing all women in a village (Bhatty 2008, 90–121). Although more inclusive than in the plains, religious practices in HP also exhibit caste discrimination (Bhatt 2010). Temples honoring the village deity are situated in upper caste hamlets, with entry for Dalits prohibited (Sharma 2016). A subset of Dalits skilled in musical performance (*bajgis*) were customarily pressured by upper castes to play drums outside temple gates to invoke the village deity.[24] Recently, the segregation of Dalit children in schools and other discriminatory practices have gained public attention.[25]

[23] As per the 2011 Census, the female labor participation rate for India was 25.5 percent. HP recorded a much higher rate of 44.8 percent.

[24] My interviews with academics and rural residents revealed that such practices have persisted. During fieldwork, I was asked to verify my caste with village priests (*pandits*) before entering temples. Dalits were excluded from these same religious sites.

[25] R., Khanna, "It's Time Himachal Owned Up to Its Caste Problem," *The Wire*, October 25, 2018. Available at: https://thewire.in/caste/himachal-pradesh-caste-discrimination. A., Nair, "Caste Still a Major Issue in Himachal Schools, Discrimination Even During Midday Meals," *CNN-News 18*, March 4, 2018. Available at: www.news18.com/news/india/caste-still-a-major-issue-in-himachal-schools-discrimination-even-during-midday-meals-1677997.html.

In sum, social relations in HP are more conducive for village collective action, especially as compared to the Gangetic plains. However, they do not approximate the horizontal ties posited by social capital theory.

Before proceeding to explore the impact of deliberative bureaucracy on the delivery of primary education, the potential significance of military recruitment in the hill region merits attention. During World War I, Punjab province, which included current day Haryana and HP, was a strategic location for military recruitment. For young officers, the exposure and informal skills acquired during their military service was transformative (Mazumder 2003). Eynde (2016) finds that colonial military recruitment positively impacted literacy rates in Punjab; however the impact on public provisioning of schooling and children's participation is weak. Nevertheless, military recruitment may have helped raise the demand for education in the hill region. According to Ministry of Defence figures for 2017–2019, military recruitment in HP was 402 officers per million and 271 for Uttarakhand, the two highest rates for India.[26] By comparison, the rate for UP was twenty-eight officers per million and only twenty-two for Bihar.[27] Some studies suggest that Himachali army officers influenced the supply side of education – for example, building schools in their villages upon retirement (Narayan 1997). Similar patterns are observed in Uttarakhand. Where retired military officers contributed to education in their villages, though their efforts were aimed at supporting private rather than government schools (Chapter 6). Moreover, in Chapter 4's study of UP little difference was found in the implementation of primary schooling in Saharanpur and Sitapur districts, though the former falls within western UP's "Jat belt," also a prime site of military recruitment.[28] While this does not diminish the possible influence of military recruitment on education demand, the connection to implementation of government schooling is more complex and calls for further analysis.

[26] Figures based on a Ministry of Defence response to Parliamentary questions on March 11, 2020. Available at: http://164.100.24.220/loksabhaquestions/annex/173/AU2849.pdf.

[27] Yet, high literacy states in southern India also exhibit relatively low recruitment into the military. Recruitment rates for Kerala and Tamil Nadu are, respectively, 36 and 23 officers per million population.

[28] Owing to their physical features, Jats, Gujjars and other agrarian castes in western UP were deemed "martial races" by the colonial administration (Mazumder 2003).

5.3 HOW DELIBERATIVE BUREAUCRACY IMPROVES ACCESS TO PRIMARY SCHOOLING

This section draws on interviews and ethnographic evidence to show how deliberative bureaucracy facilitates school coverage, provision of infrastructure and participation of disadvantaged children.[29] First, I investigate the state planning process for primary education and the ways in which deliberation leads to the adaptation of policies. I then present nested case studies of implementation at the local level, to demonstrate how deliberative bureaucracy integrates disadvantaged children, encouraging enrollment and infrastructure provision in underserved communities.

5.3.1 Planning for Local Needs

Similar to other states, the HP State Planning Board creates five-year plans, in accordance with central government planning guidelines. Line departments submit provisional plans and budget proposals to the State Planning Board and Department of Finance, which then make recommendations on fund allocation. "*Directive planning*," as a retired IAS officer put it, has been the dominant mode of development policymaking throughout India.[30] As Chapter 4 demonstrated, legalistic bureaucracy in UP directed education planning based on narrowly specified rules. In HP, by contrast, planning was driven by norms promoting deliberation. State officials used the terms "*interactive*," "*participatory*," and "*consultative*" when describing the planning process. Before submitting annual plans for legislative ratification, planning officials convened policy "working groups," informal meetings with participation from across line departments, to discuss policy goals and administrative challenges.[31] An official from the State Planning Department explained:

> The participatory planning process has been very helpful [for the state] overall ... We have been able to allocate funds and policies based on area-specific, local needs. Actually I can make a bold statement that we have made a clear

[29] Some parts of this section were previously published in my article "Bureaucratic Norms and State Capacity in India: Implementing Primary Education in the Himalayan Region," *Asian Survey*, 55.5 (2015): 882–908. I reproduce them here with permission from the University of California Press.

[30] Interview with retired IAS officer, New Delhi, June 2007.

[31] Interviews with several officials, State Planning Department, Shimla, June 2008.

shift from directive planning to more interactive planning, because there has been a great deal of flexibility given to the departments. They come back to us [the Planning Department] with their issues and then also consult with the legislative side.[32]

As another official put it, informal discussions helped "*set the agenda*" for formal plans.[33] Importantly, it gave departments an opportunity to identify how policies could be tailored to practical conditions in the field.

A similar account was given by political actors outside of the bureaucracy, including Members of the Legislative Assembly (MLAs), who were elected to the state legislature. In interviews, MLAs described their "*partnership*" (*sanjhedari*) with state officials and how routine discussions allowed them to learn about governmental initiatives and communicate information to their constituents.[34] These close interactions contrasted with state planning in UP, where bureaucrats maintained a distance from elected officials. In the words of a senior Planning Department official:

The level of consultation is a unique feature of planning here that you don't find in the rest of India. We convene regular meetings with public representatives. We request the MLAs to share their priorities and other information about their constituents' needs that would be relevant for planning. Before coming to these meetings, we ask MLAs to discuss with their constituents and local administrators at the district, block and panchayat levels what they need.[35]

Elected representatives also communicated their constituents' demands in planning meetings, working to ensure that state plans were informed by citizen needs.[36] A senior health official described his experiences working with MLAs:

Elected leaders can be very effective in connecting us to people on the ground. Some might see that as interference, but what is "interference"? It is just a word. In the end, the MLA is a public representative, and we must seek them out to understand the people's voice on the ground. And they too have to cooperate with the bureaucracy to get things done.[37]

Along with elected officials, civil society participation was also visible in state planning processes. Civil society input was deemed critical across policy domains, including primary education. Despite central government

[32] Interview with senior official, State Planning Department, Shimla, June 2008.
[33] Interview with senior official, State Planning Department, Shimla, August 2008.
[34] Interviews with several MLAs, Shimla, May–August 2008.
[35] Interview with senior official, State Planning Department, Shimla, July 2008.
[36] Interviews with several MLAs, Shimla, May–August 2008.
[37] Interview with senior official, Department of Rural Development, Shimla, July 2008.

resources for Sarva Shiksha Abhiyan (SSA), service delivery was daunting due to the mountainous terrain and dispersed habitations. As an education official explained: "*If we can achieve even 70 percent of our monitoring targets, we find that good.*"[38]

To strengthen local monitoring, the education bureaucracy partnered with civic agencies like the Himachal Pradesh Gyan Vigyan Samiti (HGVS), a civic organization working on rural education and governance. HGVS is the HP branch of the Bharat Gyan Vigyan Samiti (BGVS), a nationwide volunteer movement for education and scientific knowledge, sponsored by the central government's 1987 National Literacy Mission.[39] In a departure from other Indian states, HP's education bureaucracy granted HGVS the mandate to run a state resource center for administering adult education and village literacy campaigns. The success of literacy programming in Kerala, supported by the Kerala Sastra Sahitya Parishad, a pioneering branch of BGVS, drew national attention and encouraged state planners in HP to engage civil society in similar ways. As a retired official remarked, the partnership with HGVS was helpful since, "*the government did not have direct access to the people.*"[40] HGVS was registered in 1991 and had a local presence throughout the state.[41] Its 50,000-strong network in villages included social activists, teachers, doctors and rural youth.

Placed in charge of adult education, HGVS used its institutionalized presence in the state to communicate citizen demands and grievances. In focus group discussions, HGVS staff downplayed the adult literacy program. Rural residents, they recalled, were too preoccupied with agricultural work to concern themselves with education. Through the village literacy camps, however, parents shared their aspirations for educating their children. "*That 'I may be illiterate, but my child does not have to be,' was a sentiment that parents would often express to us*," an HGVS volunteer recalled.[42] HGVS volunteers communicated public sentiments to policymakers. When policies were perceived as unfair, the volunteers organized protests outside bureaucratic offices.[43] A senior HGVS official

[38] Interview with senior official, SSA District Project Office, Shimla, March 2010.

[39] BGVS website: www.bgvs.org.

[40] Interviews with retired IAS officers, Shimla, July 2008.

[41] Interviews with HGVS associates, Shimla (May–August 2008).

[42] Focus group discussion with HGVS fieldworkers, Respondent 3, Shimla, March 2010.

[43] I observed protests led by HGVS activists outside of government offices. For example, they held a rally outside the Forestr Department, where activists spoke out against unregulated felling of trees by timber companies.

explained: "*Sometimes we have had conflict but overall the state has been open to our support. And our participation within the state has grown so much that by now not one state government committee or program can avoid us. We must be included in any policy committee at the state level.*"[44]

5.3.2 Integrating Disadvantaged Children

Deliberative planning in HP stimulated local policy innovations that helped strengthen participation by disadvantaged children. The development of the annual academic calendar provides a compelling example. In most Indian states, primary schools follow a common academic calendar, with examinations scheduled in April and May. Amid their deliberations, state planners in HP identified the difficulties posed by a uniform academic calendar. The varying altitude and terrain created regional differences in climate and agricultural seasons. Some parts of HP had a climate similar to the plains while other areas were snowed in for months at a stretch, hindering school attendance. The timing of agricultural harvest also varied regionally. Rural children assisted their parents on the farm, especially in peak harvests months, which conflicted with their preparation for annual examinations. A retired school headmaster stated plainly: "*The exam system is unfriendly to the rural child, who has to study but also helps out with farming and domestic chores. The system sets the child up to fail.*"[45] The headmaster described how, in local planning meetings, education officials learned about the stress that the agricultural harvest placed on student attendance. Children from the poorest households missed school in the critical months leading up to examinations. Consequently, some were held back in the fifth grade, failing to transition to middle school. State planners responded by adjusting the academic calendar for different regions of the state. District administrations were granted the flexibility to alter the timing of examinations based on the local climate and agriculture harvest season, which in turn helped improve student attendance and preparation.

Local officials encouraged deliberation among schoolteachers as well, as I observed in teacher training and school monitoring visits (Figure 5.4).[46] To illustrate, consider the teacher training led by Mr. Pawar, an official

44 Interview with senior associate, HGVS, Shimla, July 2008.

45 Focus group discussion with district education officials, Shimla, February 2009.

46 In Shimla, I attended several teacher training sessions at the District Institute of Education and Training (DIET) in Shamlaghat and three block-level centers.

FIGURE 5.4 Teacher training session underway (Koti, Himachal Pradesh)
Note: Author photograph (2008).

in Mashobra block. Mr. Pawar's training sessions were no different in content from those I observed in other study states. As he narrated from a training manual, teachers recorded notes, asking few questions. However, during chai breaks and other informal interactions, Mr. Pawar asked teachers to share their practical experiences of working in the rural education system. On one occasion, Mr. Pawar went around the room asking the teachers about their first week of classes. Irregular attendance of students arose as an issue. One teacher remarked, "*The day we handed out uniforms and schoolbags, all the children showed up. But the day after, some of them went missing.*"[47] Another teacher raised doubts about parental support for education. Others commented on the lack of hygiene in rural communities. Mr. Pawar narrated one of his early experiences as a schoolteacher while posted in Mandi district. Children rarely used water to wash their hands or clean themselves after defecating, he said. Mr. Pawar had rented an accommodation in the village and offered to teach the children about hygiene. "*At that time,*" he recounted, "*to find running water in the village school was rare. The children were in the habit of using a stone* (patthar) *to clean themselves ... It took many*

[47] Participant observation of teacher training, Shimla, September 2008.

repeated attempts to convince parents to change these habits … but as the teacher, this was also my duty."[48] He used the example to stress the importance of building parental confidence in the school system.

The group's mood became somber when a teacher narrated the story of two brothers in his primary school's catchment area.[49] Sunil and Anil came from a disadvantaged community of tenant farmers. Poor health had kept them out of school. The teacher wanted to re-enroll the boys, but their advanced age was a roadblock. Mr. Pawar suggested the teacher visit the boys' home and inform their parents about SSA incentives to encourage enrollment. Later that week, the same teacher came to the block office to collect teaching materials. Mr. Pawar sought an update on Sunil and Anil. The teacher had visited their home and learned that they had physical disabilities, which made it challenging for them to interact with other students. Mr. Pawar connected the teacher with Prerna, a local NGO working with children with special needs. The teacher subsequently reported that Prerna had enrolled the brothers in a home-schooling program.

Deliberation across Departments

The examples presented so far show how deliberation percolated down to the front lines of the state, shaping how officials understood their duties and integrated disadvantaged children. As I observed, deliberation extended beyond the education bureaucracy to incorporate other state departments as well. At Shimla's southeastern edge, where the Sutlej river cuts through the Shivalik mountains, I met Govindji in a local education office. Govindji had started a program for migrant children that was later adopted throughout Shimla. After twenty years as a schoolteacher, Govindji was promoted to Block Resource Coordinator (BRC), tasked with teacher training, supervision and academic support. During his school visits, he observed children working on construction sites, which he verified with Shyam Lal, a school headmaster. Together, they identified thirty-six migrant children, mainly from Rajasthan and UP, working on construction sites. The property builders offered laborers onsite housing, but with the informal expectation that their children would assist in the construction work. Elder children were involved directly in construction, mixing cement and carrying bricks, while younger ones performed lighter tasks. As the two men narrated:

[48] Participant observation of teacher training, Shimla, September 2008.

[49] The official catchment area for a government primary school typically includes all habitations located within a kilometer distance of the school.

GOVINDJI: We tried convincing parents to send their children to school, but they were unwilling. They were worried about what might happen if the builder came to know.

SHYAM LAL: We tried hard to persuade them by offering scholarships (*vajipha*), free textbooks and uniforms, but that also didn't work.[50]

The duo approached Mr. Negi, the Additional District Magistrate (ADM) of Shimla, for assistance. Mr. Negi contacted the Superintendent of Police (SP) of Shimla, who assigned officers to meet with the parents. As Govindji narrated:

> On the SP's recommendation, we went to the local police station (*thana*) and asked for their help. An officer came with us to the worksite and told the parents that it was illegal to keep their children out of school and that they were committing a crime. People are naturally fearful of the uniform (*vardi*). The parents gave in and agreed to enroll the children.

Police officers also met with local builders and threatened to lock down construction sites if children were found working. To strengthen parents' confidence, Govindji and Shyam Lal personally delivered free textbooks and schoolbags. Thereafter, Govindji used SSA resources to create an Alternative Education Center (AEC) for migrant children. Alternative Education was a remedial program for children who had dropped out of school. However, accessing such programs was complicated because migrant households often lived in informal settlements and lacked an official address, which they needed to avail of state benefits. To work around these constraints, Govindji and Mr. Negi identified government land near the construction site to construct the center.

In a subsequent interview, Mr. Negi shared his experiences in district administration. As ADM, he was responsible for development programming as well as law and order, evident from the pile of legal files on his desk. Education was not central to his everyday work, as he noted: "*My office oversees all policy-related matters in the district, but education does not normally consume my attention.*"[51] Nevertheless, he utilized police contacts to support Govindji. As we veered to the subject of coordination between the police and other agencies, Mr. Negi offered vivid details of his experiences working across hierarchical boundaries. While posted in Chamba, an economically weak district, he learned how to interact with subordinates and ordinary citizens. In Mr. Negi's words:

50 Interview with local education official and primary school headmaster, Shimla, July 2008.

51 Interview with ADM, Shimla, August 2008.

> One positive point I have seen over the last twenty years is this ... When I started in 1986, poor ladies and chaps wouldn't come to my office for help. There was a hesitation in people to work with state agencies. But over time we learned that if you deprive Dalits, women or any weaker section of access to basic rights, then you cannot achieve overall development ... I've learned this from watching the example of my seniors. If my senior officer shuns people away from his office, then naturally that will shape how I do things. Those I worked under encouraged me to stay in close touch with my subordinates and keep my doors open to people. So, I think that's a major sign of good governance. That is where it starts.[52]

Mr. Negi's account, of learning how to administer programs and interact with local officials and citizens, was echoed in interviews with other state officials. Senior administrators were often seen to set an example of how subordinates should conduct their duties.

Mobile Schooling for Gujjars

Deliberation between administrative subdivisions also facilitated the execution of education "subplans" for interior territories and tribal populations. Established by the central government's Planning Commission, the subplan model earmarks funds for disadvantaged groups, for example, through the SC Sub-Plan Fund, ST Sub-Plan Fund and Area Development Funds. Across India, subplans have been fairly limited in scope, with state governments reporting fund utilization back to the central agencies.[53] By contrast, deliberative bureaucracy in HP used the subplan mechanism to foster "*interdepartmental coordination*" in planning.[54] For instance, officials from the Tribal Development Department worked with the Department of Elementary Education to identify the educational needs of marginalized tribal populations. Teachers and local education officials were encouraged to interact with tribal populations to learn about their customs. Cultural activities to attract tribal children, including traditional dances and musical performances, were integrated into after-school programming.[55]

The case of the Gujjars illustrates how deliberation between departments worked to improve access to primary schooling. Mr. Chauhan, an education official involved in the mobile school program, identified the difficulties of extending education to Gujjar children in Sirmaur district:

52 Ibid.

53 Interviews with retired Planning Commission officials, New Delhi, February 2009.

54 Interviews with state officials, Shimla, July 2008.

55 I observed tribal dance performances by children for school events in Shimla and Kullu districts.

"*We saw their enrollments increase at the start of the school year, but by winter they would stop coming to school ... and we didn't know where to locate them.*"[56] Senior education officials shared these observations with counterparts in the Tribal Development Department, who in turn tracked the annual migration of the Gujjars from Sirmaur to Saharanpur district in UP. The two departments organized "exposure visits" to Saharanpur. As Mr. Chauhan described:

> With support from the Department, I visited the Mohammedan [Muslim] Gujjar community in Saharanpur. The children were lagging far behind and their parents had doubts about the school system. We explained to them that SSA would provide all the necessary inputs, like books, uniforms, bags, free of cost. Many parents had not heard of SSA and the facilities available from the government, so that initial dialogue helped.[57]

Education officials from HP learned about the Gujjar community's socio-economic constraints. With departmental support, they experimented by hiring volunteer teachers from within the Gujjar community, who could work while accommodating the need for children to perform labor.

However, the appointment of volunteer teachers was contentious. Government schoolteachers were required to hold a bachelor's degree and undergo professional training. Meanwhile, volunteer teachers needed only a high school diploma. According to an official, "*Teacher selection ... that was always a sensitive issue. Employing a less qualified person appeared unfair to some permanent teachers, so we had to be careful about their sentiments.*"[58] The education bureaucracy settled on a 90-day training program and monthly stipend for volunteer teachers. The mobile schools were piloted as remedial teaching camps, operating at agreed-upon locations, often close to where Gujjar families herded their livestock. As the pilot scheme proved popular, the Department of Elementary Education pooled resources with the Tribal Development Department to expand the program. Local officials performed a comprehensive social mapping of Gujjars in HP. After a few years, the mobile schooling program became a model for service delivery to migratory populations adopted by other states as well.

The program helped initiate state efforts to recruit contract teachers, which incited backlash from regular government teachers. A new post was created for Village Para-teachers (Gramin Vidya Upasaks), hired by

[56] Interview with local education official, Shimla, March 2010.

[57] Ibid.

[58] Interview with local education official, Shimla, March 2010.

FIGURE 5.5 Primary school in a Himalayan village (Mashobra, Himachal Pradesh)
Note: Author photograph (2008).

the village *panchayat* instead of the State Public Service Commission's formal selection process. Regular teachers that I interviewed spoke of the contract-based posts as *"backdoor entry"* into the teaching profession.[59] Para-teachers organized themselves into unions and pressured the state government to convert their contracts into "regular" (permanent) teaching posts.

5.3.3 Implementing School Infrastructure

The bureaucracy's flexible interpretation of policy rules in response to practical demands was evident in the development of new schools. The construction of new schools posed distinct challenges in hilly terrain (Figure 5.5). According to SSA program rules, primary schools were required to be constructed within a one-kilometer walking distance from villages (or three kilometers for upper-primary schools). Most governments followed the central government's framework. In HP, discussions held by the Education Working Group raised the need to alter SSA rules,

[59] Interviews with numerous school teachers, Shimla district, July-August 2008.

since the hilly terrain made it more challenging for children to walk to school. A planning report submitted to the central government summarized the bureaucracy's position:

> [I]t is felt that the distance norm prescribed by the Government of India does not reflect the actual picture in the hilly terrain, as the real distance covered in hilly areas is much more, as the habitations are scattered. Unlike in the plains, one to three km in a hilly terrain often means climbing down one ridge and climbing up another and/or crossing a rivulet. All this twice a day is not easy for elementary school-going children. Hence it is felt that the government of Himachal Pradesh should formulate its own policy of providing accessibility of schools keeping the hilly terrain in mind.[60]

The education bureaucracy decided to establish new criteria for school coverage, taking into consideration the physical routes taken by children from remote villages to reach school. In interviews, officials noted that revisions to policy rules were not limited to school distance norms, but were a common feature of how they approached the implementation of central government programs.

The discussion so far may give the impression that implementation in HP had few rules supporting it. Yet, behind the bureaucracy's flexibility was a commitment to collective problem-solving, creating a distinct form of accountability within the education system. To illustrate, consider the school construction meetings that I observed in the DM's office. Mr. Dhiman, a BDO, held weekly review meetings with his associates. In one meeting, a local official identified a typical problem with infrastructure provision. Funds for a new classroom were sanctioned, but construction had stalled for six months, forcing teachers to hold classes outdoors. A month after the classroom was finished, the room's structure had caved in, nearly collapsing. An inquiry was launched, and village residents discovered that inferior quality cement had been used for the room's pillars. Mr. Dhiman engaged the group in a discussion, seeking perspectives on how local administration should respond. "*Formal proceedings will take too long!*," one official remarked.[61] Another official raised concerns about political interference in legal proceedings, recounting how in a recent building collapse elsewhere contractors used their connections to stall judicial cases. Instead, the officials found a pragmatic way to sanction the builder, by agreeing to blacklist him from future infrastructure contracts. They also agreed to cooperate against suspicious builders in the future by informing

60 Excerpt from HP State Development Report (GoI 2005, 139).

61 Participant observation, BDO meeting, Shimla, April 2010.

one another whenever such cases arose. Signaling his appreciation for the "*practical*" approach taken, Mr. Dhiman encouraged the officials to coordinate their efforts. Instead of going by the book, local officials expressed their readiness to work together through informal arrangements that were more effective.

While seeing the benefits of collective problem-solving, local officials were mindful of the downsides of having too much bureaucratic flexibility and rule-bending. The development of the primary school in Shalai, a village on the outskirts of Mashobra block, offers an instructive case. A habitation of only eighteen households, Shalai was as improbable setting for public services to reach citizens. The village was a 90-minute bus journey from Department of Education headquarters, followed by a seven-kilometer hike up a steep ravine. Shalai's primary school, built in 1998, had two teachers catering to a grand total of three students. Parents had demanded construction of the school because children had to travel four kilometers to attend school in a neighboring village. A mother recalled, "*We were concerned for our small children. They could not make the journey by themselves. Some of us took turns dropping them to school in the morning. But there was always the fear among parents that my child could fall and get injured walking home.*"[62] The women's association in Shalai organized community meetings and helped identify unoccupied land for building the school. A local education official attended the meetings and drew up a plan for the primary school.

The school had twenty-three children when it first opened. A decade later, Shalai's child population had dwindled significantly as families migrated out of the village in search of economic opportunities. Local officials issued a warning that, unless enrollment increased, the school would be closed down. Village leaders struck an informal agreement to keep the school running. Local administration would provide the teachers, the midday meal and other inputs, while maintenance costs would be covered by the village authorities. Informal arrangements like these were hardly exceptional. Throughout HP, primary schools were constructed in villages with relatively small child populations. Several schools had more staff members than students, in violation of SSA rules, which stipulated that a child population of 150 was required to qualify for a primary school.[63] Community demands, according to senior education officials,

[62] Interview with a mother, Shalai, April 2009.

[63] According to local officials interviewed, twelve government primary schools in Shimla district had more staff members than students enrolled.

led to the "*haphazard*" opening of new primary schools.[64] A retired bureaucrat who had served as education secretary summarized these perspectives: "*Schools have been opened where there is some need but not too much need … Often this has been done without proper forecasting or compliance with official norms.*"[65]

Local officials expressed similar concerns about the bending of SSA program rules. But they also appreciated the practical difficulties of providing schools in far-flung villages, which often meant that they had to cooperate with village leaders. As one official explained, a degree of local political interference was inevitable:

> With this whole decentralization push, we find pradhans have become contractors (*thekedars*). A huge network has emerged of contracting (*thekedari*) for the school building and other facilities. Then for appointing the schoolteacher and cooking staff, again it provides opportunities to dispense patronage … That is how communities are involved in school development. That is what you call a demand- or needs-based system.[66]

The process of "contracting" (*thekedari*) school construction created opportunities for local politicians to seek rents, but it also gave local communities a chance to participate in public service delivery. Returning to the example of Shalai, the village women's association petitioned the local administration to build a kitchen shed for preparing the midday meal. Subsequently, the group lobbied to have two of its members employed at the school as cooks. From the perspective of local officials, such demands were part and parcel of community involvement in service delivery.

Other officials stressed how public administration in HP had been overrun by political demands. Some explicitly referred to the state as a "*patronage-based*" system. Elected leaders and their "*intermediaries*" (*dalals*) often pressed for the construction of schools in their preferred areas. At the village-level, "*contractors*" (*thekedars*) jockeyed for government projects and construction contracts. Along with school construction, concerns about political interference in teacher transfers were commonplace.[67] The interactions I observed between senior officials

64 Interviews with several bureaucrats and elected officials in Shimla (February–April 2009).

65 Interview with retired education official, Shimla, February 2009.

66 Interview with senior official, Department of Education, Shimla, June 2008.

67 Interviews with several officials, Shimla, March–April 2010. Bureaucrats from HP have also written about patronage in public services, including the politically motivated posting of schoolteachers (Sood 2003; Sanan 2004).

and schoolteachers at the Education Directorate in Shimla were most frequently related to posting and transfer requests by teachers. On one occasion, a young teacher described the hardships she encountered while working in an interior village. She requested to be transferred to a school closer to town. Irritated by her request, the senior official noted that she had only been posted at the school for one month. "*Please consider my situation. I have not even used an approach while asking for this [transfer],*" the teacher responded.[68] By "*approach*" (*pahunch*), the teacher was referring to political connections to influence the bureaucracy, often by working through an elected representative or offering to pay a bribe. The official turned down her request and subsequently described how the politicization of teachers had caused the "*drowning*" (*beda garak*) of the primary school system.

5.4 WOMEN AT THE HELM: MOBILIZING COMMUNITIES TO MONITOR SERVICES

Section 5.3 demonstrated the impact of deliberative bureaucracy on education planning activities, school coverage and infrastructure provision. This section examines the complex tasks around monitoring primary schools. HP's schooling system is found to perform these functions comparatively well, generating higher parental satisfaction relative to other states (PROBE 1999; Das et al. 2015). In what follows, I offer field-based evidence demonstrating how deliberative bureaucracy in HP has mobilized communities to monitor schools. A distinguishing feature of public administration in HP, the education bureaucracy has effectively integrated rural women into governance processes for primary schooling, helping to enhance the quality of education services.

5.4.1 From Mahila Mandals to Mother Teacher Associations

Mahila mandals, women's village associations, have played a leading role in community governance in HP. The bureaucracy's attentiveness to the dynamics of community participation is reflected in state documents and official reports. A report by the State Planning Department devoted an entire chapter to "People's Participation." The report highlighted the importance of holding training programs, exposure visits, panchayat and

[68] Participant observation, Education Directorate, Shimla, April 2010.

NGO capacity-building activities, as well as festivals (*melas*) with local civic bodies, with the express purpose of spreading "the concept of people's participation in development planning."[69] Field observations of bureaucrats promoting participation of mahila mandals are testimony to these official statements.

Anthropological research reveals that mahila mandals in HP have long managed collective goods, including forests, water, sanitation and child welfare (Sharma 1980; Berry 2001). Mahila mandals emerged organically, often in response to ecological conditions and women's livelihood needs.[70] As men migrated out for economic opportunities, women stayed back to manage agricultural and household work. Their economic lives were tethered to forests, a critical source of fuelwood, animal fodder and medicinal plants. Because of forest depletion, however, women had to trek longer distances to gather resources.[71] In response, mahila mandals worked to enforce collective rules on the usage of trees, water and other common-pool resources. Their involvement in community decisions increased, and by the 1980s, they began forming intervillage networks. Voluntary organizations, such as Social Uplift through Rural Action (SUTRA), organized processions (*padayatras*) of mahila mandals to Shimla, where they held rallies to influence state policies affecting women, such as widow pension schemes and domestic violence laws.

State agencies took notice of mahila mandals and sought to promote their participation in policy implementation. A Department of Rural Development official observed: "*We found the mahila mandals quite helpful in our Total Sanitation Campaign. Also, we have seen them work against alcoholism and other social issues in the village. They are active within the community, and we have tried to rope them in more and more into our programs.*"[72] District administration often lacked adequate personnel and resources to monitor public services, especially in interior villages. As a BDO remarked, "We could not possibly meet our [development] targets without help from the community." Education officials likewise described how women's groups were "*aware*" (*jagruk*) about government schemes and provided valuable "*cooperation*" (*sahyog*) to

[69] Excerpt from Himachal Pradesh State Development Report (GoI 2005, 259).

[70] Mahila mandals are distinct from women's microcredit SHGs created by state agencies and NGOs.

[71] According to a study, women in HP walk thirty kilometers per month to collect wood, averaging 2.7 hours per trip (Parikh 2011).

[72] Interview with official, Department of Rural Development, Shimla, May 2010.

the local state.[73] Central programs like SSA covered capital investments, such as new school buildings, but responsibility for operations and routine monitoring fell on resource-constrained state governments. In HP, women's associations helped extend the state's infrastructural reach. As a senior SSA official narrated:

> Over the course of the [school] expansion across the state, we found that women contributed more to the primary schools. The gents were distant, either busy working or doing something else. But the women were empowered and showed more concern on a day-to-day basis ... Even far into the interior areas, like Lahaul and Spiti ... there you will find the women most active in primary education.[74]

In contrast to other social groups, the official explained, women's association members sent their children to government primary schools and thus could be relied upon to monitor services. These narratives are supported by field-based studies capturing the role of women's groups in monitoring education and health services. The PROBE (1999) report found that mahila mandals in HP contributed to school management, leading to higher student attendance and improvements in the Midday Meal Programme.[75]

The state's initiative to strengthen women's participation in education progressed in the early 2000s, when mahila mandals were awarded official recognition through the creation of Mother Teacher Associations (MTAs). Consisting of mothers whose children attended government schools, village MTAs were given authority to monitor services, liaise with local administration and report grievances. Mahila mandals in some areas had performed these activities informally, but recognition through the MTAs provided a more regular, institutionalized channel for women to voice collective demands. The political decision to adopt the MTA structure was the outcome of bureaucratic deliberations. In interviews, local education officials described their early experiences of working with mahila mandals informally. For example, the groups would contribute to school meals by organizing local vegetables from village residents, which supplemented the grains supplied by the MDM Programme. The education bureaucracy worked with civic agencies like HGVS to develop the MTA concept and pilot its administration. HGVS was asked to develop

[73] Interview with BDO, Shimla, April 2010.

[74] Interview with senior official, SSA State Project Office, Shimla, July 2008.

[75] Drèze and Kingdon (2001) find that women's groups help improve delivery of school meals as well as enrollment and attendance, especially for girls.

"model" MTAs, allowing the bureaucracy to fine-tune the system before scaling it up throughout the state. An HGVS fieldworker described the MTA pilot project as follows:

> We adopted model MTAs in the most backward villages. In the course of a few years, the MTAs turned their schools around. We showed the [Education] Department what they [the women] are capable of achieving. It was only after seeing it work in a practical way that the government came to embrace the MTA concept.[76]

The MTA model allowed mothers formal oversight of primary schools, a departure from the administrative setup in most other Indian states, which adhered to the central government's SSA program. SSA guidelines authorized Village Education Committees (VECs) to monitor primary schooling. Field observations and interviews in HP revealed that VEC involvement was limited to the oversight of school infrastructure and utilization of SSA grants. VECs rarely devoted attention to monitoring services.[77] An official from the Department of Education likewise observed:

> The VEC was created because of the school grants that must be spent for SSA. Their main emphasis was driven by spending (*kharcha*) ... But the MTA is more involved as an actual committee at the school. They [the MTA members] make sure that the school functions, that children attend and that the food they eat is nutritious. They are more active.[78]

While acknowledging the importance of VECs, education officials found that these agencies often lacked the interest or capacity to monitor education services. The pradhan of the village panchayat, who was the official head of the VEC, had the responsibility for multiple government schemes, many of which were more lucrative than primary schooling. As panchayat members themselves reported in interviews, social services like education and health were crowded out by development projects, such as village footpaths, employment and housing.[79] By formalizing the role of MTAs in routine school management, the state thus secured a reliable social partner to help monitor village primary schools.

[76] Interview with field associate, HGVS, Shimla, May 2010.

[77] Out of thirteen village primary schools visited in HP, ten had active VECs. In all ten cases, VECs were associated with "construction work" (*nirman ka kaam*) and "expenditure" (*kharcha*) of SSA grants.

[78] Interview with senior official, State Project Office, SSA, Shimla, July 2008.

[79] Similar findings emerged from observations of gram sabhas in eight villages. In none of these assemblies did questions about primary education arise.

5.4.2 Primary School Monitoring by MTAs

I now present evidence from participant observation in Shimla district to demonstrate how MTAs have practically supported the monitoring of schools. Local officials in Shimla conducted meetings and capacity-building exercises with MTAs at regular intervals, led by the SSA Gender Coordinator, an official tasked with gender-targeted programming.[80] By ensuring that dedicated personnel engaged regularly with MTA members, local administration gained exposure to the practical difficulties experienced by marginalized women and their communities. MTA members, meanwhile, gained knowledge and confidence in their abilities to participation in the school system. A district education official explained:

> Our MTAs meet on the seventh of every month. We encourage them to share any message they need to give to the government. They tell us about school repairs, problems with the midday meal, and the quality of teaching at the school. And we also pass along information on government programs and any new schemes that are coming up in education. In that way, we stay connected to local communities and they also maintain ties with the school system.[81]

Focus group discussions with MTAs largely substantiated what officials reported in interviews. I asked MTA members if they could remember when the previous meeting was held with local administration. Each of the MTAs, from different administrative blocks of Shimla, identified when the last meeting took place as well as the details of what they discussed. In all but one case, the Block Education Officer (BEO) was present at the meeting. The most common issue reported in these meetings was the paucity of teachers for science subjects. The MTAs were also vocal about teacher absenteeism and the unpredictability of school hours. Mothers often accompanied their children to school, and when teachers were either late or failed to arrive, their workdays were disrupted. These irregularities affected their livelihoods, since women often performed agricultural labor. Some of the MTAs made their own informal arrangements for childcare, with members taking turns to look after each other's children. Nevertheless, when teachers were routinely late or absent, disadvantaged households, and women in particular, paid a heavy price.

[80] I attended one such meeting in Kotkhai block in Shimla (April 2010), which brought together 279 residents from surrounding villages, mostly women. State officials gave information about the RTE Act and answered queries regarding the new legislation's provisions.

[81] Interview, BRC, SSA, Shimla, April 2010.

Deliberative processes involving MTA members, teachers and education officials provided an opportunity for addressing problems like teacher absence. The meetings held in Banyog, a panchayat on the outskirts of Shimla district illustrate the process of collective problem-solving. Banyog's administrative boundaries covered five villages, each having its own primary school and MTA. In focus group discussions, I learned that teachers had been arriving late to school since several months. In some cases, they failed to reach school until the afternoon. MTA members communicated their disapproval in a meeting, attended by the BEO and the schools' head teachers. In the discussions it surfaced that most teachers commuted from Shimla by bus. However, the bus company had changed its schedule to depart later, causing the teachers to miss the connection to another bus for Banyog. As a stopgap measure, some teachers pooled funds to hire a private taxi. Others made the connecting journey on foot. Subsequently, the BEO solicited inputs from MTAs located in nearby villages, who reported similar problems in their primary schools. After contacting the local transportation authorities, the BEO learned that the bus company in charge of the route had undergone a management change and hired new bus drivers, who were unaware of the connecting bus. The BEO described how MTAs worked with local administration to remedy the situation:

> We spoke with the [bus] company management and requested them to have the bus depart Shimla half an hour earlier in the morning. They were hesitant at first, but when we explained that the teachers had no other means [*sadhan*] to get to school, they agreed to consider changing the timing ... The MTAs were quite effective (*prabhavi*) here as well. They contacted the bus company and persuaded them [to make the changes] ... I suspect the managers had to listen if they wanted to keep the community happy![82]

The bus company managers met with the MTAs and reached an agreement to reschedule the bus to leave a half-hour earlier. Following the changes, teachers again started arriving on time to school.

The episode in Banyog was but one of several cases that I observed of practical problem-solving through deliberation between MTAs, teachers, BEOs and other local actors. Education officials in Shimla treated discussions with MTAs as a core duty. In the words of one official, "*We keep in touch with the MTAs and encourage dialogue* [charcha]. *Otherwise, the parents may lose their connection to the school.*"[83] When

[82] Interview with BEO, Shimla, April 2010.

[83] Interview with local education official, Shimla, April 2010.

FIGURE 5.6 Mother Teacher Association members (Shimla, Himachal Pradesh)
Note: Author photograph (2010).

communities brought their concerns forward, the official noted, issues could be addressed in a timely way, which prevented misunderstandings between parents and teachers from escalating.

Beyond their immediate impact on primary education, deliberative spaces gave rural women opportunities to engage regularly with the local state. Although mahila mandals were active in many parts of HP, their involvement in public services could not be taken for granted. MTA meetings allowed women to gain exposure to local agencies, interact with women from other villages and identify collective needs (Figure 5.6). The practice of vocalizing their demands to local officials also strengthened the MTA's confidence in its collective ability to exert pressure on the state. An MTA member from in Banyog underscored the transformation she had witnessed as a result of participating in school meetings:

> The men in our village are always saying to us, "You are all illiterate. What is the purpose of your group?" And we too have asked ourselves that sometimes. But when the teachers started to arrive in school on time, we didn't have to explain ourselves anymore. So what if we are not as educated? Our voice also reaches the state.[84]

[84] Focus group discussion, Respondent 2, Banyog, April 2010.

The attainment of concrete results enhanced women's confidence in local administration as well. Focus group discussions with other MTAs likewise generated narratives of increased confidence as well as heightened expectations of the state. Whereas the MTA monitoring structure granted rural women formal state recognition, deliberative bureaucratic norms helped strengthen their participation and sense of efficacy. For example, I observed MTA members take significant steps to influence local governance in Banyog, beyond primary schooling, expressing demands in village assemblies (*gram sabhas*) and other public forums. Some MTA members assumed leadership positions, becoming members of the village panchayat. Through deliberation with school agencies, members honed their abilities to monitor services and hold local administration accountable. From the perspective of local bureaucracy, MTAs helped complement state services, improving the overall functioning of primary schools.

5.5 INCLUSIVE COPRODUCTION: PRIMARY EDUCATION IN DHARMAUR

Section 5.4 showed how the education bureaucracy in HP mobilized participation from women's groups around public services and improved local monitoring of schools. This section further investigates how frontline agencies enable and sustain village-level deliberation between schoolteachers and disadvantaged households over time. Through a case study of Dharmaur, a village on the outskirts of Shimla district, I demonstrate how deliberative bureaucracy strengthens societal feedback during implementation. By encouraging an inclusive process of coproduction, the local state has helped sustain joint ownership of primary schooling with communities, leading to higher quality education services.[85]

5.5.1 Socioeconomic Characteristics and Primary Schooling in Dharmaur

Dharmaur is a relatively small village (pop. 383) situated almost four kilometers downhill from a road connecting Shimla's urban center to Mashobra Block. Table 5.2 presents the socioeconomic indicators of the village. Dharmaur was selected as a least-likely case for public service delivery, as its socioeconomic conditions are typical of remote villages

[85] The village case study is based on six weeks of ethnographic fieldwork in Dharmaur, conducted in January–March 2010.

TABLE 5.2 *Dharmaur village: Socioeconomic indicators*

Village	Dharmaur
Administrative district (block)	Shimla (Mashobra)
Population	383
Number of households	64
Distance to motor road	3.9 kilometers
Caste composition	32% General (Thakur – Rajput/Kanait) 68% Dalit (Arya, Lohar, Mochi)
House type	75% finished (*pucca*) 25% semi-finished (*semi-pucca*)
Village economy	Subsistence agriculture (wheat, rice) Animal husbandry Horticulture (flowers)
Places of worship	Devta Sthal (Hindu upper castes) Devta Sthal (Hindu SCs)
Other associations	Devta Committee (*Devta Samiti*) Women's Group (*Mahila Mandal)* Adolescent Group (*Kishore Sangathan)*

Source: Village data collected by the author.

in Shimla district. Given its small population and long distance from a road, Dharmaur attracted little government attention, and its primary school was perceived as a less desirable posting for teachers. Households earned a meagre living from farming and animal husbandry, while a few engaged in horticulture. Men earned supplementary income working as taxi drivers and restaurant and hospitality staff. The village had a large proportion of lower castes, with considerable fragmentation on subcaste (*jati*) lines. There were two village deity sites (devta sthals), one each in the upper caste and Dalit hamlets, indicating the spatial segregation of religious activities. Dharmaur had an active Devta Committee that managed religious events and festivals but unlike wealthier villages nearby, Dharmaur's committee lacked sufficient funds for a temple.

Against theoretical expectations, the government primary school in Dharmaur functioned well; on some dimensions, it performed better than schools in wealthier villages near central Shimla. The school building had been refurbished, classrooms were well lit and the walls adorned with educational materials. The bathrooms were in working order and the construction of a kitchen shed under the MDM Programme had neared completion. The school had a small library of books, which children could borrow. In my school-level observations, corroborated by parent interviews, teachers arrived on time and worked conscientiously. A household census revealed that all children in the 6–14-year age group were enrolled, and none had dropped out. Two low-fee private schools were located near the village (charging ₹250–500 per month), but only one household in Dharmaur had opted for private schooling.

5.5.2 Village Governance

Village public goods were managed by Dharmaur's panchayat, which oversaw three villages in its jurisdiction.[86] The other two villages were more populous and consisted mostly of upper castes (Thakurs). The two larger villages also had better infrastructure, such as paved footpaths and piped water. By contrast, Dharmaur's footpaths were unfinished and households had to travel long distances to fetch water. The panchayat's elected head (pradhan), Mr. Tanwar, was from an upper caste (Thakur) who lived in one of the larger villages. Most residents in Dharmaur had voted for Mr. Tanwar, but they were ambivalent about his leadership. A group of Dalit men showed me around the village while sharing their perspectives on the panchayat. As we made our way down a sloping footpath, the lack of village amenities was apparent. "*The panchayat can help*," one man observed, "*but first village residents need to come together*."[87] When I asked what "coming together" meant, he described the social changes underway in Dharmaur. Families had in the past looked after one another, sharing supplies and tending to each other's crops. With the decline of extended family households, individualism had grown. Bonds between siblings had deteriorated and disputes over landholdings increased. "*City culture* (shahr ki sanskriti) *has gained popularity … Who these days has time for their neighbors*," he remarked.[88] As we reached a bend, a second man pointed to a large house perched ahead on a hill:

> See that house over there? That is where some influential people (*bade log*) stay. They have little to do with us [lower castes]. They earn government salaries and have less concern about the land. When the electricity here goes out, it doesn't pain them. Their children attend big boarding schools far away from here … they are not in the least bothered about our [village] primary school.[89]

[86] Panchayats in HP typically include three to five revenue villages.

[87] Focus group discussion with male residents, Respondent 1, Dharmaur, January 2010.

[88] Ibid.

[89] Focus group discussion with male residents, Respondent 2, Dharmaur, January 2010.

Thakurs had better access to high-paying government jobs in Shimla, where they secured coveted posts as clerks, engineers and teachers. Likewise, the panchayat was perceived to be working for influential people (bade log), who benefited disproportionately from government schemes. "Why do you take the trouble to vote," I asked, "if the panchayat doesn't serve your needs?" The men paused, smirking at the naiveté of my question. "*Why vote?!*," one replied, "*… because when the need arises, we can approach the pradhan and seek his help. Our vote gives us access to leaders. If we don't vote, we can't expect a seat at the table.*"[90] Voting was a gateway to local leaders, who were critical in times of need.

Other residents described the material benefits of their "*personal*" (*vyaktigat*) connection to politicians.[91] Panchayat officials presented a "*means*" (*jugaad*) for obtaining ration cards, electricity connections and other resources. My observation of a village assembly (gram sabha) reaffirmed these interview narratives. Mr. Tanwar opened the assembly by reviewing various government programs: ration cards for grains and cooking oil, widow pensions and housing refurbishment funds. During the four-hour meeting, two and a half hours were spent discussing such schemes and their eligibility requirements. No mention was made of public services in Dharmaur. As the gram sabha drew to a close, a group of women seated in a corner asked the pradhan to do something about the scourge of alcoholism in the village. "*The liquor stores must be shut down!*," a woman argued. "*They are causing a menace … even our children haven't been spared.*"[92] Another woman narrated an episode of three boys who had purchased liquor on the way home from school and caused a fight, bringing shame to their families. An elderly man rose from his seat in support of the women: "*The atmosphere* [mahaul] *in the village has become unbearable … things like this shouldn't be happening every night.*"[93] A commotion erupted and Mr. Tanwar called for calm. He acknowledged their complaints and promised to relocate the liquor stores away from the village. After the gram sabha ended, I asked the residents about their experience of the panchayat. The consensus view was that the panchayat was used primarily to make individual claims. Public services such as primary education were rarely discussed. An elderly man

[90] Focus group discussion with men, Respondent 3, Dharmaur, January 2010.
[91] Interviews with several residents, Dharmaur, January–March 2010.
[92] A woman in the gram sabha, Dharmar, March 2010.
[93] An elderly man in the gram sabha, Dharmaur, March 2010.

who had spoken during the gram sabha approached me, eager to share his perspective. "*If you want to learn about the primary school, you must talk to the women's association* [mahila mandal] ... *They are the ones getting things done for the village.*"[94]

In Dharmaur, I collected oral histories through focus group discussions with elderly women, who described how the mahila mandal came into being in the 1970s.[95] The group was initiated informally by a few Dalit women who supported each other through collective agriculture and labor sharing. During the harvest season, they helped pick each other's crops. They also created a joint system of childcare, taking turns looking after each other's children. In cases of medical emergencies and other unexpected events, they provided assistance, pooling resources for medicines and hospital treatment. During the monsoon season, when storms and landslides wrought damage, the women would clear village footpaths and help rebuild each other's homes.

In the 1980s, the mahila mandal drew wider participation from village households. The depletion of forests put an immense burden on women, who were forced to undertake longer, riskier journeys to collect firewood and other resources. A woman from the group recounted the story of her niece, who suffered a fatal injury while trekking far away to collect grass. On her return journey, she slipped and hit her head against some rocks. Her family found her lying unconscious. They rushed her to a medical clinic, but she succumbed to her injuries. As the woman narrated:

> After the accident, we decided that something needed to be done. The responsibility for collecting wood and grass always fell on us [women] ... and we were suffering. We had to protect our forest (*apna van*), otherwise it would get more difficult for us ... We brought families together and called meetings in the village. We discussed how much each family could take (from the forest) and agreed on which parts were off limits ... Turn-by-turn, each family monitored the forest. If someone was caught, we held an assembly (*chaupal*) and shamed them.[96]

The need to protect "*our forest*" (*apna van*) resonated strongly with households in Dharmaur and gradually, they developed informal rules for resource usage. Likewise, informal rules were established for managing village waterbodies and grazing areas for livestock.

94 Interview with an elderly man, Dharmaur, March 2010.

95 Focus group discussions with elderly women, Dharmaur, February–March 2010.

96 Focus group discussion with elderly women, Respondent 5, Dharmaur, February 2010.

In the early 1990s, HP's Department of Education worked with volunteers from HGVS to promote adult literacy initiatives. HGVS fieldworkers visited Dharmaur in 1994 to conduct literacy camps, which drewsupport from the mahila mandal. According to a man who had volunteered in the program, "*The mahila mandal had organized everyone in the village. They took charge of the government's literacy campaign* (saksharta abhiyan). *They found people who were more aware* (jagruk) *and helpful in the village.*"[97] An Adult Literacy Center was established in Dharmaur in 1996 with the help of mahila mandal members, who organized meetings in their homes. A permanent space for the Center was built through donations collected by the group. Some years later, HGVS fieldworkers approached the district administration to register Dharmaur's women's association so that the group would have official recognition as a nonprofit agency. They also helped the group open a bank account. The mahila mandal became a nucleus of village activities, while HGVS provided guidance on accessing state programs. A retired state official who had helped administer literacy camps in Shimla explained the rationale for supporting women's groups:

> When the NLM [National Literacy Mission] started in Himachal Pradesh, we were doubtful that the public would respond [positively] to the program ... But I saw first-hand the hard work of the local volunteers and the support given by the mahila mandals ... For the literacy center, or any governmental scheme, to run properly, it had to be embraced by the community. So we took the decision to get the mahila mandal's registered ... They would benefit from having official recognition (*pehchan*), and it made it easier for us to include them in our programs.[98]

Soon, the group expanded to twenty eight member from different households, though others connected informally through extended kinship ties. The Adult Literacy Center gave the residents of Dharmaur exposure to government services. For example, monthly newsletters from HGVS disseminated at the Center gave updates on public schemes, such as sustainable agriculture. As women's association members gained confidence, their attention shifted to other domains, including health and education. The group connected with local health authorities and spread information about government immunization drives throughout the village. They invited Anganwadi workers, who were trained in child development and nutrition, to advise expecting mothers on safe deliveries and neonatal health. When Anganwadi workers were conducting

[97] Interview with a male resident, Dharmaur, February 2010.
[98] Interview with retired state official, Shimla, July 2008.

rounds of the village to screen for pregnancies and childbirths, the mahila mandal helped them identify families requiring assistance. In 1998, an Aanganwadi Center was established in Dharmaur. A young member of the mahila mandal was hired as an ASHA health extension worker, a source of pride for the group.

5.5.3 Inclusive Coproduction of Primary Schooling

The mahila mandal took interest in education, but the everyday governance of primary schooling was daunting. Most members of the group were illiterate, having completed only a few years of formal schooling. An elderly member recounted: "*When we were children, there wasn't any emphasis on educating girls. Most of us hadn't studied beyond primary [level] … We were hesitant to get involved with the primary school.*"[99] The group focused initially on improving physical access to the school. The worn-out footpath leading to the school was also used for taking cows out to graze. Twice a year, they cleared the footpath of weeds and obstructions that could cause children to slip. Although the school was functioning well during my field visits, parents described the deficiencies at the school during earlier years. Most critically, they found the teaching unreliable. On some occasions, children would return home right after lunch because the teachers had left early. A father in the village narrated:

> Before the mahila mandal became active at the school, nobody raised their voice. The schoolteachers used to come late to school and fail to teach. And when parents complained, they would shoo us away. They would tell us that, "*We work for the government, not for you. It's not our duty to teach.*"[100]

Parents reported other problems as well. For example, the school had no electricity or piped water connection. Classrooms were dimly lit, making it difficult for children to read. Those needing to use the bathroom had to instead go out into the fields. The lack of working bathrooms impacted adolescent girls the most, causing some to avoid coming to school.

The mahila mandal organized a meeting between parents and teachers to air grievances. The discussion turned sour when a parent broached the topic of teacher absence and low quality education. A mother recalled, "*We asked the teachers to explain why classes started late and ended early. They didn't like that we questioned them … They told us that*

99 Focus group discussion with women's association, Dharmaur, January 2010.

100 Interview with an elderly father, Dharmaur, February 2010.

illiterate people [anpadh log] *should know their place* [aukat]."[101] With no immediate resolution, the women's association undertook a half-day journey to report the matter to the district education office in Shimla. They were encouraged to find education officials receptive to their concerns. The officials advised them against filing a formal complaint since administrative processes were tedious and could create animosity. They suggested instead that the group hold another parent–teacher meeting, in the BEO's presence. Not knowing what to expect, the parents felt hopeful after meeting with education officials, who listened and offered a "*fair response*" to their concerns.

A second meeting was held at Dharmaur's primary school. However, this time the panchayat pradhan and Mr. Kaushik, the BEO, also attended. Parents communicated their frustrations with the poor quality of teaching. The teachers shared concerns as well, such as their being inundated by paperwork, which cut into their teaching time, as well as a lack of parental support with homework assignments. Mr. Kaushik acknowledged the administrative burden on teachers, but he reproached them for being absent. According to a mother who had attended the meeting, "*Kaushikji repeatedly asked them [the teachers] why they were absent, but they fell silent ... He told them that they were responsible for teaching and had a hand in our children's futures.*"[102] Mr. Kaushik, she narrated, gave an example of a teacher who was transferred for dereliction of duty and lost the "*esteem and respect*" (*man-samman*) of the community. He also called attention to the growing preference for private schooling, citing the public school system's failures. "*The teachers got the message...,*" a mother remarked. "*They promised to come to school regularly and pay more attention to teaching. And we [parents] agreed to pay more attention to our children's homework.*"[103] The parent–teacher meetings helped strengthen parents' faith in the government school, and accordingly, they worked to re-establish ties with the teachers. The meetings also raised confidence in their collective abilities to participate in education service delivery. As the head of Dharmaur's mahila mandal observed:

> Initially, we were hesitant to work things out with the schoolteachers. But the positive response from the education department [*shiksha vibhag*] helped build our confidence ... We could see things improving when our children would

[101] Interview with a father from Dharmar, February 2010.
[102] Focus group discussion with parents, Dharmaur, February 2010.
[103] Focus group discussion with parents, Dharmaur, February 2010.

come home and tell us that "*Madam [the teacher] came early this morning and checked our notebooks*" ... We visit the school regularly now, and if the teachers show up late, we tell them with love, "*Please come on time!*"[104]

Other parents noted that, while meetings were contentious, they helped bridge the distance (*duri*) between parents and teachers. Parents became more comfortable approaching the teachers for assistance and sought ways to contribute to the Midday Meal Programme.

Households in Dharmaur took initiatives to follow up with district administration on other issues raised in school meetings. Since the school building lacked electricity, classes were held outside in daylight hours, an arrangement that became untenable during the monsoons. Mr. Kaushik coordinated with the mahila mandal and village panchayat to have engineers fix the electricity connection. Inaugurating the school's first day with electricity, the mahila mandal held a celebration, where they publicized the joint contributions of village residents, Mr. Kaushik and other local officials. Witnessing real results (*parinam*) from their collective efforts, parents were encouraged to invest further in the school. For example, they pooled village resources to help maintain the school's playground. A mother noted the contributions of residents:

Our women's association [mahila mandal] got the wiring done for electricity at the school ... And their efforts have continued. One year later, they raised funds from within the village to hire an additional teacher at the primary school, collecting more from better-off families and less from poor families. They got people together to help re-paint the school and build an additional classroom. Some even gave their own labor (*shram dan*).[105]

The women's association was not allowed to collect school fees, but households were willing to make voluntary donations, which complemented school development grants from SSA. Funding drives for Dharmaur's "*village school*" (*gamv ka school*) became a regular feature of village social events. For example, during *Barsakhi*, a festival marking the arrival of spring, households repainted their homes. Cultural programs were also held at the school, including a play enacting stories of Durga Mata, the Hindu goddess associated with the new season. The mahila mandal organized families to help repaint the school for *Barsakhi*. A member of the association remarked, "Barsakhi *reminds everyone that this is our school,*

[104] Focus group discussion with women's association, Dharmaur, February 2010.
[105] Interview with a mother, Dharmaur, March 2010.

and it must undergo improvement *(sudhar), in the same way that we refurbish our homes.*"[106]

Community involvement in schooling helped improve the dynamic between teachers and parents, with positive effects on education services. According to a parent, "*Our relations with teachers have also improved. One of the teachers even helped to enroll disabled children in our village.*"[107] Teachers drew inspiration from parental efforts, which motivated them to devote extra time to after-school activities:

> The parents have contributed in areas where we get less support [from the state]. Recently, they helped us send children to represent the school at the district volleyball tournament. They also raised local funds to purchase sports equipment for children and a carom board as well ... The teachers from this area decided to come together and hold competitions between nearby schools.[108]

Joint efforts by teachers and community members thus yielded practical benefits for the school. MTA members showcased the school's achievements to the wider community. For example, they publicized when school-children from Dharmaur excelled in exams or sports competitions.

For its efforts, Dharmaur's mahila mandal gained further recognition through the creation of an MTA. Mr. Kaushik, who organized quarterly meetings with the MTAs in his administrative block, had Dharmaur's MTA formally registered. The association conducted village-wide campaigns to alert parents of the need to participate in meetings. They also requested households to support the school's midday meal by donating fresh vegetables, to supplement the government-provided rations. To help facilitate MTA meetings at the school, teachers requested funds from local administration for new furniture and refreshments during meetings. Sustaining community participation at the school was taken as a collective responsibility, shared by education officials, schoolteachers and parents.

The case study of Dharmaur has demonstrated the sequence through which deliberative bureaucracy harnessed societal input to strengthen the delivery of primary education. The presence of an active women's association and other forms of village-wide collective action provided the social basis for coproduction. However, it took the routine involvement of frontline officials to build and sustain confidence among disadvantaged

[106] Interview with a women's association member, Dharmaur, March 2010.

[107] Interview with a parent, Dharmaur, March 2010.

[108] Interview with a teacher, Dharmaur, February 2010. Carom is a popular game played in India, similar in concept to billiards.

households to work with teachers, monitor education and communicate gaps in services to local administration. Having experienced tangible benefits from engaging with local administration, particularly in moments of adversity, households in Dharmaur took collective ownership of the government school, and through their complementary investments, enhanced the quality of services.

5.6 CONCLUSION

This chapter has shown how deliberative bureaucracy stimulates broad coverage of primary schooling along with higher quality education services. Despite having the same formal administrative structures of other states, bureaucracy in HP has developed a distinct set of informal bureaucratic norms that approximate the deliberative model theorized in Chapter 2. The historical analysis in this chapter revealed that deliberative bureaucracy emerged through elite collective action, spurred by HP's unfavorable political and fiscal conditions in the initial period of state formation. Based on a multilevel analysis of implementation, deliberative bureaucracy is found to have made a decisive impact on the implementation of primary education. Bureaucratic commitment to deliberation has contributed to HP's educational lead within India, notwithstanding weak initial conditions and a challenging geographic terrain. Deliberation incorporated bureaucrats from across ranks and divisions, elected officials, civic organizations and other members of society, including the least advantaged citizens. Fieldwork revealed how deliberation operates on a range of administrative tasks, from planning and infrastructure provision by state-level agencies, to local monitoring alongside women's associations, to quotidian interactions between frontline officials and communities. As a result, the state has learned to adapt primary education programming to the needs of heterogeneous communities, producing innovations like the mobile schooling program for Gujjars.

The evidence in this chapter also demonstrates how deliberative bureaucracy works to strengthen societal coproduction of services. State planners in HP encouraged agencies like HGVS to engage in education programming, extending fiscal support and integrating them institutionally within the adult literacy program. At the local level, deliberative bureaucracy's problem-centered orientation allowed frontline officials to "see" informal women's associations as legitimate partners, and in turn, find ways to encourage and sustain their participation over time (Scott 1998). Frontline officials promoted village-level deliberation as well, helping to mediate conflicts between parents and teachers. These officials learned, along the way, that public fora, such as panchayats and VECs, often excluded women and overlooked collective issues such as primary education. Through the establishment of MTAs and other deliberative spaces in villages, the coproduction of services was made more regular and inclusive, yielding higher quality education

These findings on deliberative bureaucracy in HP vary widely from the legalistic model of bureaucracy in UP. As shown in Chapter 4, women's associations and subordinate castes in UP also attempted to participate in school governance, but they experienced administrative burdens and had to struggle to have their demands heard through official grievance procedures. In HP, meanwhile, the bureaucracy helped strengthen participation by marginalized groups, encouraging more capacious forms of societal feedback. Rural women were not simply allowed to monitor schools, but actively supported in the process, enhancing their collective capabilities.

While this chapter has provided crucial evidence for how deliberative bureaucracy works in HP, it raises questions about the viability of deliberative bureaucracy in other settings. Compared to other Hindi belt states, HP is less populous, has more inclusive caste and gender norms, as well as a two-party political system, factors that likely supported the maintenance of deliberative bureaucracy. Whether and how deliberation can work in a context such as UP, where divisive ethnic politics, patriarchy and caste inequalities are deeply entrenched, remains to be established. Chapter 7 addresses these issues through a study of institutional reforms in UP that were designed to stimulate deliberation for women's empowerment. Before proceeding with that task, Chapter 6 further elucidates the mechanisms of my theory through the comparative case of Uttarakhand. Despite having similar geographic and socioeconomic features as HP, Uttarakhand has not achieved comparable results in primary schooling, especially with respect to the quality of services. The comparison with HP permits us to investigate how *different* bureaucratic norms operate in otherwise *similar* sociopolitical contexts, while addressing alternative explanations, including those centered on gender norms and village social capital.

6

Norm Persistence

Exit, Voice and Bureaucratic Inertia

> Nowadays, every official talks about "*people's participation.*" But the administrative structure (*dhancha*) tells the people something else. It tells them: "*You stay seated, we are running everything*" ... And so communities have become hesitant to step forward. They have come to believe that their participation is not needed.
>
> – Political activist involved in Uttarakhand's statehood movement[1]

6.1 INTRODUCTION

Chapter 5 demonstrated the positive dynamic that deliberative bureaucracy unleashed for the delivery of primary education in Himachal Pradesh (HP). This chapter analyzes education delivery in the neighboring state of Uttarakhand. The contextual comparison between Uttarakhand and HP offers a critical test of my theory of implementation. Adjacent states in the western Himalayas, Uttarakhand and HP have similar geographies, agrarian economies, income levels, caste composition and other sociodemographic features. Importantly, village caste and gender norms are comparable as well, enabling the identification of causal mechanisms. The comparison also enables testing of the argument about bureaucratic norms against key alternative explanations, such as social capital. Uttarakhand's social movement history and rich tapestry of village associations creates relatively permissive conditions for societal collective action around public services.

1 Interview by author, Almora, September 2009.

Furthermore, I leverage the historical changes occasioned by Uttarakhand's political separation from Uttar Pradesh (UP) to study how bureaucratic norms persist across time. Uttarakhand was carved from UP in 2000 into a separate state, a rare opportunity for governing elites to reshape bureaucratic norms. Bhuwan Chandra Khanduri, Uttarakhand's first chief minister, remarked at the time that the new state was a culmination of "the long-cherished aspirations of the people of the region."[2] Following Uttarakhand's exit from UP, the state decentralized governance and expanded the number of administrative districts and legislative assembly constituencies, improving the prospects for citizens to express voice. Freed from the yoke of UP's multiparty system and divisive caste politics, Uttarakhand embraced a two-party system, similar to the one in HP, with the Bharatiya Janata Party (BJP) and Congress Party alternating in power.

The formation of Uttarakhand was enabled by progressive social movements as well as an historical legacy of administrative and educational development. In 1951, Uttarakhand's literacy rate of 18.9 percent was slightly above the national average (18.3 percent). As late as 1981, literacy in Uttarakhand (46.1 percent) exceeded that in HP (42.5 percent). Yet, Uttarakhand's performance in primary education is comparatively disappointing. Though not far behind HP with respect to enrollment and infrastructure provision, the functioning of schools and quality of services is markedly worse in Uttarakhand. As noted in Chapter 2, a high proportion of schools have only a single teacher and quality indicators remain weak. Compared to HP, outcomes for student learning in Uttarakhand are considerably worse, even though its adult literacy rate is not far behind HP's.

What accounts for the relative underperformance of Uttarakhand's primary education system, especially when it comes to the quality of services? I suggest that the persistence of legalistic bureaucratic norms in Uttarakhand after state formation has contributed to highly uneven policy implementation. My argument about norm persistence builds on the historical institutionalist insight that critical junctures lessen constraints on state actors, creating windows of opportunity for them to refashion the rules of the game (Capoccia and Kelemen 2007). Policymakers from Uttarakhand sought to utilize this window to learn and integrate HP's

[2] "With Hopes and Fears," *Frontline*, September 1, 2000. Available at: www.frontline.in/static/html/fl1717/17170350.htm.

"best practices" in public service delivery. Nevertheless, legalism has continued to influence the collective understandings and behaviors of state officials. Through interviews with senior and frontline bureaucrats, civic agencies and citizens, I connect the persistence of legalism to the overwhelming fear among policymakers about political interference and the need to protect the bureaucracy through hierarchical discipline and chain of command.

Residents of Uttarakhand have applied exit and voice in various ways to seek improvements in public services and, more broadly, in governance (Hirschman 1970). After exiting from UP to create their own state, citizens used collective voice mechanisms to demand better services from local administration. However, as indicated by the political activist quoted above, the aspirations of the public remain unfulfilled. As I demonstrate through local-level fieldwork, legalistic bureaucracy in Uttarakhand has produced administrative barriers for village-level agencies and citizens seeking to hold schools accountable for services. Repeated attempts by communities to secure quality services have contributed to a diminishment of societal expectations of the state, inducing exit from government schools. Consequently, I observed that rural communities have collectively mobilized to support substitutes, such as nongovernmental tutoring and private schools. The findings reveal how the relational dynamics between bureaucracy and citizens stimulates exit from government services and a shift to non-state service provision (Cammett and MacLean 2014).

This chapter proceeds as follows. Drawing on historical and field-based materials, I first explore the political process behind Uttarakhand's separation from UP, a critical juncture for state elites to reshape bureaucratic norms. I also explore Uttarakhand's social movement legacy, led by rural women and village associations, which provided an enabling environment for societal coproduction of services. Evidence from interviews with state and societal actors, however, demonstrates the persistence of legalistic bureaucracy. Next, I analyze how legalism influences the performance of complex tasks, including bureaucracy's management of teachers and community oversight of primary education services. Through village-level fieldwork, I show that community efforts to monitor schools are thwarted by local administration's rigid adherence to uniform rules and procedures, weakening the coproduction of services, gradually inducing exit from the government school system.

6.2 THE CREATION OF A NEW STATE

Uttarakhand (pop. 10.1 million) separated from UP on November 9, 2000, to become India's twenty-seventh state. Located between the Shivalik hills and the Himalayan range, Uttarakhand is mountainous and landlocked, with HP to the west, Nepal to the east, China's Tibetan region to the north and the plains (*terai*) area on the southern border with UP (see Figure 6.1). Uttarakhand's thirteen administrative districts are organized into two administrative divisions, Garhwal and Kumaon. This section examines the critical antecedents leading to the formation of Uttarakhand (Slater and Simmons 2010). The political importance of Uttarakhand, or "UP hills" as the region was called, can be traced back to British occupation. Deemed a "martial race" by colonial administrators, the hill population was conscripted into the military, forming two highly decorated contingents, Garhwal Rifles and the Kumaon Regiment. Uttarakhand also contributed to India's nationalist movement, with several senior leaders hailing from Almora district.[3]

Equally, Uttarakhand became a recognized site for India's bureaucratic and educational development, housing preeminent institutions for training elite civil servants and military brass. The Indian Military Academy, the principal institute for military officer training, was established in 1932 in Dehradun, Uttarakhand's state capital. The Lal Bahadur Shastri National Academy of Administration, where the elite Indian Administrative Service (IAS) corps is trained, was founded in 1959 in the hill town of Mussoorie. The exclusive Doon School, modeled after British boarding schools, was established in Dehradun in 1935. The town of Roorkee became a leading center of higher education that included the University of Roorkee, established in 1847 and subsequently recognized as an Indian Institute of Technology in 2001. Yet, behind these revered institutions, political resistance and mass discontent with governance had brewed as well, which, as discussed below, helped unleash pressures for a new state.

6.2.1 Peasant Resistance and Mobilization

The first critical antecedent to Uttarakhand's separation from UP was the emergence of social movements and village associations committed to forest protection and local governance. The social capital literature

[3] These included Govind Ballabh Pant, UP's first chief minister, and Narayan Datt Tiwari, who served as chief minister of both UP and Uttarakhand.

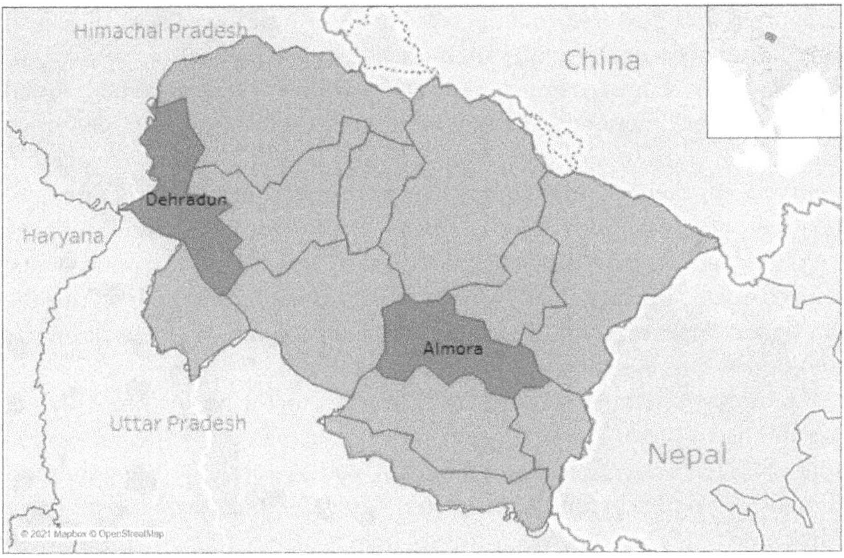

FIGURE 6.1 Study map of Uttarakhand
Note: Main study districts are highlighted.
Source: © Mapbox, © OpenStreetMap.

suggests that having dense civic associations improves governmental effectiveness (Putnam, Leonardi and Nanetti 1994). According to Census of India data, the density of officially recognized associations is 7.7 per 100,00 people in Uttarakhand and 4.3 in HP.[4] Based on an apparently low associational density, one might infer that social capital is weak in the Himalayan region.[5] However, informal associations have greater purchase in much of rural India and are a better indicator of social capital in the Himalayan region as well (Krishna 2003). Anthropological studies have demonstrated the importance of informal institutions of cooperation in Uttarakhand (Berreman 1972; Fisher 1978). Dependency on natural resources for rural livelihoods provided the material basis for social cooperation. Berreman's (1972) village ethnography suggests that both upper and lower castes in Uttarakhand's Garhwal region owned land, performed agricultural labor and exchanged resources. Village deity (*devta*) worship and cross-caste participation in religious functions

4 Population Commission of India figures drawn from 2001 Census. Available at: http://ngo.india.gov.in/ngo_stateschemes_ngo.php.

5 Surveys in India likewise report low levels of membership in civic associations (Chhibber 2001).

supported social cohesion, though the exclusion of lower castes has also been documented (Alter 2016). Informal forest councils (*van panchayats*) in Uttarakhand emerged in the early twentieth century. The colonial state's encroachment on land and restrictions on forest use sparked resistance from indigenous communities (Guha 2000). Peasants engaged in *dhandak*, a practice of noncompliance with government rules. For example, they would publicly declare their nonpayment of taxes.[6] Under the 1931 Forest Council Rules, the colonial state recognized van panchayats, which became operational throughout Uttarakhand. Research reveals the continued importance of these institutions for the management of forests and other common-pool resources (Agrawal 2001).[7]

Quotidian resistance to the state accelerated in the postcolonial period, exemplified by the 1970s Chipko movement. The movement emerged following the 1927 Forest Act. Colonial agencies seized forests and permitted logging by private contractors, while denying local communities forest usage rights. Peasant protests against the commercialization of forests in the Garhwal region inspired local movements throughout the state (Pathak 2020). Their livelihoods under threat, the peasants sought to protect trees from being axed by private companies. Famously, they wrapped their arms around trees as a protest tactic, earning the movement its name, "Chipko" (meaning "stick to" in Hindi). Rural women, who were directly impacted by deforestation, were key protagonists in the movement. As Jain (1984, 1788) writes,

> Women being the sole in-charge of cultivation, livestock and children, lost all they had because of recurring floods and landslides. The message of the Chipko workers made a direct appeal to women who were able to perceive the link between their victimisation and baring of the mountain slopes by commercial interests.

Chipko protesters demanded state recognition of forests as protected lands. Their voices reached New Delhi as well, as Prime Minister Indira Gandhi met movement leaders and issued a fifteen-year ban on commercial exploitation of trees. Beyond its immediate policy impacts, Chipko left a legacy of women's mobilization and collective resistance to rules (Guha 2000). Women involved in the movement helped establish village associations to manage forest resources and

[6] Guha notes that dhandak was predicated on the relationship between the king and public, revealing the "democratic character" of peasant communities (2000, 67–68). Similar protest tactics, known as *dum* or *dujam*, were applied by peasants in HP.

[7] Forests account for 63 percent of Uttarakhand's land, a source of fuel, fodder and medicinal herbs (Mehta 2005).

other collective goods (Sarin 2001; Sharma and Sudarshan 2010). Women's associations sprouted up throughout the state, influencing village governance.

6.2.2 Pahari Dissatisfaction

The Chipko movement also gave voice to regional identification and public dissatisfaction with existing policies, shaping societal pressure for a new state (Mawdsley 1998; Tillin 2013, 98–100). A second critical antecedent to Uttarakhand's statehood, hill residents (Paharis) expressed mass dissatisfaction with public administration under the UP state government. Prior to independence, hill principalities had their own systems of taxation, land-ownership and civil law (Sati and Sati 2000). Under UP's administration, the hill region was subjected to policies and administrative processes that were disconnected from the needs of its population. According to a regional scholar, Pahari alienation was exacerbated by "[t]he callous attitude of Lucknow in imposing every plan formulated without any consideration to the topographical distinctness of the hills" (Kumar 2000, 93–94). It is noteworthy, however, that the UP government had undertaken special planning efforts for Uttarakhand. In 1974, the UP Hill Development Department was created, with its own ministerial representative and budget under the Uttarakhand Sub-Plan. Additionally, public expenditures in hill districts were substantially higher on a per capita basis than in the plains, a gap in public spending that increased over successive five-year plans (Mehta 2000: 83–84). Public infrastructure in the hills was more developed as well. Table 6.1 presents comparative indicators for public infrastructure in UP and Uttarakhand in 1991–1992, when the movement for a separate state began to peak. Compared to the plains, villages in Uttarakhand had better access to schools, health centers and electricity. Funding for social services, like education and health, was considerably higher as well. In the Ninth Five Year Plan period (1997–2002) social services drew the highest share (30 percent) of the Uttarakhand Sub-Plan budget (Kumar 2000, 63). On indicators of education spending, Uttarakhand performed no worse than HP. For example, per capita public outlays in the Seventh Five-Year Plan (1985–1990) were slightly higher in Uttarakhand (₹2,223) than in HP (₹2,171). Expenditure data must be interpreted with caution, since services are costlier to provide in hilly areas, but the indications are that public services were relatively well resourced in Uttarakhand.

TABLE 6.1 *Public infrastructure in Uttar Pradesh and Uttarakhand (1991–1992)*

	Uttar Pradesh	Uttarakhand
Metaled road per 1,000 sq. km of area (km)	256	227
Number of schools per 100,000 people		
Primary	57	144
Senior basic	11	30
Higher secondary	5	19
Medical facilities per 100,000 people		
Allopathic hospitals and dispensaries	3.4	12.4
Hospital beds	50.3	121.8
Primary health centers	2.4	3.6
Subcenters and Maternity service centers	16	27.5
Electricity		
Per capita consumption (kWh)	170.5	217.1
% Villages electrified	73.9	73.5

Source: Data from UP State Development Reports, as reported in Papola (2000).

Although the Pahari population had low numerical representation in UP's state assembly, political leaders from Uttarakhand were pivotal in the state government and public administration. The hill districts outperformed UP plains districts on socioeconomic and development indicators.[8] Yet, the UP government was perceived as being distant and neglectful of Pahari demands. Planning under the UP Hill Development Department failed to address the geographic conditions in the hills. As Mehta (2000, 87) has observed,

> The basic problem with development plans for Uttarakhand is not the lack of general awareness of the problem of hill areas, nor the lack of sincerity on the part of the central and state planners, but rather the absence of an integrated and region-specific approach to thinking about, planning for, and implementing these development programs.

[8] By contrast, when HP separated from Punjab in the 1970s, the hill region's underdevelopment was an acute concern highlighted by movement leaders (Chapter 5).

Annual economic plans drafted in Lucknow were applied to Uttarakhand as if it were an extension of the Gangetic plains. Scant attention was paid to the hill ecology and informal institutions, leading to perceptions that Uttarakhand needed "autonomy to plan for its own development" (Joshi 1995, 46).

Citizen grievances triggered demands for statehood in the 1950s, which were led by Puran Chand Joshi, a Communist Party leader from Almora district. Popular demands for separation were sporadic, but these were dismissed by the central government on the grounds that a hill state would be financially unviable. The Uttarakhand Kranti Dal (UKD), a regional party established in 1979, was committed to statehood and mobilized support for increasing Pahari representation in UP's state assembly. In 1994, the UP government passed a resolution to create the state of "Uttaranchal," the name assigned to the hill region by plains people. The proposal was, however, turned down by the central government.

The third critical antecedent to state formation in Uttarakhand was the creeping influence of caste politics from the plains areas. In 1994, UP Chief Minister Mulayam Singh Yadav passed a resolution extending reservations to Other Backward Classes (OBCs). Numerically predominant in the Gangetic plains, OBCs represented a small fraction of Uttarakhand's population (Aggarwal, Agrawal and Gupta 1995, 7). Meanwhile, the new policy reserved 27 percent of seats in government and educational institutions for OBCs. Adding this to existing reservations for SC (15 percent) and ST (7.5 percent) groups would mean that 50 percent of posts were reserved. The change stoked fears that hill-based government jobs and economic opportunities would be swallowed up by plains residents, marginalizing the Pahari population further (Mawdsley 1996, 205). Perceived as a serious threat, OBC reservations, according to a UKD political activist, would have "*practically excluded the hill population*" from public employment and higher education.[9] The UKD organized demonstrations against expanding reservations, garnering public support for state separation.

Given the public's demands, the eventual separation of Uttarakhand in 2000 offered a political opportunity to governing elites to reform public administration. Previously, the hill districts had sent 19 legislators to the UP state assembly, less than 5 percent of its 424 assembly seats. The

[9] Interview with political activist, Almora, October 2009.

political map of Uttarakhand was redrawn to create seventy constituencies, each electing its own MLA to the state assembly in Dehradun, the state capital. Uttarakhand was also unchained from UP's fragmented, caste-driven party system, and instead it adopted a two-party system led by India's two main national parties. As Chapter 4 noted, in the 1990s, the Samajwadi Party and Bahujan Samaj Party in UP brought lower castes into the electoral fold. The political emphasis on lower-caste populations in the plains contributed to a sense of *Pahari* marginalization. The hill population identified more with the BJP and the Congress Party, as witnessed in the 2002 state elections. The Congress Party won thirty-six of the seventy assembly seats, while the BJP won nineteen seats. Exit polls from Uttarakhand's first state election showed that 57 percent of voters considered development the most important electoral issue (Kumar 2002, 82). However, the UKD, which spearheaded the statehood movement, won only four seats. Subsequent state elections saw continued support for India's national parties, as Uttarakhand appeared to consolidate its two-party system, similar to the one in HP.

With these political shifts, Uttarakhand's administrative structure also underwent important changes, which had the potential to alter bureaucratic norms. The original eight administrative districts were reconfigured into thirteen districts. Dehradun became the political capital and administrative center, bringing bureaucracy closer to the public. Moreover, Uttarakhand's bureaucracy no longer relied on the recruitment of officials from the plains, many of whom did not identify with the local population and viewed working in the hills as a "punishment posting."[10] The newly formed Uttarakhand Public Service Commission oversaw the recruitment of bureaucrats and local public functionaries, including schoolteachers. Bureaucrats from the UP cadre of the IAS were given the option to remain in UP or join the Uttarakhand cadre. Those who moved to Uttarakhand were given incentives for promotion.[11]

Uttarakhand's separation from UP was expected to bring about significant improvements in governance.[12] Led by committed state elites, a subnationalist party, bottom-up social movements and mass political

[10] Interviews with several IAS officers, UP and Uttarakhand, 2009–2010. Also see: "IAS officers reluctant to Opt for Uttaranchal," *The Hindu*. September 9, 2000. Available at: http://hindu.com/2000/09/09/stories/02090007.htm.

[11] Interviews with several IAS officers, UP and Uttarakhand, 2009–2010.

[12] In a related vein, Singh (2016) demonstrates that subnationalist parties and movements triggered social policy expansion in south Indian states.

support, the creation of Uttarakhand offered an unparalleled opportunity to refashion bureaucracy for public service delivery. Indeed, a chief argument for Uttarakhand's formation was to bring administration closer to the public and improve bureaucratic responsiveness. No longer constrained by UP's divisive caste politics, Uttarakhand's leadership was in a better position to mobilize state action for programmatic services.

6.3 THE PERSISTENCE OF LEGALISTIC BUREAUCRACY

This section demonstrates how legalistic bureaucratic norms have persisted in Uttarakhand. Following the formation of a smaller, more decentralized state, governing elites explored deeper institutional reforms. As I find, however, concerns about political interference and corruption reinforced legalistic rule-following, dampening initiatives for change. These findings draw on interviews with serving and retired bureaucrats as well as participant observation of local administration. State officials interviewed had spent their careers in the UP and Uttarakhand bureaucracies, and thus offered a unique perspective on institutional persistence. Bureaucratic perspectives are supplemented by interviews with members of civil society and political activists, providing a worms eye view of institutional continuity.

6.3.1 Reinforcing Legalism

The persistence of legalism is evident from the accounts of senior state officials. After Uttarakhand's formation, state planners were eager to identify new approaches to policy implementation. There was political support within the state to improve administrative practices around service delivery for the hill region. According to a Department of Health official:

> There was a feeling among the leadership [of the state] that we wanted to implement policies in a new way. Though initially we followed the same structure as in UP, the discussion came up that we should do things differently. Teams were put together to visit other hill states like Himachal Pradesh and Jammu-Kashmir, and they came back with some new ideas.[13]

Bureaucrats in charge of social policy sought to learn how HP administered services effectively within the Himalayan context. Policymakers drew the lesson that an "*integrated approach*" was needed to encourage

[13] Interview with senior official, Department of Health, Dehradun, August 2009.

greater coordination across line departments and geographic divisions of the state.[14]

Accordingly, administrative changes for primary education were introduced. The Department of School Education was given the mandate for both primary and secondary schooling, previously overseen by two separate departments. District Education Officers (DEOs) were assigned to oversee both levels of schooling, to support students as they made the transition to higher grades. Additionally, close coordination between primary and pre-primary education services was encouraged. The latter was overseen by the Department of Women and Child Development. According to new policies, Anganwadi centers, which supported early child development and nutrition, were to be relocated to primary school campuses and supported by the Department of School Education. By integrating Anganwadi centers with primary schools, state officials sought to improve the educational readiness of young children and streamline school enrollment. Moreover, because Anganwadis supported child immunization drives, primary schools were deemed appropriate locations for administering child health services. A senior official remarked on the effort to strengthen interagency coordination:

> Since our UP days, there was no integration across departments, so everyone would work in isolation. We saw during our visits in Himachal Pradesh that different offices worked well together … On similar lines, a new organizational structure was envisaged [in Uttarakhand] to coordinate between child nutrition, health and education. Instead of keeping them apart like before, we adopted a structure that tied the different [governmental] functions together.[15]

Other officials noted that "*convergence*" across government departments was needed to improve the efficiency of services.[16] However, putting convergence into practice was challenging, especially for schoolteachers, Anganwadi workers and other frontline agents, who had to take on new roles and responsibilities. These difficulties arose in HP as well, which prompted state officials there to introduce pre-primary education incrementally. Early child development and preschool services were merged over a fifteen-year timespan. Senior officials in HP deliberated with frontline workers, village residents and women's associations, who

[14] Interviews with several state officials from the Departments of Health, School Education and Rural Development, Dehradun, August 2009.

[15] Interview with state education official, SSA State Project Office, Dehradun, August 2009.

[16] Interviews with several state officials, Dehradun and Almora, August–November 2009.

gradually learned how to adjust practices to better integrate programming across departments.

In Uttarakhand, by contrast, preschool services were established in one fell swoop. Responsibilities of frontline workers were enlarged significantly, without their full understanding or input. In focus group discussions, Anganwadi workers perceived preschool services to be a diversion from their core mandate. As one put it, "*Teaching preschool children is the duty of the Education Department, not ours.*"[17] The job expectations of Anganwadi workers were reinforced by senior state officials, who pressured them to meet the rules for child development as well as nutrition targets. Preschool was a more ambiguous task that redefined the Anganwadi Center's core responsibilities. As another Anganwadi worker remarked, "*Our basic duty is no longer recognizable to us.*"[18] Similar concerns were expressed by senior officials in the Department of Women and Child Development:

> The [preschool] centers are fine in theory, but our mission is not teaching children. I would not expect an Anganwadi worker to interrupt a schoolteacher who is running a class to ask for help with the preschool ... In the same way, I would not expect my colleague in the Education Department to interfere in our work.[19]

The official appreciated the connections between early child health and education; he even cited the Pulse Polio campaign as an example of effective interagency coordination. However, he found that integrating responsibilities too much risked creating "*confusion and conflict*" between departments.[20] Likewise, Department of Education officials noted that teachers already had too many administrative duties and that public health work detracted from their core teaching mandate.

The reaction within the state bureaucracy to reforms that would have integrated responsibilities across departments is understandable in light of existing norms, which encouraged the maintenance of hierarchical boundaries. After the formation of Uttarakhand, among the most visible changes noted by state officials was the "*closing of distance*" between administrative levels of the state, as well as between state agencies and citizens.[21] These changes were perceived to bring some benefits. Under

17 Focus group discussion with Anganwadi Workers, Almora, September 2009.
18 Focus group discussion with Anganwadi Workers, Almora, August 2009.
19 Interview with official, Department of Women and Child Development, Dehradun, August 2009.
20 Ibid.
21 Interviews with several state officials, Dehradun and Almora, Uttarakhand, August–November 2009.

the UP bureaucracy, frontline officials had fewer opportunities to interact with senior bureaucrats. Now that state- and district-level agencies were in closer contact, information exchange and monitoring happened more smoothly. As a senior education official observed:

> Things are different now that we have a small state. Information from here can go straight to the officials at the top. During the UP days, nothing ever reached Lucknow or Allahabad. But today, if something is needed, I have direct links to the Directorate. I can even tell you what the district education officer in Pithoragarh [a remote district] is doing right now.[22]

With the closing of distance, routine administrative processes, such as the dispersal of funds and dissemination of bureaucratic orders and circulars, involved fewer delays and hindrances. Greater accessibility of senior officials also made it easier for subordinates to communicate their concerns upward.

On the other hand, a more decentralized state was also perceived to conflict with norms requiring adherence to rules and hierarchical boundaries. Local officials, who in the past interacted less frequently with senior officials, were now in regular contact with the secretariat. Senior officials, who had been steeped in the UP administrative system, found themselves having to answer a growing number of queries from subordinates. A senior education official reflected:

> We separated from UP, why? Because we were geographically different and we were tail-enders, far away from Lucknow ... And a small state means what? It should mean better administration. Now there is greater access to officials like the Director and Secretary [of Education]. That is helpful, but only up to a limit. Having more access is not positive when procedures and chain of command gets broken. In that way, I feel we were much better off as part of UP.[23]

Other officials interviewed conveyed a similar worry that citizens' access to the state posed a threat to legalistic order. The new state assembly had many more legislators, granting public "*too much access*" to the state, which was seen to encourage rule-bending.[24] Frontline functionaries sought greater access as well. Teachers, for example, demanded a greater say over work conditions, while teachers unions were lobbied to weaken administrative oversight of the teaching profession. An education official noted:

[22] Interview with state official, SSA State Project Office, Dehradun, September 2009.

[23] Interview with senior state official, Department of Education, Dehradun, September 2009.

[24] Interview with state official, Department of Women and Child Development, Dehradun, August 2009.

> Before, when we had our Education Directorate in UP, no teacher would think of approaching us. All their concerns would flow through official channels. But with greater access to the state, things can happen backhandedly.[25]

Frontline functionaries were perceived to be more outspoken in meetings, which senior bureaucrats viewed with suspicion. A retired official, who had held several senior posts in the UP administration, narrated his experience of participating in an administrative reforms committee in Uttarakhand. According to him, the growing pressure from local-level officials in policy discussions represented a "*breakdown of order*," which needed correcting.[26]

District officials were also conflicted by administrative changes in Uttarakhand. In focus group discussions they described the challenges of balancing pressures from senior bureaucrats against what they thought were legitimate requests of schoolteachers for postings and transfers. As a local education official noted, he could face penalties when answering teachers' transfer requests:

> Now if I try to press the matter [of teacher transfers] too much, senior officials will interrogate me. "*Why aren't you obeying orders?*" they will say. And if we share our ideas or suggest making changes [to the rules], they respond by throwing more paperwork (*kagazi kaam*) at us.[27]

When questioning administrative rules, local officials experienced overt and subtle pressures. In some instance, supervisors would single out local officials during meetings.[28] The assignment of extra "*paperwork*" (*kagazi kaam*), something that local education administration routinely demanded from schoolteachers, was a clear signal that senior officials were dissatisfied.[29] Pressures to document all decisions intensified due to growing concerns over administrative accountability and corruption, in policy arenas beyond education as well. As Mathur (2016) describes in her ethnographic study of bureaucratic practices in Uttarakhand, district administration was overwhelmingly guided by accountability demands, which encouraged the proliferation of paperwork. For example, in implementing the National Rural Employment Guarantee Scheme, local

25 Interview with state official, Department of Education, Dehradun, August 2009.

26 Interview with retired official, Dehradun, August 2009.

27 Interview with Block Education Officer, Almora, September 2009.

28 Observations of multiple meetings with local education bureaucracy, Almora and Dehradun, September–November 2009.

29 Interviews with block-level education officials, Dehradun and Almora, September–October 2009.

officials faced singular pressures to generate what she calls "transparent-making documents," a practice that aimed to prevent "leakages" in the system (2016, 95). Taken in sum, the interviews with state and local officials point to the persistence of legalistic pressures within the state, creating resistance to changes in bureaucratic norms.

6.3.2 How Civil Society Experiences Legalistic Bureaucracy

This subsection takes us beyond state boundaries to explore how citizens and civil society agencies in Uttarakhand experienced bureaucracy during the first decade of state formation. Interviews and participant observation with civic agencies suggest that public administration was seen as a continuation of the "*UP-style*" of administration, as noted by several respondents. The experiences of Uttarakhand Seva Nidhi (USN), an agency with more than twenty-five years of experience in rural development, are instructive. Having operated under both the UP and Uttarakhand state governments, USN had established credibility with the administration. Headquartered in Almora district, the organization was founded by Dr. Lalit Pande, a social worker and environmentalist who was well versed in the workings of UP's bureaucracy.[30] Under India's National Education Policy of 1986, USN was appointed a nodal agency for environmental education, and created instructional materials and textbooks for government schools.[31]

USN also engaged in grassroots programming in the hill region, focusing on community development, women's empowerment, early child education and environmental sustainability.[32] It operated through a network of community-based organizations and women's associations (*mahila mangal dals*) in more than 500 villages across Uttarakhand. USN supported the development of women's groups, helping them to organize and collectively express community needs. In the 1990s, USN established village preschool centers (*balwadis*), managed entirely by local communities. USN provided technical inputs, training for preschool instructors, monitoring and academic support, while women's associations oversaw the provision of land and labor and routine operations. Though they lacked official recognition

[30] Dr. Lalit Pande agreed to be identified for this study.

[31] During my fieldwork, USN's environmental education workbook, *Hamari Dharti, Hamara Jivan* (Our Land, Our Life) was being used by government schools in Uttarakhand.

[32] For more information on USN, see www.sevanidhi.org.

from the Department of School Education, the balwadis operated as *de facto* primary schools. They also served as community spaces for women and other village residents to discuss collective needs.[33]

Like other civil society organizations in Uttarakhand, USN's program team was optimistic about the new state. The village women's groups they supported also aspired to gain state recognition for their community-based development work. However, they found Uttarakhand's bureaucracy stifling in many ways. The balwadi program was supported under the 1986 National Education Policy, with assistance from the central government's Ministry of Human Resource Development (MHRD). A program manager at USN recalled that UP's education bureaucracy at the time was "*neither a support to us nor a hindrance.*"[34] However, after the formation of Uttarakhand, the education bureaucracy sought to establish its grip over civil society organizations. Those failing to conform to administrative rules were issued penalties; some were even shut down.[35] USN's balwadi program was among those affected by these changes. The program did not meet Department of School Education rules concerning the operational timings and locations for preschool centers. As noted earlier, the initiative for "convergence" of child health and education services required preschools to be situated near government primary school campuses. Meanwhile, USN's balwadi centers operated according to the needs of local communities. Women's association members – often these were mothers whose children attended balwadis – had agreed on the locations and timings for the centers. However, the bureaucracy's strict enforcement of rules meant that balwadis could no longer operate under Uttarakhand's preschool program. A program manager from USN narrated her experiences working with bureaucracy:

> When Uttarakhand broke off from UP, we were very positive. We wanted to work more closely with the state, and we tried being proactive. But instead of supporting our work, we found the bureaucracy questioning us. They would come up with any number of technicalities about our approach that did not fit with official rules and requirements.[36]

The bureaucracy in Uttarakhand, she went on to suggest, was driven by "*concern for its rules, and nothing more.*"[37] By contrast, she emphasized

33 For more information on the balwadi program, see USN (2001).

34 Interview with senior associate, USN, Almora, October 2009.

35 Interview with several senior officials, Department of School Education, Dehradun, July 2009.

36 Interview with senior program manager, USN, Almora, October 2009.

37 Interview with senior program manager, USN, Almorap, November 2009.

how the organizational norms guiding USN gave paramount importance to community participation in decision-making. Operational decisions for the balwadi program were made by communities, ensuring that households could fully utilize the centers. Typically, balwadis were located in areas that mothers found suitable for their children. As I observed during village visits, women's association members came to rely on balwadis for childcare and education services.[38] Each morning, they would leave their young ones at the centers before heading to the agricultural fields to perform labor. Program flexibility encouraged community ownership of balwadis. For example, in some villages, balwadis doubled as community centers where panchayat meetings were held, or as guest houses for weddings and social functions.

The balwadi program's more flexible approach to administration conflicted with the education bureaucracy's strict adherence to rules. The Department of School Education issued a directive that all preschool centers operating under the government's policy had to be relocated to the nearest primary school campus. The directive was applied equally to state-run Anganwadi centers and preschool centers managed by recognized non-state agencies.[39] From the perspective of USN and its network of women's associations, the state's uniform application of rules undid twenty years of community organizing around education, all in one sudden move. The handling of the balwadi program was seen as but one example of the bureaucracy's tendency to apply policy rules without regard for the practical work conditions of community-based organizations. According to a USN program manager:

> The bureaucracy cannot say that "*your organization is good or different.*" They have to follow a standard rule ... And once you get kicked out by the [administrative] system, that's it ... you are out.[40]

Other USN employees drew the lesson that Uttarakhand's bureaucracy had "*no concern about the quality of NGOs*" and that community-based approaches to development were given little merit.[41] Consequently, USN avoided further partnerships with government departments, and instead, redesigned programs to work more closely with philanthropic agencies.

[38] Based on field observations in eight villages in Almora District, August–October 2009.

[39] In interviews, Department of Education officials praised USN for its work in environmental education. However, they felt compelled to apply directives evenly, giving no special consideration for USN's balwadi program.

[40] Interview with senior associate, USN, Almora, October 2009.

[41] Interview with associate, USN, Almora, October 2009.

USN's experiences with Uttarakhand's education bureaucracy were not unique. Other civic agencies and residents interviewed offered similar accounts of the administrative barriers involved in working with government departments. Consider the case of Mr. Dangwal, a retired government teacher with twenty-five years of experience doing grassroots work in Almora. As a political activist, Mr. Dangwal became involved in Uttarakhand's statehood movement in the 1970s. Subsequently, he worked on various community development programs. He recalled his experiences of the World Bank's Swajal project, a water and sanitation program overseen by the UP Water Corporation (Jal Nigam) in the 1990s. Mr. Dangwal and his collaborators worked with village residents to identify sustainable water sources and install safe water lines in villages. However, when the time came to coordinate with the UP bureaucracy, Mr. Dangwal noted, state officials often disregarded community input:

> The Jal Nigam had demarcated the forests and water sources according to maps that did not fit with the situation we saw on the ground. As a result, 90 percent of the water lines they created in our villages did not work. Instead of listening to communities, they pushed the people aside and worked by their own rules.[42]

Mr. Dangwal's experiences are even more telling considering that he had an insider's grasp of the state bureaucracy. Having held administrative posts at a leading government high school in Almora, he understood the practical difficulties of building community ties through the school system. In 2001, Mr. Dangwal founded a grassroots NGO that assisted rural communities in multiple domains, including livelihoods, forest management and early child education. The NGO helped establish women's associations and supported their efforts to monitor government primary schools. Village Education Committees (VECs) and other state-sanctioned local bodies, he observed, often worked against women's interests and participation.[43] Because men had migrated out of Almora for work, responsibility for looking after education fell increasingly on mothers. Yet, in his experience, the notion of "*people's participation*" in service delivery was divorced from the social realities that rural communities, and women in particular, encountered.

[42] Interview with social activist, Almora, October 2009.

[43] On bureaucracy's indifference to the needs of women in Uttarakhand, see Joshi (2005). A study of Swajal also finds community engagement was "totally ignored from the implementation phase onwards" (Centre of Development Studies 2000, 2).

6.4 "RATIONALIZING" SCHOOLTEACHERS

I have shown so far that legalistic bureaucratic norms persisted after the formation of Uttarakhand, notwithstanding the political opportunity for norm change. This section investigates the ways in which legalism influences the performance of complex tasks, in particular the management of teachers and oversight of services in primary schools. As detailed in Chapter 2, Uttarakhand has a high incidence of single-teacher schools and comparatively weak learning outcomes. Based on participant observation and interviews in two study districts (Dehradun and Almora), I argue that bureaucratic adherence to rules has hampered the state's ability to monitor teachers effectively. Furthermore, ethnographic evidence from the village level suggests that grievance redressal mechanisms have imposed administrative burdens on disadvantaged households, making it more difficult for them to hold teachers accountable.

6.4.1 Teacher "Rationalization": From Dehradun to Almora District

The high prevalence of single-teacher schools has been a concern for education officials in Uttarakhand. Although the state has a favorable ratio of students to teachers at the aggregate level, the geographic distribution of teachers is heavily lopsided. Single-teacher schools are located mainly in the interior hills, while urban areas and roadside villages are oversubscribed with teachers. A Department of Education official explained, "*If you look at it closely, our [teacher to student] ratio is one of the best in the country ... What we need to do now is rationalize these teachers. And for that we have a policy to send teachers to deficit regions.*"[44] Education officials attempted to reverse the tide through what they called "*rationalization*," that is, policy rules for allocating teachers to underserved village. Moreover, to promote accountability, formal grievance procedures were instituted so that parents could report errant behavior. According to another official:

> Most teachers want to get transferred from the interior hills to the lower hills and plains. Transfers are not happening from the plains back up to the hills. We felt that teacher transfers must be two-way. It should not be like rainwater flowing down the hills ... We instituted a rationalization policy barring teachers from migrating down to the plains. We prepared a list of teachers who had been

[44] Interview with official, Department of School Education, Dehradun, July 2009.

serving continuously in plum locations, like Dehradun and Haridwar, for the last fifteen years. They were asked to serve in more remote areas. We also blocked the movement of teachers to city centers and schools located in roadside villages.[45]

The rationalization of teacher appointments was instituted uniformly throughout the state, albeit with limited input from teachers. I asked education officials whether mechanisms existed to determine if teachers were satisfied with their postings. The question raised eyebrows. "*Teachers need the stick* (danda)," an official stated bluntly.[46] The idea of consulting teachers before posting them to schools was not accepted practice. Conversely, senior officials saw districts administration as being too "*approachable*" and "*loose*" (*dhila*) in its dealings with teachers, which may have encouraged teachers to manipulate rules.[47]

Soon after the rationalization policy was instituted, I observed the interactions between teachers and local officials in Dehradun's district education office. Teachers often brought requests challenging transfer orders, in some cases working through political intermediaries. District officials that I interviewed overwhelmingly supported rationalization. The policy rules provided a safeguard in case teachers brought complaints against officials. For example, officials could be accused of being "*prejudiced*" (*pakshpat*) in their handling of transfer requests. As a local official explained:

> Ever since it [rationalization] was announced, we've had a long line of teachers coming here every day asking for a transfer ... They are using any means possible to work around the policy. But I keep telling them that my hands are tied. Teachers are unhappy with it. But they see that I am only applying the policy given to me. Nobody can blame me for doing my job.[48]

Rationalization did not prevent teachers from trying to secure their favored postings. Dehradun's district education office had a backlog of teacher complaints, challenging their transfer orders. Some teachers came accompanied by relatives and associates, indicating their "*approach*" the local parlance for having political connections.[49] To illustrate, as I observed in the district education office, a teacher arrived one morning

45 Interview with education official, Dehradun, August 2009.

46 Interviews with several state officials, Department of School Education, Dehradun, August 2009.

47 Interviews with several state officials, Dehradun, July–September 2009.

48 Interview with local education official, Dehradun, July 2009.

49 Teachers frequently used the term "*approach*" (in English) when speaking to officials, rather than the associated Hindi term (*pahunch*).

with her brother. She sat quietly, while her brother tried persuading officials to transfer her from an interior village school to one that was closer to Dehradun. Indicating his "*approach*," he supplied the names of two local politicians whom he had consulted on the case. The education official heard his request and advised him to return later so that senior officials could review the case. The official later shared his interpretation of the incident:

> You saw that brother and sister sitting here this morning? She is a schoolteacher, and he [her brother] came along to play politics (*netagiri*) on her behalf. Last time she came asking for a transfer because her children were studying in Dehradun. This time, her bother came and mentioned his political contacts ... I have sent them both away, but how long can it continue? This is the third time I have seen her this month ... You just watch and see ... next time they will come with the transfer order. Someone [an official] on top will instruct me on what to do.[50]

After handling many such cases, local officials were cognizant of systemic loopholes in the rules. For example, some teachers made bogus medical claims, supplying "fake" (*farzi*) notes from doctors indicating an injury, to secure comfortable posts. "*That is the kind of malfeasance we wanted to stop*," remarked another official.[51] In response, the education bureaucracy adopted more stringent oversight measures:

> We took the matter out of the hands of local officials. We informed schoolteachers and doctors that they must appear before a medical board at the state level. We told them that transfer requests made on medical grounds would be subject to the medical board's decision. This sent the message that they cannot evade our scrutiny.[52]

By tightening the oversight of teacher transfers, senior officials also sought to send a message to local administration about the need to ensure swift and unflinching application of the rules. Some teachers delayed their transfer orders by filing counter-petitions with the Department of School Education. Manipulation of the rules undermined rationalization. Transfer delays were costly to schools needing additional teachers, with posts lying vacant for months together.

On the other hand, teachers questioned the fairness of rationalization. Cases emerged of teachers with disabilities being transferred to interior villages, which placed local administration in a quandary. The concern

[50] Interview with local official, district education office, Dehradun, July 2009.
[51] Interview with state official, Dehradun, August 2009.
[52] Ibid.

over being seen as "*impartial*" (*nishpaksh*) had to be balanced with consideration for the legitimate welfare needs of teachers. District officials bristled at accusations of their being "*callous*" (*kathor*) toward teachers. On the other hand, granting exceptions to the policy rule could damage their reputations with higher-ups in the education bureaucracy. A district official described the predicament:

> They [senior officials] have come up with a good policy. But I doubt it can work across the entire state. We are out here explaining to the teachers that we cannot make any concessions for anyone ... But how do I explain to a sixty-year-old headmaster who has difficulty walking why he was transferred to a school in some far-flung village? How do I tell him that I cannot do anything for his case? And there are many, many cases like his.[53]

News of such cases circulated among teachers in Dehradun and was widely discussed at teacher union meetings as well. The feeling of unfairness among teachers made it more difficult for local officials to secure their cooperation on other matters, such as administration of the mid-day meal.[54] Nevertheless, almost all officials interviewed favored a strict interpretation of the rationalization policy rules, seen as a necessary correction to bureaucracy laxity. Moreover, failing to demonstrate commitment to the rules could invite "*scolding*" (*dant*) from superiors, or even harsher penalties. Some officials cited the example of a colleague who was seen as being less stringent in his adherence to the policy. He was subsequently transferred from Dehradun to a remote location near the Tibetan border.

Due to its proximity to the state secretariat, one may suppose that Dehradun's local administration faced heightened pressures to follow departmental rules. I conducted similar fieldwork in Almora, far away from departmental headquarters. I found, however, that education officials in Almora were no less inclined to apply the "*stick*" (*danda*) on teachers. In focus group discussions, officials shared the difficulties of balancing departmental obligations with their concern for individual teachers. These officials interacted frequently with teachers at work, but also in social gatherings, as well as informally over evening tea in the marketplace. They understood teachers' daily grievances and found it difficult to apply a uniform policy for rationalization. An official described his predicament:

53 Focus group discussion with local education officials, district education office, Dehradun, July 2009.

54 Interview with teacher union member, Dehradun, August 2009.

Take the primary school at the end of that road. It has 96 children, but only one person teaching. The headmaster has been asking us to send an additional teacher, again and again, for the last year. But it is on the roadside, so the issue of "*sugam-durgam*" [accessible versus remote school location] comes up, and rationalization doesn't allow it. I brought this issue up once before at the district, but if I press harder, it will draw too much attention.[55]

He showed me the official list of "*accessible*" (*sugam*) and "*remote*" (*durgam*) primary schools in Dwarahat. The classification was based on the walking distance between the school and the nearest road. The school he had been referring to had ninety-six students, but its proximity to a road prevented it from receiving additional teachers. I subsequently visited the school, which was overflowing with students.[56] The head teacher was frustrated with having to manage classes alone. He also appreciated the departmental pressure on local bureaucrats: "*What can they do. This area is considered accessible* (sugam). *Rules come from above, and they must follow them. They have to send their monitoring report back to Dehradun. I can't blame them.*"[57]

Most teachers I interviewed in Almora openly stated their objections to rationalization as well as other aspects of bureaucratic oversight by the Department of School Education. I met with teachers in between their sessions at the training center (Figure 6.2). I also interacted with them on their way to and from school, at tea stalls and bus stands, settings that facilitated more candid conversations. Teachers expressed their exasperations over how the education bureaucracy treated them. The uniform approach to rationalization was perceived as being unfair and nontransparent. Politically connected teachers, who were adept at circumventing the rules, seemed to always find the most favored postings. A teacher summarized the sentiments of his colleagues:

They [the Department of Education] tell us the policy is transparent. But how do we know that? They make all the decisions in Dehradun. Nobody asks us what we think about it. Even the higher ups in the union have no say. The teachers who are involved in politicking (*netagiri*) ... only they seem to benefit. The common teacher (*aam adhyapak*) ... has to face the rules no matter what ... So that means that we should also just look out for ourselves.[58]

[55] Interview with BRC, Almora district, November 2009.
[56] Field visit to primary school, Dwarahat, Almora, October 2009.
[57] Interview with headmaster of primary school, Almora, October 2009.
[58] Focus group discussion with government school teachers, Almora, November 2009.

FIGURE 6.2 Teacher training center (Almora, Uttarakhand)
Note: Author photograph (2009).

Skepticism was reinforced by cases of young, able-bodied teachers obtaining desirable posts. Meanwhile, those with disabilities and medical ailments were sent to interior villages. These incidents undermined teachers' faith in the administration.

The leaders of teacher unions expressed similar misgivings about rationalization. Unions also encountered administrative barriers when attempting to negotiate terms with senior officials, which made it difficult to secure union loyalty from teachers. Many teachers had opted to work outside of union mechanisms, using personal connections instead. A union leader explained:

> The problem is like this ... Since I am the local head of the union, I want to unite the teachers and form a single voice (*ekta*). The government order said no new transfers to roadside schools for three years. But then just four months later we found that those who were connected [politically] were getting transfers. The 10 to 15 percent involved in politicking (*netagiri*), those teachers can get things done ... The rest are affected by this. They are left wondering, "*Who is listening to us?*" And when we [the union] can't get things done for them, they look for other means [*jugaad*].[59]

[59] Interview with local leader of teacher union, Almora, September 2009.

The union's credibility was undercut by its inability to strike bargains on behalf of all teachers. Meanwhile, the education bureaucracy was perceived as lacking the ability to distinguish between legitimate requests and cases of "politicking" (*netagiri*) by teachers. Like their counterparts in Dehradun, teachers in Almora would leave the district education office in disappointment. In one striking example, parents from a village had advocated on behalf of a teacher, petitioning the local administration *not* to transfer her to a different school.[60] However, local officials had strict orders to post the teacher to an interior village, since she had spent the Last six years at a roadside school. What was seen by the bureaucracy as consistency in applying the rules was experienced by teachers (and parents) as the arbitrary use of state authority. Many teachers were left feeling insecure about their positions.

Education officials recognized that rationalization may have come across as opaque and inflexible to teachers. Teachers were given little advance information about their transfer orders. The ambiguity in the process also created opportunities for politicians to intervene, and sometimes manipulate teachers. In interviews, teachers described having "*tie-ups*" with local politicians, in the hope of influencing bureaucratic decisions. Politicians charged fixed rates for assistance with transfers, at a cost of ₹50,000–200,000, between two and ten times a teacher's monthly salary.[61] There was no guarantee, moreover, that payments would lead to the desired result. Politicians sometimes asked teachers to render services in return for help. For example, teachers were asked to campaign for politicians in target villages, an activity that is illegal. The extent of these practices was difficult to determine, but most teachers I interviewed found it important to maintain political connections. In a focus group discussion, a teacher described how he and his colleagues had tied up with a local politician:

> Vidhayakji [the MLA] came around asking us to get things done for him. We agreed, or else we could risk getting transferred. We don't know what the status is of our [transfer] cases. So, we tied up with him in the meantime. We are hoping that, one way or another, it will help ... Our transfer hasn't happened yet, so maybe it is helping.[62]

[60] Based on field research conducted in Dhaula village Almora, October 2009.
[61] Interviews with several teachers, Almora, September–November 2009.
[62] Focus Group Discussion with teachers, Almora, November 2009.

As others likewise noted, political tie-ups were murky. Some teachers diversified their risk through a multipronged strategy, involving informal political connections, union representation and formal applications to the Department of School Education all at once. Yet, few teachers I spoke with expected a fair "*hearing*" (*sunwai*) from the state.[63] The formal administrative process encouraged them to bypass the bureaucracy and take an informal "*approach*" to advance their interests.

6.4.2 School Accountability in Pujari Village

I have so far examined how schoolteachers respond to administrative demands for accountability. This subsection takes the analysis down to the village primary school, to consider the role of parental oversight of education services. It investigates how legalistic bureaucracy shapes local accountability practices through a case study of primary schooling in Pujari village. I selected Pujari as a field site because village-level variables impacting the delivery of public services pointed in its favor.[64] Situated on the main bus route to the administrative block of Dwarahat, Pujari's primary school was accessible to teachers and administrators. Further, Pujari had a cohesive community of relatively well-educated upper-caste households. The village was home to *Pujaris*, high-ranking Brahmins who performed religious rites. The Pujaris valued education and households took pride in having civil servants, teachers and military officers among their family members. Residents possessed small landholdings for subsistence farming, and in sync with the pattern in Almora, young men had migrated from the village for employment and would send remittances back home. A village census that I conducted revealed that almost 90 percent of men had migrated out, while women, children and elderly relatives remained in the village.

Pujari had an attractive primary school building. A wooden signboard on the front gate read "Sarva Shiksha Abhiyan," the government's Education for All program. The school had a playground with a fountain at the center of the courtyard and two hand pumps for water on each side. Classrooms were decorated with paintings of flora and fauna from the Kumaon region. Separate bathrooms for girls and boys had been recently installed. The school's head teacher, Kamla Devi, informed me that local officials took an interest in the school. For example, they

[63] Interviews with several teachers, Almora, September 2009.

[64] I lived for three months near Pujari village, Almora, September–November 2009.

had requested her to submit photographs documenting the completion of construction work, an indication of the bureaucracy's rule-oriented approach to infrastructure provision.

Despite its welcoming exterior, services at the primary school were in disarray, to the distress of parents. Ms. Devi often arrived late to school. On occasion, she would be absent without warning. Parents would find her in the office, leaving students unsupervised. During my own school visits, Ms. Devi rarely stepped outside of her office to teach. Classes were disorganized and the children had little guidance on how to complete their assignments.

School dysfunction in Pujari was not for want of community oversight. Village residents were well versed in collective action. For example, they managed the Mahadev temple, a religious site that attracted visitors from across Almora. The temple, situated on the bank of a stream that ran through the village, also had a hermitage (*ashram*), where traveling monks (*sadhus*) could stay. According to the village residents, the temple was built on an auspicious site, which was a resting place visited by the Pandavas, protagonists of the ancient Hindu epic *Mahabharata*. Residents jointly managed the temple and ashram, providing food and clothing to visiting monks. In a similar way, they mobilized collectively around education. As village elders recounted, in the early 1900s households in Pujari established one of Almora's first primary schools, located at the ashram. Education was provided by priests (*pandits*) and funded through household donations. The community also made demands on the state for education. A full decade before independence, Pujari's residents petitioned public authorities for a primary school, which was established in 1938.

Pujari had an active women's association (mahila mangal dal), which took shape in the early 1990s. The association pooled its resources to create an informal preschool (balwadi) for children of different ages. The balwadi also became a center for community gatherings and discussions. Problems at the government primary school were discussed in women's association meetings, which they presented at quarterly VEC meetings convened by the elected head (*pradhan*) of the village panchayat. Meanwhile, Ms. Devi shared the difficulties of having to teach five grades by herself, in addition to her administrative work. She had requested her department to appoint an additional teacher but had not received a response. In turn, the women's group took its own initiative to organize funds from the village and hire an additional teacher, who informally assisted Ms. Devi. However, Ms. Devi's absences became more frequent and the assistant teacher was left in charge of running classes at the school. After a child was injured at school, the women's association made a formal complaint against the head teacher. As a mother recalled,

> We did everything we could to get Kamla Deviji [the head teacher] to take her teaching duties seriously ... One day, children were climbing the tree in the courtyard (*aangan*) during school hours, and one of them fell and broke his arm ... A few of us [mothers] went to the school and demanded that she take responsibility, or else we would make a complaint against her. "*Go ahead*," she told us, "*I am a government servant. I do not work for you!*" From that day forward, we took matters in our own hands and filed a complaint in Dwarahat [at the block education office].[65]

Ms. Devi responded by lodging a legal case against the women's association for harassment under the SC-ST Prevention of Atrocities Act, a law that protected disadvantaged groups from harassment and assured prompt judicial action. Parents in Pujari expressed a combination of surprise and concern over the legal case. As one father remarked, "*The law and administration are there only to protect the teacher. All the while, our children are the ones being mistreated by the school system.*"[66]

To avoid having to go to court, the women's association withdrew its complaint. However, a few vocal mothers decided to keep fighting and visited the district education office in Almora, determined to hold the teacher accountable for her lapses. A mother described the reaction from district officials: "*They showed little support for our cause. Instead, they turned around and questioned us about our motives for monitoring the teacher. They told us that we had no official authority and could not set foot on the school's premises, unless Madamji [the head teacher] called us there for a meeting.*"[67] Angry and humiliated by the experience of engaging with local officials, mothers in Pujari found it futile to put additional energy into monitoring the primary school. Summarizing the sentiments of the group, one mother stated: "*Why should we risk legal repercussions when the department* (vibhag) *won't even acknowledge our presence at the school!*"[68]

Subsequently, I interviewed education officials in Almora, who offered a different perspective on teacher malpractices. In the district education office, they showed me the backlog of cases filed by teachers. One official

[65] Focus group discussion with women's association, Pujari, October 2009.
[66] Interview with a father, Pujari, November 2009.
[67] Focus group discussion with women's association, Pujari, November 2009.
[68] Ibid.

recalled having to answer thirty-seven information requests from senior administrators during the previous month, all related to legal cases involving teachers. Pointing to a stack of legal files, he said: "*These are teacher-related cases that are ongoing … and this [pile] is only from the previous month!*"[69] Cases involving caste-based harassment were considered highly sensitive, since they could easily escalate into judicial action and stoke political conflicts. When I asked the official how parents registered complaints about teaching, he cited the Department of School Education's official grievance procedures. On further probing, he conceded: "*The administration's grievance procedures can be cumbersome. Our local officials also find them complex. But we ultimately have to follow the procedures, or else we can run into bigger problems … We can be accused of bias (pakshpath) and get summoned to the secretariat.*"[70]

In sum, local officials in Dehradun and Almora used policy rules to limit political interference in bureaucratic decisions. However, the adherence to rules also created tensions and conflicts, which were detrimental for service delivery. A commitment to legalism led senior officials to tighten the reins on local administration, which constrained the ability of frontline officials to negotiate disputes between teachers and parents. In response, teachers used administrative procedures as well as informal networks to influence bureaucratic decisions. Administrative channels were utilized by parents as well, as indicated in the case of Pujari. However, these mechanisms also created administrative-legal barriers that worked against parents, weakening community oversight of primary schooling.

6.5 STATE-INDUCED SUBSTITUTION: PRIMARY EDUCATION IN SARKOT VILLAGE

The previous section demonstrated how legalistic bureaucratic norms have shaped the management and oversight of schoolteachers, impacting local administration's responses to the demands of teachers and parents. This section investigates the mechanism of societal feedback, the expectations and collective strategies of citizens, which shape service delivery. Through the village case study of Sarkot, I demonstrate how community participation in primary schooling evolves in response to legalistic bureaucracy. With a history of social cooperation between

[69] Interview with local education official, Almora, September 2009.
[70] Ibid.

castes, encompassing village associations, including a dynamic women's group, Sarkot was a likely setting for village social capital to enhance service delivery. Drawing on ethnographic evidence, including interviews and oral histories with residents, I found that household collective action helped enhance the functioning of Sarkot's primary school. However, as community expectations grew, demands for quality education services were met with administrative roadblocks. Tracing local state–society interactions over time, I found that households in Sarkot gradually altered their approach to education by coproducing substitutes, such as private tutoring. Notwithstanding robust village social capital, I observed that legalistic bureaucracy tends to diminish societal expectations of the local state and induce a shift toward private education.

6.5.1 Village Socioeconomic Characteristics

A medium-sized village, Sarkot (pop. 503) had socioeconomic characteristics positively associated with higher quality public services (Table 6.2).[71] Located in the administrative block of Dwarahat, Sarkot is twelve kilometers from the town center. The government primary school, a short distance uphill from a road leading to Dwarahat, was accessible to local administration. Teachers noted in interviews that Sarkot's primary school was a coveted post. All households owned small tracts of agricultural land, used for terrace farming (Figure 6.3). Farming revolved around subsistence crops, such as corn and *madua,* a hearty finger millet. Most households had at least one member employed in government service, posted as teachers, engineers, police constables and military officers. The village census I conducted indicated that 42 percent of families had migrated out of Sarkot, most of whom resettled in Haldwani and Rudrapur, large towns near the plains. Men for the most part lived outside of the village, while women and elderly householders resided in Sarkot. Financial remittances from family members working outside Sarkot were a major source of household income.

The strength of community bonds in Sarkot was palpable dring my fieldwork. The village had two hamlets (*toks*). The majority upper caste (Thakurs) population lived in a large hamlet, while Dalits lived in a smaller hamlet on the opposite side. A stream ran between the

[71] Socioeconomic features of Sarkot based on a village household census and interviews.

TABLE 6.2 *Sarkot village: Socioeconomic indicators*

Village	Sarkot
Administrative district/block	Almora, Dwarahat
Population	508
Number of Households	131
% Households migrated out	42
Distance to motor road	0.4 kilometers
Caste composition	71% General (Thakur, Brahmin) 29% SC (Arya, Lohar)
House type[1]	85% finished (*pucca*) 15% semi-finished (*semi-pucca*)
Village economy	Subsistence agriculture (wheat, finger millet, soya bean, lentils) Animal husbandry
Places of worship	Devta Sthal (Hindu upper castes) Devta Sthal (Hindu SCs)
Other associations	Devta Committee (*Devta Samiti*) Forest Council (*Van Panchayat*) Women's Group (*Mahila Mangal Dal*) Women's Self Help Groups (SHGs)

Source: Village data collected by the author.

FIGURE 6.3 Aerial view of village terrace farms (Almora, Uttarakhand)
Note: Author photograph (2009).

two hamlets, partitioned further by a new road leading to Dwarahat. Their physical separation notwithstanding, relations between the two castes were cordial and households cooperated in multiple domains. The construction of Sarkot's footbridge was a visible marker of social cooperation. The footpath for crossing the stream had succumbed to damage during the monsoons. Households pooled resources and labor to build a small bridge (*pul*) above the stream. An elderly woman recalled, "*The families* [from both sides of the bridge] *were always tied together ... The bridge too was built through everyone's collective assistance* (sabka sahyog)." According to other residents I interviewed, the bridge was emblematic of how families came together for everyone's collective welfare. Some contrasted the solidarity (*ekta*) in Sarkot with the casteism (*jatiwad*) they encountered while interacting with residents of the UP plains. Communal bonds were also palpable among village associations. Oral histories shared by village elders revealed that Sarkot had a forest council (van panchayat) that managed the surrounding forests over multiple generations.

Sarkot also had a women's association (mahila mangal dal) that had been operational for twenty years, with substantial membership from both caste groups. Additionally, two women's Self Help Groups (SHGs) were engaged in collective savings. Social cooperation across caste lines manifested in village governance of public goods. For example, in deciding where to place the government primary school, households came together to find a mutually beneficial location. Thakurs agreed to construct the school near the Dalit hamlet, since it was closer to the main road, making it easier for teachers to travel to the school. Thakur children, as I observed, hiked down from their hamlet each day to reach school, crossing the stream and agricultural fields to reach the school.

6.5.2 Primary Education in Sarkot

Sarkot's primary school had an attractive campus, with good infrastructure and facilities. Established in 1958, the building had been upgraded recently to meet Right to Education [RTE] Act infrastructure standards, adding three new classrooms, a kitchen, boundary wall and separate bathrooms for boys and girls. The school had thirty-eight students (twenty girls and eighteen boys) enrolled and their attendance was regular. However, Mr. Joshi, the headmaster, was the only teacher posted at the school. A second teaching post was sanctioned but it remained vacant, to Mr. Joshi's exasperation. "*We have tried again and again, but we are unable to do anything about the lack of teachers.*"[72] In his office, Mr. Joshi showed me a Department of Education order restricting teacher transfers to roadside schools.

At the time of my field visit, reliance on the government school system had dwindled in Sarkot. Distressed by the lack of teaching, some households sent their children to private, fee-based tutoring, while others depended entirely on private schools. During my visits to the government school, I observed that the day would begin with students being lined up for attendance, and then singing patriotic songs. The veneer of order dissipated when Mr. Joshi assembled the students into grade-wise groups, handing each group an assignment. He would then retire to his office to complete the attendance register and other administrative work. By late-morning, children could be found running around the campus unattended. The gong of a metal plate (*thali*) signaled the lunch break. Occasionally, I observed children in the kitchen, assisting with preparation of the midday meal.

Teaching resumed after lunch recess, when Mr. Joshi made his rounds of the classrooms to check students' notebooks. On one occasion, a group of enthusiastic fourth graders asked if I could review their math and Hindi assignments. Their command of the material was impressive. I asked if anyone in their families assisted them with their homework. "*We go to Kailash bhaiya's school in the afternoon*," one girl replied, pointing to a small building across the road. Kailash was a college graduate who ran a private tutoring center. Twenty-two children from Sarkot attended Kailash's center. Fees were subsidized by a local NGO, the Society for Environmental Education and Rural Development (SEED), run by Dwarahat residents. SEED's members included retired teachers and public servants committed to community-based development.[73] They supported village programs and training for local governance, education, environmental conservation and women's empowerment.

In interviews, parents compared the government primary school with "Saraswati Shishu Mandir," a low-fee private school that had been managed by Mr. Nautiyal, a retired army officer.[74] Residents praised Mr. Nautiyal, for his earnestness: "*Nautiyalji came back [to Sarkot] after years of being away. Immediately, he wanted to do something for the village. The government* (sarkari) *school was languishing, and families were desperate to educate their kids. So, he dedicated himself to running*

[72] Interview with school headmaster, Sarkot, November 2009.

[73] To learn more about SEED, see http://seedsunadi.blogspot.com

[74] Parents I interviewed reported spending ₹135–550 per month on private school fees.

Shishu Mandir."[75] Shishu Mandir operated for two years, but abruptly closed when Mr. Nautiyal left Sarkot seeking medical treatment for a family member. On a walk to the Shishu Mandir building, a group of fathers shared their apprehensions about the government school system. In one father's words,

> Our government (sarkari) primary school is in a bad state. The Shishu Mandir was better. At least it employed a full staff of four teachers. It ran for only two years and then stopped because Masterji (Mr. Nautiyal) moved from the area ... So now I'm sending my children once again to the government school. But the headmaster there hardly has time to teach ... You will find the kids running around here and there. He's too busy with paperwork and other duties to pay attention to them.[76]

The lack of teaching in government schools was a serious concern for parents. Many perceived that the headmaster was too busy managing the midday meal and administrative duties, and could not devote enough time to teaching.

Households in Sarkot struggled with the decision to exit the government school. Those employed in service professions had exposure to private schooling, prompting them to question the poor condition of the government school. An army officer who had returned to Sarkot was in a quandary about sending his children to the village government school: "*We all studied at the same school. But this time I visited the school and met with Mr. Joshi. Things didn't look right to me. We are thinking about shifting the children to the [army] base where I'm posted and enrolling them in a private school.*"[77] Meanwhile, less advantaged households conveyed a sense of helplessness. Neither could they afford private schooling in Dwarahat, nor could they pack up and leave to seek schooling elsewhere. A father who was engaged in agricultural work remarked, "*We care for our children, but our livelihood depends on this land. Education has become a business* (vyapar). *The expenses do not end with fees. There are books, stationary and daily transport* (aane jaane ka kharcha). *For us, all of this isn't possible. We are sending our children to Kailash's school, in the hope that they will learn something there at least.*"[78] For poor households, seeking private tutoring from Kailash was not an educational enhancement, but a substitution strategy to cope with the lack of teaching in the government school.

[75] Interview with a resident, Sarkot, December 2009.
[76] Interview with a father, Sarkot, November 2009.
[77] Interview with an army officer, Sarkot, December 2009.
[78] Interview with a father, Sarkot, October 2009.

6.5.3 Community Mobilization: The Women's Association in Sarkot

Poor quality education in Sarkot's primary school could not be attributed to a lack of community involvement. Sarkot's *gram panchayat* had procured Sarva Shiksha Abhiyan (SSA) funds to upgrade school infrastructure, evident from new construction. The women's association, whose members came from nearly all village households, held regular meetings and collected private contributions for schooling. The group emerged in the late 1980s to address women's collective needs, including the acute problem of water scarcity. A member of the association explained,

> We faced big problems with water. Many of the water sources (*pani ke srot*) around us had dried up and we looked for alternatives. Depending on the rains, some farms in our village would dry up, while others would overflow with water, causing damage to the crops. As a group, we agreed to jointly manage water. If there was too much water in one family's farm, the rest of us would collect water from there. And next time when that family had less water, we would provide extra water collected from others' farms. With that understanding, we depended on each other for help.[79]

The women's association also developed informal arrangements to regulate firewood and forest grass collection, which became depleted from overgrazing by livestock, requiring women to walk longer distances and bear greater physical risks. The association agreed on limits for grass collection and took turns monitoring forest usage. Households that collected too much grass or entered prohibited areas were brought before the group and penalized. Through collective management, Sarkot's forest gradually regenerated, bringing much-needed relief to the village.

The women's association operated informally for several years before gaining formal recognition in 1994, with assistance from SEED. Having observed women's groups emerge throughout Dwarahat, SEED members offered organizational and leadership training to help the groups address collective needs. In Sarkot, daycare for children was identified as a critical need by young mothers, who performed the strenuous labor of child rearing along with agricultural and household work. In partnership with USN, the environmental organization in Almora introduced earlier, SEED supported the creation of preschools (balwadis) throughout Dwarahat. In 1998, the women's association inaugurated a balwadi in Sarkot. The center, which provided childcare and preschool services, became an all-purpose community center (*samuday kendra*) for residents.

[79] Focus group discussion with women's association, Sarkot, November 2009.

FIGURE 6.4 Women's association members performing ceremonial dance outside a preschool center (Dwarahat, Uttarakhand)
Note: Author photograph (2009).

Households jointly managed the center and children from different castes availed of its services. Physical space was donated by a family in Sarkot, while the women's association donated labor (*shram dan*) to construct and decorate the center (Figure 6.4). Preschool services were run by two women who had recently completed high school. Children were educated informally at the balwadi for more than a decade. In 2009, the women's association converted the balwadi into an after-school center (*sandhya kendra*) for children. The sandhya kendra was operational during my field visits. A college student from Sarkot operated the center in the afternoons. Through songs, games and other activities, she encouraged children of different ages to participate. Mothers were at ease knowing that their children spent afterschool hours in a safe environment.

Community action in Sarkot eventually shifted to the government primary school. The SSA program in Uttarakhand gave VECs authority over school management. Sarkot's VEC coordinated with local administration to monitor provisioning of school infrastructure, teaching materials, textbooks and other SSA inputs. However, the VEC failed to function as a committee. Led by the panchayat pradhan and Mr. Joshi, the head teacher, issues of education quality were rarely addressed in meetings. Although parents were VEC members, their participation was irregular and decisions were often taken without their input. A parent on the VEC observed, "*Meetings happened without our knowledge. We only got to know about decisions much later, when Masterji [Mr. Joshi] came to us asking for our signatures.*"[80] As other residents noted, Mr. Joshi and the pradhan controlled the VEC, and since their cooperation was needed to secure SSA resources, parents were reluctant to challenge him.[81]

The women's association tried participating in VEC meetings as well. However, women in Sarkot were customarily excluded from "government" (sarkari) meetings. An association member recounted: "*We would never attend official meetings or sit alongside the men. We didn't even know that meetings took place at the primary school.*"[82] The balwadi center, on the other hand, grew into a space for women to discuss public issues, raising their confidence to speak alongside men. Another association member described the transformation that took place among women:

> Everyone, including us [women] doubted that we could manage affairs at the primary school ... But now the situation has reversed. We all come forward and attend school meetings. Now the women don't let the men speak![83]

Confident members of the women's association took on leadership roles at the government school, voicing their demands to Mr. Joshi and local education officials. As I learned in interviews, Mr. Joshi habitually came late to school and would remain in his office throughout the morning, neglecting to teach. He also used to extract fees from parents to cover the cost of school facilities, including a desktop computer, which was rarely used. Although it was illegal for government primary schools to charge fees, parents felt compelled to pay.

The women's association pressured Mr. Joshi to stop charging fees, and to arrive on time and look after the students. They also monitored mid-day meal preparation to ensure food quality. Foodgrains, they learned, failed to reach the school on time. To their dismay, parents discovered that Mr. Joshi was making the children carry sacks of grain to school from a nearby storehouse (godam). A father noted, "*The little children*

[80] Interview with a mother on the VEC, Sarkot, November 2009.

[81] According to SSA policy rules, the secretary of the VEC (the head teacher) was a signatory on funding requests.

[82] Focus group discussion with women's association, Sarkot, November 2009.

[83] Ibid.

would climb uphill, carrying heavy sacks (boris) *of grain on their backs. There was a huge uproar ... 'Why are our children being made to carry grains to school?', parents asked.*" The women's association used official grievance procedures, lodging complaints about the midday meal to local administration. Subsequently, education officials from Dwarahat made unannounced inspections of the school and reported problems with the midday meal. "*When the officials came, Mr. Joshi was put on alert,*" a mother remarked.[84] The administrative response raised the confidence of parents in Sarkot.

6.5.4 State-Induced Exit

Parents in Sarkot wanted quality education for their children. Exasperated by the lack of teaching at the government school, the women's association organized a march (*padyatra*) to Dwarahat to voice their concerns to local administration. They held demonstrations (*pradarshan*) outside the education bureaucracy's office, chanting the slogan, "*We want education, not handouts*" (*Hamein bhiksha nahin, shiksha chahiye*). The slogan referred to the Midday Meal Programme, which became an emblem of uneven service delivery by the state.[85] Although households relied on the meal program, some parents felt that it was a "*handout*" (*bhiksha*) that diverted state attention away from "*education*" (*shiksha*). The group demanded to have an additional teacher posted to the school along with an updated curriculum covering science subjects. Local officials advised the parents to submit an official request through the local VEC, warning them against interfering with administrative procedures.

Instead, the group turned inward, organizing village funds to hire an additional teacher at the school. They appointed a high school graduate, who taught at the school for five years. Eventually, she moved on after getting married. Having seen the limitations of informal teaching arrangements, the women's association raised the matter again with local administration. They demanded additional teachers for science, mathematics and English, which were seen as critical subjects. The group traveled to Dwarahat to meet local officials multiple times in the span of three months. Each time, their demands fell on deaf ears. The head of the women's association recounted:

84 Interview with a mother, Sarkot, December 2009.

85 Interviews with parents, Sarkot, December 2009.

> We went to the [administrative] block to complain about the lack of teaching going on at the primary school. But not one officer came to help us. Nobody from the Department [of Education] listened to what we had to say. We even had the *gram pradhan* write letters to the administration, but we received no response. The situation became hopeless at the government school ... Now everyone is going after private school.[86]

Following the poor results of collective action, many households opted for private schooling in Dwarahat or even further away.

However, collective action in Sarkot did not dissipate. Households continued to participate in panchayat assemblies *(gram sabhas)* and to assist one another through labor sharing and in weddings and other social functions. Activities of the women's association also persisted. For example, they coordinated with other villages to adopt rainwater harvesting techniques. They also participated in village politics, supporting one of their members to run for office in panchayat elections. While collective action continued, households shifted their efforts away from issues of government schooling, which which they no longer saw as a fruitful arena for investing their precious time and community resources.

Local education officials in Dwarahat had a different understanding of the state's responsibility to communities. From their perspective, the bureaucracy was required to follow rules for teacher postings. The request for an additional teacher conflicted with the state's rationalization policy, which gave interior (durgam) villages priority over more accessible (sugam) villages like Sarkot. A blanket stay was issued by the Education Department on all teacher transfers to roadside primary schools. Sarkot's primary school did not qualify for additional teachers and would need to wait until the stay order was lifted. An education official living in Dwarahat sympathized with parents in Sarkot, but noted that his office was merely "*applying the rules*" for teacher allocation.[87] To demonstrate consistency, local administration had to override community demands. Bureaucratic commitment to rules, he noted, is what ensured that schools received the midday meal and other facilities.

Some officials expressed misgivings about having women's associations and other village organizations involved in the governance of local services, since these groups were sometimes enmeshed in local politics. For example, women's associations in Sarkot and other nearby villages organized votes during panchayat elections and collected funds to

[86] Interview with head of the women's association, Sarkot, December 2009.

[87] Interview with local education official, Dwarahat, December 2009.

support assembly candidates. Officials narrated instances where local politicians prodded women's associations to make illegitimate demands on district administration, which became more frequent near election time. In their view, village associations were vulnerable to "*misuse*" by politicians seeking votes.[88] Others flagged concerns over the partisanship of community groups and cited the case of a women's association leader in Dwarahat who campaigned for state assembly elections. Community participation in school governance had to be controlled through administrative rules and hierarchical boundaries, these officials suggested, or else community participation could undercut the state's policy goals.

6.6 CONCLUSION

This chapter has analyzed the persistence of legalistic bureaucracy and its effects on primary schooling in Uttarakhand. It has advanced the book's argument in several ways. First, the chapter offered evidence substantiating the theorized link between legalistic bureaucracy and uneven implementation of primary education. By controlling for the influence of geography, colonial land institutions, agrarian economy, social inequalities, as well as caste and gender norms, the contextual comparison between Uttarakhand and HP helped isolate the causal mechanisms by which bureaucratic norms drive implementation in the Himalayan region. The comparative underperformance of Uttarakhand's primary education system was connected to the persistence of its legalistic bureaucracy. On the one hand, a rule-based orientation helped ensure that primary schools in Uttarakhand received the necessary inputs, such as infrastructure, SSA incentives and the midday meal. However, the strict application of teacher rationalization policies and administrative grievance procedures ultimately thwarted community oversight, reducing school accountability to parents.

Second, village-level fieldwork addressed the alternative explanation centered on social capital theory. Building on historical and ethnographic literatures on forest management and the environmental movement in Uttarakhand, I leveraged contextually appropriate indicators of village social capital to show how village women's associations in the Kumaon region mobilized collectively for public goods. In contrast to highly unequal and socially fragmented village relations in UP, villages in Kumaon

[88] Interview with local official, Almora, January 2010.

exhibited relatively cooperative intercaste relations and village-wide solidarity. As the case studies of Pujari and Sarkot indicate, community ties supported collective action for primary education. In both cases, moreover, legalistic bureaucracy allowed the monitoring of schools, encouraging parents to register complaints through official grievance redressal systems. Concerned parents used these processes to exercise voice, but this did not lead to higher quality education services. Rather, repeated interactions with local administration discouraged households and gradually induced their exit from the government school system, as shown most strikingly in Sarkot. The local state–society dynamics reported in this chapter does not diminish the importance of village social capital in the Himalayan region. Community norms and networks remain integral to social life, the provision of collective goods and, not least of all, joint management of the Himalayan region's fragile ecosystem. However, the findings provoke more careful thinking about the interactive effects of bottom-up collective action by society and bureaucratic norms within the state. The latter are shown to guide the understandings and behaviors of frontline officials, shaping their responses to societal demands. When it comes to providing quality public services in rural India, village collective action is critical, but how the state responds to it can vary. Frontline institutions can either support or stymie community efforts to monitor services, thereby impacting tangible social outcomes (Krishna 2003).

Finally, I have shown how legalism persists in a bureaucracy after the critical juncture posed by the formation of a new state. The creation of Uttarakhand made decision-making more decentralized, affording the public greater access to local government and administration. However, legalistic bureaucracy resisted deeper institutional changes and maintained substantial barriers to civic participation in governance and public services. The foregoing findings on norm persistence must be tempered by the acknowledgment that Uttarakhand is a relatively new state. Bureaucratic norms may yet shift, as the state bureaucracy becomes acclimated to community demands and undergoes generational turnover in the composition of its human resources. That said, given the rapid growth of private schooling in Uttarakhand, the window of opportunity for the state to harness societal input in public services may well be diminishing.

7

Norm Change

Conflict and Commitment on the Front Lines of Reform

7.1 INTRODUCTION

Chapters 5 and 6 showed the divergence in bureaucratic norms between Himachal Pradesh (HP) and Uttarakhand, which helped account for differences in the implementation of primary schooling across the two Himalayan states. Deliberative bureaucracy in HP encouraged collective problem-solving, motivating frontline officials to undertake complex tasks and support local monitoring by women's associations, which together strengthened the quality of services. By contrast, Uttarakhand's legalistic bureaucracy adhered closely to rules, which facilitated gains in infrastructure, but hampered execution of complex tasks and placed excessive burden on rural women and marginalized households, inducing many to exit from government schools and seek private substitutes. The contextual comparison between the two states helped pinpoint how bureaucratic norms sustain societal participation–or fail to–during service delivery. However, the analysis was confined to the Himalayan region, a part of India with relatively lesser inequality and more inclusive caste and gender norms, allowing for more robust village collective action. Questions remain, therefore, as to whether and how bureaucracy can support the delivery of education services in less favorable socioeconomic environments. Additionally, the evidence presented thus far strongly suggests that bureaucratic norms persist, despite changes in the formal institutional environment, raising questions of how norms change.

In this chapter, I address these questions through the analysis of institutional reforms in Uttar Pradesh (UP) and Bihar. Whereas Chapter 4 demonstrated how legalistic bureaucracy in UP reinforces preexisting caste and gender inequalities, here I examine institutional reforms designed to tackle these inequalities through a case study of Mahila Samakhya, a program designed for women's empowerment. Introduced by the central government in the 1990s, the case of Mahila Samakhya in UP demonstrates how deliberative bureaucracy works in a setting of heightened socioeconomic inequality (Heller and Rao 2015). Through ethnographic observations, interviews and focus group discussions, I find that Mahila Samakhya fostered a subculture of deliberation that countered legalistic bureaucracy, enabling frontline workers to undertake complex tasks and activate societal participation during service delivery. Unlike village women's associations in the Himalayan region, which emerged organically, Mahila Samakhya purposively mobilized Dalit women to identify collective needs and challenge village structures of caste and patriarchy, a process rife with social conflict. Through routine deliberation with households and mediation of village conflicts, Mahila Samakhya frontline workers helped integrate Dalit girls into school and adapt education programming to their needs.

While the Mahila Samakhya reforms were initiated by India's central government, reforms in Bihar were driven by the state's political and bureaucratic leadership. After a period of protracted institutional decline, Bihar experienced a political turnaround in the early 2000s. Building on the electoral mobilization of lower castes, political leadership of the "new Bihar" distanced itself from the clientelism and corruption of previous regimes, worked with bureaucracy to strengthen law and order, and in turn, contributed to impressive growth in the economy and public services (Singh and Stern 2013; Chakrabarti 2013). Governing elites promoted legalistic reforms to encourage bureaucratic discipline. Field research conducted in two districts shows that while clientelistic practices continued to operate, bureaucratic commitment to legalism contributed to large gains in enrollment, school infrastructure and other inputs. On the other hand, state efforts to improve the education of quality through innovative teaching practices were less successful. Drawing on interviews and focus group discussions with schoolteachers and frontline administrators, I find that the administrative flexibility required for adopting innovative pedagogical practices conflicted with the bureaucracy's adherence to rules.

In demonstrating the importance of bureaucratic conflict and commitment on the front lines of the state, this chapter speaks to theories of endogenous institutional change (Hacker 2004; Tsai 2006; Falleti and Riofrancos 2018). In both UP and Bihar, governing elites introduced changes by "layering" reforms onto existing institutional structures

(Hacker 2004, 248–249). And in each case, the shift in bureaucratic norms was partial and generated conflicts for frontline workers. In UP, the central government encouraged deliberation by layering the Mahila Samakhya program within the Department of Education. Operating as an island of deliberation within UP's legalistic bureaucracy, Mahila Samakhya frontline workers experienced routine conflicts. Given the UP state government's weak political support for Mahila Samakhya, the program's reach was circumscribed within certain geographic and administrative pockets of the state. In Bihar, the political conditions for bureaucratic norm changes were more propitious. Committed state leadership spearheaded a significant (albeit incomplete) shift away from clientelism toward legalistic bureaucracy. However, initiatives for improving education quality floundered, despite unwavering political support from the chief minister as well as technical expertise from development economists, educationists and civil society organizations. The stalling of education quality improvements in Bihar suggests the limits of reforms that overlook the institutional demands on teachers and other frontline workers.

This chapter is organized as follows. First, I examine the origins of Mahila Samakhya's program in UP and showcase its distinct, gender-oriented approach to public administration. I then show how Mahila Samakhya has supported the implementation of residential schooling for disadvantaged girls through local deliberation. Next, I explore the institutional turnaround in Bihar and the political currents underlying the shift toward legalistic bureaucracy. I show how the emphasis on bureaucratic discipline led to sizable gains in schooling inputs and enrollments, but hampered the uptake of classroom teaching practices aimed at improving education quality. I conclude by reflecting on the implications of frontline worker conflict and commitment for the process of bureaucratic norm change.

7.2 MAHILA SAMAKHYA IN UTTAR PRADESH: DELIBERATION, SOCIAL CONFLICT AND GIRLS' EDUCATION

This section analyzes institutional reforms that encouraged a shift toward deliberative bureaucracy in UP.[1] Established in the 1990s, Mahila

[1] Some parts of this section were previously published in my article, "Social Conflict on the Front Lines of Reform: Institutional Activism and Girls' Education in Rural India." *Public Administration and Development*, 42.1 (2022): 95–105. I reproduce them here with permission from John Wiley & Sons.

Samakhya is a government program for women's empowerment, operating under the Department of Education, with a mandate to promote girls' education. Drawing on ethnographic fieldwork, including village-level participant observation, interviews and focus group discussions in three administrative districts (Mathura, Saharanpur and Sitapur), I find that deliberation within Mahila Samakhya has catalyzed the implementation of education programming for disadvantaged girls. In what follows, I first examine how Mahila Samakhya's UP branch facilitated deliberation in settings of entrenched social inequality, suggesting the importance of institutional activism by frontline workers. I then demonstrate how local deliberation between frontline workers, schoolteachers and disadvantaged households has improved the delivery of girls' education programming. Finally, I reflect on the tensions arising from Mahila Samakhya's deliberative model and the challenges of sustaining frontline worker commitment in the context of UP's legalistic bureaucracy.

7.2.1 Mahila Samakhya Uttar Pradesh: Deliberative Bureaucracy for Women's Empowerment

Integrating disadvantaged girls into the school system is a major challenge confronting the state, more so in places like rural UP, where deeply entrenched gender and caste hierarchies militate against social inclusion. Reflecting on the difficulties of providing mass education within India's unequal social order, the 1986 National Policy on Education proclaimed: "The empowerment of women is possibly the most critical precondition for the participation of girls and women in the educational process."[2] Mahila Samakhya is an institutional reform program that arose out of the 1986 policy, through consultations between the Ministry of Human Resource Development (MHRD), state governments, Indian civil society agencies, international organizations and experts on gender and education.[3] Conventional approaches to public administration were considered ill-suited to redressing India's gender imbalances in education. The Mahila Samakhya program thus adopted "women's empowerment" (*mahila sashaktikaran*) as a guiding principle. The program was designed with a multilevel governance structure. Mahila Samakhya's National Project Office reported to the MHRD in New Delhi, advised by a National

[2] National Policy on Education (1986), Government of India. Available at: www.education.gov.in/en/mahila-samakhya-programme.

[3] On the development of the Mahila Samakhya program, see Ramachandran (2014).

Resource Group with expertise in education, health, gender and law. A State Project Office operated under the Department of Education at the state level to guide the activities of district-level teams. With funding from the central government and external agencies, Mahila Samakhya was piloted in Gujarat, Karnataka and UP in 1988 and later extended to 11 states and 130 districts.

A hybrid institution, Mahila Samakhya was designed to have official state authority along with managerial autonomy over its internal operations. The Mahila Samakhya Uttar Pradesh (MSUP) branch functions under the aegis of UP's Department of Education but retains administrative control over personnel decisions and local programming. MSUP became operational in 1990 in five districts, later expanding into 19 districts, 77 blocks and 5,853 villages across the state (IIM-A 2014). Program villages were chosen based on an assessment of poverty and social marginalization and typically had a high share of Scheduled Caste (SC) and Scheduled Tribe (ST) populations. MSUP has worked on various issues affecting rural women and supports government programming for disadvantaged girls. Forging an organizational identity distinct from the education bureaucracy was central to MSUP's development. MSUP diverged from UP's legalistic model of bureaucracy; instead it was oriented toward undoing "*the processes and dynamics of patriarchy*" that excluded women and girls from equal participation in the public sphere.[4] Attention to gender inequality was inscribed into MSUP's administrative processes, including hiring decisions, training and gender-based programming.

At the heart of its gender-oriented approach, MSUP developed a grassroots network of women's associations (*mahila sanghas*) throughout its coverage area. These *sanghas* are village organizations working for women's collective interests, and their members are mainly landless and Dalit, though they can include other lower castes and Muslims as well. In contrast to the Self Help Groups (SHGs) promoted by Indian NGOs and government agencies, which focused narrowly on micro credit, MSUP sanghas were conceived as "pressure groups," sources of countervailing power that challenged social discrimination at the intersection of caste and gender. The creation of sanghas was facilitated by MSUP local fieldworkers (*sahyoginis*), women living near target villages, who often had disadvantaged backgrounds. Each fieldworker was assigned to oversees activities in a cluster of ten villages, where they supported sanghas and

[4] Interview with senior official from Mahila Samakhya, Lucknow, January 2009.

implemented women's programming. MSUP also had district teams, who managed field activities and coordinated with local administration.[5]

Commitment among MSUP frontline workers to the mission of women's empowerment was strengthened through personnel decisions, training and organizational processes. Along with education credentials, the application and interview process at MSUP emphasized communication skills and a demonstrated ability to work with disadvantaged women.[6] The importance of communication was reinforced in organizational meetings, as I observed in three study districts. Meetings in each district covered different thematic issues but had a common format. A typical meeting began with folk songs celebrating women's capabilities. Fieldworkers sat on the floor in a circle with senior district team members. The flattening of organizational hierarchy helped foster discussion, irrespective of age, rank and level of education. Fieldworkers were encouraged to share their experiences with sangha women in villages, to interrogate MSUP's program activities, and importantly, to freely express disagreements with senior staff. Strategies for how to support sangha women in villages were discussed frequently. District team meetings were similarly conducted during monitoring visits by MSUP officials stationed in Lucknow. In two district monitoring visits that I attended, state-level officials sat on the floor with fieldworkers and participated in meeting rituals. They gave special attention to village-level experiences and actively sought fieldworkers' perspectives on the practical difficulties of supporting sangha women.

For fieldworkers, socialization into the practice of deliberation was transformative. Virtually all fieldworkers that I interviewed described the strains of having to "*adjust*" to norms of group-based discussion. Many reported having to acquire new "*habits of speaking*" (*bolne ki adatein*), narrating in detail how they learned to express themselves and disagree with others. Deliberation was viewed as an alien concept and articulating their own perspectives was an uncomfortable activity for fieldworkers, something they needed to hone with practice. Alongside the training conducted internally by MSUP, frontline workers gained confidence in their capacity to deliberate while working externally with sangha women. Through a gradual process, village-level deliberation was aimed at empowering sangha women. Fieldworkers "*entered*" rural communities

[5] Jandhyala (2014) describes Mahila Samakhya's process for creating sanghas.

[6] Interview with MSUP officials, Lucknow and Sitapur 2009. Also see Ramachandran (2014, 51–55).

and built organizational ties with women incrementally. The formation of sanghas took between six and twelve months and required repeated and intensive village discussions. Initially, fieldworkers had to put the women's empowerment agenda to one side; instead they worked to identify the more immediate needs of rural women and their families. A retired MSUP official with experience working across the state explained:

> When we would first enter a rural community, we would have no agenda. We would just try to understand the system within the community. If we started talking about "gender," "education" and "rights" they [the village] would throw us out ... So we would go there and try to understand the community and its needs first.[7]

The tactics fieldworkers employed for establishing community ties varied somewhat depending on the geography and sociocultural context of each district. In Chitrakoot district, for example, fieldworkers connected with women through the prism of water scarcity, a recurring crisis in the drought-prone region of Bundelkhand, where women and girls were responsible for collecting water. Meanwhile, in Bahraich district, where annual flooding made it difficult to access services, fieldworkers helped women identify various coping strategies. Gradually, they inched toward more controversial topics, such as the discrepancy in agricultural wages of women and men. Socially sensitive topics, such as domestic violence and child marriage, were broached only after fieldworkers had built a trusting relationship with the sangha women.

Fostering deliberation among sangha members took considerable time and required fieldworkers to train women on how to conduct public meetings, slowly building their confidence in speaking and self-expression. Fieldworkers promoted village-level deliberation by connecting sangha women's practical needs to MSUP's mandate for girls' education. In each village, fieldworkers established a women's literacy center (*mahila saksharta kendra*). The centers taught basic literacy and numeracy skills in a practical fashion, such as how to read signs to catch a bus. Additionally, the literacy centers served as public spaces where women could meet and discuss issues outside the restrictive confines of their homes. While discussing their collective needs, sangha women also learned about public programs, such as schemes for upgrading village footpaths and sanitation. As sanghas matured, fieldworkers introduced the topics of girls' education and health. Sanghas were mobilized

[7] Interview with former State Project Director, Mahila Samakhya, Lucknow, January 2009.

to conduct school enrollment campaigns, identify barriers to attendance and support girls who were at risk of dropping out. When the physical safety of women and girls emerged as a key concern, MSUP fieldworkers encouraged collective problem-solving to find practical ways of addressing it. In focus group discussions conducted in nine villages across the three study districts, sangha women consistently observed that physical insecurity when traveling to school acted as a deterrent for lower-caste girls. In four of the villages, sanghas had worked with MSUP fieldworkers to form youth groups comprising adolescent girls (*mina manch*) and boys (*sathi sangathan*).[8] The groups met after school to support educational activities in their villages. In some groups, children were paired to walk together to school, with older children accompanying younger ones. In Saharanpur district, where problems of alcoholism and domestic violence surfaced, MSUP supported the creation of an informal women's court (*nari adalat*) managed by sangha women. I observed that the court held regular hearings and made decisions on cases affecting women, sometimes in collaboration with village authorities and local law enforcement.[9] Police agencies drew on witness testimony and collective decisions from the women's court, an example of how sanghas engaged in the coproduction of women's security.

The mission to empower women and challenge patriarchal norms was furthered by MSUP's commitment to deliberation. MSUP staff were encouraged to interpret policies in a flexible way, to address practical conditions on the ground. A senior official explained: "*We are constantly planning, revising and adapting, so our work stays engaged with the field … and in the field, new challenges keep coming.*"[10] The importance attached to deliberation was evident from MSUP's personnel decisions, training and administrative processes. For example, the qualifications required for the fieldworker (*sahyogini*) position included not only formal credentials but also communication skills, the ability to consider alternative viewpoints and, crucially, a demonstrated capacity to work with disadvantaged women.[11] The importance of deliberation was reinforced in how meetings and institutional decisions

[8] Focus group discussions with sangha members (Mathura, Saharanpur and Sitapur), January–April 2009.

[9] Participant observation of women's court proceedings and police officer interviews in Saharanpur (February–March 2009).

[10] Interview with senior MSUP official, Lucknow, January 2009.

[11] Interview with MSUP officials, Lucknow, January 2009. On Mahila Samakhya's approach to staff selection, see Ramachandran (2014, 51–55).

were conducted. From sahyoginis all the way up to district leadership, MSUP's local agents were encouraged to give perspectives on policies and question ordinary practices. To illustrate, in a meeting I attended in Mathura, MSUP staff members sat together on the floor in a circle, with no distinctions made based on rank, age or experience. The meeting opened with songs, and then staff members took turns describing field experiences, identifying achievements as well as roadblocks to their work. Fieldworkers shared their experiences with village sanghas and discussed strategies for how to overcome social barriers to women's collective action.

Mobilizing Dalit women to challenge patriarchy and caste norms brought MSUP fieldworkers into conflict with village men and upper castes. Most fieldworkers themselves came from rural, socioeconomically disadvantaged households. Traveling confidently through village hamlets, their physical mobility and assertiveness challenged patriarchal norms that restricted women to the confines of the home. Fieldworkers would also get involved in village caste conflicts while engaging with sanghas. In focus group discussions, nearly all fieldworkers narrated experiences of harassment from upper castes. Fieldworkers who were Dalit recalled the angry glances, insults and threats they encountered when walking through upper-caste hamlets, often from men. Upper-caste fieldworkers, meanwhile, risked being ostracized by members of their own caste. Working closely with Dalit women, they breached norms forbidding close interactions and sharing of meals with different castes. Fieldworkers took these challenges in their stride, observable from their confidence in village-level meetings.

However, managing caste conflict was hardly straightforward. Fieldworkers noted how the political assertiveness of Dalits had grown in recent years. As discussed in Chapter 4, the Bahujan Samaj Party's rise amplified the electoral representation and political consciousness of Dalits in UP. Dalits (including sangha women) were encouraged to speak in public spaces, attend village assemblies (*gram sabhas*) and demand inclusion in matters of village governance. These changes sparked a counterreaction from upper castes. More than half of the fieldworkers I spoke with reported experiencing a backlash from village upper castes. The backlash could take multiple forms, including public insults, vandalism and the defacing of Dalit homes and community centers (*samudayak bhawans*). For example, in two separate villages in Mathura, Dalit women informed me that human feces was left at the doorstep of sangha meeting spaces. In a third village, I learned that feces were left outside the kitchen shed of a government primary school, after a sangha woman, who was Dalit, was hired to cook the midday meal. According to the sangha women I interviewed, the denigration of these spaces was intended to silence and intimidate Dalits.

According to MSUP fieldworkers, upper-caste backlash was a response to the growing assertiveness of Dalit women, an inescapable part of challenging the status quo. Additionally, the public nature of caste conflict helped signal MSUP's commitment to supporting Dalit women and combating social discrimination, something that sangha women also noted in focus group discussions. Fieldworkers observed that village conflicts helped them identify bold women, who were willing to take risks. Social conflict thus performed important functions. After identifying "*confident women*" (*himmatwali mahilaen*), fieldworkers encouraged them to take on leadership roles in sanghas.[12] The fear of conflict, however, continue to pose concerns for safety and compelled some Dalit women to drop out of sanghas. When threats became serious, involving physical violence against fieldworkers and sangha members, senior MSUP officials took direct administrative action. They used MSUP's legal standing within the state to report incidents to law enforcement agencies and issue legal notices to village *panchayats*. These actions sent a strong warning about the consequences of violating the law, including the SC-ST Prevention of Atrocities Act, which criminalized caste-based discrimination.

7.2.2 The KGBV School Program for Disadvantaged Girls

Having examined Mahila Samakhya's organizational aims and deliberative In the previous subsection, I now analyze how the agency has promoted the education of disadvantaged girls. I examine MSUP's implementation of the Kasturba Gandhi Balika Vidyalaya (KGBV) scheme, a national program launched in 2004 for adolescent girls who dropped out before completing the eighth grade. KGBVs were residential girls' schools that provided free education, meals and accommodation, along with healthcare and other social services. The program targeted girls from underprivileged backgrounds, including Dalit, tribal and Muslim communities. KGBV schools were established in educationally backward blocks, localities with below-average literacy for women and compratively high

[12] Interviews with MSUP fieldworkers, Sitapur district, June 2009.

gender disparities in education. The KGBV scheme was designed to help students complete eighth grade and transition to the secondary level of schooling, the equivalent of high school in India.[13] The state of UP had 746 KGBV schools overseen by the Department of Education, along with 33 KGBV schools managed by MSUP.

I conducted fieldwork in four KGBV schools run by MSUP. The schools were well-functioning learning environments. Students appeared healthy and engaged in classroom and extracurricular activities.[14] Health and nutrition were core components of programming in KGBV schools. Upon enrollment in school, a health profile was created for each student and checked regularly. Girls were frequently malnourished, making it difficult to engage in classes. While screening their physical development, KGBV teachers observed a transformation in girls' classroom participation. During a class session I observed, teachers asked students to share their career aspirations. A Dalit girl stood up and stated with poise, "*I want to be prime minister of India.*"[15] She went on to note that, if a Dalit woman could govern India's largest state (referring to Mayawati, the erstwhile chief minister of UP), then why could she not lead the country. MSUP's teachers actively supported girls' participation and self-expression. Student progress was monitored regularly and discussed with parents at quarterly intervals. Parents who I interviewed expressed a high degree of satisfaction with the KGBV schools, notwithstanding their initial apprehensions about residential schooling.

Building on its women's empowerment agenda, MSUP established a "*gender-sensitive*" teaching model in KGBV schools.[16] As per MSUP's internal policy, teachers were hired through a competitive application process that prioritized two dimensions: (1) "aptitude," covering academic qualifications, professional experience and achievements; and (2) a "gender" component that assessed candidates through interviews and written work on their understanding of patriarchy and ability to work with disadvantaged women. After selection, KGBV teachers were put through a rigorous training program informally referred to as "*de-learning.*" The concept of de-learning was linked to socio-psychological theories of gender discrimination. The training aimed to change standard

[13] The KGBV program was recently extended to cover grades 9–10. See http://samagra.mhrd.gov.in/kgbv.html.

[14] As a participant observer, I engaged with the KGBV students and held activity sessions on self-defense and Hindustani classical music.

[15] Interview with girls, KGBV school visit, Sitapur, July 2009.

[16] Author interview with senior MSUP officials, Lucknow, March 2009.

teaching methods and perceptions that reinforced gender stereotypes.[17] Whereas the conventional approach to teaching in government schools emphasized rote learning from textbooks and the completion of the grade-wise curriculum for exams, MSUP's teacher training promoted participatory methods and attention to gendered power dynamics in the classroom.[18] Teachers were encouraged to discuss competing viewpoints with students and question the depiction of how women and girls in textbooks. In interviews, KGBV teachers noted that training provided by MSUP departed significantly from their previous teaching experiences based on the regular curriculum. As one teacher put it, teaching in the KGBV required "*listening, instilling confidence in students, and helping them find their own 'awaaz' [voice].*" The objective, she explained, was to "*transform the girls, within the classroom and out in the village.*"[19]

MSUP's innovative programming for KGBV schools also relied on trust between fieldworkers and disadvantaged households. The process of identifying adolescent girls who had dropped out of school and persuading their parents to re-enroll them was daunting; frequently, it resulted in conflicts within households and between village groups. In interviews, parents recounted their unpleasant experiences with the government school system, which in some cases compelled girls to drop out. For example, Dalit girls risked being harassed by upper-caste boys while walking to and from school. Stories of sexual assault and other forms of gender-based violence circulated in villages. Dalit children also experienced insults from upper caste students as well as schoolteachers. As some parents noted, teachers would use abusive language when scolding children, calling them "*good for nothing*" (*nikamma*) and unfit for studies.[20] Participant observation conducted in government primary schools corroborated these perceptions. In several schools, I observed teachers asking Dalit students to mop floors, sweep the veranda and make tea. These indignities left parents skeptical about KGBV schools. Sending adolescent girls away from home also raised fears of mistreatment, even sexual abuse.[21] To allay parental concerns, MSUP fieldworkers

[17] Interviews with MSUP officials, Lucknow, February 2009.

[18] Interviews with government school teachers, multiple districts, January–March 2009. See Saxena and Mehrotra (2014) for a discussion of Mahila Samakhya's approach to teaching, which bears resemblances to the critical pedagogy of Paolo Freire (1970).

[19] Interview with teacher at KGBV, Sitapur, March 2009.

[20] Interviews with parents in study villages, Mathura, Sitapur and Saharanpur, February–April 2009.

[21] Several parents cited girls' safety as a significant barrier to participation in the KGBV program.

and sangha women visited households and cited positive examples of educated girls from within the same caste communities. In a village in Mathura, for instance, a Dalit fieldworker tried to build confidence in parents by sharing her personal experiences, describing her initial misgivings about sending her own daughter to the KGBV school.[22]

Along with intensive communication, MSUP identified ways to adjust KGBV program rules to make schooling more attractive to disadvantaged households. In a KGBV school in Sitapur district, MSUP fieldworkers joined hands with sangha members to learn why parental participation had been low at school meetings and family visitation days, normally Sundays. They learned that rural households traveled to the town center on Mondays, when the local market was open. The KGBV experimented by shifting the weekly school holiday from Sunday to Monday, allowing parents to complete market errands and meet their daughters in school the same day. The small change in rules lessened the burden of participation for disadvantaged households saving them the time and expense of an additional journey into town. Subsequently, teachers reported an increase in visits from parents and greater engagement in parent–teacher meetings. In the school principal's words, "*We have brought the community to the KGBV.*"[23] Likewise, in focus group discussions, parents showed appreciation for the adjustments made by KGBV staff, who sacrificed their Sundays to facilitate parent–teacher meetings.[24] Households reciprocated by engaging in social functions at the school, contributing to religious festivals and enrichment activities.

Maintaining trust with parents brought challenges for the KGBV program as well. In Saharanpur district, MSUP tried to integrate girls from the Deobandi community, a conservative Muslim sect. In many cases, girls would be removed from school after the fifth grade because formal schooling was thought to interfere with religious teachings.[25] MSUP fieldworkers belonging to the same religious community described the difficulties of persuading family members, especially men, to enroll their daughters in the KGBV school. As one remarked: "*Sensitizing men to the issues [of girls' education] and listening to their concerns was necessary to gain the household's trust.*"[26] Fieldworkers reassured parents

[22] Participant observation with MSUP fieldworker, Mathura, February 2009.
[23] Interview with school principal, KGBV, Sitapur, March 2009.
[24] Focus group discussion with parents at KGBV, Sitapur, March 2009.
[25] This sentiment was expressed in interviews with parents in Deobandi Muslim households in Saharanpur.
[26] Interview with MSUP fieldworker, Saharanpur, February 2009.

about the KGBV's recognition of different faiths, noting, for instance, the facilities available for Muslim students to hold daily prayers (*namaz*). They also stressed the offering of Urdu language classes, which some parents found attractive.[27] District staff in Saharanpur also sought help from local religious leaders to encourage girls' enrollment. These efforts produced mixed results. As MSUP fieldworkers acknowledged, the integration of Muslim girls remained a challenge for them. They also found it more difficult to mobilize participation from sangha members belonging to the Deobandi community. If they pushed too far, they risked spoiling their relations with target households. Maintaining MSUP's standing within the community thus remained a source of tension for fieldworkers.

In some situations, fieldworkers were compelled to take a stronger stand. Where deliberation alone seemed ineffective, they applied administrative-legal mechanisms, leveraging MSUP's official recognition and credibility within the state. In Mathura district, for example, some caste communities practiced "double marriage," which involved having a pair of sisters married off together. Double marriage allowed families to save money on dowry and wedding costs. The younger of the two sisters, often too young to even realize that she was being married, would be forced to quit school. To counter such practices, MSUP district staff mobilized sangha members to raise awareness in village gatherings, where they highlighted the injustice and illegality of double marriage. I attended one such gathering in Mathura's Chhata block, where fieldworkers stressed the benefits of delaying marriage and enabling girls to complete higher levels of education. They also discussed the legal ramifications of child marriage, pointing to cases of police action taken in nearby villages. The gathering turned into a shouting match. Some residents challenged fieldworkers for interfering in private family affairs. The public argument brought to light an egregious case of a twelve-year-old girl, who was taken out of school after her relatives promised her hand in marriage to a middle-aged man from another village. MSUP fieldworkers visited the girl's home, and after failing to persuade her parents to cancel the marriage, they lodged a complaint with the police. As a legally recognized agency, MSUP relied on its official standing to report child marriage and other violations of law. Pursuing legal action was risky, however, and could backfire. Fieldworkers resorted to using the law enforcement mechanism only in rare and exceptional cases, it being fully

[27] MSUP fieldworker perspectives were corroborated by interviews I conducted with Muslim households in study villages in Saharanpur district.

cognizant that such a step could sow distrust and weaken ties within their target communities.

7.2.3 Sustaining a Deliberative Subculture Within a Legalistic Bureaucracy

In this subsection, I examine how MSUP maintained a subculture of deliberation while operating within UP's legalistic bureaucracy. Before proceeding, though, it would help to consider alternative explanations for why MSUP's programming for girls' education may have been effective. The evidence presented suggests that MSUP frontline workers induced conflict within society. Alternatively, one may suppose that MSUP's administrative resources are what contributed most to implementation.[28] Local bureaucracies in India are often pressed for resources, which constrains their ability to implement public services (Aiyar and Bhattacharya 2016; Dasgupta and Kapur 2020). In that regard, MSUP-run schools likely benefited from additional administrative support and resources. Yet, UP's Department of Education also received an infusion of resources under Sarva Shiksha Abhiyan (SSA), with dedicated funds and personnel for gender programming, including district-level gender coordinators. The UP state government has a poor record of utilizing central government funds earmarked for social programs such as girls' education, raising questions about the links between resource allocations and implementation. It is noteworthy, moreover, that MSUP resources were allocated not only for education, but also to a broad set of activities: women's health, law, security, village governance, etc. KGBV schools sought to address multiple, interconnected barriers to girls' education, including health and nutritional deficits, suggesting that *how* resources got utilized also mattered for the quality of implementation.

A second explanation highlights the importance of institutional autonomy from political interference (Geddes 1994; Evans 1995). Research on institutional "pockets of effectiveness" suggests that autonomy from patronage politics helps sustain relatively high levels of bureaucratic performance in developing countries (Leonard 2010; Roll 2014; McDonnell 2020). In India's primary education sector, politicization of teacher postings and transfers is found to undermine quality services (Béteille 2015). Within UP, the politicization of government teachers and their unions is

[28] On the importance of administrative resources for policy enforcement in developing countries, see Amengual (2016).

shown to weaken school accountability (Kingdon and Muzammil 2012). Given these conditions, MSUP's autonomy from the education bureaucracy was a boon, since it provided institutional space for the agency to formulate goals and instill frontline worker commitment to women's empowerment. Autonomy was supported by MSUP's legal status as a semiautonomous agency. In that sense, MSUP likely benefited from legalistic bureaucracy's commitment to hierarchical boundaries. MSUP frontline staff also relied on the agency's legal standing to press for state action on behalf of women and girls. District teams, whose members included lawyers, were conversant with UP's administrative-legal processes, which they utilized often to advance their work.

However, autonomy can only partially account for how MSUP overcame societal hurdles and effectively implemented girls' education reforms.[29] Department of Education officials referred to MSUP as a government program, but MSUP staff had neither the civil service protections nor the high salaries associated with public employment. Moreover, institutional autonomy was not simply granted by law, but instead had to be claimed and fought for on an ongoing basis. MSUP staff often challenged bureaucratic rules that curbed their operational autonomy and routinely got embroiled in conflicts with UP state officials. Challenging the wider bureaucracy and its rules formed part of MSUP's institutional repertoire. As MSUP fieldworkers narrated:

RESPONDENT 1: District administration is wedded to their rules (*sarkari niyam*). However many times we may try to clarify our requests [for support], it doesn't matter. They will keep finding rules to tie our hands.

RESPONDENT 2: And neither are we willing to bow down to state officials![30]

The gulf between MSUP's activist stance and the legalistic orientation of UP state officials led to frequent disagreements. Moreover, MSUP fieldworkers identified strongly with the marginalized communities they served. They supported sangha women when they voiced collective demands on district administration. In Sitapur, for instance, sangha women from different villages joined hands to lodge complaints about teacher absenteeism. MSUP fieldworkers stood alongside them as they protested outside district education offices.[31] Support from the education bureaucracy was irregular and often contingent on the individuals

[29] As McDonnell (2020, 135–164) suggests, protection from political interference does not guarantee that bureaucratic norms encouraging high performance will take root.

[30] Focus group discussion with MSUP fieldworkers, Saharanpur, March 2009.

[31] Participant observation, Sitapur and Saharanpur, February–April 2009.

occupying positions of authority.[32] Senior MSUP officials in Lucknow often came to the defense of frontline staff.[33] For example, they made formal representations to government line departments and coordinated with district officials to maintain administrative support for fieldworkers. A senior MSUP official explained:

> Resistance to the way we work is very stiff. From here [MSUP's state office] we network with Government of UP agencies and try to orient the bureaucracy about our work ... At times, we get support from District Magistrates ... but maintaining their support is never easy.[34]

Other senior MSUP officials narrated the difficulties of operating as a semi-autonomous agency, emphasizing the tensions of having state institutional authority but also challenging that selfsame authority.[35] MSUP sometimes induced conflicts with the Department of Education as well, for example, by altering KGBV program rules, which broke with the education bureaucracy's commitment to legalism. The department held teacher training at set intervals and applied the state-mandated training curriculum. At MSUP, meanwhile, teacher training was an "*ongoing process*" that was continuously updated with input from gender program experts.[36] An official from the Department of Education expressed misgivings with MSUP's approach:

> You can't segregate yourself from the mainstream system. The [government's education] schemes provide you with a framework to elaborate on and experiment. But the point is that you need to implement things as per the scheme. Don't deviate from the scheme.[37]

To "*deviate*," the official elaborated, meant flouting the standards for teacher training, KGBV school timings, examinations and other departmental rules. MSUP officials saw deviation in a different light. In an environment of patriarchy and caste-based exclusion, the bureaucratic commitment to rules was seen as further marginalizing rural women and girls. Like sangha women, who challenged village hierarchies, MSUP district staff and fieldworkers referred to themselves as "*pressure groups*"

32 Interviews with MSUP fieldworkers, Saharanpur, February 2009.

33 Interviews with MSUP fieldworkers, Saharanpur, February 2009.

34 Interview with MSUP state official, Lucknow, March 2009.

35 Sharma (2008) identifies the tensions in MSUP's status as a semi-autonomous agency. See also Ramachandran (2014), an education expert who narrates her experience of "walking a tightrope" between Mahila Samakhya and the state bureaucracy.

36 Interview with senior official, MSUP State Project Office, Lucknow, January 2009.

37 Interview with senior official, Department of Education, Lucknow, December 2010.

inside the bureaucracy, interrogating its rules and conventions.[38] Conflict with local officials was a source of pride for fieldworkers and reinforced their identity as institutional activists.

MSUP's activist orientation helped sustain frontline worker commitment under adverse conditions. Senior MSUP officials set an example through their own institutional activism, which came in the form of advocacy work. For example, they sought state permission to allow KGBV schools to impart vocational training, including mechanical (*mistri*) skills, conventionally treated as men's work.[39] In a longer advocacy battle, they pressured the UP state government for years to alter KGBV program rules, to permit the residential schools to operate up through the secondary level of education. After completing the eighth grade, KGBV graduates would return to their villages, and in many cases, experienced difficulties joining secondary school. MSUP fieldworkers helped enroll KGBV graduates, but the barriers to girls' participation in higher grades of school were daunting. Disadvantaged girls in particular found it difficult to access secondary schools, which were often too far away. For over a decade, senior MSUP officials petitioned UP's political leadership and the Department of Education for policy changes. Finally, in 2019, the UP government acceded to their demands and extended the KGBV program up to grade twelve.[40] In that way, MSUP's institutional activism went beyond the implementation of reforms to influence the making of social policy. The field-based study of Mahila Samakhya's programming in UP suggests that deliberative bureaucracy can work, even in contexts of social inequality, to support programmatic reforms for girls' education.

7.3 BIHAR: LEGALISTIC BUREAUCRACY AND THE UNFINISHED AGENDA FOR QUALITY EDUCATION

Located to the east of UP, in a densely settled part of the Gangetic plains, Bihar (pop. 104.1 million) is India's third most populous state (see map in Figure 7.1). Bihar is also among India's poorest states and a laggard on multiple dimensions of economic and social development.[41] Child

[38] Interviews with local MSUP staff (multiple districts), January–July 2009.

[39] I observed two KGBVs provide skills training in mechanical (*mistri*) work.

[40] See "54 KGBVs in UP to offer free hostels to girls up to class 12," *Indian Express*, November 22, 2019. Available at: www.hindustantimes.com/education/54-kgbvs-in-up-to-offer-free-hostels-to-girls-of-up-to-class-12/story-iFF5MVe7wLoyGmdPjVCaSL.html.

[41] According to the World Bank, 34 percent of Bihar's population lives below the poverty line. See "Bihar: Poverty Growth and Inequality," *India States Briefs*, World Bank. Available at: www.worldbank.org/en/country/india/brief/india-states-briefs-bihar.

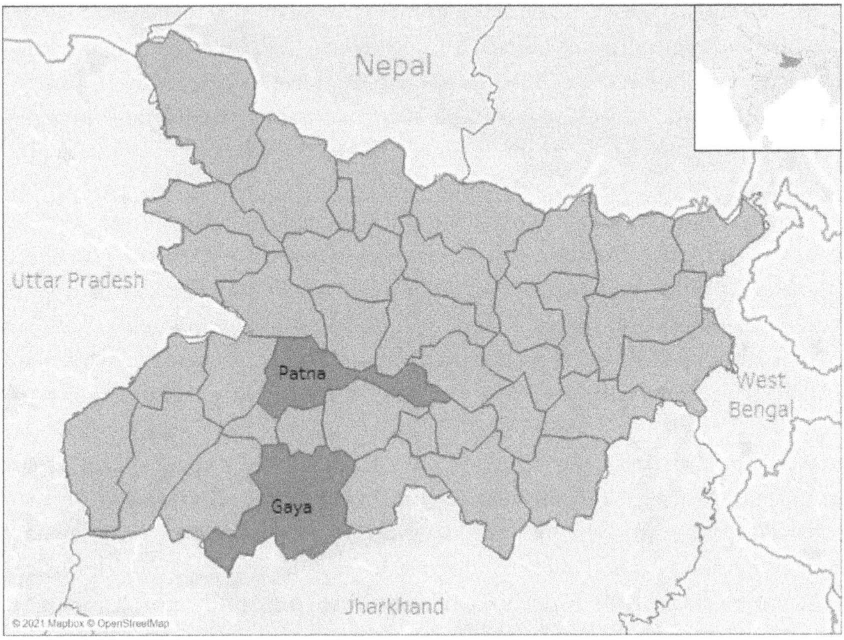

FIGURE 7.1 Study map of Bihar
Note: Main study districts are highlighted.
Source: © Mapbox, © OpenStreetMap.

welfare indicators in Bihar are among the worst globally. Nearly half (48.3 percent) of the children under five years of age are stunted (NFHS-4 2015–16). As shown in Chapter 2, schoolchildren in rural Bihar exhibit exceedingly poor literacy and numeracy. These deprivations follow from decades of misgovernance and failures in public service delivery, which are connected to Bihar's tortuous political history, marked by feudalism, lawlessness, caste violence and corruption. Given frequent breakdowns of public order, observers pegged Bihar as a failed state, epitomizing the "crisis of governability" in India (Kohli 1990).[42]

For multiple reasons, then, one does not expect the state to deliver primary education effectively in Bihar. However, since the early 2000s, Bihar has undergone a remarkable reversal. Political leadership representing a broad coalition of lower castes came to power on an agenda to reform the state. Arresting the state's institutional decline, the Bihar

[42] On Bihar's deteriorating state capacity in the 1990s, see Mathew and Moore (2011, 5–6). Also see "Special Report: An Area of Darkness," *The Economist*, February 21, 2004.

government achieved impressive changes in law and order and social welfare programming. As Singh and Stern suggest, however, the reforms in Bihar can be seen as "both a glass half full and a glass half empty" (2013, xxvii). Despite some notable improvements, government primary schools in Bihar have exhibited exceedingly poor quality services, producing stagnant learning outcomes.

This section seeks to explain the mixed results of state initiatives in Bihar to improve the delivery of primary education. Drawing on three months of field research, along with an analysis of official documents and secondary literature, I find that Bihar's governing elites led an extraordinary shift in bureaucratic norms. The state moved away from neo-patrimonial rule and encouraged bureaucratic commitment to legalism. However, I argue that political support for quality education was stifled on the front lines of the state, where expectations about administrative "discipline" and rule compliance dominated reform efforts, weakening the uptake of innovative classroom practices by schoolteachers. This section begins by exploring the sociopolitical factors leading up to Bihar's institutional turnaround, which I suggest was the culmination of an endogenous process of institutional change. Next, I connect the shift toward legalistic bureaucracy to subsequent developments in primary schooling, including the noteworthy gains in enrollments and the provision of infrastructure and teaching inputs. Amid these changes, I find that legalistic bureaucracy in Bihar has also resisted reforms that were designed to enhance the quality of education services, contributing to the stagnation of student learning in government schools.

7.3.1 Forging an Institutional Turnaround: From "Jungle Raj" to the "New Bihar"

Among the BIMARU states of northern India – an acronym for the less developed Hindi belt states – Bihar stands out for its underperformance. There are profound historical and political reasons for Bihar's underdevelopment. Colonial institutions in Bihar were in many respects similar to those in UP. Under the land revenue system of *zamindari*, the state bureaucracy reinforced upper-caste dominance. In the colonial estate of Darbhanga, for instance, local administration was controlled by upper castes, who constituted a large proportion of "Circle Managers," officials in charge of revenue collection within their administrative divisions (Henningham 1983). Circle Mangers were supported by frontline staff, from the *tehsildar* down to the *patwari*, who maintained village land records. Collusion between local officials and landowners was a well-institutionalized feature of Darbhanga's land revenue system (Henningham 1983, 43–45). Taking advantage of mass illiteracy, patwaris extracted rents from peasants and altered land records to favor upper-caste notables, a system that propagated the economic dependency of tenant farmers and landless laborers. Zamindari was abolished under the 1950 Bihar Land Reforms Act, the largest landholdings confiscated by the state. However, land ceiling and tenancy regulations were poorly enforced and zamindars continued to operate *de facto* (Jannuzi 1974, 37–41). Informal practices of moneylending, at exorbitant rates of interest, tied peasants into knots of intergenerational debt and labor bondage (Sharma 2005).

Exploitative economic relations were interlaced with Bihar's highly stratified caste system. Upper-caste landowners (Brahmin, Bhumihar, Rajput and *Kayastha*) comprised 20 percent of the population, but they dominated state politics and educational institutions (Verma 1991, 1142). Tenant farmers and merchants, from a heterogeneous swathe of middle and backward castes (Yadav, Kurmi, Koeri and Baniya), were the majority (60 percent) of Bihar's population. At the bottom of the social hierarchy, agricultural laborers belonged to various Dalit *jatis*, or subcastes (Chamar, Dusadh, Dom, Pasi and Musahar); they were mostly landless and economically dependent on upper castes. Hierarchy and discrimination were inscribed into the very names given to jatis in Bihar. Bhumihar meant "landowner" while Musahar translated literally to "rat-eater." Downtrodden castes practiced untouchability among each other as well. The state eventually recognized Mahadalits, the most oppressed among Dalit castes, as a separate administrative category. Feudalism and discrimination continued into the postcolonial period. Upper castes controlled the state politically and held coveted posts in education, the judiciary and police (Jha 1970). Clientelism became entrenched as landowners acted as intermediaries between peasants and local administration.

The Congress Party governed Bihar with a majority of assembly seats in the 1950s and 1960s. However, factional rivalries and upper-caste infighting hindered the functioning of the party (Roy 1966). Conflicts between rival castes and frequent splits in the succession of leadership undermined governance. In a pattern akin to the fractious politics of neighboring UP, the Bihar Congress Party saw internecine conflicts and the cycling of state leadership. Political currents took a new course in the 1970s as regional parties representing Other Backward Classes (OBCs) rose to power.[43] OBC membership in the state legislature increased from 8 percent in 1962 to 20 percent in 1971, while upper-caste membership decreased from 58 to 45 percent.[44] As OBC farmers began acquiring agricultural land, their growing economic clout led to conflicts with Bhumihars and other upper castes.[45] Social conflict intensified as different caste groups raised private militias to protect their economic interests, policing the land as well as social boundaries.[46] The political assertion of OBCs and Dalits led to retributive violence against subordinate castes, "to remind them of their lowly status and to create segregation between pure and impure castes within society" (Nandan and Santhosh 2019, 429). Along with caste conflict, politics in Bihar became associated with crime and corruption.[47] Having amassed significant wealth in the 1970s, OBC farmers mimicked the political tactics of upper-caste landlords, using surplus resources "to enter networks of politicians, bureaucrats and criminals which allowed them to appropriate development resources on a large scale" (Wilson 1999, 318).

Political mobilization of OBCs reached new heights under Lalu Prasad Yadav. A charismatic politician, Yadav led the assault against upper-caste hegemony. He underscored the humiliations that downtrodden groups had suffered at the hands of upper-caste landlords. Demands for social dignity became a clarion call for OBC and lower-caste voters. The political aim of securing dignity (*samman*) for lower castes was juxtaposed against the goals of public order and development, expressed forcefully in the slogan, "*Vikas nahin, samman chahiye*" (We want dignity, not development). Yadav's narrative around dignity

43 OBC parties were inspired by socialist leaders of the farmers' movement (Roy 1970). The Congress Socialist Party was founded in 1934 in Patna, where socialist leader Ram Manohar Lohia also founded the Samyukt Socialist Party.

44 The percentage of OBC MLAs peaked at 31 percent in 1968, under B.P. Mandal's government. Belonging to the Yadav caste, Mandal was India's first OBC chief minister. Mandal also chaired the national commission that called for extending caste-based reservations in public employment to OBCs.

45 OBCs benefited from anti-zamindari laws, acquiring land previously belonging to upper-caste landlords (Sharma 2005).

46 Caste militias exemplified the "privatization of law and order" in Bihar (Das 1986). Mobilized in response to Maoist peasant uprisings, armed militias like the Bhumi Sena, run by Kurmis and the Bhumihar-sponsored Ranvir Sena, became ensnared in caste conflicts as well (Louis 2002; Kumar 2009).

47 Witsoe (2011; 2013) describes the interplay between politics and corruption in Bihar. Vaishnav (2017) focuses on Bihar as an example of the wider criminalization of Indian politics.

was a milestone in Bihar's political trajectory, as it mobilized the poor against upper-caste landlords.[48] Emphasizing dignity politics, Yadav popularized the slogan "*Bhurabal hatao*" (Remove upper castes), a play on Prime Minister Indira Gandhi's campaign slogan "*Garibi hatao*" (Remove poverty).

The intermingling of caste politics, crime and corruption also reached new heights under Yadav, who served as Bihar's chief minister from 1990 to 1997. Over this period, India's economy grew at 6 percent annually, while Bihar's growth rate was stuck at 2.7 percent. Yadav used his political position to assert OBC control over the state machinery, evidenced by the frequent transfer of upper-caste bureaucrats. He appointed OBCs (especially Yadavs) out of turn to key administrative posts, leaving many positions vacant for extended periods. Recruitment of frontline functionaries (e.g., schoolteachers, health workers and police officers) also lay dormant. Political interference in bureaucratic decisions was commonplace and public resources remained underutilized by line departments. In 2002, Bihar's finance department reported that 20 percent of central government fiscal transfers had been left unspent. As Mathew and Moore (2011) suggest, *non*-implementation of public policy under Yadav was more than a byproduct of caste conflict; it was a deliberate political strategy to render the state ineffectual.

Yadav's Bihar became practically synonymous with corruption. After he formed a new party, the Rashtriya Janata Dal (RJD), Yadav resigned in 1997 amid a scandal over the embezzlement of $285 million from the state exchequer.[49] Subsequently, he installed his wife, Rabri Devi, as Bihar's chief minister, through whom he continued to exercise political control. The Yadav regime (1990–2005) helped mobilize OBCs, Muslims and other downtrodden groups, but its politics of identity was often exclusionary, benefiting Yadavs in particular more than other castes. The rural poor in Bihar saw little improvement in their quality of life. The Yadav regime also cemented Bihar's reputation as a "Jungle Raj." Administrative rules were often flouted and public order crumbled under the weight of clientelism and corruption. Violent crimes, such as kidnapping and murder, became normalized. The state bureaucracy,

48 On the politics of dignity in Bihar, see Roy (2013). On Yadav's anti-development politics, see Witsoe (2013). Bhu-ra-ba-l was an acronym for upper castes – Bhumihar, Rajput, Babhan (Brahmin) and Lala (Baniya) – accused of exploiting the poor.

49 After prolonged investigation, Yadav was convicted for the infamous "Fodder Scam" in 2013.

as an observer put it, had "withered away" and public services were emasculated (Sharma 1995, 2587).

On the verge of institutional collapse, Bihar underwent a dramatic reversal when political changes swept the state in 2005. Nitish Kumar and his Janata Dal United (JDU) party came to power by stitching together a coalition of lower castes left behind by Yadav's regime, together with Bharatiya Janata Party (BJP) support from upper-caste voters. While associated with insurgent corruption, the electoral mobilization of underprivileged groups in Bihar was also a political achievement. In a state with long-standing upper-caste hegemony, corruption was itself part of Yadav's "social justice" agenda; by partaking in the spoils of the state, numerically dominant lower castes were politically included (Witsoe 2011). Lower-caste mobilization was also an important precursor to political efforts to reform Bihar's bureaucracy and systems of local administration. In 2000, Bihar's most prominent Dalit leader, Ram Vilas Paswan, launched the Lok Janshakti Party (LJP). Meanwhile, the OBC leader Nitish Kumar began organizing Mahadalits, a group that continued to be exploited during Yadav's tenure, into a separate voting bloc (Ahuja 2019, 110–115). Dalits, rural women and other social groups that had remained marginalized during Yadav's reign now became the beneficiaries targeted by state programs.

Kumar's government sought to differentiate itself from prior regimes by highlighting "*good governance*" (*sushasana*), understood in terms of administrative discipline and anti-corruption measures (Mukherji and Mukherji 2013). Kumar tightened oversight of the police and introduced legislation against criminality, which signaled the government's seriousness about law and order. The Bihar Special Courts Act of 2009 established fast-track courts for trials of well-known criminals. The Bihar Lokayukta Act was an anti-corruption measure that enabled swift prosecution of bureaucrats suspected of corruption. The law also allowed for the confiscation of property of bureaucrats if they were found to have assets disproportionate to known sources of income. Bureaucratic discipline was tied politically to the state government's emphasis on public service delivery. To monitor frontline administration, Kumar's regime introduced a program called Janata ke Darbar men Mukhyamantri (Chief Minister in the People's Court). An open court (*darbar*) was instituted weekly in Kumar's residence, inviting citizens to register complaints and petitions, which were dispensed speedily. The Janata Darbar was formalized and linked to a digital platform under Bihar's Public Grievance Redressal Act. The new law called for efficient public service delivery, guaranteeing a response to citizen requests within a specified time. From my observations in two Bihar districts (Patna and Gaya), I found the Janata Darbar had been enthusiastically adopted by district administration. On the assigned day, long queues would form outside the District Magistrate's (DM) office, as citizens of various social backgrounds arrived to lodge claims on local administration. The DM would hear citizens' demands and direct line departments to respond swiftly, often on the spot.[50] The emphasis on bureaucratic discipline extended to social services as well (Verma, Gupta and Birner 2018; Banerji 2015). To strengthen implementation of the Integrated Child Development Services (ICDS), a national program for early child nutrition and health, Bihar introduced strict monitoring and reporting of gaps in services. A system of random inspections of village ICDS centers was instituted and stringent penalties were imposed on errant officials, which included suspension for absenteeism and other irregularities.[51] State efforts to inculcate bureaucratic commitment to rules was matched by the activities of civil society organizations and social activists from below, who used the Right to Information Act and other accountability mechanisms to demand prompt services from the state (Verma, Gupta and Birner 2018; Jha 2018).

Although the impact of governance reforms on policy outcomes appears to have been mixed, the reform agenda resonated with Bihar's voters (Vaishnav and Swanson 2015; Kumar and Ranjan 2009). The 2010 state assembly election was billed as a watershed victory for Kumar, whose JDU alliance with the BJP won 206 of 243 seats. Lalu Yadav's RJD and alliance partners were decimated, mustering a mere twenty-five seats. The election was read by many as a victory for development (*vikas*).[52] Kumar had campaigned vigorously on a good governance platform, explicitly connecting primary education and other social programs to the effort to combat corruption. At a political rally in 2010, Kumar highlighted the state's new anti-corruption legislation. Public servants found guilty of amassing disproportionate assets, he proclaimed, would be sent to jail and their confiscated properties would be converted into government schools.[53] Intrigued by these developments,

[50] Participant observation, Patna and Gaya districts, December 2013–January 2014.

[51] Verma, Gupta and Birner (2018) report that 250 Anganwadi Sevikas (ICDS workers) were suspended by the Social Welfare Department in 2009–2010 and another 167 were suspended in 2011–2012.

[52] "From Goonda Raj to Vikas Raj," NDTV News, November 24, 2010. Available at: www.ndtv.com/assembly/nitishs-bihar-from-goonda-raj-to-vikas-raj-440147.

[53] "More from Nitish: Homes of Corrupt and Jailed Officials Will be Used as Schools," *Indian Express*, November 2, 2010. Available at: https://indianexpress.com/article/india/latest-news/more-from-nitish-homes-of-corrupt-and-jailed-officials-will-be-used-as-schools.

international researchers arrived to document the "New Bihar" (Singh and Stern 2013). Some changes brought (cautious) optimism, but material deprivations and governance challenges continued to afflict the state. Bihar was no longer considered a failed state. However, it continued to display massive deficits in the quality of public services. According to Dr. Rukmini Banerji from Pratham, a globally recognized education NGO with extensive experience working in Bihar, "[T]here is political will at the top and there are aspirations and demands from below. It is the middle of the delivery system that is rusted and needs overhauling and repair. The need is to understand the nature of the rust in the system" (2011, 39). In what follows, I delve into the "rust" to demonstrate how the commitment to legalistic bureaucratic norms helped facilitate Bihar's school expansion but at the same time, constrained the implementation of quality-enhancing education reforms.

7.3.2 Primary School Expansion

Reestablishing law and order was a central pillar of Kumar's regime. The police, social services and other frontline departments were under pressure to demonstrate "discipline" and observe rules.[54] The state government assigned high priority to discipline within the education sector in particular. After decades of accumulated neglect, Bihar's primary school system was pressured to "catch-up" with other Indian states (Banerji 2011, 34). The *Economic Survey of Bihar* in 2007–2008 reported that almost a quarter of Bihar's public expenditure went toward education, while two-thirds of all social spending was devoted to the primary level of education. These fiscal allocations were utilized by the education bureaucracy to achieve progress in primary school expansion. Between 2004 and 2012, the number of government primary schools increased from 54,061 to 69,911 and more than 100,000 new classrooms were built. A concerted recruitment drive saw the number of government schoolteachers increase by 50 percent, from 233,887 to 349,538.[55] Disadvantaged students received targeted incentives – free textbooks, uniforms and scholarships conditional on enrollment – under SSA. Between 2005 and 2010, the percentage of out-of-school children aged 5-14 years fell from 20.1 to 6 percent. Special initiatives were launched for girls' education. Notably, the Chief Minister's Cycle Scheme (Mukhya Mantri Cycle Yojana) provided a free bicycle to

[54] Interviews with senior bureaucrats, Patna, December 2013.
[55] Figures from District Information System for Education. Available at: www.dise.in.

girls conditional on their enrollment in secondary school. The program earned media attention and research demonstrated its positive impact girls' participation in school.[56]

Girls' education was an important plank within the state government's policy platform for gender-targeted programming. A community-based anti-poverty program known as Jeevika (meaning "livelihood") was introduced in 2006, with the aim to improve rural livelihoods through the formation of women's Self Help Groups (SHGs).[57] SHGs of ten to fifteen women were established in villages; they received state grants and training to enable group-based savings. Once the SHGs matured, they were assisted with opening bank accounts and eventually federated into larger associations. Studies show that Jeevika brought significant economic and social gains to rural women and their households.[58] Though they were not expressly created for education, SHGs created under Jeevika became involved in monitoring primary schools.[59] From interviews with schoolteachers and parents in four villages, I learned that SHG members supported enrollment campaigns for their local primary schools.[60] They mobilized to improve girls' enrollment in particular, disseminating information to disadvantaged households on the incentives and gender-targeted schemes offered by the government. The Department of Education took the step of including SHG women in the official membership roster for the Village Education Committees (VECs) overseeing primary schools, though village-level implementation was uneven.

Bihar's rapid gains in enrollment and school infrastructure provision occurred in a context of unprecedented political support for primary education. Chief Minister Kumar himself presided over planning meetings with Department of Education officials.[61] Leading educationists, international researchers and civil society organizations were invited to share policy recommendations for improving service delivery. The state government

[56] A study observed a 32 percent increase in secondary school enrollment among girls exposed to the program vis-a-vis a control group (Muralidharan and Prakash 2017).

[57] Jeevika was officially known as the Bihar Rural Livelihoods Project. For more information, see http://brlp.in/.

[58] These gains include better access to credit (Datta 2015) as well as a shift in gender norms (Sanyal, Rao and Majumdar 2015).

[59] Interviews with district education officials, Patna and Gaya districts, January 2014.

[60] Village-level fieldwork in Patna and Gaya districts revealed that while SHGs were involved in school monitoring, their participation was ad hoc and not well institutionalized.

[61] Interviews with senior education officials and civil society representatives, Patna and New Delhi, December 2013.

entered into partnerships with philanthropic agencies and leading education NGOs, such as Pratham and the Azim Premji Foundation, that provided technical expertise on teacher training and curriculum reform. In interviews, representatives from these organizations remarked on the "*unwavering commitment*" of Bihar's state government to education reform. They also noted the bureaucratic leadership's "*openness to ideas*" from NGOs and researchers.[62] The Bihar state government's political commitment to primary education can be contrasted with the lackluster governmental support in neighboring UP (Drèze and Gazdar 1996; Singh 2016, 148–171). As noted earlier, education reforms in UP were mainly driven by central government agencies, with little initiative taken by UP's state government.

Despite the heightened political commitment in Bihar, I observed remarkable similarities in bureaucratic norms across UP and Bihar, particularly at the local level. Field research in Patna and Gaya districts revealed that implementation of education reforms in Bihar was facilitated by the shift in bureaucratic norms toward legalism. Rapid expansion of schooling was driven by intensive, "*mission-mode*" efforts to achieve universal access and school infrastructure targets.[63] A tight inspection system was introduced to ensure that policy inputs reached schools, a departure from the "*leakage*" often observed in Bihar's social programs. Bihar's Department of Education set ambitious targets and monitored the chain of local implementation, from the administrative district and block down to the schooling "*cluster*," which consisted of ten to twelve primary schools.[64] To supervise primary schools, a cadre of Cluster Resource Centre Coordinators (CRCCs) was established and given clear targets for enrollment, midday meal provision and other inputs. These frontline officials reported back regularly to education officials in the district. In a focus group discussion, CRCCs reported an increase in hierarchical oversight, which they perceived as a welcome departure from the past. Summarizing the group's sentiments, an official remarked:

> Overall, I can say that our motivation level has increased. Now the DM's office together with the DEO [District Education Officer] conducts a review of the CRCC. Before, there was never a review of the CRCC ... Did the textbooks reach the school or were they lost in the [monsoon] floods? Nobody knew or paid attention to our work.[65]

[62] Interviews with representatives from Pratham and Azim Premji Foundation, New Delhi and Patna, December 2013.

[63] Interview with senior official, Department of Education, Patna, December 2013.

[64] Interviews with senior officials, SSA State Project Office, Patna, January 2014.

[65] Focus group discussion with CRCCs, Gaya, January 2014.

Other officials similarly stressed the importance of more stringent, routinized monitoring meetings held by district administration. Another CRCC remarked:

> Now, the nature of our meetings is very different. CRCCs who do not perform are given a strict warning. Those who do well are given awards and recognition in front of everyone. This motivates others.[66]

In interviews, district education officials admitted that their earlier practices had been lax. For example, they would remain in their offices and send written orders or collect data from CRCCs over the phone. "*How accurate was the data, who could say?*" an official reflected.[67] Now, they were instructed to conduct field visits in person and ensure that records were accurate, which I witnessed first-hand through participant observation.

The process of "*inspection*," a term district officials used to describe local monitoring, was anchored heavily in administrative rules. In a typical inspection visit to a CRCC office, district officials would scrutinize administrative registers and tally the data collected from schools. The CRCC would normally prepare records in advance, but with unannounced inspections becoming more frequent, they felt the pressure to be extra diligent with record-keeping.[68] Records pertaining to various schooling inputs and performance metrics – student and teacher attendance, the midday meal, and distribution of textbooks, uniforms and SSA incentives – could be scrutinized at a moment's notice. Frontline officials who maintained tidy records were viewed favorably by the Department of Education, earning praise for being "*high performers*."[69] Meanwhile, those who appeared lax (*dhila*) or failed to maintain adequate records risked facing "*serious and direct action*" from senior officials.[70] The demands of legalistic bureaucracy, meted out through inspections and record-keeping, had a cascading effect on bureaucratic behaviors further down the hierarchy. According to a time-use study, CRCCs in Bihar normally spent four to five hours per day in the field visiting schools (Aiyar, Dongre and Davis 2015). During school visits, they prioritized

66 Similar changes are reported by Aiyar, Dongre and Davis (2015).

67 Interview with education official, Patna, December 2013.

68 Focus group discussion with CRCCs, Gaya, January 2014.

69 Interview with senior state official, Department of Education, Patna, December 2013.

70 Interviews and participant observation with local education officials, Patna and Gaya districts, December 2013.

the inspection of administrative records and tabulation of data on attendance, the midday meal and other performance targets. Less time was allocated toward providing teachers with academic guidance, or advising them on other complex tasks, such as encouraging parental engagement in school.

7.3.3 The Stalling of Education Quality Reforms

As the primary school expansion gained pace, the Bihar government turned its attention to the quality of education services. Despite the success of enrollment campaigns, student attendance was irregular and the quality of services woeful. According to ASER surveys, between 2007 and 2011 the attendance of children in government primary schools was stuck in the range of 50–59 percent (Banerji 2011, 174). Another study reported that nearly half the primary school teachers in Bihar could not perform basic teaching tasks correctly (Kingdon and Banerji 2009). Responding to these deficiencies, in 2013 Bihar's state government launched Mission Gunvatta (MG), or Mission Quality, a program designed to improve learning outcomes. The MG program was developed with education experts and NGO partners, including Pratham. Overambitious school curricula in India had left children struggling to acquire foundational skills (Pritchett and Beatty 2012). First-generation learners were at the greatest risk of falling behind, becoming disillusioned with school and dropping out. Taking a fresh, innovative approach, the MG program was designed according to principles of "Teaching at the Right Level" (TaRL). The TaRL methodology, which involved tailoring instruction to the learning levels of students, was validated through field experiments by education researchers and endorsed by Nobel Prize-winning economists at the MIT Jameel Poverty Action Lab (J-PAL) as a best practice approach for improving foundational learning.[71] A departure from conventional, grade-wise teaching in India, the MG program regrouped children (in grades three to five) according to their learning levels and provided two hours of remedial instruction each day.

The MG program had much going for it. Bihar's chief minister and senior education officials were committed to quality reforms. The program's design drew on the experiences of Indian civil society and

[71] For more information on TaRL, see "Teaching at the Right Level to improve learning," J-PAL. Available at: www.povertyactionlab.org/case-study/teaching-right-level-improve-learning.

cutting-edge techniques recommended by international researchers. The MG program was honed further through local initiatives in a few Bihar districts, such as Jehanabad, where district administration had proactively engaged with Pratham to pilot education reforms.[72] After a baseline assessment of learning levels, Pratham worked with CRCCs in Jehanabad district to implement the TaRL methodology, providing training and in-school support. Six months later, early results from the Jehanabad pilot were encouraging. Of the children who were exposed to the intervention, the percentage that could read increased from 30.8 to 72.3 percent.

With critical elements in place – political attention from state leadership, administrative resources and technical expertise and endorsement from local education officials – the Bihar government attempted to scale up the MG program. Yet, the program suffered from administrative bottlenecks and eventually stalled. A standard account from the implementation literature might hypothesize that the reforms were frustrated due a lack of effort or commitment by frontline agents, including district officials, CRCCs and teachers.[73] However, field-based evidence suggested otherwise. The officials that I interviewed expressed their commitment to improving the quality of education and CRCCs took their academic support roles seriously. In my observations of training sessions in Gaya district, CRCCs had become well versed in TaRL methods and were motivated to guide teachers on the novel approach. In focus group discussions, CRCCs shared their own ideas an how to adapt teaching according to the learning levels of students. For example, some CRCCs noted the importance of building solidarity within student groups. Others recommended ways to reduce the frustration (*nirasha*) and stigma (*kalank*) that children may have experienced when assigned to weaker groups, especially older children who were grouped with younger ones.[74] Primary school teachers, painted so often as demotivated and apathetic, also showed enthusiasm for TaRL. In interviews, several teachers highlighted the usefulness of new teaching materials and methodologies. Others noted that the training led by Pratham was helpful for their everyday classroom teaching. Although it was challenging to deliver group-wise remedial education, teachers found it more manageable with practice. Many teachers reported feeling inspired by the visible improvements they observed in students. Virtually

72 The Padho Jehanabad pilot program began in August 2012 in 224 schools in two administrative blocks of the district (Banerji 2015).

73 Pressman and Wildavsky (1984).

74 Focus group discussion with CRCCs, Gaya, January 2014.

all the teachers I interviewed contrasted the MG program's "practical" approach with the "textbook" (*kitabi*) training that they received from the Department of Education.[75]

Despite the collective efforts of teachers and CRCCs, teaching practices promoted under the MG program ultimately failed to get integrated into the classroom. A chief reason for this outcome, I suggest, is that the MG program's flexibility conflicted with the administrative pressures for rule-following under a legalistic bureaucracy. Schoolteachers experienced discord between the novel teaching practices and what they understood to be their "*main duties*," namely, executing the official curriculum and covering the mandatory subjects in time for end-of-year examinations.[76] Left to grapple with the conflict between the two approaches, teachers reverted to the familiar terrain of rule-based teaching practices. Rule-following was reinforced by the school inspection system, which sent a strong signal that teachers were liable for maintaining administrative records and answering information requests swiftly. CRCCs reported similar conflicts between the demands of the school inspection regime and their academic support roles. The MG program assigned CRCCs the responsibility to observe classroom teaching and provide teachers guidance on applying the pedagogical methods of TaRL. These visits presented opportunities for mentorship discussions with teachers, what TaRL practically meant for their work, how it conflicted with (or complemented) existing practices and how TaRL could be adapted in different school environments. But CRCCs experienced administrative pressures from within the education bureaucracy to follow rule-based monitoring guidelines instead, which pointed to a different set of priorities. Rather than supportive discussions, monitoring visits emphasized the review of school records, documentation and fulfillment of the state-mandated curriculum.

The emphasis on rule compliance was reinforced by pressures from district administration. Shadowing district officials, I observed that if a CRCC was suspected of inflating student enrollment figures or fabricating school data, known as "*bungling*" (*ghapla*), district officials called the head teacher of the school straightaway to ascertain the "*ground-level situation*" (*zamini stithi*).[77] Likewise, when discrepancies arose between the school headmaster's records and the CRCC's

[75] Interviews with primary school teachers, Gaya, December 2013–January 2014.

[76] Interview with primary school teacher, Gaya, December 2013.

[77] Interview with Block Education Officer, Gaya, December 2013.

administrative reports, a stern warning was isssued to both individuals. CRCCs who made repeated errors received official notices of censure from the Department of Education; a negative mark could be placed in their personnel files. The demands of district education officials and CRCCs had a cascading effect on the expectations and behaviors of schoolteachers, who learned to work according to similar norms.[78] For example, CRCCs were asked to maintain notebooks to record observations during school visits, which were periodically reviewed by district officials. Teachers reported in interviews that they were more occupied with record-keeping and other "*administrative duties*," limiting the time they could devote to quality teaching practices.[79] The system of school inspections reinforced the value of rule compliance and record-keeping.[80] To preempt suspicion from education officials, teachers kept records well prepared and responded promptly to requests for administrative data. However, when teachers attempted to apply the new classroom teaching methods, the emphasis on rule compliance created conflicts. In a focus group discussion, a teacher described the conflicts she had experienced:

> When we attended the [MG Program] trainings, we were told one thing—that we should give group-wise teaching. We need to split the children into different groups and then teach them according to their level ... But then once we return to school, we hear something different from the administration. We are told to complete the curriculum. We have to report on our administrative duties and submit every form required in our paperwork (*kagazi kaam*). Even for this program [MG Program], we have to prepare data in different formats for inspection by the CRCC and the department. As for group-wise teaching, that gets left far behind.[81]

Compliance-based monitoring was geared toward the preparation of administrative forms and registers, such as those for school enrollment and the midday meal. Expectations of teachers were reinforced by district education officials. Teachers who devoted more time to classroom activities and engagement with parents risked being seen as underperformers

[78] A field-based study of the MG pilot program in Bihar's Jehanabad district similarly found that "tight monitoring" and "discipline" were the primary modes through which CRCCs were mobilized by the bureaucracy to support teachers (Aiyar, Dongre and Davis 2015, 38–40).

[79] Interview with primary school teachers, Gaya, December 2013.

[80] In other words, the Bihar education reforms encouraged what Honig and Pritchett (2019) refer to as "thin accountability" within the school system.

[81] Focus group discussion with primary school teachers, Respondent 2, Gaya, December 2013.

if they were caught unprepared during a school inspection. Liaising with community members to address problems at the school was seen as "*extra work*" (*anya kaam*), not a central duty.

Legalistic bureaucracy's emphasis on rules was one of several potential factors that made it difficult to adopt new teaching practices. Another plausible explanation comes from the political economy literature on public goods and accountability. In settings of low information, elected officials may have incentives to prioritize activities that are "visible" to voters, credit for which can be attributed to executive actions (Mani and Mukand 2007; Bueno de Mesquita and Stephenson 2007). Harding and Stasavage (2014) extend these arguments to primary education in Uganda, observing that political executives are more likely to abolish school fees than provide schooling inputs or make quality improvements. One might infer from the outcome in Bihar that state leadership put in less effort toward quality improvements in education. However, field-based evidence for this claim is wanting. In their study of Bihar's reforms, Aiyar, Dongre and Davis observe that Kumar "staked his personal political capital on improving elementary education" (2015, 14). The MG program was politically visible, executed with high publicity, alongside other programmatic initiatives by the state. Chief Minister Kumar himself attended the launch of Pratham's annual ASER survey, where Bihar's weak learning outcomes were publicly reported. In a bold move, the state government began administering competency tests for newly recruited teachers, based on materials from the fifth grade syllabus. Of the 43,477 teachers who took the exam in 2013, almost 24 percent failed, an outcome widely publicized by state and national media.[82] Teachers who continued to fail the exam after multiple attempts were threatened with termination, a politically risky move for the state government.

Another possibility is that administrative resource constraints made it impossible for teachers to undertake the multiple tasks required of them. In their study of Block Development Officers in India, Dasgupta and Kapur (2020) observe that juggling multiple tasks with insufficient resources leads to "bureaucratic overload," weakening local agency effectiveness. Their argument is plausible, especially when considering that the growth in enrollments in Bihar led to increased class sizes, making it

[82] Singh, S., "Reality Check: In Bihar, Every 4th Primary, Middle Teacher Failed Class V-level test," *Indian Express*, November 28, 2013. Available at: http://archive.indianexpress.com/news/reality-check-in-bihar-every-4th-primary-middle-teacher-failed-class-vlevel-test/1200529/.

more difficult for teachers to manage group-wise teaching. Likewise, the state's rapid teacher recruitment drive made it more difficult to ensure the quality of teachers, which was found to be wanting in many cases.[83] Along with resource constraints, teachers I interviewed pointed to the socioeconomic realities of the government school system, which made group-wise teaching particularly difficult. The children enrolled in government schools were largely first-generation learners and received little parental support. In one teacher's words, "*Our situation is not like in private schools. Here, the children need extra time and attention. They get no help with homework from their parents.*"[84] Given these complexities along with resource constraints, it is unsurprising that teachers put more energy into completing administrative duties, which had a clearer endpoint and yielded a physical record of their efforts.

Under similar resource constraints, MSUP's frontline workers also performed multiple complex tasks. Some of these tasks, such as mediating village caste conflicts and reintegrating Dalit girls into school, were arguably more challenging than group-wise teaching. But whereas the MSUP organization routinely discussed work-related conflicts with frontline agents, who were in turn supported by state- and district-level officials, government teachers in Bihar were left to cope with conflicts on their own. The MG program required teachers to give attention to individual students, identify differences in learning levels and adapt their teaching to each student group. Student progress was to be monitored through regular contact with parents. These complex tasks created new problems and conflicts for teachers. Their capacity to deal with these conflicts was limited, however, by a legalistic bureaucracy, which understood the mandate for quality education as a matter of following rules.

7.4 CONCLUSION

This chapter has examined institutional change in UP and Bihar. By tracing the partial shift in bureaucratic norms within each state and their subsequent impact on the delivery of primary education, it has advanced the book's arguments in several ways. The case of Mahila Samakhya

[83] S. Mishra, "Bihar's Bitter Lesson in Teacher Recruitment," *Business Standard*, July 19, 2014. Available at: www.business-standard.com/article/economy-policy/bihar-s-bitter-lesson-in-teacher-recruitment-114071900764_1.html.

[84] Focus group discussion with government teachers, Gaya, December 2013.

showed how deliberative bureaucracy works in a highly unequal context, far removed from the ideal conditions for deliberation to flourish (Heller and Rao 2015). To make deliberation more inclusive, MSUP fieldworkers challenged rural hierarchies and encouraged Dalit women to mobilize around their collective interests. Through joint problem-solving with households, they found ways to integrate Dalit girls into school and support their education. UP's entrenched inequalities made deliberation more challenging for MSUP frontline workers, who were called upon to mediate social conflicts on a regular basis. These findings help us understand how street-level bureaucracies redress inequalities during service delivery, impacting how marginalized citizens experience the local state (Brodkin 1997; Maynard-Moody and Musheno 2012). Whereas existing research has treated conflict as a burden that street-level bureaucrats seek to avoid (Piore 2011), the study of MSUP suggests that conflict is unavoidable on the front lines of reform. Conflict can even play a constructive part in reform implementation, by making social injustices public and encouraging the formation of solidaristic ties among marginalized groups.

The case of MSUP also suggests the importance of frontline worker commitment for sustaining institutional change. The impetus behind the Mahila Samakhya program came from India's central government, working in concert with domestic civil society and international organizations. Mahila Samakhya was designed to challenge conventional public administration and draw state attention to the needs of women and girls. Mahila Samakhya pushed back against legalistic bureaucracy in UP, demonstrating the kind of robust "bureaucratic activism" that has been observed in other places, including Brazil's health and environmental sectors (Abers 2019; Rich 2019).[85] By creating deliberative spaces for fieldworkers to discuss and interrogate status quo arrangements in society, MSUP helped sustain institutional activism. Moreover, senior MSUP officials advocated for frontline workers and sangha women, pressuring district administration to support women's causes.

MSUP forged a distinct organizational identity, anchored around deliberation for women's empowerment. However, it should be noted that deliberation was confined to geographies and administrative offices where Mahila Samakhya had an operational presence. I found little evidence that

[85] As Abers writes, bureaucratic activists "[s]truggle daily to discover institutional opportunities and vulnerabilities, to work around rules, and to find the time to organize with each other in defense of ideas they believe in" (2019, 40).

deliberation spilled over to influence wider bureaucratic practices in UP. As a mode of institutional reform, MSUP was "layered" within the Department of Education, an approach that benefited the new agency but also had drawbacks. MSUP appealed to its legal status as a semi-autonomous organization to claim official authority, while retaining internal control over personnel, training and local programming. MSUP also benefited from the repertoires developed by its district and village fieldworkers, who learned to use legalistic tactics, such as administrative orders and petitions, to advance organizational goals. At the same time, being situated inside the Department of Education, MSUP had to work to protect its organizational autonomy. Conflicts with UP's legalistic bureaucracy were more challenging given the limited political support for Mahila Samakhya within the state government.

Bureaucratic norm change took place differently in Bihar. Under committed state leadership, Bihar's government sought to uphold bureaucratic order, discipline and rule-following, instigating a major shift in a state bureaucracy that was long plagued by clientelism and corruption. Although clientelistic practices did not disappear, including in the hiring of teachers, the movement toward legalism faciliated the state's anti-corruption efforts and improvements in law and order. Bureaucratic rule-following extended to social sector programming as well. In the primary education sphere, legalistic bureaucracy supported infrastructure provision and helped strengthen the enrollment of disadvantaged children.

The Bihar case also brings to the fore the difficulties of instituting quality education reforms on the back of legalistic bureaucracy. Despite political support, external expertise and civil society input, the introduction of new pedagogical practices saw limited success. Administrative oversight of schools improved discipline within the system, but the pressure to observe rules clashed with novel classroom practices that called for flexibility and experimentation. Schoolteachers' were held accountable for compliance with administrative rules and record-keeping, which conflicted with pedagogical innovations, dampening their commitment to education quality reforms.

PART III

COMPARATIVE EXTENSIONS AND IMPLICATIONS

8

The Argument in Comparative Perspective

8.1 INTRODUCTION

Part II presented evidence for my theoretical argument based on multilevel comparative field research in northern India. The analysis showed that the historical divergence of bureaucratic norms has contributed to subnational differences in the implementation of primary schooling in four Hindi belt states. Part III extends the book's argument to other empirical contexts and explores its implications for scholarship and policy. This chapter considers the plausibility of my argument beyond northern India. The four cases examined are the south Indian state of Kerala, along with China, Finland and France. These cases were chosen for theoretical reasons, to test different aspects of my theoretical argument in very different political economy contexts. I have a relied on a close reading of secondary literature examining the education system, bureaucracy and implementation processes in each setting.

Before proceeding with the analysis, some caveats are necessary. The abridged discussion of cases here is not intended to substitute for careful empirical investigation. I have no desire to extend my argument beyond what can be demonstrated empirically. Indeed, my objective in this book has been to signal the painstaking attention to research design and data collection that is needed to study bureaucratic norms and trace comparative their effects on implementation across different sociopolitical contexts. My aims here are therefore more modest. I seek to establish the plausibility of my theory outside northern India and to suggest directions for future research. At first glance, the inclusion of country-level cases may seem odd given the book's focus on subnational variation across Indian states. Following Singh (2017), I intend to show how a theoretical framework developed through subnational comparative research can yield insights for comparative scholarship on national systems of education and social welfare provision, with an eye toward fostering dialogue between these approaches. To be sure, the discussion of country-level cases overlooks large, within-country variations and historical nuances. The literature that I reference accentuates the central tendencies of bureaucracy in each country, but pays less attention to subnational differences in bureaucratic norms.

This chapter's discussion progresses as follows: I first examine Kerala, a recognized leader in education and health that has outperformed other Indian states, attaining social indicators that rival middle-income countries (Lieten 2002; Singh 2011). Kerala has a history of social movements by subordinate castes and classes, along with a comparatively successful project of democratic decentralization (Heller 1999; Isaac and Heller 2003). Less appreciated, I suggest, is how Kerala's deliberative bureaucracy has helped strengthen community participation in public services. Next, I investigate China, a country that defies social scientific thinking on institutions and development. Scholars have investigated the Chinese state's capacity for implementation through mechanisms of "adaptive governance" (Heilmann and Perry 2011) and "directed improvisation" (Ang 2016a). Building on their work, I argue that China offers theoretical lessons for how deliberative bureaucracy shapes social policy implementation in the absence of democracy. Third, I extend my argument to advanced economies by comparing the performance of school education in France and Finland, which have similar levels of public spending on education, but divergent outcomes. Finland's school system has gained prominence among OECD countries for producing superior learning outcomes that are more equitably distributed across socioeconomic groups. France's school system, meanwhile, produces learning outcomes closer to the OECD average, with relatively uneven outcomes between socioeconomic groups. Drawing on experimental governance and public administration scholarship (Sabel et al. 2011; Peters 2021), I suggest that deliberative and legalistic bureaucratic norms have generated distinct policy implementation patterns across these countries, contributing to the varied performance of their school systems.

8.2 DELIBERATIVE BUREAUCRACY WITH SOCIAL MOVEMENTS: REVISITING THE "KERALA MODEL" OF SOCIAL DEVELOPMENT

The southern coastal state of Kerala (pop. 33.4 million) has earned international acclaim for being a model of social development at a relatively low level of income. Many researchers have been struck by the differences in public service delivery and social welfare outcomes in Kerala and Hindi belt states (Drèze and Sen 2002; Singh 2015). The comparison has helped accentuate the distinctiveness of the "Kerala model" of social development (Lieten 2002). Kerala has also had distinctive historical conditions and sociopolitical features that are not replicated in northern India. In 1951, Kerala's literacy rate of 47 percent was already more than twice the all-India average of 18 percent. Kerala maintained its lead, and by the 2011 Census, recorded a literacy rate of 94 percent. The rural–urban divide in primary school access and enrollment was closed in the 1990s, long before the central government launched Sarva Shiksha Abhiyan (SSA). In 1999, more than 90 percent of rural Keralites lived in villages served by a primary school and 87 percent had access to middle school, against national averages of 80 percent and 45 percent, respectively (NFHS-2 2000). By then, Kerala's enrollment rate for girls and boys (ages 6–17) was on par at 91 percent, compared to 61.4 percent for girls and 77.3 percent for boys at the national level. Kerala's primary school system is found to produce superior learning outcomes, as 65.2 percent of rural fifth graders have a demonstrated ability to read and 45.9 percent can perform simple division, well above the national averages of 41.7 percent and 24.8 percent (ASER 2013).

To explain Kerala's superior performance in mass education and other social programs, scholars have pointed to the historical importance of social movements by subordinate castes and classes, reinforced by leftist government and a robust civil society (Heller 1999), along with the solidaristic ties of Malayali subnationalism (Singh 2016). Missing from existing accounts is an appreciation for how bureaucratic norms in Kerala have evolved to support social policy implementation. Based on historical and secondary sources, I suggest that state-building processes in Kerala promoted deliberation between bureaucracy and societal actors, which has in turn supported Kerala's superior educational performance. In contrast to the politics of elite cooperation in HP, deliberative governance in Kerala was forged through a combination of elite cooperation and societal conflict. By supporting local deliberation and citizen participation in service delivery, deliberative bureaucracy in Kerala has helped institutionalize conflict and steer it toward programmatic ends (Mansuri and Rao 2013, 90–91).

At first glance, the superior performance of primary schooling in Kerala can be attributed to multiple factors. Kerala's coastal geography and settlement patterns are more conducive to public service provision, allowing for maritime trade and financial remittances from migrants. Kerala is also among India's most densely settled states (Bhat and Rajan 1990). The 2011 Census shows that more than 92 percent of rural Keralites reside in villages with populations exceeding 10,000, compared to only 8.7 percent for the rest of India. Higher rural population density lessens administrative costs and raises political incentives for providing education, mitigating the urban bias in service provision. Also, the historical beneficence of Kerala's political leadership encouraged more generous public spending. The princely states of Travancore and Cochin had socially progressive leadership supporting mass education. In 1817, Gowri Parvathi Bai, Queen of Travancore, declared, "The state should defray the entire cost of the education of its people," a bold proclamation for any government at the time (Ramachandran 1997, 268). Regrettably, the policy statements of progressive leaders were not always matched with attention to implementation (Sen 1992). Public funding for mass education reached notable levels by the nineteenth century's close, but gender-and caste-based exclusion limited societal participation (Mathew 1999).

Another oft-cited explanation is that Christian missionaries introduced English-medium education and opened formal schooling to women and lower castes, targeting marginalized groups (Tharakan 1984; Sen 1992; Mathew 1999). Missionaries in Travancore, for example, set up boarding schools for girls and children of lower-caste slaves, despite protests by upper-caste landlords (Mathew 1999, 2814–2815). Although the direct impact of missionaries on mass education was diluted by their limited geographic presence, they were pivotal in bringing caste injustices to light, creating the ideological space for social reform movements (Singh 2011, 284). The Christian message of equality, combined with fears of mass conversion, provoked religious competition from upper-caste Hindus. An historical study of social welfare in Travancore found that "the state was under considerable pressure from upper caste groups to open their own Hindu schools, for the missionary schools quite rightly were viewed as venues for the conversion of lower castes to Christianity" (Desai 2005, 472).

A discussion of mass education in Kerala must give consideration to its legacy of bottom-up social movements challenging caste and class hierarchies, a defining feature of the state's political development (Jeffrey 1975; Herring 1983; Menon 1994; Heller 1999). Kerala's elaborate caste system was one of the most oppressive ones in India. All castes below the Namboodiris, the highest-ranking Brahmin subcaste, were considered polluted and had restrictions imposed on their physical movement. The lowest castes suffered extreme humiliations; along with untouchability, these included "unapproachability," which made the mere act of being seen by upper castes a punishable offense (Nossiter 1982, 25–27). Slavery of Dalits was common as well in the colonial period, and it persisted in some forms, such as bonded labor, even after independence (Sivanandan 1976).

In the backdrop of caste oppression, mass movements challenging hierarchy and discrimination arose in the late nineteenth century. These movements raised political awareness among lower castes, who learned to articulate injustices to the state (Sen 1992, 263). An example is the Ezhavas, a lower caste that constitutes 22 percent of Kerala's population. Denied entry into Hindu temples, the Ezhavas were discriminated against in schooling and employment. Upper-caste teachers and students boycotted classes to avoid making contact with Ezhava students (Mathew 1999, 2817). An Ezhava social movement arose in 1903 with the creation of the Sree Narayana Dharma Paripalan Yogam (SNDP), Kerala's first caste association. SNDP promoted religious and secular education, while also working to secure Ezhavas access to Hindu temples (Jeffrey 1975). The movement stressed the importance of literacy and economic self-help. Ezhavas also learned to demand their rights from the state, establishing the link between access to formal schooling and social mobility.

If pre-independence social reform movements stimulated political demands from below, the communists in Kerala aggregated these demands into a coherent, class-based political movement. The world's first democratically elected communist government, the Communist Party of India secured a majority of assembly seats in the 1956 state elections. More than simply collecting votes, Kerala communists operated as a "social movement party," Heller writes, "occupying the trenches of civil society, building mass-based organizations, ratcheting up demands, and cultivating a noisy but effective politics of contention" (2000, 511). The CPM government led by E.M.S. Namboodiripad adopted a pro-poor policy platform, which included agrarian land and labor reforms. Kerala communists institutionalized societal demands in class-based terms and directed them toward the state, offsetting the destabilizing nature of class conflict. In addition to class movements, Singh (2016) demonstrates that a shared Malayali subnational identity motivated political elites to invest in social policies, while celebrating Kerala's distinctive language and cultural traditions. For example, subnationalism was promoted by political elites during the Aikya Kerala (United Kerala) movement, which secured statehood for Kerala under the central government's 1956 States Reorganisation Act. Malayali subnationalism, Singh argues, also triggered increased public spending on primary education and health. Faced with a common external enemy (non-Malayali Brahmins), political elites formed a cross-caste coalition, and in turn, were motivated by subnationalism to prioritize social welfare.

If state programming for primary education was a product of Kerala's class-based mobilization and subnationalist politics, how services reached citizens effectively requires further explanation. Kerala's bureaucracy is institutionally similar to those in other Indian states. Indian Administrative Service (IAS) officers occupying senior posts in Kerala's administration are recruited from across India. Under service deployment rules, the vast majority of IAS officers belong to other states and are inculcated with a national outlook through training and promotion processes, which, by design, reduce the scope for subnational identification with a particular province. It is similarly unclear why class mobilization in Kerala led to participatory governance arrangements for primary education. The northeastern state of West Bengal, which experienced uninterrupted leftist government rule for over thirty years, has also been effective at poverty alleviation (Kohli 1987; Echeverri-Gent 1992). However, its performance in primary education and health has remained abysmal (Mullen 2011). West Bengal's Communist Party of India (Marxist) (CPM) used the bureaucratic machinery to cement its electoral dominance, stifling political competition and dissent from civil society (Desai 2001). West Bengal also scores highly on the subnationalism scale, but the bonds of Bengali identity have not yielded superior education and health outcomes.

A fuller understanding of Kerala's education performance requires an examination of the norms that emerged within the bureaucracy, and specifically, how state agencies learned to work with societal actors to provide services. As a first step, we must consider the historical state-building process, which shaped the nature of school governance in Kerala. A distinctive feature of state formation in Kerala, bureaucratic norms emerged in a setting in which *non*-state provision of social services was substantial. Historically, private provisioning comprised a larger part of Kerala's education system. State programming was introduced only after religious authorities and lower-caste reform movements were well entrenched in the education sphere. Although the number of private schools was insufficient to guarantee universal coverage, the presence of multiple, competing non-state service providers allowed the state to experiment with mixed forms of public and private governance. In the princely state of Travancore, for example, a significant share of public expenditure on education went toward subsidies for private schools run by Christian missionaries and Hindu caste societies. As Tharakan (1984) observes, missionary education depended on state grants-in-aid to private schools. The Queen of Travancore's 1817 proclamation that the state would bear the cost of education carried an important rejoinder that granted the state control over school *management*. In settings where rural education catered to different castes and religious denominations, centralized political control of schooling was highly controversial. Religious authorities were wary of administrative intrusion by the state in the affairs of schools. The state's response to the concerns of private school bodies was remarkable. As an historian of Kerala has noted, the Travancore government took the decision not to interfere with existing school management structures; traditional headmasters were instead incorporated into the government school system (Jeffrey 1987). "By preserving the old schools," Jeffrey observes, "the Travancore government retained the trust of elders willing to send their charges to institutions run by known and respected masters" (1987, 453). The incorporation of traditional schools in Travancore contrasted with the approach taken by the princely state of Cochin. In the 1890s, the government of Cochin adopted a strict regulatory stance toward the traditional school system, which fell into decline, contributing to a deterioration in literacy.

During the first half of the twentieth century, Kerala's bureaucracy engaged in both cooperation and conflict with private school authorities. The assertion of state control in 1910 led to a drop in the number of private schools, while the subsequent relaxation of state control saw the swift reappearance of private schools (Lieten 1977, 6–7). Conflict was intense between the bureaucracy and Kerala's church authorities, who competed for institutional oversight of schooling. By the late 1950s, Kerala had 9,500 primary and secondary schools, more than 60 percent of which were privately managed. As Jeffrey observes, "Nearly 70 per cent of corporate private managements were Christian (though schools run by individuals were overwhelmingly Hindu)" (1992, 155). Government primary schools in turn expanded in the 1960s, doubling in number. Nevertheless, by 1970–1971, the percentage of privately managed schools remained high, at 61.7 percent (Lieten 2002, 57). Given large public outlays on private schooling, the state kept close tabs on how church authorities ran the school system. The bureaucracy sought to instill uniform standards and professionalize teaching, thought it also needed buy-in from private schools.

Alongside the bureaucracy, the CPM sought to exert control over primary schooling, in part to secure ideological dominance over schooling curricula. Church authorities were suspicious of communist political interference. In 1957, Kerala's communist-led government proposed a compromise education bill, which granted private management control of day-to-day administration while retaining state control over school inspections and curricular supervision, the latter responsibilities handed to the education department. The 1958 Kerala Education Act was adopted by the state legislature, albeit with an important amendment acknowledging the protection of minority (i.e. Christian and Muslim) rights under the Constitution. The Act's provisions applied only to government schools and private-aided schools that received state financial support. An important stipulation was that private-aided schools were required to hire teachers from a government-approved roster. Teachers were paid directly by the government, a provision that aimed to protect teachers from unscrupulous school management. Non-aided private schools, those opting out of state financial support, continued to operate autonomously while having state recognition.

The Kerala Education Act bred conflict between the state and church authorities. Church leaders, who feared the spread of secular education, lodged protests against proposed revisions to textbooks. They were joined by members of the Kerala Provincial Congress Committee (KPCC), who argued that the Act was an attempt to spread communist ideology (Lieten 1977, 10). Controversy surrounding the Act may have contributed to the downfall of the CPM-led government in 1959. Nevertheless, the education policy withstood multiple changes of government. The bureaucracy continued to oversee private schools, which in practical terms meant that officials had to learn how to coordinate with religious authorities and community associations, whose interests at times conflicted with those of the state. These experiences of working with non-state agencies impacted bureaucracy's orientation toward societal participation but also paved the way for reforms granting local communities greater voice in school management.

The bureaucracy's catalytic role in encouraging societal participation in service delivery is equally apparent from Kerala's more recent decentralization reforms. Following the 73rd and 74th constitutional amendments, Kerala has led India in establishing Panchayati Raj Institutions and devolving funds and substantive decision-making authority to village councils. Kerala's panchayat reforms were spearheaded by the communist government in 1996, which came to power on the pledge to decentralize state authority.[1] As Isaac and Heller (2003) find, decentralization initiatives also depended critically on the bureaucracy, which worked with non-state agencies to strengthen societal involvement in state planning. As they argue, "The Kerala State Planning board formulated, designed and drove the Campaign for Democratic Decentralization. In doing so, the Board has relied on a stock of practical knowledge, ideas and experiences drawn from twenty-five years of local-level experiments conducted by NGOs" (Isaac and Heller 2003, 80). Studies also indicate that the Kerala Sastra Sahitya Parishad (KSSP) – the People's Science Movement – helped the state integrate local knowledge for planning purposes (Isaac and Franke 2000; Véron 2001). A grassroots organization created in the 1960s by retired teachers and other professionals, KSSP grew into a mass "people's movement" for scientific thinking. The group supported the National Literacy Mission during the 1980s and 1990s and worked with local administration on the Total Literacy Campaign in Kerala's Ernakulam district.[2] These efforts earned Ernakulam the distinction of being India's first "fully literate" district and a national model of state–society collaboration (Rao 1993; Tharakan 2004). In his analysis of Kerala's literacy campaign, Tharakan notes, "In Ernakulam there remains an unquantifiable factor regarding the role played by the district administration and its personnel which went far beyond the call of duty. The attitudinal change that resulted in such participation has certainly persisted in the administration, leading to better results in the delivery of welfare and development programmes" (2004, 77). The bureaucracy's ability to learn from local experiments helps account for how the Ernakulam experiment was later scaled up throughout Kerala.

Kerala's bureaucracy institutionalized KSSP's role with the implementation of *panchayat* reforms. As Heller notes, "The presence of a KSSP

[1] The political history of panchayat reforms in Kerala is examined by Heller (2005).

[2] In a parallel vein to KSSP's work in Kerala, Chapter 6 shows how the Himachal Gyan Vigyan Samiti supported rural literacy in Himachal Pradesh by promoting deliberation between local officials and citizens.

cell within the Planning Board has helped embed this state agency in social movement structures," creating "new nonpartisan institutions of participation that build on civic associationalism" (2001, 154). Through its network of more than 6,000 volunteers, KSSP has provided technical support and assistance with fiscal decentralization.[3] The state bureaucracy undertook an elaborate training program, covering thousands of state and local officials, described as "one of the largest non-formal education programs ever undertaken in India" (Isaac and Heller 2003, 83). Consequently, Kerala's panchayats are more likely to have functional village assemblies (*gram sabhas*) and draw high levels of citizen participation (Besley, Pande and Rao 2007). Bureaucratic deliberation has thus made democratic decentralization comparatively deeper in Kerala.

This section revisited the Kerala model in light of my theoretical argument. The discussion pointed to the political process of state-building in a context of private schooling, religious pluralism and routinized conflict between government and religious authorities. The Kerala bureaucracy's historical engagement with non-state agencies enabled joint management of schools. In a setting of social movements by subordinate groups, two-party competition and leftist government, the state bureaucracy's policy experimentation during literacy campaigns, followed by decentralization in the 1990s, helped consolidate deliberative ties between local administration and civic bodies. Bureaucratic norms promoting inclusive deliberation, incorporating marginalized social groups in local governance, helped sustain the efforts of KSSP and other civil society groups. Deliberation between state and society has thus improved the quality of education services in Kerala and enhanced bureaucratic responsiveness to the needs of the least advantaged.

8.3 CHINA: HOW DELIBERATIVE BUREAUCRACY WORKS IN A NON-DEMOCRACY

In contrast to Kerala, the case of China raises questions as to whether and how deliberative bureaucracy works in the absence of democracy. Few countries have challenged mainstream social scientific thinking on institutions and development as much as China has. China's embrace of global capitalism *sans* conventional rule of law and Weberian state

[3] Almost 40 percent of Kerala's public expenditure on development projects is routed through panchayats, affording ordinary citizens a direct say in how public funds get utilized within their localities.

institutions continues to puzzle scholars. Research comparing China and India has highlighted differences in the management and growth of their economies. China's more open and dynamic market, steered by an organized party-state, has been contrasted with India's fractious democratic federation and more rigid "License Raj" bureaucracy (Bardhan 2010; Chibber 2003). When India gave up its autarkic, planned economy in the 1990s, China had already become a global economic powerhouse (Mukherji 2014). However, the comparative human development performance of the two countries has not received due attention. China has gone far ahead of India in improving the quality of life for its people, arresting rural poverty, illiteracy and infant mortality (Sen 2011).

The comparison between India and China in the primary education arena is particularly instructive. In the 1950s, the countries had comparable levels of education, with India's literacy rate of 18 percent slightly below China's rate of 20 percent. However, China's education expansion happened at a much faster pace in the next three decades. By 1980, India's literacy rate of 40 percent was surpassed by China's rate of 65.5 percent (World Bank 2020). China achieved universal enrollment in primary schooling in the 1970s, while it took India until the early 2000s. China also made significant progress in tackling education inequalities. In 1981, the ratio of rural to urban literacy in India was 54 (per 100), rising to 61 in 1991. Over that period, China's ratio climbed from 76 to 90 (Drèze and Loh 1995). Similarly, the ratio of female to male literacy in China was 78 (per 100) in 1991; in India it was only 61. By 2018, China's gender gap in literacy vanished and India's ratio improved to 85 (World Bank Group 2021). China is now at the cusp of having full adult literacy. Meanwhile, India's road to catching up remains a long one.

China's superior education performance may seem puzzling given its authoritarian political system. Leading theories of political economy expect democratization to encourage redistribution in favor of the poor (Meltzer and Richard 1981; Boix 2003; Acemoglu and Robinson 2006). Numerous studies associate democratic regimes and political competition with increased public spending on primary schooling, as well as greater enrollment and other positive outcomes (Brown 1999; Lake and Baum 2001; Brown and Hunter 2004; Stasavage 2005; Ansell 2010).[4] On the other hand, historical examples abound of non-democratic regimes that provided mass education, from Meiji Japan to modern Turkey.

[4] Others question democracy's pro-poor tendencies (Ross 2006).

A study of 109 countries over a 200-year period finds that democracy produces little or no effect on primary school enrollment, and that in most cases, state provision of primary schooling was introduced *prior* to democratization (Paglayan 2021). There can be multiple motivations for non-democracies to promote mass education. Not all of these motivations are related to human capital development, such as extending state control over the political beliefs and ideologies held by citizens (Pritchett 2003). Setting aside the various political purposes for non-democracies to provide primary education, questions remain as to how these policies get implemented.

There are many potential factors behind China's superior implementation of primary schooling, some continuing since the Maoist period, if not earlier in history. An underappreciated factor, I suggest, is the presence of deliberative bureaucracy in China. Political philosophers associate deliberation with democratic forms of government and substantive citizen participation in decision-making (Cohen 1989). China may appear, then, an unlikely place for deliberative bureaucracy to flourish. Yet, deliberation has historical importance within China's party-state.[5] Central and provincial elites in the Chinese Communist Party (CCP) exert authority and top-down hierarchical control over governmental decisions. However, they have also been open to persuasion and have responded to policy ideas and experiences from below, including from local deliberative fora. He and Warren (2011) theorize the concept of "authoritarian deliberation" and trace its lineage within China's political development. In authoritarian deliberation, "powers of decision are concentrated, but power holders enable communicative contexts that generate influence (responsiveness to claims and reasons) among the participants. Power holders are influenced in their decisions by the reasons generated by communication among participants and/or by the legitimacy of the process of reason-giving" (He and Warren 2011, 274). Functionalist accounts suggest that deliberative mechanisms provide state officials information about public sentiments, facilitating negotiation with society, as well as legitimacy for policy decisions. Deliberation encourages "*willing* compliance" among citizens for state policies, lessening the costs of authoritarian control (He and Warren 2011, 280).[6]

[5] On deliberation within the Chinese context, see He (2006).

[6] The argument linking authoritarian deliberation to state legitimacy and citizen compliance has parallels to Levi's (1988) notion of quasi-voluntary compliance.

Deliberation with societal groups during public service delivery has also enabled the Chinese state to make inroads into civil society.[7]

Deliberative politics was institutionalized in China in the 1980s with the enactment of decentralization, village elections and other participatory reforms.[8] However, deliberative practices have an older pedigree in Chinese political thought and were later adopted by Mao, who emphasized "learning from the people through direct engagement with their conditions and struggles" (He and Warren 2011, 276).[9] Along with "deliberation," the concepts of "pragmatism," "experimentalism" and "adaptation" appear in the scholarly lexicon of Chinese governance. Heilmann and Perry (2011) explore the Chinese party-state's capacity for "adaptive governance," an ability to experiment and learn from unfamiliar and changing circumstances, which they argue has facilitated economic and social development.[10] The experimental approach to policy development in China has been associated with Mao's embrace of pragmatism. "In line with his practice-based epistemology," Heilmann notes, "Mao held that policy implementation, not policy debate, provided the crucial device for learning and innovation" (2008a, 8).[11]

Decentralized administration sets the stage for local policy experiments, which, importantly, are guided from above by national and provincial agencies (Heilmann 2008b; Ang 2016a). Despite its unitary political system, China is administratively among the most decentralized countries in the world (Landry 2008). City, county and township governments are responsible for funding and implementing public services. Along with formal decentralization, informal bureaucratic norms promote experimentation by local officials. As Heilmann elaborates: "Most experimental efforts are set off by local policymakers ... Encouragement and protection extended by senior leaders to local experimenters, a mechanism of informal 'policy hedging,' is a major determinant of pioneering

7 Teets suggests that "collaboration between local government and private entities to deliver public services also serves as a mechanism to bring the party closer to society in a way that defuses the potential threat to government authority presented by civil society" (2012, 19).

8 Participatory reforms have included village representative assemblies and elections, consultative meetings in municipalities and deliberative polling.

9 He (2014) traces the advent of deliberative politics in China to traditional Confucian practices of consultative decision-making.

10 Heilmann and Perry (2011) surmise that adaptive governance is a consequence of China's having experienced three decades of revolutionary mobilization.

11 Heilmann (2008a, 18–20) locates the influence of pragmatic philosopher John Dewey on Mao's thinking about governance.

behavior on the local level" (2008b, 9). Rather than top-down political control, senior officials guide lower-level functionaries and enable them to take risks.

The significance of informal bureaucratic norms in the Chinese state is drawn out in a compelling fashion by Ang (2016a), who demonstrates how state officials have improvised with society to address practical challenges of development. Ang advances a theoretical framework of "directive improvisation," a set of behavioral norms motivating entrepreneurial behavior by bureaucrats on a range of development problems. Improvisation, she argues, is not idiosyncratic or spontaneous, but *directed* by senior officials, who articulate policy mandates in ways that balance national goals against subnational differences. In addition to the "hardware" of a decentralized authoritarian state, Ang emphasizes the institutional "software" facilitating adaptation, namely, administrative guidance and flexibility, as well as the rewarding of successful policy adaptation. To illustrate, she describes the puzzling behavior of Mr. Zhou, the principal of a public elementary school (Ang 2016a, 103–104). In a display of entrepreneurship, Mr. Zhou upgraded the school's infrastructure into a state-of-the-art facility, drawing on schoolteachers' savings and a bank loan secured against their property. His unorthodox behavior broke with administrative rules on fundraising, but helped solve a practical problem, contradicting stereotypes of the shirking bureaucrat. In a related example, Paine (1992) describes how local bureaucracy in China helped address the urban housing shortage, which had negatively impacted teachers. In the mid-1980s, 32.3 percent of elementary and secondary schoolteachers lacked access to housing, creating irregularities in the teaching force. Education officials cooperated with other public and private agencies to address the matter. In one locale, school administrators negotiated a pragmatic solution with a nearby factory, agreeing to admit a section of workers' children in exchange for the construction of new housing.

These examples from the education sector point to general features of the Chinese bureaucracy. Problem-oriented deliberation by local administration (city, county and township) is supported by central and provincial governments. Consider China's comparatively successful implementation of agricultural reforms.[12] In the 1970s, most agricultural households

[12] Bardhan (2010, 51) observes that land reforms in China were implemented far more effectively than in India, which has a higher incidence of rural landlessness.

belonged to communes, whose output was based on predetermined prices and production targets. To meet their targets, some communes gave households individual farm plots and let them retain output beyond predetermined quotas. After selling the required output at fixed prices to the state, any residual output could be sold at market prices, allowing households to earn profits from their labor. The household responsibility system, as it came to be known, created marginal incentives for households to produce more, enabling subsequent market reforms (Lin 1988). Notably, the household responsibility system arose organically through local experimentation by communes. Successful experiments were identified by local leadership, emulated elsewhere and later endorsed by the central leadership. Xu describes how "proto-types" of the household responsibility system emerged in the 1970s (2011, 1111–1113). Land contracting experiments were attempted by local officials in Anhui and Sichuan, with support from provincial governors. The management of political risks associated with experimentation is noteworthy in this case, since land reforms were illegal and incurred heavy penalties. After experiments were validated in the 1980s, the central government extended these reforms nationwide. Similar bureaucratic processes supported the growth of rural industry through township and village enterprises, the creation of a "manager responsibility system" to reform state-owned enterprises, and the introduction of special economic zones to attract foreign investment and trade. These reforms were not conceived in Beijing and imposed all over China. Instead, they emerged as subnational initiatives and were tested in geographic pockets before being scaled up countrywide.

The bureaucratic mechanisms that Ang and other scholars describe have an affinity with the flexible, problem-based orientation of deliberative bureaucracy theorized in this book. The cases of Himachal Pradesh (HP) (Chapter 5) and Mahila Samakhya in Uttar Pradesh (UP) (Chapter 7) brought out the importance of deliberation within India's public agencies. In this respect, however, Chinese bureaucracy far exceeds its Indian counterpart. A bureaucratic culture of deliberation in China is sustained with support from central and provincial governments. By contrast, central government agencies in India have exhibited a "culture of rule-following," which, as Chhibber (2002) observes, limits their capacity to undertake complex development tasks and coordinate with society. Along with differences in bureaucratic culture, formal administrative structures vary decidedly between the two countries. In comparison to China, administrative decentralization in India has been much shallower.

The Indian state is highly centralized with respect to fiscal responsibilities and social policy implementation, barring a few subnational exceptions, such as Kerala. At the subnational level, legalistic bureaucracy in states like UP has prevented education officials from pursuing practical responses to citizen grievances. As we saw in Chapter 4, local education officials in UP who attempted to innovate experienced institutional setbacks and had little support from senior officials. In that sense, the Indian state operates more like a conventional "rule-of-law" system, which, as Heilmann notes, "virtually rules out discretionary and experimental administrative measures" (2008b, 9). Successful policy experiments in India are less likely to receive encouragement from state leadership, weakening the prospects for institutional learning and scaling up of local innovations. It is not surprising, then, that policymakers in India refer to its governance landscape as a "graveyard of pilots."[13]

This brief foray into China's social development suggests that deliberative bureaucracy's promise is not reserved for democracies. This is not to deny the value of democracy and the political freedoms it affords. If bureaucratic deliberation is well institutionalized in China, the constraints posed by its authoritarian political system are considerable. In particular, the mechanism of societal feedback during implementation is weakened when citizens cannot freely organize and voice collective demands on the state. In India, the political dynamics unleashed by democratic elections, associational freedoms and protection of civil liberties are more conducive to societal involvement in policy implementation. Even in underperforming states like UP, democratic processes have increased the scope for women and lower castes to mobilize collectively. By contrast, China's authoritarian system limits deliberative bureaucracy's ability to fully incorporate societal feedback, especially when it comes from underprivileged groups who lack preferential access to the party-state.[14] China's authoritarian restrictions, particularly state suppression of public criticism, can lead to major policy mistakes, as witnessed in the Great Famine (Drèze and Sen 1989). Moreover, authoritarianism can weaken society's ability to exercise voice collectively on an everyday basis. Tsai's (2007) study of rural public goods provision shows, for example, that while village temple groups can hold local officials accountable, village

[13] Interview with retired state official, New Delhi, December 2013.

[14] On the other hand, Tsai (2007) finds that village solidary groups hold local officials accountable for public goods provision. Likewise, O'Brien and Li (2006) observe that Chinese citizens challenge local officials by appealing to higher-level agencies.

church groups lack the same opportunity since the Chinese party-state closely regulates churches, prohibiting local officials from participating in them. The limits of authoritarian deliberation are perhaps further revealed in the recent period of market-oriented reforms, which have brought unmatched economic prosperity but with heightened inequality and diminished progress in basic health and education.[15] As Bardhan (2010, 104–116) observes, the collapse of local public finances and growing privatization of public services has widened China's class divisions and regional disparities. Likewise, Ang notes, the Chinese bureaucracy's profit orientation "has exacerbated unequal access to essential services and provoked public resentment" (Ang 2016b, 14). Thus, while deliberative bureaucracy in China has facilitated extraordinary gains in economic and social development, how the political system addresses these mounting concerns is yet to be seen. This brief foray into China's development suggests that the concept of deliberative bureaucracy has analytical reach beyond democracies such as India, and merits further attention in comparative research on the state and service delivery.

8.4 FINLAND AND FRANCE: VARIETIES OF BUREAUCRACY IN ADVANCED ECONOMIES

This section considers the book's argument in the context of advanced economies through a comparison of school education in Finland and France. The theory connecting bureaucratic norms to differences in policy implementation pertains primarily to weak institutional environments, where the gap between formal rules and bureaucratic behavior is often substantial (Levitsky and Murillo 2009). In advanced economies, states tend to have greater legal and fiscal capacity, improving the likelihood for public services to be well implemented (Besley and Persson 2014). Citizens in these countries will also tend to have better material conditions and more knowledge of their rights, raising the demand for quality services. Yet, even wealthy countries encounter hurdles when implementing education services, as evidenced by the OECD's Programme for International Student Assessment (PISA). A well-recognized international assessment for education, PISA measures the aptitude of fifteen-year-old students in reading, mathematics and science. Learning improvements

[15] See the data on China in Drèze and Sen (2002) as well as the discussion by Evans and Heller (2015, 703–707), who connect China's earlier gains in social development to its egalitarian socialist model.

in OECD countries have been marginal since PISA's first round in 2000, despite major public outlays for education.[16] In the 2018 PISA round, 24 percent of students from OECD countries scored below the minimum proficiency level in mathematics and 12 percent did so in reading (Crato 2021). Against these disappointing results, there is significant variation across OECD countries in average PISA test scores as well as disparities in the achievement gap between different socioeconomic groups. Finland is a leading performer on PISA, having comparatively superior learning outcomes across students of different socioeconomic categories. France, meanwhile, is a middling performer among OECD countries, with relatively high inequality in learning outcomes across students.

What explains the variation in education services and associated learning outcomes between the two countries? In what follows, I suggest that differences in bureaucratic norms help account for some of the variation in learning, especially among the least advantaged student cohorts. It should be noted at the outset that student achievement is determined by a multitude of factors, some operating outside of the school system. Student socioeconomic background–conditioned by factors such as parental education and work status, household income, family immigration status–explains to a large extent the individual and cross-national variation in learning (Hanushek and Woessmann 2011). Yet, the magnitude of the effect of socioeconomic factors on learning varies between countries, suggesting that schooling systems have an important influence on student achievement. As Woessmann writes, "The considerable differences in student achievement across countries are systematically related to differences in the organization and governance of school systems" (2016, 3). Quantitative indicators of schooling provision, such as public expenditure per student and class sizes, are important up to a threshold, but have less of an impact on learning outcomes than one might expect (Schleicher 2018, 20). Education researchers are therefore paying more attention to "nonresource institutional features of school systems," such as teacher training and incentives, but also school governance, monitoring and accountability systems (Hanushek and Woessmann 2011, 138).

Before proceeding, it is important to validate the comparison between France and Finland. The Varieties of Capitalism literature has shown how different institutional configurations for the economy and welfare state

[16] A. Jack, "Rich-Nation Education Splurge Fails to Deliver Results," https://www.ft.com/content/6e9e0534-129d-11ea-a7e6-62bf4f9e548a *Financial Times*, December 3, 2019. Available at: www.ft.com/content/6e9e0534-129d-11ea-a7e6-62bf4f9e548a.

produce varying patterns of skill development (Hall and Soskice 2001; Thelen 2004; Iversen and Stephens 2008; Busemeyer 2014). Their many differences apart, France and Finland have similar levels of public spending on education – 5.4 percent and 5.9 of GDP, respectively – and social spending overall is also comparable (Busemeyer 2014, 125–126). France's welfare state lies near the cluster of Scandinavian countries, where education is regarded as "a complementary addition to social policy" (Busemeyer 2014, 134). State commitment to education in France diverges from the approach taken by liberal market economies like the United Kingdom, where education is largely privatized. And yet, inequalities in student achievement are considerable in France, and may be even worse than in the United Kingdom (Duru-Bellat and Suchaut 2005; Doyle 2021). There are, at the same time, important differences in the formal institutions governing school education in Finland and France. While recognizing these differences, I suggest that bureaucratic norms may also contribute to the variations in education delivery and learning outcomes between the two countries.

8.4.1 Finland

Finland stands out among advanced economies for its high-performing and egalitarian public education system. Finnish students perform comparatively well on the PISA test in reading, science and mathematics.[17] Finland also exhibits a more equitable distribution of learning outcomes across socioeconomic groups. The bottom quintile of Finnish students outperform their peers in other countries on PISA by a considerable margin, helping to raise Finland's aggregate achievement level.[18] Disparities in learning, between different schools and individual students, are among the lowest in the OECD. Geographic location and family background are also less important determinants of student performance. Public spending on education does not fully explain these superior results, as learning outcomes improved even when education spending somewhat declined (Sahlberg 2007, 161).

What, then, are the institutional factors that help to account for the superior performance of Finland's school system? Sabel et al. (2011) outline a combination of formal and informal mechanisms for deliberation and collective problem-solving, which enable systematic tailoring

[17] The average Finnish student is 40 percent of a standard deviation ahead of the average American student.

[18] Other countries with better performing bottom quintile of students include South Korea and Canada.

of services to the needs of individual students. Their analysis starts by recognizing that learning is a highly complex, idiosyncratic process that varies across individuals. Education services have to be customized to the diverse needs of individual students, and continuously monitored and updated as circumstances change. Further, they note the growing heterogeneity of student populations throughout the world, owing to increased participation of girls and immigrant children, for instance, making the customization of education more important. Last, they suggest, education has to be made available to students as early as possible, since the acquisition of foundational reading and arithmetic skills in early years has a cascading effect on subsequent achievement.

The Finnish school system has met the challenge of providing high-quality, customized education in several ways. First, the early detection and treatment of learning difficulties – this begins before children enter primary schooling – is facilitated by a network of child health clinics. University researchers along with clinicians and teachers work together to codevelop tools for diagnosing learning difficulties, along with materials and training programmes for remedial teaching. Second, Finnish schools are supported by a Student Welfare Group (SWG). This multi-professional association oversees the physical and psychological welfare of individual students, tracks their progress and monitors the learning environment in schools. SWG membership can include the school principal, psychologist and nurse, a regular and special education teacher, a social worker and student advisor. Systematic reviews of classes and individual students take place at least once a year, with more frequent meetings held for addressing school-wide challenges. Third, a cadre of special education teachers and assistants work in consultation with other professionals and civic bodies to create customized syllabi and pedagogy for individual students. Through continuous review of student progress, teaching content and techniques are updated according to changing circumstances.

Institutional practices around education, including cross-sectoral coordination and continuous review, are supported by bureaucratic norms promoting deliberation and local flexibility. Deliberative governance of education was historically tied to Finland's school reform movement of the 1960s and 1970s, starting with the 1968 School System Act, which guaranteed free primary education. The new legislation created comprehensive schools, where mixed-ability students were taught together for nine years. Training reforms raised the mandatory qualifications for primary school teachers and helped establish education as a university subject (Simola 1993). The National Board of General Education (NBGE) oversaw reform implementation throughout Finland, from decisions on the curriculum and textbooks to the creation of new schools. The most important decisions were centralized, with the education minister setting standards for teacher qualifications and class sizes, while granting provincial officials the authority over teacher hiring decisions. Meanwhile, decentralization in the 1990s gave schools greater autonomy over instruction and teachers the freedom to decide on lesson plans. As Wiborg notes, "The national curriculum ... became much less detailed and prescriptive, and allowed municipalities and schools to adjust it in order to meet local needs" (2017, 175). Local planning and consultation were facilitated through municipal education committees, enabling local officials to propose different models of school reform in accordance with central mandates. Teachers and university representatives participated in reform committees that oversaw implementation of school-level changes. Characteristic of "the Nordic way," the legal mandate to establish SWGs arrived relatively recently (Sabel et al. 2011). Nor were there state-mandated rules for SWG membership and functioning. Rather, SWGs developed informally through collaborations between teachers and other education stakeholders.

It should be noted that deliberation in the schooling system has operated in the backdrop of Finland's corporatist system, which facilitates bargaining by interest groups, including the country's powerful teacher union.[19] During decentralization, the teacher union sought representation within the Ministry of Education's working groups, strengthening its "already-close proximity to the state apparatus" (Wiborg 2017, 176). Teachers have engaged in both formal and informal modes of deliberation strategically, for example, to secure better terms of employment.[20] These observations remind us that strategic actors can use deliberative platforms in self-interest. That said, routinized deliberation between parents, teachers and administrators has also fostered trust in the education system, enabling joint problem-solving at the local level and customized service delivery.

8.4.2 France

Whereas Finland's school system leads the international league tables, France performs near the OECD average. Inequalities in education achievement

[19] On deliberation and interest group representation within corporatist systems, see Mansbridge (1992).

[20] A critical view suggests that Finnish teachers have engaged in deliberation to block reforms (Simola 2005, 461–463; Wiborg 2017, 178).

in France are also more pronounced. Since the first PISA round in 2000, the performance of the bottom quintile of French students has declined, while the results of the top performers have improved (Dobbins and Martens 2012). Disparities in achievement between socioeconomic groups are particularly stark. In the 2018 PISA round, French students in the top and bottom quartiles of socioeconomic status had a gap in reading of 107 points, much larger than the OECD average gap of 88 points (Doyle 2021, 4–5). Economically disadvantaged students appear less hopeful of succeeding in school. For example, one in five high-achieving students from disadvantaged backgrounds reported that they did not expect to complete tertiary education, compared to one in thirteen among more privileged students. By contrast, in Finland and other leading countries in PISA (e.g. South Korea and Canada), overall country performance correlates positively with lesser disparity between better and worse performing pupils.

France's lackluster showing on PISA has gained attention in research and policy circles. Some have critiqued the French assessment regime, while others have sought to understand why achievement is weak among disadvantaged students (Pons 2016). Nearly 40 percent of French students have to repeat a grade, against the international average of 5 to 10 percent. French students trail their OECD peers in terms of their academic level, with differences becoming more apparent by age fifteen, which is when PISA is administered (Duru-Bellat and Suchaut 2005). Demands have arisen for a more proactive policy approach, including calls to emulate the "Finnish model," known for its flexibility and attentiveness to underperforming students (Dobbins and Martens 2012).

Disparities in student learning in France bring the administration of its school system into focus. An important feature of the French state, bureaucratic centralization has long shaped the governance of education (Archer 1979). The central government holds decisive authority at all levels of education, consistent with principles of uniformity in governance (Suleiman 1974). French students are taught under a common curriculum set by the *Bulletin official del' Éducation nationale* and are expected to pass national standardized tests. Uniform approaches to teaching, resource allocation and evaluation are celebrated as indications of the national state's commitment to equality. Through centralized administration of schooling, the French state has also sought to inculcate in students the ideals of civic republicanism, such as equality and uniformity (Corbett 2002). In addition to formal centralization, Peters (2021, 54–74) underscores the importance of France's legalistic bureaucracy. Legalism in France embodies the notion that public administration is defined by law and that the bureaucrat is "first and foremost a legal official" (Peters 2021, 58). Administrators are expected to apply the law uniformly across cases, preserving the collective interests of society above the private concerns of individuals.

Peters traces legalism back to the Napoleonic system of governance, which sought to ensure administrative control as it extended public services over a large territory. The state was envisioned as a dominant, unifying force that could overcome social divisions. Legalistic bureaucracy sought to project consistency in policy responses and the equal treatment of citizens.[21] A prime example of legalism, according to Peters, is the *Counseil d'Etat*, whose function is "to monitor the legality of administrative actions, and to approve or disapprove the actions of public servants" (2021, 59). The legalistic approval process aims to achieve centralized control over bureaucratic agencies, influencing routine accountability practices. Public expenditures are overseen by the *Cours des comptes* (Court of Audit), an auditing agency that pursues legality by holding a court. Having a "court" within the state to monitor that very state's adherence to law embodies the notion of legalistic accountability. The French state also makes wide use of "inspectorates," government agencies charged with monitoring the activities of other agencies (e.g. schools and prisons) and reporting on malfeasance. These disparate elements, Peters suggests, present a coherent sum of legalistic bureaucracy. They also contrast with other bureaucratic ideals, such as New Public Management, which underscores the importance of managerial performance.

Elements of legalistic bureaucracy condition everyday practices within France's school system. Sharpe's (1992) comparative ethnography of two primary schools in a northern French town captures how bureaucratic commitment to uniformity and equal treatment percolate down into the classroom. Despite the different socioeconomic conditions of each school, Sharpe observes remarkably similar patterns of behavior and pedagogy. Teachers in both schools adhered to administrative prescriptions and rarely discussed the differing educational needs of individual students. or even the differences across classrooms, which were "almost invariably

[21] Although he does not weigh into the origins of legalistic bureaucracy in France, Peters gestures to Tilly's (1986) account of the "contentious French." A centralized, rule-oriented bureaucracy was a response to the challenges of governing a mobilized society given to engaging in strikes, demonstrations and class-based conflicts.

regarded as homogeneous groups" (Sharpe 1992, 336). Connecting these behaviors to French traditions of civic republicanism, Sharpe observes: "Schools are therefore expected to offer every child exactly the same curriculum and exactly the same pedagogy irrespective of who they are, where they live, or even, within limits, whatever abilities they may have or lack" (Sharpe 1992, 339).

Homogeneity in teaching practices is reinforced by bureaucratic norms that identify teachers as members of the national civil service. Teachers are seen first and foremost as employees of the Ministry of Education in Paris, not of the local governments or school districts in which they work. Teachers understand themselves to be "civil servants," an orientation that reinforces uniformity in service provision (Peters 2021, 61). Relations between the education bureaucracy and schools are hierarchical. Schools are expected to collate administrative data and their pedagogical duties are circumscribed under centralized guidelines. Higher administration has a virtual monopoly on evaluating its own performance; it relies on its own statistical indicators to measure the relevance of its decisions and grants a limited role to local-level actors (Laforgue 2007). Although recent education reforms have increased formal autonomy among schools, heads of schools face the risk of hierarchical sanctions for engaging in experimentation and failing to comply with rules (Laforgue 2007; Doyle 2021). Consequently, opportunities for multi-stakeholder deliberations, such as those facilitated by Finnish SWGs (involving the nurse, social worker, principal and special education advisor), are severely curtailed in the French education system. This is detrimental to weaker students, who stand to benefit most from these deliberative mechanisms (Dobbins and Martens 2012). Finally, the top-down policymaking process, which operates without deliberation, prevents trust-building and stymies the communication of feedback from local stakeholders. Political confrontations and strikes have, consequently, become a primary means for influencing governmental policy directives. The risk of political obstruction creates hesitation within the government to entertain experimental reforms, contributing to a policy environment that is less adaptive to emerging needs.

These administrative features of French education bear resemblances to the legalistic bureaucratic norms observed in northern India. Teachers that I interviewed commonly referred to themselves as "government workers" (*sarkari karamchari*), accountable upward to the state rather than to the communities they served. To maintain their civil service protections and other employment conditions, teacher unions have pressured state governments to centralize decision-making and limit the scope of reforms that would increase community oversight of schooling (Béteille, Kingdon and Muzammil 2017). Compared to India, education reforms in France have gone much further in decentralizing school administration and making services responsive to communities.[22] School headmasters and local councils enjoy greater autonomy to plan and utilize budgets. Nevertheless, administration of teaching personnel, national curriculum and other aspects of education policy remain centralized. According to Dobbins, teacher unions in France have pressed for the dilution of reforms, leading to "pseudo-decentralization" of education (2017, 100). The state's ability to experiment with new approaches has been curtailed and local agencies are prevented "from adapting solutions and financial means to local needs" (Dobbins 2017, 107). While recognizing the potential benefits of *de jure* decentralization, Peters suggests, decentralization in France "does little to alter the legalistic nature of public administration" (2021, 59). Education reform in France thus provokes questions as to whether and how decentralization's promise can be achieved under a legalistic bureaucracy, even in a wealthy and vibrant democracy.

8.5 CONCLUSION

In this chapter I have placed the book's arguments in comparative perspective, examining how legalistic and deliberative bureaucratic norms operate and shape public service delivery in cases outside northern India. The investigation of Kerala's comparative achievements in education revealed that deliberative bureaucracy is most responsive to citizens where social movements and political competition help sustain democratic articulation of subaltern demands (Sandbrook et al. 2007). The case also suggested how state-building processes can influence contemporary service delivery, emphasizing bureaucracy's historical engagement with non-state education providers, an underappreciated attribute of social development in Kerala. Bureaucracy in Kerala learned how to work with religious authorities, private schools and civil society organizations that provided social services, establishing mechanisms for the joint management of schools and co-governance of public goods more broadly. These

[22] Schmidt (1990) suggests further that France's informal systems of governance granted authority to local officials, countering centralization. Decentralization reforms in the 1980s formalized these norms, though education was among the slowest ministries to decentralize authority.

observations point to the need for further research investigating how, in the process of state-building, bureaucracies learn to govern public services and forge relationships with non-state service providers (Cammett and MacLean 2014; Ansell and Lindvall 2021).

In contrast to Kerala, the Chinese case explored how deliberative bureaucracy functions in a non-democratic context. Mechanisms of policy adaptation in China's education system (and other policy domains) revealed unanticipated parallels with India, highlighting the importance of deliberation by higher-level agencies to support local experimentation. The provisional observation, that bureaucratic commitment to deliberation has facilitated the implementation of public services in China, in some ways more effectively than it has in India, merits further study. The comparison of school education in Finland and France pointed to the advantages of deliberation for improving the education of underprivileged students in advanced economies. The case of Finland suggested how deliberative governance supports customized education services, encouraging cross-sectoral coordination to identify and respond to individual needs, thereby enabling students from different social backgrounds and learning levels to succeed. Meanwhile, the case of France showed how legalistic bureaucracy encourages uniformity in the implementation of education services, but at the same time leads to inequalities in achievement between students from different geographies and social classes. While the findings are tentative and require deeper investigation, the comparative analysis of Finland and France suggests that informal bureaucratic norms matter for the implementation of high quality education, even where formal institutions are strong.

9

Conclusion

Reimagining Bureaucracy for Inclusive Development

9.1 INTRODUCTION

This book was animated by the puzzling differences in the implementation of primary education in northern India. Subject to the same national policies, constitutional-legal framework, administrative structures and electoral institutions, it sought to explain why and how bureaucracies in some cases have delivered primary education more effectively than others. The theory and evidence presented underscores the importance of bureaucratic norms–unwritten rules that influence the behavior of state officials and their relations with citizens. Through a multilevel comparative study, I have shown that bureaucratic norms vary systematically across north Indian states and help account for variation in service delivery. The findings stress the advantages of deliberative bureaucracy, which encourages a problem-based orientation, over legalistic rule-following bureaucracy. Deliberative bureaucratic norms were shown to enable state officials to undertake complex tasks, coordinate with society and adapt policies to local needs, yielding higher quality education services. These findings are impressive considering that rural north India is not where one would anticipate bureaucracy to function well in the first instance.

In highlighting the impact of bureaucratic norms on implementation, I should stress that my argument also recognizes the significance of other factors. Policy implementation is a causally complex process. The research design took alternative explanations into account, including geography, colonial land institutions and the agrarian economic structure. Chapter 2 also took note of prominent political explanations, operating at different levels of analysis, that could influence implementation. My findings at the state level accord with research demonstrating that two-party competition in India is more conducive for social service provision than fragmented, multiparty systems (Chhibber and Nooruddin 2004; Nooruddin and Simmons 2015; Thachil and Teitelbaum 2015). However, in contrast to prior work, which shows how electoral incentives influence levels of social spending, I suggest that party systems can also operate through administrative mechanisms, influencing how officials plan and utilize public resources. Furthermore, research at the village level investigated social capital's bearing on community monitoring of schools (Krishna 2003). Sociocultural norms and inequalities were observed to influence collective action by marginalized groups. Nevertheless, my fieldwork revealed that bureaucratic norms can shape the nature of village collective action over time, leading to differences in the coproduction of services and local accountability of schools.

In this concluding chapter, I review my findings and contributions to the fields of comparative politics, development and public administration. The theoretical framework, anchored in bureaucratic norms, brings institutionalist perspectives on the state and social policy together with insights from literatures on street-level bureaucracy and local collective action. The conceptual interweaving of meso-level institutional processes with the micro-politics of service delivery yields a new understanding of bureaucracy and its connection to human development. Along with scholarly contributions, I explore policy implications, particularly for reform efforts to enhance primary education and other frontline public services in developing countries.

9.2 BRINGING BUREAUCRACY BACK IN

Bureaucracy does not often inspire praise. Researchers have cast bureaucracy as "inefficient, lazy, incompetent, wasteful, inflexible, unaccountable, and inhumane" (Olsen 2008, 14).[1] These negative assessments motivate drives for reform, such as New Public Management, which calls for private sector-style contracts and incentives (Dunleavy and Hood 1994). Bureaucracy is also found wanting from the perspective of democratic accountability, as noted by calls for collaborative and network-based governance (Ansell and Gash 2007; Bevir 2010). The literature on distributive

[1] See Du Gay (2000).

politics in developing countries is no less pessimistic about bureaucracy's constructive potential. Bureaucrats are portrayed as cogs in the wheels of clientelism (Kitschelt and Wilkinson 2007). State agencies that deliver social services are seen as egregious sites of patronage and political interference (Brun and Diamond 2014). Under conditions of weak state capacity, mechanisms of democratic competition are found to yield "visible" gains in school enrollment, but little improvement in the provision of schooling inputs, services or learning outcomes (Harding and Stasavage 2014). Along these lines, Indian democracy is weighed down by a bureaucracy that is deemed to be captured and corrupt, incapable of executing its core functions (Wade 1982; Iyer and Mani 2011).

Nevertheless, as I have shown, bureaucracy is not everywhere the same in India. This book departs from the pessimistic view of public agencies in developing countries, bringing to the fore the remarkable differences in bureaucratic performance within the Hindi belt, a region associated with clientelism and patronage politics (Chandra 2004; Keefer and Khemani 2004). Delivery of education services poses a particularly difficult test for bureaucracy given chronic political neglect of primary education in this region, as well as the absence of leftist government and subaltern movements demanding social rights (Heller 1999; Ahuja 2019). During twenty-eight months of field research, I observed local administrators and teachers travel great distances to ensure that primary education reached villages. Even in rural Uttar Pradesh, where identity politics and ethnic targeting are thought to divert public resources away from programmatic ends, bureaucrats committed to legalism used their discretion to direct resources to primary schools in need. It is all too easy to overlook the effort of bureaucrats laboring quietly from a sense of duty. Instead, my approach builds on scholarship exploring the possibilities for bureaucracy to function well amid institutional weaknesses and political constraints (Uphoff 1994; Grindle 1997; Tendler 1997; Chand 2006).

There are, of course, many instances where bureaucracy falls short. In India and elsewhere, citizen encounters with the state can end in frustration. Such cases, considered throughout this book, often get framed as examples of bureaucratic shirking and corruption (Klitgaard 1988). Yet, deficiencies in service delivery can occur even when officials abide by policy rules. Collapsing all such cases as instances of corruption depends on an overly stylized view of implementation and bureaucratic discretion, which distorts empirical reality more than it clarifies it. Discretion is deemed to be problematic because, theoretically, it provides rent-seeking opportunities. However, discretion is a necessary feature of public service work and, in some cases, it is preferable to administrative control (Tendler and Freedheim 1994; Piore 2011; Honig 2018). That is not to say that bureaucrats always apply discretion in public-spirited ways; they can and do succumb to the temptations of rent-seeking. It is inappropriate, however, to treat discretion as synonymous with rent-seeking. Nor is it obvious that more and tighter rules are a bulwark against misuse of discretion.[2] As Gupta (2012) shows, conscientious adherence to rules and procedures in India can generate the opposite effect, leading officials to apply "red tape" and deny citizens essential services. Instead of assuming that discretion is harmful, my framework of legalistic and deliberative bureaucratic norms helps decipher alternative ways in which discretion can be applied in various administrative tasks.

The pessimism surrounding bureaucracy is in part due to the paucity of field-based investigations of public agencies in developing countries. In India, few empirical studies catalog the internal dynamics of the state and its ordinary relations with citizens. I have attempted to help fill this void. My analysis of the striking variation in policy implementation by education bureaucracies in India joins recent studies of state capacity in developing countries (Piore and Schrank 2008; Schrank 2009; Canales 2014; Amengual 2016; Ang 2016a; Williams 2017; Bersch 2019; Dasgupta and Kapur 2020; McDonnell 2020). Whereas others have emphasized the role of policy entrepreneurs, administrative resources and formal structures of the state, my argument underscores the stark differences in the norms that guide state officials on how to understand their duties. As I have shown, bureaucracies in India with identical formal administrative structures have developed very different informal norms that shape their internal operations and external ties with society. There is more than one bureaucratic ethos.

The advantages of integrating norms into the analysis of bureaucracy can be gleaned from the vibrant debates on state capacity in the United States. On the one hand, public agencies in the United States have historically been depicted as weak and politicized (Novak 2008). Formal bureaucratic structures are shown to bend to the political will of elected officials and interest groups (Moe 1989). At the same time, studies identify vast differences in the informal norms and culture of public agencies in the United States (Kaufman 1967; Wilson 1978; DiIulio 1994). These

[2] For a critique of the faith often placed in well-specified policy rules, see Sabel (2012) and Fukuyama (2013).

differences in norms can have political implications. As Carpenter (2001) demonstrates, executive agencies like the US Postal Service used their discretionary authority to build an organizational culture of performance. They created network ties with societal groups and earned a reputation for innovative work, which over time allowed them to loosen the shackles of political control and secure their autonomy. These debates suggest that bureaucracy is not merely an instrument for political ends, but an institution bound by norms, with political authority in its own right.

9.3 DELIBERATION AND THE DEVELOPMENTAL STATE

This book contributes to comparative scholarship on the state and inclusive development. The developmental state literature has demonstrated how bureaucracy has facilitated industrial development and economic growth in East Asia (Haggard 2018). *Inclusive* development, however, calls for administrative mechanisms that support the expansion of human capabilities (Sen 1999). There is a need, therefore, to reorient our understanding of the developmental state toward the provision of public services, in particular mass education and health (Evans and Heller 2015; Evans, Huber, and Stephens 2017). Accordingly, my argument has cast the spotlight on quotidian bureaucracies that coproduce primary education with citizens (Ostrom 1996). Coproduction of services is a cognitively difficult, transaction intensive and politically challenging work, presenting "wicked problems" for the state (Andrews, Pritchett and Woolcock 2017; Peters 2017). Beyond the technical details of policy design, the inclusive development agenda warrants a fundamental rethinking of bureaucracy and its relationship with society, and marginalized citizens in particular, who are asked to participate in coproduction.

I push the developmental state literature forward by offering a new theory centered on differences in bureaucratic norms that advances our understanding of bureaucracy's role in inclusive development. Chapter 2 theorized the ideal types of bureaucracy–legalistic and deliberative– and delineated the mechanisms whereby they generate differences in policy implementation. Subnational comparative field research in four north Indian states (Chapters 4–7) provided evidence for the material impacts of bureaucratic norms on the delivery of primary education. These divergent bureaucratic norms were shown to spark very different orientations among officials, influencing how they understand their policy mandates, apply discretion and encourage societal input. The empirical findings suggest that deliberation is a central component of developmental states oriented toward human capability expansion.[3] Although legalistic bureaucracy was shown to succeed at codified tasks, such as enrollment and the provision of schooling inputs, deliberative bureaucracy performed far better on complex tasks of school monitoring and teaching, yielding higher quality education services. Deliberative spaces for collective problem-solving by senior and frontline administrators, schoolteachers and parents enabled "thick" information exchange and coordination, as demonstrated through the case of Himachal Pradesh, allowing the state to adapt education policies to meet diverse local needs.

In arguing for the significance of bureaucratic norms, I do not discount the importance of formal Weberian institutions. Bureaucratic autonomy, corporate coherence and commitment to impartial rules are important restraints against corruption, predation and other pathologies (Evans and Rauch 1999; Rothstein 2011). Rule-following is encouraged by *esprit de corps*, a corporate culture supported by meritocratic selection, training and promotion (Levi and Sherman 1997, 332–333). Where formal state institutions are comparatively weak and politicized, creating a bureaucratic ethos of rule-following remains a first-order challenge, as McDonnell (2020) observes in her study of public institutions in Ghana. McDonnell demonstrates that "pockets of effectiveness" within the state depend on bureaucratic subcultures that build commitment to administrative rules and boundaries, countering political pressures. Seen from this angle, the presence of legalistic bureaucracy in parts of northern India is a noteworthy achievement. Nevertheless, when it comes to the challenges of inclusive development, bureaucratic commitment to rules is not enough. To implement quality services, bureaucracies need to solve complex problems and adapt to local needs, which is best achieved when bureaucratic norms encourage robust deliberation.

My book's arguments about bureaucracy and inclusive development are based on evidence from India's primary education sector. However, the theoretical framework of bureaucratic norms offers insights for other policy arenas as well. Ever since Gunnar Myrdal's (1968) depiction of India as a "soft state," scholars have cataloged its bureaucracy's uneven performance across policy functions. The Indian state has been variously described as "weak-strong" (Rudolph and Rudolph 1987), "failed developmental" (Herring 1999), "Sisyphean" (Kapur and Mukhopadhyay

[3] These findings also lend empirical support to Evans' (2004; 2015) recommendation for incorporating deliberation into the developmental state.

2007) and "flailing" (Pritchett 2009). These formulations suggest that Indian bureaucracy has the potential to achieve development goals by virtue of its semi-Weberian design, but it falls short of its theoretical promise owing to societal demands, resource constraints and particularistic politics. Pritchett's (2009) notion of a "flailing" state adds another dimension to the assessment, highlighting the disconnect between the "brains" of Indian bureaucracy, the elite agencies that formulate policy, and its "limbs," the frontline agencies tasked with implementation. There are likely many reasons for this disconnect. My argument demonstrates that institutional barriers to deliberation are one critical source of dysfunction, while the social distance that legalistic bureaucracy creates between state planners and lower-level functionaries is another.[4] These barriers are reinforced by legalism's penchant for upholding hierarchical divisions and written documentation as a mode of internal communication, which can disempower frontline workers and divert their energies away from solving citizens' practical needs.[5]

Equally, it may be that the elite agencies constituting the "brain" of the Indian state are not as well functioning as they appear. Chibber (2002; 2003) has demonstrated that a bureaucratic culture of rule-following in elite economic institutions, such as the Planning Commission, stifled interagency coordination and weakened the execution of industrial policy in the decades following independence. Despite having capable officers from the Indian Administrative Service, who drew up sophisticated five-year plans, Chibber finds that an excessive reliance on formal rules and procedures undermined policy implementation. On the other hand, there are also moments where bureaucratic norms support interdepartmental coordination. Indian bureaucracy is not always flailing. As Kapur (2020) observes, the periodic administering of elections in India brings disparate arms of the state together on a massive scale, with intensive coordination among the police and other agencies. He notes puzzling discrepancies in state performance as well, such as the remarkable strides India has made in eradicating polio, even as public health systems languish. More research is needed to identify the causes of uneven bureaucratic

[4] Elsewhere, I have shown that the organizational culture of police agencies creates communication barriers and social distance between elite officers in the Indian Police Service and the rank-and-file constabulary posted in the field (Mangla and Kapoor 2021).

[5] Aiyar and her collaborators refer to this phenomenon as "the post office state" (Aiyar, Dongre and Davis 2015; Aiyar and Bhattacharya 2016). On the Indian bureaucracy's fealty to written documents, see Raman (2012) and Mathur (2016). For related work on bureaucracy in Pakistan, see Hull (2012).

performance in India.[6] Bureaucratic norms, I submit, merit consideration alongside other plausible factors.

These examples from outside the primary education domain also cast doubt on the proposition that rational-legal norms are always the surest path to effective state performance. Perhaps the most striking example of divergence from rational-legal norms comes from China. The Chinese bureaucracy's contributions to economic and social development are bewildering from the vantage point of Weberian bureaucracy. Alternative models of public administration have been proposed, theorizing norms that vary widely from the Weberian rational-legal ideal (Rothstein 2015; Ang 2016b; Heilmann and Perry 2011). Explored in Chapter 8, Ang's (2016a) account of "directed improvisation" underscores the importance of bureaucratic flexibility and local adaptation for poverty reduction. Her argument resonates with my conception of deliberative bureaucracy, albeit with the difference that my framework also highlights how different bureaucratic norms activate alternative pathways for societal feedback. The emphasis on feedback also brings out the advantages of democratic arrangements, especially the freedom to associate and voice dissent. The brief examination of China in Chapter 8 does not consider subnational differences in bureaucratic norms, the study of which would enrich our understanding of Chinese bureaucracy.

My argument linking state action to societal feedback during implementation also advances scholarship on embeddedness, the state–society linkages associated with high performing developmental states (Evans 1995). Instead of industrial capitalists, however, inclusive development requires bureaucracy to connect with mass publics. Chapter 2 theorized societal feedback as a dynamic process of interaction between citizens and local bureaucracies. When citizens seek public services, they learn how local agencies function, and, gradually, form expectations and collective strategies. Legalistic bureaucracy embeds itself through officially recognized channels, such as Village Education Committees (VECs), encouraging citizens to monitor services and voice demands through systems for grievance redressal. However, these channels impose administrative burdens on citizens, which limit the state's ability to "see" and respond adequately to societal demands (Scott 1998). Meanwhile, the problem-based orientation of deliberative bureaucracy motivates state officials to discuss

[6] Along with norms, Mukherji (2014) suggests that the policy ideas of bureaucrats are a driver of economic reform. See also Mehta and Walton (2014).

BUREAUCRATIC NORMS

SOCIOECONOMIC INEQUALITY	**Legalistic**	**Deliberative**
High	***Episodic coproduction*** • Community mobilization around services is fragmented and episodic E.g. UP (Ch. 4); Bihar (Ch. 7)	***Conflictual coproduction*** • Community mobilization around services induces social conflict and elite backlash E.g. Mahila Samakhya in UP (Ch. 7)
Low	***Substitutive coproduction*** • Community mobilization gets redirected toward (private) substitutes E.g. Uttarakhand (Ch. 6)	***Inclusive coproduction*** • Community mobilization guided toward complementary inputs to public services E.g. Himachal Pradesh (Ch. 5)

FIGURE 9.1 Regimes of coproduction

policy problems with societal groups, including informal associations, enlarging the spaces for marginalized citizens to monitor services and communicate demands.

The difficulties of promoting substantive citizen participation in public service delivery are well recognized, especially in contexts of social inequality (Fox 2007; Houtzager and Acharya 2011; Heller and Rao 2015). The design of this study accounted for regional differences in socioeconomic inequality within northern India. Inequality was considered both in terms of the agrarian economy, by incorporating land-ownership patterns (Bardhan, Ghatak, and Karaivanov 2007), and with respect to gender and caste relations (Agarwal 1997). My comparative field research gave rise to four theoretically distinct local-level patterns, or what I call "regimes" of coproduction (Figure 9.1). The matched-pair comparison of HP (Chapter 5) and Uttarakhand (Chapter 6) identified differences in coproduction within the western Himalayas, a region with relatively less inequality. Deliberative bureaucracy in HP supported *inclusive* coproduction, broad-based societal participation and complementary investments from communities, helping to bind households to government schools. In Uttarakhand, by contrast, legalistic bureaucracy provided a platform for societal input, but gradually induced communities to seek *non*-state services, a pattern of *substitutive* coproduction. Community efforts to hold government schools accountable were frustrated, compelling households to seek private tutoring and exit for non-state services. Village collective action in Uttarakhand did not diminish, but instead shifted away from government services to support private and "hybrid" forms of education provision (Cammett and MacLean 2014; Post, Bronsoler, and Salman 2017). Legalistic bureaucracy is thus shown to induce privatization.[7] The divergent patterns of coproduction observed in the two Himalayan states are more striking given that the case-study villages had similar levels of social capital, evidenced by membership in village-wide women's associations, shared religious practices and other forms of social cooperation (Krishna 2003). Village collective action was found to enhance education services in both states, but differences in bureaucratic norms had a significant impact when it came to sustaining community participation and investment in government schools.

In the Gangetic plains, where inequality is higher, marginalized citizens encountered greater hurdles to participation in service delivery. Compared to the Himalayan region, social relations in UP villages were more fragmented and unequal on economic, caste and gender lines. Households still came together at various junctures to monitor primary schooling, but they were discouraged by their experiences with VECs and district administration. Collective action around schooling did not cease entirely, but proceeded in spurts, following a pattern of *episodic* coproduction. These observations from UP echo Ostrom's (1996) findings about the fragile nature of coproduction in rural Nigeria. As she observes, "[v]illages that had demonstrated their capabilities to engage in collective action were discouraged by government officials from active engagement in the education of their children" (1996, 1076). However, comparative findings from within UP suggest the possibilities for an alternative path. The study of Mahila Samakhya's programming on girls' education in Chapter 7 demonstrated how deliberative bureaucracy helps to sustain the robust engagement of marginalized groups. Frontline

7 For an institutional analysis of state-induced privatization in India's education system, see Davies (2018).

workers mobilized Dalit women and countered village hierarchies to promote public deliberation, a process that induced social conflict and backlash from upper castes.[8] Through deliberation, Dalit parents learned that their engagement in school meetings meant something. The pattern of coproduction nevertheless remained *conflictual*. Mahila Samkhya frontline workers mediated conflicts, serving as "pressure groups," to counter societal inequalities and challenge conventional norms in the bureaucracy.

The four coproduction regimes that I have outlined capture theoretical differences in local state–society relations impacting policy implementation. They also point to the bureaucratic mechanisms that help invigorate coproduction in hierarchical settings. Where coproduction is conflictual, for example, frontline officials must take an activist stance to support marginalized groups when they make claims on the state. The significance of bureaucratic activism in support of disadvantaged groups is further demonstrated in comparative research from Latin America. Abers (2019) shows how activism took hold in Brazil's environmental bureaucracy, motivating officials to challenge rules and support contentious causes. Similarly, Rich (2019) finds that the health bureaucracy in Brazil fostered societal activism, forging a state–civil society coalition to combat AIDS. These and other Latin American cases reinforce the point us that coproduction is a political process requiring active support from the state (Baiocchi 2003).

Understanding why bureaucratic norms and cultures diverge across settings requires us to engage with the comparative history and politics of state-building (Slater 2010; Soifer 2015; Centeno et al. 2017).[9] Historical evidence suggests that the political conditions for deliberative bureaucratic norms to thrive are relatively rare. At its normative core, deliberation involves a submission to the constraints of public reason (Rawls 1996, 212–254). The political commitment to deliberation means, at minimum, that bureaucracy must be willing to listen and respond to reasonable demands from the public. However, state elites are reluctant to submit to such demands, more so when they are made by the least advantaged (Acemoglu and Robinson 2006). In HP, deliberative bureaucracy emerged from the historically specific process

[8] Brulé (2020) makes an insightful argument about elite backlash during the implementation of laws protecting women's property rights in India.

[9] See also the work on political settlements, which emphasizes power configurations and conflicts underlying bureaucratic reforms (Khan 2010; Hickey, Sen and Bukenya 2015).

of state-building, where elite cooperation was spurred by political marginalization and the acute need for central government resources. Elsewhere in India, programmatic social movements have been critical to the forging of deliberative institutions, as in the case of Kerala (Heller 1999). Explored briefly in Chapter 8, Kerala's deliberative bureaucracy has supported mass education and the deepening of local democracy. The success of these projects was also contingent on historical social movements led by subaltern groups as well as civil society organizations (Isaac and Heller 2003). Where social movement politics has not materialized, deliberative bureaucracy's reach is more likely to be restricted to geographic and administrative pockets of the state, as witnessed in the case of Mahila Samakhya in UP. Additional research is needed to identify the political factors that enable deliberative bureaucracy to take root and flourish more fully.

This book's arguments pertain mainly to bureaucracy and public services in developing countries. However, increased global attention to economic inequality and social discrimination suggests that inclusive development has also become a matter of concern for advanced economies (Hacker 2006; Lieberman 2011; Case and Deaton 2020). My theoretical construct of deliberative bureaucracy builds on scholarship examining how deliberative and pragmatic governance arrangements can address complex policy problems in North America and Europe (Cohen and Sabel 1997; Fung 2006; Ansell 2011; Sabel and Zeitlin 2012; Moffitt 2014). Public administration scholars have similarly called for a rethinking of how bureaucracy can support vulnerable groups in these regions (Nabatchi 2010; Maynard-Moody and Musheno 2012; Brodkin 2016). Extending my argument to OECD countries, Chapter 8 offered a comparative sketch of school education in Finland and France. The comparison proposed, albeit provisionally, that differences in bureaucratic norms help account for variation in the performance of school systems across the two countries, leading to differences in student achievement. Finland's superior and more equitable achievement results were tied to deliberation by Finnish Student Welfare Groups as well as education and health agencies, encouraging "individualized service delivery" (Sabel 2012). In France, meanwhile, legalistic bureaucracy has pressed for centralized control and uniformity of education delivery, lessening the school system's capacity for local adaptation. More research is needed to establish these propositions. The comparative study of bureaucratic norms opens up new avenues for future research on inclusive development within and across countries.

9.4 POLICY IMPLEMENTATION AND SOCIETAL FEEDBACK

My argument about bureaucracy's conditioning effects on citizens contributes to scholarship on policy feedback. This rich body of work has demonstrated the downstream political effects of social policies, which gradually can transform the landscape of mass politics (Pierson 1993; Mettler 2002; Campbell 2005; Kumlin and Rothstein 2005). I extend the insights of this literature to the terrain of public services in developing countries, where policy *implementation* generates its own politics (Grindle 1980). Further, my emphasis here is on mundane forms of participation beyond elections, driven by the collective needs of underprivileged groups (Davies and Falleti 2017). Though relatively rare, studies of policy feedback in developing countries have the potential to transform our understanding of local governance and state–society relations.[10] Holding India's national primary education policy framework constant, I have shown that subnational differences in bureaucratic norms lead education officials to interpret the same policies in radically divergent ways, which in turn leads to very different citizen experiences of local bureaucracy. Examining this causal chain helps us understand why similarly placed social groups in India come to "see" the state so differently (Corbridge et al. 2005).

My argument for how bureaucratic norms induce varied societal responses during implementation brings policy feedback into conversation with public administration scholarship (Moynihan and Soss 2014). I find that legalistic bureaucracy triggers compliance-oriented school monitoring and administrative grievance procedures, creating opportunities for parents to register complaints. However, these channels impose administrative burdens that are disproportionately stacked against the least advantaged, making it harder for them to hold public service providers to account (Goetz and Jenkins 2005; Herd and Moynihan 2018). I also find that legalistic bureaucracy reproduces caste inequalities and stigmas in the process of monitoring services, which can dissuade marginalized groups from following up on complaints. As Chapter 4 showed in the case of UP's Midday Meal Programme, local bureaucracy's rule-based interpretation of food "hygiene" comingled with dominant village narratives of caste-based pollution, which disempowered Dalit women and rendered futile their collective efforts to monitor school meals. By contrast, ordinary experiences of the local state enhanced the confidence

[10] For important exceptions, see Maclean (2010) and Auerbach and Kruks-Wisner (2020).

of rural women in HP as well as among Dalit women attached to UP's Mahila Samakhya program.

Attention to local bureaucracy's conditioning effects on societal participation invites a corrective to the conventional view that residents of northern India are apathetic about primary education and other collective goods. Studies of public service provision in UP, Bihar and other Hindi belt states point to a deficit of political "awareness" among rural residents, whose "apathy" and "inertia" are cited as a cause for implementation failures (Drèze and Gazdar 1996; Lanjouw and Stern 1998; World Bank 2003, 44–45; Singh 2016, 168–172). My argument reverses the direction of causality. Field research in villages across UP suggests that poor households were aware of deficiencies in government primary schools, that local monitoring was taking place and that parents did communicate grievances to the local state. However, their voices were muffled by a thicket of bureaucratic rules and procedures that weakened school accountability.[11] Societal "apathy" was not the cause of implementation failures but the *consequence* of concerned parents engaging in "active citizenship" through which they acquired practical knowledge of the local state.[12]

To be sure, the obstacles to societal monitoring of public services in the Hindi belt remain significant. The findings of this study concur with prior research identifying the difficulties in achieving substantive participation in collective institutions, especially among marginalized groups (Mansuri and Rao 2013). As Appadurai (2015) notes, behind a chain of participation, there often lies a string of performative failures. The question is whether such failures bring incremental gains that enlarge the aspirations of the poor. In that sense, this study suggests that cautious optimism regarding the possibilities of state-induced societal feedback in settings of inequality is warranted. Chapter 7 demonstrated that Mahila Samakhya's frontline workers encouraged village-level deliberation and supported Dalit women during public conflicts. Dalit households experienced greater confidence in their abilities to participate in school governance.[13] These positive dynamics filtered down into classrooms as well, encouraging Dalit girls who had previously dropped out of school to aspire for a better future.

[11] These observations accord with Gupta's (2012) ethnographic account of local administration in UP.

[12] Kruks-Wisner's (2018) argument about "active citizenship" in rural Rajasthan offers a powerful critique of the citizen apathy thesis. Also see Houtzager and Acharya (2011).

[13] These findings offer evidence for Herd and Moynihan's suggestion that "[p]ositive interactions with the state can increase citizen confidence and knowledge of opportunities, and allow them to develop participatory skills" (2018, 29).

This book's comparative examination of societal feedback across northern India suggests the benefits of combining field research with an historically situated analysis of subnational bureaucracies. I build on the methodological approach advanced by MacLean (2010) in her study of the state and citizenship in Africa. Drawing on village-level fieldwork and oral histories, Maclean identifies how the state in Ghana and Cote d'Ivoire spawned vastly different informal institutions and practices. In a similar way, my comparative ethnography of rural India identifies divergent societal responses to state bureaucracy. In the absence of historical data and written records, interviews and focus group discussions with village elders were a window into the histories of collective action in villages.[14] Without intensive fieldwork and attention to the temporal dimension of societal feedback, the political activities of marginalized groups can be missed.

9.5 STREET-LEVEL BUREAUCRACY AND THE INSTITUTIONS OF COLLECTIVE WELFARE

Scholarship on street-level bureaucracy has shed important light on the quotidian practices of the state (Lipsky 1984; Brodkin 1997; Maynard-Moody and Musheno 2003; Piore 2011; Zacka 2017). My argument advances this literature by situating the micro-politics of frontline service work within a multilevel comparative analysis of bureaucratic institutions. Tracing implementation processes over multiple tiers of the Indian state reveals the two-way interactions between citizens, frontline agencies and higher-level authorities.[15] This approach complicates the well-worn dichotomy between "top-down" administrative control and "bottom-up" discretion posited in the implementation literature (Sabatier 1986; Matland 1995).[16] The behavior of local officials, I find, is contingent on bureaucratic norms established upstream in the administrative hierarchy. Supervisory officials stationed in state capitals (or district headquarters) reinforce norms through their routine communications with subordinates, influencing how the latter understand their duties.[17] As shown in

[14] Also see Auerbach (2018) on the use of informal archives for reconstructing the administrative history of slum settlements in India.

[15] Bussell (2019) likewise demonstrates how the uneven provision of services at the local level in India induces citizens to seek support from higher-level officials.

[16] O'Brien and Li (1999) similarly question the "top-down" versus "bottom-up" dichotomy in their study of implementation in rural China.

[17] These findings support prior research showing that state-level factors help account for *local* variation in public goods provision in India (Banerjee, Iyer and Somanathan 2007).

Chapter 4, monitoring of the Midday Meal Programme by local officials in UP reflected a narrow, "accounting-based" interpretation of the policy, as propagated by state planners in Lucknow. By contrast, Mahila Samakhya's frontline workers in UP (Chapter 7) saw health and nutrition programming as integral to girls' education, a more capacious interpretation, encouraged by senior officials through gender-oriented training. I also find that street-level bureaucrats help sustain norms collectively from below. Local education officials in HP (Chapter 5) supported bureaucratic deliberation by seeking out village women's groups during adult literacy campaigns. These same officials later coordinated with state planners to experiment with models of school governance involving mother teacher associations.

The empirical findings also suggest the ways that frontline worker commitment and conflict supports processes of institutional persistence and change (Mahoney and Thelen 2010). Institutionalist scholars of different theoretical persuasions have recognized that the rules of the game are not merely applied, but also interpreted by officials, who can have conflicting ideas and interests (March and Olsen 1989; Mantzavinos, North, and Shariq 2004; Thelen 2004; Schmidt 2008). In that sense, not only do street-level bureaucrats achieve policy outputs, they also enact norms and practices that can reinforce, enhance or subvert institutions over time.[18] In developing countries, where informal rules often have greater purchase, the interpretive work of frontline agents helps to build and consolidate state institutions (Helmke and Levitsky 2004). For example, the institutional "layering" of the Mahila Samakhya program within the education bureaucracy sparked conflicts inside the state and between women's associations and local administration. While mediating such conflicts, frontline workers advocated for local-level changes in norms, which over time contributed to a shift in formal rules that expanded residential schooling for disadvantaged girls. In a contrasting case, local administration's commitment to legalism in Bihar was found to have frustrated the efforts of policymakers to institute innovative pedagogical reforms in classrooms. These findings accord with prior work on institutions of collective welfare, such as Falleti's (2010b) study of health reforms in Brazil, which point to gradual processes of

[18] Sheingate (2014) suggests that institutional analyses may profit from linking the study of frontline agencies with institutional processes at higher levels of the state. The significance of interactions between institutional levels is also suggested by research on multilevel governance (Hooghe and Marks 2003; Piattoni 2010).

change. Future research may go even further to connect street-level bureaucracies with comparative and historical institutional processes and probe the linkages between frontline work and the ideas and strategies of political actors located in the higher echelons of the state.

9.6 POLICY IMPLICATIONS

This study of bureaucratic norms carries policy implications, particularly for the reform of education and other public services. Developing countries throughout the world are in the midst of a learning crises (World Bank 2018). As the UN Millennium Development Goals program reached a close in 2015, 193 countries extended the pledge for "inclusive and equitable quality education" under the Sustainable Development Goals (SDG) program. To realize SDG 4 (Education), governments and international donor agencies have committed to ensuring that all children, including first-generation learners, acquire foundational skills in the early years of schooling (Beeharry 2021). These pronouncements are noteworthy and have the potential to transform the lives of millions of children. They also present daunting challenges for policymakers and practitioners. Meanwhile, the COVID-19 pandemic has taken an immeasurable toll on human life and economic livelihoods, while wreaking havoc on school systems worldwide (UNESCO 2021). The pandemic has also brought attention to the critical need for strengthening frontline state capacity.

Amid these concerns, the policy advice given to developing countries has also undergone important changes. The earlier impulse to recommend a universal policy blueprint (or the "right" institutions) was criticized for imposing unrealistic demands on developing country governments, while ignoring their sociopolitical contexts (Evans 2004; Grindle 2004). More attention is now accorded to the historical conditions of institutional development (Acemoglu and Robinson 2012). Micro-level research has aimed to guide reforms incrementally through local experimentation (Banerjee and Duflo 2011). International donor agencies have also put more resources into strengthening community participation in development (Mansuri and Rao 2013). These important shifts notwithstanding, the policy advice for public sector reform in developing countries has remained focused on technical, efficiency-oriented fixes, performance metrics and the tightening of formal rules. This advice stems from an intellectual paradigm favoring top-down control and private sector incentives, with an aim to limit shirking and the misuse of discretion (Brinkerhoff and Brinkerhoff 2015).

The recognition that bureaucracies have their own informal norms and cultures prompts a different approach to institutional reform. To achieve high quality public services, bureaucracies need to embrace norms that encourage vigorous deliberation and problem-solving. Rather than simply tightening rules, a more productive approach would be for policymakers to first take stock of the range of administrative tasks associated with implementation for a given policy context, anticipate points of ambiguity, interdepartmental coordination and societal engagement, and the power differences and conflicts these may occasion.[19] To overcome implementation hurdles, especially around complex tasks, bureaucrats need room to "puzzle," which means having opportunities to discuss and learn through iterative experiments and partial changes (Heclo 1974). The institutional space for deliberation must extend beyond elite policy circles to include street-level bureaucrats, as well as citizens and non-state agencies. Local administration in particular needs to be empowered to take risks, communicate ideas, and interrogate status quo arrangements. By supporting problem-oriented discussion on the front lines of the state, policymakers can integrate local knowledge, what Scott (1998) has referred to as *metis*, into the implementation process.

Deliberation, as described here, may be an alien practice that conflicts with existing bureaucratic norms. In such cases, initiating collective discussions in well-defined institutional spaces would allow officials to gain familiarity with deliberation, before extending it widely. A related approach would be to identify positive deviants within an agency and enable them to build deliberative spaces (Andrews 2015). It should be noted, however, that positive deviation can also spawn conflict, and reformers may therefore need greater support and flexibility from external agencies. Where bureaucratic deliberation has arisen organically as a norm, policymakers should exercise care not to disrupt it. Reforms in these cases may focus on reinforcing and scaling up deliberation, for example, by institutionalizing discursive spaces between geographic and administrative units of the state. The opportunity to expand deliberation is likely to be greater in moments of political stability, when the climate for politicians and bureaucrats to cooperate for state-building is more favorable. It may be tempting to seize these moments to execute reforms rapidly, in a wholesale manner. However, the lessons of this book caution

[19] These policy implications resonate with the Problem-Driven Iterative Adaptation framework of Andrews, Pritchett and Woolcock (2017). However, my theoretical framework emphasizes power differences and conflicts in reform implementation.

against introducing deliberative reforms with haste.[20] State-building is a political process that unfolds over the longue durée. Building deliberative bureaucratic norms is not a one-off intervention but requires incremental and continuous engagement. Moreover, to sustain a shift in bureaucratic norms, participation from across the administrative hierarchy is needed, including from frontline agents.

While these policy implications focus on informal norms, formal authority and incentives clearly matter as well. Well-designed monitoring and incentive schemes can, in some cases, improve the quality of services (Muralidharan and Sundararaman 2011; Duflo, Hanna and Ryan 2012). However, an exclusive emphasis on formal rules and pecuniary rewards may dampen the intrinsic motivation of bureaucrats (Banuri and Keefer 2013; Rasul and Rogger 2018).[21] Top-down managerial pressures may induce perverse behaviors as well, as Honig (2018) observes in his study of foreign aid organizations, leading frontline agencies to suspend their own judgment and instead comply with rules and narrow performance metrics. Such risks loom large in the education field, where pressures to adopt global "best practices" amplify the seduction of "looking like a state," while camouflaging the underperformance of school systems (Pritchett, Woolcock and Andrews 2013). Greater attention to bureaucratic norms may help identify the institutional dynamics that support (or discourage) the uptake of incentives and performance measurement schemes, enabling such initiatives to achieve their potential.[22]

My study also has implications for institutional reforms aimed at fostering societal participation in development. These reforms, which include decentralized governance and community-based development, promise to enhance citizen voice and local accountability, though evidence of their impact is mixed (Bardhan and Mookherjee 2006; Mansuri and Rao 2013). An experimental study of VECs in eastern UP illustrates the challenges of community mobilization in unequal settings (Banerjee et al. 2010). After it provided information on learning outcomes to parents and employed "best practice guidelines" to stimulate their engagement, the intervention yielded no improvement in monitoring or the quality

[20] Bersch (2019) likewise argues for the advantages of "puzzling" rather than wholesale "powering" through of reforms.

[21] Incentive schemes can also fail to sustain behavioral changes (Banerjee, Duflo and Glennerster 2008; Dhaliwal and Hanna 2017). On intrinsic motivation in the public sector, see Perry and Vandenabeele (2015).

[22] See the discussion in Khemani (2019) on the constructive links between bureaucratic norms and incentives.

of education services. These results may be read as a failure of societal participation. Taking bureaucratic norms into consideration, however, the lackluster results are not surprising (Fox 2015, 349). Under a legalistic bureaucracy, voicing complaints through VECs will tend to generate administrative burdens on marginalized citizens, while doing little to mitigate the social stigmas and reprisals that may come with complaining. To make participation more meaningful, attention to what Fox (2015) calls the "vertical" dimension of accountability is required. Citizens need institutional backing to question frontline service providers, which means that local agencies must work to mitigate practical obstacles that come in the way of such questioning. Otherwise, VECs are likely to achieve little more than rule compliance and "thin accountability" within the school system (Dubnick and O'Kelly 2005).

To make local accountability "thick," higher-level bureaucracies have a critical part to play in strengthening societal input. It is not by coincidence that some of the more effective social programs in developing countries assign a prominent role to central bureaucracies, including Mexico's *Progresa* and Brazil's *Bolsa Família*, both of which are administered by federal agencies (Sugiyama and Hunter 2013; Weitz-Shapiro 2014, 153–164). Central agencies may help curb local clientelistic interferences, but also guide and support bureaucratic problem-solving, lessons that Tendler (1997) identified in her research on public health reforms in Brazil. Through deliberation with lower-level agencies, central agencies reinforce the purpose of local participation, helping to align local practices with programmatic goals.

Turning specifically to India's primary education system, this study offers policy guidance for Indian states as they gear up to implement the new National Education Policy (NEP). Enacted in 2020, the NEP is a bold policy document. It acknowledges the shortcomings of government schools, evidenced by the rapid growth of low-fee private schools targeting poor households (Kingdon 2020). Replacing the previous policy of 1986, the new NEP calls for an overhaul of the education system, with changes to school curriculum, pedagogy, governance and regulation. Foundational literacy and numeracy in the early years of schooling are emphasized, along with systems of assessment to measure and track learning outcomes. The NEP recognizes the need to shift classroom pedagogy and assessment away from the traditional emphasis on rote learning and compliance with overambitious school curricula (Pritchett and Beatty 2012). Instead, it encourages the mastery of concepts and analytical skills. These classroom-level changes will require updates to teacher training as well as continuous administrative support. Noting the importance of early child development, the NEP calls for universal preschool services. Centers specializing in childcare and nutrition support under the Integrated Child Development Services (ICDS) program will be repurposed to provide pre-primary education. Anganwadi workers, frontline agents managing ICDS centers, will be assigned new responsibilities for delivering preschool education.

Like so many social policies crafted in New Delhi, realizing the NEP's promise will turn on the actions of state governments and local administration. The policy will also require investment in augmenting the state's capacity to deliberate. For example, pre-primary education will require interagency coordination between the Departments of Education and Women and Child Development. Moving past conventional school curricula to support foundational learning means that teachers will need to adapt pedagogical approaches to the diverse needs and learning levels of different students. From the experience of past reforms, it appears that legalistic bureaucracy in India can institute changes involving compliance with rules and well-specified targets, but it faces difficulties in instituting pedagogical innovations, which belie easy codification through rules (Aiyar et al. 2021). Detailed policy blueprints are unlikely to achieve the necessary shift in bureaucratic understandings and behaviors, and may even have the opposite effect, as seen in prior attempts to adopt "Teaching at the Right Level" (TaRL) in Bihar. The adoption of TaRL faltered, not due to poor policy design or even a lack of political will within the Bihar government, but because frontline administration and schoolteachers were ill-prepared to embrace pedagogical practices that conflicted with existing administrative rules and curricular requirements.[23] Looking ahead, a more promising approach would be to encourage state governments to adapt NEP rules according to their varying contexts and also grant local districts and schools the flexibility to experiment with curricular changes based on the practical needs of students and teachers. Central agencies may continue to serve important functions, providing guidelines for local adaptation and institutionalizing processes for deliberation and learning across states and local districts.

A final set of implications pertain to education reforms in response to the COVID-19 pandemic. Owing to the public health crisis, school systems have faced prolonged closures, compounding inequalities in access

[23] See Chapter 8 for discussion of education reforms in Bihar, as well as Aiyar, Dongre and Davis (2015).

and learning. Disproportionate learning losses have been experienced by children from low-income backgrounds, particularly those lacking access to technology, online resources and educational support at home (UNESCO 2021). India, which has experienced one of the longest school closures in the world (17 months or longer in some states), has seen a decline in student participation and learning, among girls in particular (ASER 2021). Unless mitigated, this crisis may cause irreparable damage to the education and life chances of millions of children. Given the pandemic's unequal impacts, education researchers have argued for more personalized instruction for children of different social backgrounds (Reimers 2021). Relatedly, there are calls to institute remedial education as a regular feature of schooling, to ensure that all children gain foundational skills (Beeharry 2021). For personalized and remedial education to succeed, policy efforts must also go toward augmenting bureaucratic capabilities to deliberate and adapt local programming. Equally, the pandemic has made clear that public health, education and other social services are interlinked. Building societal resilience raises the need to strengthen deliberation between different frontline services and agencies.

At the same time, the pandemic has opened spaces for reform, encouraging new practices and the uptake of educational technology (EdTech). India is becoming a leader in digital learning tools, with sizable investments going into EdTech start-ups.[24] We have yet to see where the growth of EdTech ultimately leads. I would caution against either celebratory or cynical readings of technology's potential to transform public services. In India, the reality is that almost a third of rural households with children of school-going age do not own smartphones (ASER 2021). There is a digital divide even within households owning smartphones, as girls and younger children face greater barriers to access. Meanwhile, household access to smartphones has been improving and some Indian states have adopted digital platforms to monitor government schools and foster communication between teachers and parents. Others are using digital technologies to provide teachers pedagogical training and support for customized learning. While some technological interventions appear promising, we are only starting to learn about their impact on teachers and students (Muralidharan, Singh and Ganimian 2019; Cilliers et al. 2022). From a system-wide governance perspective, digital

[24] "Educational Technology Is Coming of Age during the Pandemic: Nowhere More so than India," *The Economist*, November 11, 2020. Available at: www.economist.com/international/2020/11/11/educational-technology-is-coming-of-age-during-the-pandemic.

communication technologies may support deliberation within schooling systems, though the quality of interactions they facilitate remains an open question. Technologies may also weaken deliberation, for instance, by reinforcing a culture of compliance with technical standards and metrics for thin accountability (Honig and Pritchett 2019). Along with improving access, much will depend on the social practices surrounding the use of technologies as they become embedded within education systems.

9.7 IN CLOSING

This book has put forward a new argument for what makes bureaucracy work, especially for the least advantaged. In contrast to explanations emphasizing formal rules and structures of the state, I have highlighted differences in bureaucratic norms, an underappreciated but critical feature of public institutions that shapes how officials behave and relate to citizens. I developed and tested my argument connecting the divergence in bureaucratic norms to variation in the implementation of primary schooling across northern India. Based on a multilevel comparative analysis, I have shown that bureaucratic norms have meaningful effects on the delivery of primary education, with further consequences for how citizens experience the local state. This concluding chapter has shown how my argument may advance scholarly debates in comparative politics, public administration and development. I have explored policy implications as well and suggested how reforms might encourage bureaucratic deliberation in a sustainable manner to help address the need for quality education. There has been a profusion of research on distributive politics and public goods provision in developing countries. Much of this work paints a bleak portrait of bureaucracy, and understandably so. In India, ordinary experiences of the state are often disappointing, more so in the case of services like primary education. Yet, as I have tried to show, bureaucracy has multiple faces. The same agencies that succeed on some tasks can flounder on others. Agencies can also go beyond the call of duty and achieve results that exceed our expectations. From a distance, the vagaries of bureaucracy can appear arbitrary, but when investigated up close, significant patterns emerge.

We still have much to learn about when, why and how bureaucracy works in developing countries, and why some agencies do so more effectively than others. I have suggested that a comparative, multilevel approach to the study of policy implementation can illuminate important aspects of these puzzles. The politics of implementation covers a vast terrain and multiple policy arenas. This book has explored the understudied arena of primary education, a public service that touches many people's lives. As I have shown, primary schools are political sites, where state bureaucracies project authority and impart lessons of citizenship (Bruch and Soss 2018). The delivery of primary education is also intimately tied to the political development of modern states (Ansell and Lindvall 2020). To grasp these political dynamics requires us to appreciate bureaucracy as an institution and take cognizance of the norms that bind it.

Appendix: Researching Bureaucracy and Frontline Public Services

The empirical findings of this book are drawn from comparative field research conducted in four states and multiple local study sites in northern India. To trace the implementation process, I employed qualitative field methods over multiple levels of the state, from bureaucratic agencies in state capitals, to local administration in rural districts, and ultimately, the village primary school. Researching bureaucracy and frontline public services ethnographically presents many challenges, more so in settings of entrenched inequality, such as rural India. This Appendix details my methodological approach. First, I discuss the rationale behind multilevel field research and the variety of qualitative methods employed. I then describe the data collection process, how I "entered" field sites and ensured the quality of ethnographic and interview evidence. I describe the selection procedures for study participants and the sample summary of interviews and focus group discussions (FGDs) conducted. Finally, I give a summary of the local-level field sites that were studied.

A.1 MULTILEVEL FIELD RESEARCH

This book examines policy implementation up close. I conducted qualitative field research over multiple administrative levels of the state and local field sites (see Figure A.1.). In each of the four states, I lived within or nearby field sites while collecting primary data. Through my full-time presence in the field, I became immersed in the sociopolitical context of service delivery, allowing for a first-hand understanding of public administration and the rural school system. I used multiple methods to apprehend the inner workings of the state, including interviews,

State level	***1. Elite policy decisions, planning and monitoring functions*** • Interviews with state bureaucrats from across subdivisions of the bureaucracy, state politicians, civic agencies and education policy experts • Participant observation of state planning meetings and routine monitoring and appraisals of primary school system

↓

District level	***2. Local planning, monitoring and administrative support*** • Interviews and FGDs with district education officials, school teachers, union officials and members of local civic agencies • Participant observation with local administrators engaged in infrastructure provision, teacher training and monitoring activities

↓

Village and School level	***3. Frontline service delivery, community oversight and coproduction*** • Participant observation with subdistrict administrators and teachers involved in service delivery and monitoring of schools • Ethnographic study of education and local governance in villages and routine operation of government primary schools • Interviews, FGDs and oral histories collected of teachers, parents, other village residents, women's groups and other associations

FIGURE A.1 Multilevel field research summary

FGDs, participant observation of local bureaucracies and village- and school-level ethnography. Each method had its strengths and limitations. Ethnographic fieldwork was invaluable, but it was intensive and limited the number of field sites that I could visit. Through interviews, I reached a wider set of study participants across locations. Participant observation offered evidence of quotidian behaviors and relations that could not be fully apprehended through second-hand accounts. These methods complemented each other, and triangulating between them strengthened the validity of the findings (Denzin 2012). For example, participant observation with state officials offered descriptive evidence of bureaucratic norms, but also informed the questions that I asked in follow-up interviews. Crucially, ethnographic fieldwork allowed me to understand the social context of interview respondents, ensuring that the interview evidence and inferences drawn from it were accurate.

Moving iteratively between methods aided in the identification of bureaucratic norms, helping to systematically rule out alternative explanations for observed behaviors. To determine whether a bureaucratic norm was at work, I needed evidence that state officials abided by informal rules or standards of behavior, and that they understood each other's actions with reference to those standards. I also needed evidence that actions consistent with (or in violation of) informal rules had consequences, for example, by eliciting social approval (or disapproval). As Brinks writes, "Rules must have both normativity – in the limited sense that they provide a standard of conduct – and facticity – in the sense that they are actually enforced" (2006, 204). Observing patterns of behavior that appear consistent with a norm was therefore not enough. Nor was it sufficient to rely entirely on interview narratives. Both pieces of evidence were needed to establish the presence of norms.

In addition, I sought interviews and FGDs with a diverse set of respondents, allowing for varied and competing accounts of bureaucracy and primary education. More than just the number of respondents, I paid attention to the quality of data from interviews and FGDs. Interviewing to uncover behavioral motivations is known to present difficulties and can generate biases (Tilly 2004). However, attention to interview quality can vastly improve the reliability of responses, helping to uncover motivations (Small and Cook 2021). For example, when trying to establish the presence of a bureaucratic norm, I probed interviewees by asking for concrete examples and posing counterfactuals. Participant observation complemented these interview strategies, as it allowed me to identify concrete issues and challenges that interviewees likely experienced in their local contexts.

An initial round of open-ended interviews offered evidence for how state elites interpreted the policy mandate for primary education. My access to senior bureaucrats was facilitated through academic and personal contacts, though I also made unmediated requests to meet with officials, which sometimes succeeded. These interviews alerted me to high-level political and administrative challenges of implementation. In subsequent rounds of fieldwork, I used semi-structured interviews to probe officials on more specific policy matters. In addition to bureaucrats, I interviewed other policy elites, including elected officials and political party workers, as well as various non-state actors, including members of civic agencies, social activists, academics and education experts.

Elite interviews provided crucial information, especially for the initial stages of implementation. Tracing implementation processes further down required fieldwork in rural districts and villages. District-level data collection had three main components. I conducted in-depth interviews of local politicians and party workers, civic leaders, local bureaucrats and schoolteachers. I used semi-structured questionnaires, but I gave respondents the room to provide their own meanings and interpretations, following their cues in conversation. To supplement interviews,

I conducted FGDs with schoolteachers, local bureaucrats and village residents. The FGDs probed selected themes in more depth, such as the political pressure exerted by village elites and the difficulties of holding teachers accountable. FGDs allowed respondents to discuss topics with peers and express points of agreement and contention that one-on-one conversations might have missed. FGD respondents often built on each other's cues to broach sensitive topics, such as discrimination against lower-caste children, or forms of corruption, such as the marketplace for teachers to acquire fake (*farzi*) BEd degrees. Disagreements during FGDs also alerted me to conflicts between bureaucratic norms, as well as how norms were experienced differently by different actors.

Interviews and FGDs were designed to allow state and societal actors the opportunity to articulate understandings, expectations and duties of the state, in their own words. I listened closely for instances where actions were framed with an appeal to bureaucratic norms. I also probed respondents to identify alternative sources of motivations, such as pressure from politicians as well as societal attitudes regarding the government school system. Face-to-face interviews have the risk of introducing social desirability bias, especially when they cover sensitive topics (Krumpal 2013). To alleviate this risk, I applied techniques used in social anthropology and organizational studies (Hammersley and Atkinson 1995). I met with schoolteachers and bureaucrats multiple times, to build familiarity and communicate my understanding of their work environment, before requesting an interview. Rapport-building happened "off-site," for example, when I joined officials on walks between their meetings, over cups of chai with teachers at tea stalls or on buses traveling between villages and market centers. These informal interactions helped me connect interview themes to the social world of my respondents. Most of the bureaucrats and teachers that I spoke with were remarkably forthright about the shortcomings of the government school system, as well as their own constraints. Many government teachers lamented that poor households were increasingly turning to low-fee private schools. Bureaucrats and schoolteachers acknowledged the lack of attention to quality education services. If anything, these respondents may have overstated their limitations.

The interviews brought out meanings, perspectives and experiences of officials in a conversation mode. To learn how bureaucratic norms operated *in situ*, I conducted participant observation of local education bureaucracies in the main study districts. As a participant observer, I spent considerable time with local officials who were posted in the district and block administrative offices for primary education. Participant observation had three main components. First, inside the administrative offices, I recorded the interactions among local officials, as well as between them and schoolteachers, parents and other citizens. Seated at the reception area or inside a bureaucrat's office, I quietly witnessed the daily functioning of the local education bureaucracy, observing local officials dispensing their ordinary duties. I attended meetings for planning and monitoring, where implementation problems were discussed and decisions reached. I also watched attentively whenever teachers, parents, contractors and other visitors came to district education offices to seek support or lodge complaints related to schools.

Second, I undertook participant observation outside administrative offices, joining local bureaucrats in their ordinary field activities. These included the distribution of textbooks, uniforms and other inputs, teacher training, monitoring the Midday Meal Programme and routine school inspections. I experienced at first-hand how training and monitoring take place, and the priorities that get communicated to schoolteachers. Third, I visited the teacher training centers located in my study districts, known as the District Institutes for Education and Training (DIETs). Within each DIET, I observed teacher training sessions on a larger scale, along with the informal interactions between primary school teachers, trainers and other local officials. Fourth, I attended meetings and rallies for primary education organized by the education bureaucracy, local civic agencies and village associations. These in-depth observations of the primary school system helped contextualize and further substantiate interview evidence for bureaucratic norms. They also informed the questions I asked in follow-up interviews.

To fully trace the effects of bureaucratic norms, I needed to visit the site of service delivery, the rural primary school. This stage of my field research involved the collection of ethnographic data from government primary schools and the adjoining villages to which they catered.[1] I first gained familiarity with school head teachers, village leaders and other local residents. I made frequent visits to the primary school, observing how it functioned on a daily basis. I interviewed the key individuals involved in running the school, including teachers, other employees (e.g. cooks for the Midday Meal Programme) and members of the Village Education Committee, an association of parents and teachers in charge

[1] Although my fieldwork focused on the government school system, in most villages I also visited the nearest private schools, where I conducted teacher interviews.

of school management. In many instances, I helped tutor students in subjects such as English and mathematics, both during and after school hours. My participation in schooling helped build trust with parents and other community members.

In the study villages, I first used Participatory Rural Appraisal techniques to map the major social groups and their access to public goods and services. Indian villages are organized into hamlets, usually stratified on caste and subcaste lines. To grasp village power dynamics, I met regularly with caste groups living in different hamlets. I undertook a complete census of households from each hamlet, spending ten days going house to house to interview family members. These interviews, which lasted 45 minutes on average, provided essential data on household education levels, economic status and schooling decisions. Some interviews involved multiple family members speaking with me as a group. Families were candid in describing their experiences with the primary school system. Delving further into certain themes, I conducted in-depth interviews with a wide range of village respondents. These included the elected *pradhan* (head) of the village *panchayat*, members of the school's management committee, retired schoolteachers, other public employees and, most importantly, the parents of children attending primary school. In addition, oral histories shared by village elders, including retired schoolteachers and local state employees, provided a rich source of citizen perspectives on the evolution of local politics, bureaucracy and primary schooling. To supplement interviews, I conducted FGDs with parents and other village residents. I also performed participant observation of village institutions and community associations, documenting how they operated on a regular basis. This involved attending *gram sabhas*, the public assemblies held by the panchayat, as well as meetings of village women's associations, youth clubs and temple societies. As I learned in the course of field research, women's groups were often at the forefront in monitoring primary schools. I conducted additional interviews with these groups, honing in on the role of women in village governance, as well as the diversity of their experiences when seeking assistance from the local state.

Finally, to investigate the origins and persistence of bureaucratic norms, I collected oral histories from state officials and consulted archival sources. The archival research was performed at the Nehru Memorial Museum and Library in New Delhi as well as the libraries attached to the state legislative assemblies located in each of the states' capital cities (Shimla, Dehradun, Lucknow and Patna). I drew on a wide range of government documents, which included reports of various commissions on public administration, education and other policy domains (from 1882 until 2010), the reports and minutes of meetings of government advisory groups and the written assessments of educationists and other policy experts. While government sources reflected the "official" perspective of state elites, I also drew on memoirs, newspaper editorials and the writings of retired officials, education reformers and social activists, who, in many cases, challenged the extant policies and administration of primary schooling. Where possible, I collected oral histories of these individuals as well, which provided information about the relationships that evolved between bureaucrats, politicians and civil society. The combination of archival materials and oral histories painted a vivid portrait of how bureaucratic norms emerged and propagated over time.

A.2 QUALITATIVE DATA: INTERVIEWS AND FOCUS GROUP DISCUSSIONS

The qualitative data for the study was collected over twenty-eight months of field research in four north Indian states. I visited Uttar Pradesh (UP), Himachal Pradesh (HP) and Uttarakhand between 2007 and 2011 and Bihar during 2013–2014. In total, I conducted 507 interviews with state actors, which included 176 local bureaucrats and 144 government school teachers, as well as many state politicians and village officials. I interviewed 346 non-state actors in total, which mainly included village residents, but also representatives from civic agencies, teacher unions and international organizations. In addition, I conducted 103 FGDs of local bureaucrats, government school teachers, village women's groups and other village residents. A summary of interviews and FGDs is given in Tables A.1 and A.2. Interviews lasted for 70 minutes each on average, ranging between 60 and 90 minutes. FGDs had between 4 and 12 participants, with 7 participants on average. Each FGD typically lasted for 110 minutes, though the length varied between 90 and 140 minutes. The identities of the study participants have been kept anonymous, unless a respondent explicitly asked to be quoted, in accordance with ethnographic research protocols (Reyes 2018). To protect the identities of state officials and schoolteachers, I do not reveal their names, specific job titles, or other personally identifiable information when quoting them. Instead of their actual names, I use pseudonyms to indicate important social features (e.g., gender, caste and religion) of the study respondents.

TABLE A.1 *Interviews in India*

	Number of Interviews
State actors	
Central bureaucrats[1]	16
State bureaucrats	81
Local bureaucrats	176
State Legislative Assembly members	17
Other state politicians	32
State political party officials	22
Government school teachers	144
Elected village officials	19
Subtotal	507
Non-state actors	
Private school teachers	13
Teacher union leaders	12
Unelected village leaders	13
Village residents	216
Civic agency officials	55
Social activists	8
International agency officials	16
Educationists and policy experts	13
Subtotal	346
Total	**853**

Notes:
1. "Central bureaucrats," "state bureaucrats," and "local bureaucrats" refer to state officials posted in the three different administrative tiers of the Indian state.
Source: All interviews conducted by author.

TABLE A.2 *Focus group discussions in India*

Participants	Number of Focus Group Discussions
Local bureaucrats	14
School teachers	22
Village women's associations	25
Other village residents	42
Total	103

Source: All FGDs conducted by author.

I undertook the interviews after establishing trust with respondents, particularly teachers and parents. Interviews with schoolteachers often took place "on-stage," inside primary school buildings and campuses where they worked. For many teachers, the interview was the first time that someone had inquired about their work conditions. I also performed teacher interviews "off-stage" in other locations, say, while riding buses (*badi gari*s) and shared minivans (*choti gari*s) with teachers on their way to and from school, or while having chai at local tea stalls after school (Goffman 1959). These interviews alerted me to the social life of teachers. As it happened, India's official decadal census was being administered around the time of my field research. Government school teachers are deputized to enumerate households for the census. Interactions with teachers during their census data collection afforded an opportunity to discuss their experiences working with underprivileged households. Teachers also shared what "literacy" (*saksharta*) meant to them and how they determined that someone was literate for the census. Most interviews lasted between sixty and ninety minutes, though some lasted longer than two hours. In addition, several interviewees, frontline officials and schoolteachers in particular, were interviewed more than once. This allowed me to incorporate details from participant observation into the interviews, making the questions more concrete for my respondents.

All interviews, FGDs and other qualitative research for this book were conducted by me primarily in Hindi. Interviews of senior bureaucrats and other elites in the capital cities were conducted in both Hindi and English. I had the advantage of being a native Hindi speaker, with familial roots in northern India. My grasp of language allowed me to hold seamless conversations with respondents and follow cultural references that communicated my competence. Though I could understand it without difficulty, I found it challenging to speak in "*shudh*" (pure) "*sarkari bhasha*" (administrative language), a version of Hindi that is peculiar to government officialdom in northern India. For my interview questions, I learned to incorporate administrative terms along with colloquial phrases from the Hindi dialects and regional languages used in different research sites. These included variants of Pahari in HP, Kumaoni in Uttarakhand, Braj Bhasha in western UP, and a regional variant of Hindi interwoven with Bhojpuri, a language of eastern UP and Bihar. In full disclosure, I often stumbled while trying to grasp the niceties of the colloquial tongue. In those moments, my interviewees showed exceptional patience and good humor.

With an ethnographic ear, I listened carefully to what my respondents were saying, taking equal note of what they were *not* saying. Some of the richest data sources were unplanned conversations that happened by chance around my interviews. For example, in a typical interview conducted in an education official's office, I may have overheard intermittent exchanges between him and other officials, phone calls from politicians and village residents and disagreements among schoolteachers standing outside his office. Staying aware of these interactions helped me piece together what was actually happening inside and around the local education bureaucracy. I used a field diary and learned to take detailed notes quickly, using a mixture of Hindi and English to capture the context and meaning of key phrases. The ideas and experiences conveyed by my respondents made fuller sense when they were recorded in their mother tongue. I then transcribed written field notes to my computer, again in a combination of Hindi and English, either the same night or in batches at the end of each week.

I was attuned to the ways in which my positionality and social background colored my interactions in the field. As a foreign-educated, upper-caste male raised in an urban environment, I was more privileged than most of my research subjects. My privileges became visible while doing village-level field research and interacting with poor households, whose members often had little formal education. Compared to the experiences of marginalized citizens, I could access schoolteachers and local administrators with relative ease. At time, my ability to access the state was overestimated by my interviewees. Some sought my assistance in accessing local state agencies. These interactions alerted me to the salience of caste (along with gender and class) identities when engaging with the local state. My caste identity came up frequently in conversations with village residents and local officials. I was asked sometimes about my last name, which is uncommon in much of northern India. Throughout this region, the last name is a marker of family lineage (*gotra*) and indicates a person's *jati*, or subcaste. Where my *jati* was readily identified, it sometimes helped me gain access to interviewees and entry into field sites, including village temples and other spaces.[2] My caste also facilitated interviews with schoolteachers, village leaders and local bureaucrats, some of whom introduced me to their wider social networks.

[2] In Western UP, where my gotra (last name) is more common, my caste background helped me build rapport with some interviewees, and in one case, it helped me obtain administrative data from local education officials.

At the same time, I was cognizant of the limitations of my social background for ethnographic fieldwork, especially when it came to accessing the least advantaged. In villages of northern India, poor households, Dalits and women frequently experience discrimination by more privileged social actors. I therefore had to put extra effort toward building trust and confidence with these respondents. Fortunately, I had the opportunity to undertake specialized training in Participatory Research Appraisal (PRA) techniques, which I had learned how to apply in villages of eastern UP before embarking on the fieldwork for this book (Chambers 1994).[3] I learned practical techniques for establishing rapport with marginalized social groups. For example, when I visited the homes of Dalits, I made it a point to ask for a glass of water and promptly drink it. The act of drinking water broke with conventional norms of purity and pollution, a small but meaningful step that signaled my willingness to set aside caste boundaries.[4] Often, rural households offered me chai, which I learned to politely accept.[5] I was equally cognizant of my privileges as a man in rural India. Interviews and FGDs with women's association members were conducted in public spaces deemed safe and appropriate by my study participants. Though I was normally offered a chair or woven cot (*charpai*), I insisted on sitting with study participants on the ground.

My attentiveness to the quality of interviews and other data collected during field research carried into data analysis and the drafting of ethnographic materials (Van Maanen 1988). After transcribing my field notes, I did an initial coding of qualitative data based on emergent concepts and themes. Most of the fieldwork was conducted in Hindi, but my notes were in a combination of Hindi and English. I chose to keep all quotes from interviewees in their original Hindi version. I then created supplementary notes for interpreting the quotes before settling on an English translation. Where interview notes generated conflicting meanings and interpretations, say about specific policy, I chose to embrace the conflict and sought additional evidence for either interpretation, often by

[3] I learned PRA methods through a UNICEF research internship program in 2006. The training was delivered by skilled fieldworkers from grassroots organizations in UP, specializing in rural development, health and education.

[4] I observed these and other trust-building practices from community-based fieldworkers who interacted regularly with rural women and households.

[5] A Dalit father in a UP village remarked, "I am just happy that someone has come to our house to sit and speak with us about our children's schooling" (Saharanpur, May 2009).

comparing across data sources. I was most confident when the evidence from interviews, FGDs and participant observation aligned. In that way, I sought to triangulate across qualitative data sources whenever possible during the analysis. This allowed me to identify the most stable and consistent interpretations of bureaucratic norms and other themes around implementation across my study sites.

A.3 LOCAL STUDY SITES IN NORTHERN INDIA

The research for this book uncovered differences in the bureaucratic norms operating in four states in northern India. The logic of selecting the states was discussed in Chapter 1, along with the study's multilevel research design. To summarize, UP served as a theory-building case from the Gangetic plains. HP and Uttarakhand were a matched-pair cases to test the theory in the Himalayan region. Mahila Samakhya in UP and the institutional reforms in Bihar were selected to test the mechanisms and impact of norm change in the Gangetic plains. Here, I explore the rationale behind the selection of *local* research sites, the administrative districts and villages where I conducted intensive field research. Local-level cases were selected keeping in mind the broader multilevel comparative design of the study examining implementation across north Indian states. Table A.3 summarizes the local-level field sites visited for the study. Table A.4 presents a list of the study villages that were visited for protracted fieldwork.

Indian states are large and internally heterogeneous. The choice of rural districts and villages to include in a study becomes crucial, particularly in small-N case study research, which relies on intensive engagement in fewer field sites. Acquiring social competence to collect qualitative data in field sites takes time and there are only so many settings that the researcher can adequately cover. To facilitate district selection, I held extensive discussions with state and local officials, academics, education experts and civil society agencies. After shortlisting candidate districts, I made preliminary field trips to "soak and poke," visiting primary schools and meeting with district officials and schoolteachers (Fenno 1978).

District and village selection was most challenging in UP, given its population size and internal diversity. Regions of UP vary remarkably with regards to their socioeconomic conditions, caste relations and local politics. Despite these internal differences, my preliminary fieldwork revealed striking similarities in how local agencies functioned in UP. To test emergent hypotheses about bureaucratic norms, I followed Mill's

TABLE A.3 *Local field sites in India*

State	Districts[1]	Blocks	Villages	Schools[2]
Uttar Pradesh	Agra	2	3	4
Uttar Pradesh	Bhadohi	2	3	3
Uttar Pradesh	Lucknow	2	1	5
Uttar Pradesh	Jaunpur	3	3	3
Uttar Pradesh	Lalitpur	2	4	3
Uttar Pradesh	Mathura	2	4	4
Uttar Pradesh	Mirzapur	2	3	3
Uttar Pradesh	**Saharanpur**	4	8	11
Uttar Pradesh	**Sitapur**	4	8	10
Himachal Pradesh	Kullu	1	2	1
Himachal Pradesh	**Shimla**	4	6	11
Himachal Pradesh	Sirmaur	1	2	2
Uttarakhand	Dehradun	3	2	5
Uttarakhand	**Almora**	4	9	12
Uttarakhand	Pithoragarh	1	1	3
Bihar	Gaya	2	4	6
Bihar	Patna	1	1	3
Total sites visited	**18**	**41**	**64**	**89**

Notes:
1. Districts listed were visited by the author for ten days each on average. Districts highlighted in bold were visited for protracted study of three months (or longer) each.
2. "Schools" refers to government primary and middle school visits. In highlighted districts, private schools were also visited.

TABLE A.4 *Study villages in India*

State	District	Block	Village[1]
Uttar Pradesh	Saharanpur	Balia Kheri	Panchal
Uttar Pradesh	Saharanpur	Muzaffarabad	Langra
Uttar Pradesh	Sitapur	Pisawan	Sarai Khan
Uttar Pradesh	Sitapur	Biswan	Dimapur
Himachal Pradesh	Shimla	Shimla (Rural)	Dharmaur
Himachal Pradesh	Shimla	Theog	Kandhar Ghat
Uttarakhand	Almora	Dwarahat	Sarkot
Uttarakhand	Almora	Dwarahat	Pujari

Notes:
1. Village names have been changed to pseudonyms to ensure the anonymity of research subjects.

Method of Agreement (George and Bennett 2005). I selected two UP districts that were "least similar" on key political economy variables affecting public service delivery (e.g. income level and economic growth, caste structure and colonial land institutions) but had similar patterns for the implementation of primary schooling. I chose Saharanpur district, located in western UP's comparatively developed, high-growth agricultural belt, along with Sitapur, a district with comparatively weak social indicators located in the less developed Awadh region of central UP. I spent approximately five months in each district for data collection. To supplement in-depth fieldwork, I conducted shorter field visits in seven districts, each trip lasting from eight to fourteen days (ten days on average). These seven districts were located in all four sociocultural regions of UP. Including them in the study added breadth to the fieldwork, helping to establish the external validity of findings beyond the two major study districts.

The logic of district selection in the Himalayan states of HP and Uttarakhand followed Mill's Method of Difference. I adopted a "most-similar" case design by selecting two districts (Shimla in HP and Almora in Uttarakhand) that matched on key political economy factors but had different primary schooling outcomes (George and Bennett 2005). In addition to common geography, agrarian economies and caste structures, these districts were directly administered by the British and were prime sites of military recruitment. The comparison thus accounted for the possible long-term effects of colonial institutions on the bureaucracy and delivery of education (Iyer 2010). In addition, both districts were prime sites for military recruitment, a factor associated with increased demand for education (Eynde 2016). I conducted intensive local-level fieldwork lasting approximately six months in each district. To substantiate the findings, I visited two additional districts, one each in HP and in Uttarakhand, where I spent two to three weeks. Lastly, as Bihar was included for the study of bureaucratic norm change within the state, district selection was relatively straightforward. I selected Patna as an urban district that was relatively developed, along with Gaya, a less developed rural district (Gaya). Field visits in Bihar were comparatively brief, lasting ten days in each district, and focused on the uptake of institutional reforms for primary education.

After extensive field visits and interviews with state and local officials, I selected two villages in each of the main study districts for ethnographic study. Table A.4 provides the list of villages where I conducted protracted fieldwork, spending a minimum of four weeks per village. Names of villages have been changed to protect the identities of study participants. These villages were selected for theoretical purposes to enable nested comparisons and address alternative explanations. Village selection accounted for distance from urban commercial centers and major roads, level of income, population size, caste composition and local economic system. Most were located an hour or more by bus from commercial centers and required walking long distances on unpaved footpaths for two miles, or in the Himalayan region, hiking similar distances in forests. The preceding empirical chapters contain further details on village selection and sociodemographic characteristics. For want of space, not all study villages find mention in the book and many details gleaned from qualitative research have been left out. It is my hope, nevertheless, that the field-based evidence provided sufficiently captures the variation in bureaucratic norms and their divergent effects on the delivery of primary education across rural north India.

References

Abadzi, H. 2002. *India: Education Sector Development in the 1990s: A Country Assistance Evaluation*. Washington, DC: World Bank.

Abers, R. 2019. "Bureaucratic Activism: Pursuing Environmentalism Inside the Brazilian State." *Latin American Politics and Society* 61 (2): 21–44.

Accountability Initiative. 2013. *PAISA District Surveys: Mid-Day Meal Scheme (2012)*. New Delhi: Centre for Policy Research.

Acemoglu, D., S. Johnson, and J. Robinson. 2001. "The Colonial Origins of Comparative Development: An Empirical Investigation." *American Economic Review* 91 (5): 1369–1401.

Acemoglu, D., and J. Robinson. 2006. *Economic Origins of Dictatorship and Democracy*. New York: Cambridge University Press.

Acemoglu, D., and J. Robinson. 2012. *Why Nations Fail: The Origins of Power, Prosperity and Poverty*. New York: Crown Books.

Afridi, F. 2011. "The Impact of School Meals on School Participation: Evidence from Rural India." *Journal of Development Studies* 47 (11): 1636–1656.

Agarwal, B. 1997. "Environmental Action, Gender Equity and Women's Participation." *Development and Change* 28 (1): 1–44.

Agarwal, B. 2010. "Does Women's Proportional Strength Affect Their Participation? Governing Local Forests in South Asia." *World Development* 38 (1): 98–112.

Aggarwal, J., S. Agrawal, and S. Gupta. 1995. *Uttarakhand: Past, Present, and Future*. New Delhi: Concept Publishing Company.

Agrawal, A. 2001. "State Formation in Community Space? Decentralization of Control over Forests in the Kumaon Himalaya, India." *Journal of Asian Studies* 60 (1): 9–40.

Agrawal, A., and A. Chhatre. 2006. "Explaining Success on the Commons: Community Forest Governance in the Indian Himalaya." *World Development* 34 (1): 149–166.

Ahluwalia, M. 1998. *Social, Cultural, and Economic History of Himachal Pradesh*. New Delhi: Indus Publishing Company.

Ahuja, A. 2019. *Mobilizing the Marginalized: Ethnic Parties without Ethnic Movements*. New York: Oxford University Press.

Ahuja, A., and P. Chhibber. 2012. "Why the Poor Vote in India: 'If I Don't Vote, I Am Dead to the State'." *Studies in Comparative International Development* 47 (4): 389–410.

Aiyar, Y., and S. Bhattacharya. 2016. "The Post Office Paradox." *Economic and Political Weekly* 51 (11): 61.

Aiyar, Y., V. Davis, G. Govindan, and T. Kapoor. 2021. "Rewriting the Grammar of the Education System: Delhi's Education Reform (A Tale of Creative Resistance and Creative Disruption)." Research on Improving Systems of Education (RISE) Working Paper.

Aiyar, Y., A. Dongre, and V. Davis. 2015. "Education Reforms, Bureaucracy and the Puzzles of Implementation: A Case Study from Bihar." International Growth Centre Working Paper.

Alam, A. 2007. *Becoming India: Western Himalaya under British Rule*. New Delhi: Cambridge University Press.

Alter, A. 2016. *Dancing with Devtas: Drums, Power and Possession in the Music of Garhwal, North India*. London: Routledge.

Ambedkar, B. R. 1989 [1955]. *Thoughts on Linguistic States*. Aligarh: Anand Sahitya Sadan.

Amengual, M. 2016. *Politicized Enforcement in Argentina: Labor and Environmental Regulation*. New York: Cambridge University Press.

Amsden, A. H. 1989. *Asia's Next Giant: South Korea and Late Industrialization*. New York: Oxford University Press.

Anand, I. 2016. "Dalit Emancipation and the Land Question." *Economic and Political Weekly* 51 (47): 12–14.

Anderson, B. 1991. *Imagined Communities: Reflections on the Origin and Spread of Nationalism*. London: Verso.

Andrews, M. 2015. "Explaining Positive Deviance in Public Sector Reforms in Development." *World Development* 74: 197–208.

Andrews, M., L. Pritchett, and M. Woolcock. 2017. *Building State Capabilities*. Oxford: Oxford University Press.

Ang, Y. Y. 2016a. *How China Escaped the Poverty Trap*. Ithaca, NY: Cornell University Press.

Ang, Y. Y. 2016b. "Beyond Weber: Conceptualizing an Alternative Ideal Type of Bureaucracy in Developing Contexts." *Regulation & Governance* 11 (3): 282–298. doi: 10.1111/rego.12123.

Ansell, B. 2010. *From the Ballot to the Blackboard: The Redistributive Political Economy of Education*. New York: Cambridge University Press.

Ansell, B., and J. Lindvall. 2013. "The Political Origins of Primary Education Systems: Ideology, Institutions, and Interdenominational Conflict in an Era of Nation-Building." *American Political Science Review* 107 (03): 505–522.

Ansell, B., and J. Lindvall. 2020. *Inward Conquest: The Political Origins of Modern Public Services*. New York: Cambridge University Press.

Ansell, C. 2011. *Pragmatist Governance: Re-imagining Institutions and Democracy*. New York: Oxford University Press.

Ansell, C., and A. Gash. 2007. "Collaborative Governance in Theory and Practice." *Journal of Public Administration Research and Theory* 18 (4): 543–571. doi: 10.1093/jopart/mum032.

Appadurai, A. 2002. "Deep Democracy: Urban Governmentality and the Horizon of Politics." *Public Culture* 14 (1): 21–47.

Appadurai, A. 2015. "Success and Failure in the Deliberative Economy." In *Deliberation and Development: Rethinking the Role of Voice and Collective Action in Unequal Societies*, edited by P. Heller and V. Rao, 67–83. Washington, DC: World Bank Group.

Archer, M. S. 1979. *Social Origins of Educational Systems*. London: Sage.

Arnold, D. 1979. "European Orphans and Vagrants in India in the Nineteenth Century." *Journal of Imperial and Commonwealth History* 7 (2): 104–127.

ASER. 2013. *Annual Status of Education Report 2012 (Rural)*. Mumbai: Pratham Resource Centre.

ASER. 2015. *Annual Status of Education Report 2014 (Rural)*. Mumbai: Pratham Resource Centre.

ASER. 2021. *Annual Status of Education Report 2021 (Rural)*. Mumbai: Pratham Resource Centre.

Attri, V., and H. Bhattacharya. 2019. "Assembly Elections 2017–2018." *Studies in Indian Politics* 7 (1): 100–129.

Auerbach, A. 2018. "Informal Archives: Historical Narratives and the Preservation of Paper in India's Urban Slums." *Studies in Comparative International Development* 53 (3): 343–364.

Auerbach, A. 2019. *Demanding Development: The Politics of Public Goods Provision in India's Urban Slums*. New York: Cambridge University Press.

Auerbach, A., and G. Kruks-Wisner. 2020. "The Geography of Citizenship Practice: How the Poor Engage the State in Rural and Urban India." *Perspectives on Politics* 18 (4): 1118–1134.

Auerbach, A., and T. Thachil. 2019. "Cultivating Clients: Reputation, Responsiveness, and Ethnic Indifference in India's Slums." *American Journal of Political Science* 64 (3): 471–487.

Auyero, J. 2011. "Patients of the State: An Ethnographic Account of Poor People's Waiting." *Latin American Research Review* 46 (1): 5–29.

Ayres, I., and J. Braithwaite. 1995. *Responsive Regulation: Transcending the Deregulation Debate*. Oxford: Oxford University Press.

Azam, M., and G. Kingdon. 2013. "Are Girls the Fairer Sex in India? Revisiting Intra-Household Allocation of Education Expenditure." *World Development* 42: 143–164.

Baccaro, L., and K. Papadakis. 2009. "The Downside of Participatory-Deliberative Public Administration." *Socio-Economic Review* 7 (2): 245–276. doi: 10.1093/ser/mwn030.

Baier, V. E., J. G. March, and H. Saetren. 1986. "Implementation and Ambiguity." *Scandinavian Journal of Management Studies* 2 (3–4): 197–212.

Baiocchi, G. 2003. "Emergent Public Spheres: Talking Politics in Participatory Governance." *American Sociological Review* 68 (1): 52–74.

Baiocchi, G., P. Heller, and M. Silva. 2011. *Bootstrapping Democracy: Transforming Local Governance and Civil Society in Brazil*. Stanford, CA: Stanford University Press.

Banerjee, A., R. Banerji, J. Berry et al. 2015. "Teaching at the Right Level: Evidence from Randomized Evaluations in India." NBER Working Paper 22746.

Banerjee, A., R. Banerji, E. Duflo et al. 2007. "Can Information Campaigns Raise Awareness and Local Participation in Primary Education?" *Economic and Political Weekly* 42 (15): 1365–1372.

Banerjee, A., R. Banerji, E. Duflo, R. Glennerster, and S. Khemani. 2010. "Pitfalls of Participatory Programs: Evidence from a Randomized Evaluation in Education in India." *American Economic Journal: Economic Policy* 2 (1): 1–30. doi: 10.1257/pol.2.1.1.

Banerjee, A., and E. Duflo. 2011. *Poor Economics: A Radical Rethinking of the Way to Fight Global Poverty*. New York: Public Affairs.

Banerjee, A., E. Duflo, and R. Glennerster. 2008. "Putting a Band-Aid on a Corpse: Incentives for Nurses in the Indian Public Health Care System." *Journal of the European Economic Association* 6 (2–3): 487–500.

Banerjee, A., and L. Iyer. 2005. "History, Institutions, and Economic Performance: The Legacy of Colonial Land Tenure Systems in India." *American Economic Review* 95 (4): 1190–1213.

Banerjee, A., L. Iyer, and R. Somanathan. 2007. "Public Action for Public Goods." In *Handbook of Development Economics*, edited by T. P. Schultz and A. S. John, 3117–3154. Amsterdam: Elsevier.

Banerjee, A., and R. Somanathan. 2007. "The Political Economy of Public Goods: Some Evidence from India." *Journal of Development Economics* 82 (2): 287–314.

Banerji, R. 2011. "Challenging Bihar on Primary Education." *Economic and Political Weekly* 46 (11): 33–39.

Banerji, R. 2015. "How Do Systems Respond to Disruptive Pedagogic Innovations? The Case of Pratham in Bihar." Research on Improving Systems of Education (RISE), Working Paper 15/002.

Banuri, S., and P. Keefer. 2013. "Intrinsic Motivation, Effort and the Call to Public Service." World Bank Policy Research Working Paper No. 6729.

Bardach, E., and R. Kagan. 1982. *Going by the Book: The Problem of Regulatory Unreasonableness*. Philadelphia, PA: Temple University Press.

Bardhan, P. 2010. *Awakening Giants, Feet of Clay: Assessing the Economic Rise of China and India*. Princeton, NJ: Princeton University Press.

Bardhan, P., M. Ghatak, and A. Karaivanov. 2007. "Wealth Inequality and Collective Action." *Journal of Public Economics* 91 (9): 1843–1874.

Bardhan, P., and D. Mookherjee. 2006. *Decentralization and Local Governance in Developing Countries: A Comparative Perspective*. Cambridge, MA: MIT Press.

Barnard, C. 1938. *The Functions of the Executive*. Cambridge, MA: Harvard University Press.

Barro, R., and J. Lee. 2015. *Education Matters: Global Schooling Gains from the 19th to the 21st Century*. New York: Oxford University Press.

Bates, R. H. 1981. *Markets and States in Tropical Africa: The Political Basis of Agricultural Policies*. Berkeley: University of California Press.

Battilana, J., and S. Dorado. 2010. "Building Sustainable Hybrid Organizations: The Case of Commercial Microfinance Organizations." *Academy of Management Journal* 53 (6): 1419–1440.

Becker, G. 1964. *Human Capital: A Theoretical and Empirical Analysis*. 2nd Edition. New York: Columbia University Press.

Beeharry, G. 2021. "The Pathway to Progress on SDG 4 Requires the Global Education Architecture to Focus on Foundational Learning and to Hold Ourselves Accountable for Achieving It." *International Journal of Educational Development* 82: 102375.

Benhabib, S., and P. Linden-Retek. 2018. "Judith Shklar's Critique of Legalism." In *The Cambridge Companion to the Rule of Law*, edited by J. L. Meierhenrich. Cambridge: Cambridge University Press.

Berreman, G. 1972. *Hindus of the Himalayas: Ethnography and Change*. Delhi: Oxford University Press.

Berreman, G. 1979. *Himachal: Science, People and "Progress."* Copenhagen: International Work Group for Indigenous Affairs.

Berry, K. 2001. "The Group Called Women in Himachal Pradesh." *Himalayan Research Bulletin* 21 (2): 62–69.

Bersch, K. 2019. *When Democracies Deliver: Governance Reform in Latin America*. New York: Cambridge University Press.

Bertelli, A., and C. Smith. 2010. "Relational Contracting and Network Management." *Journal of Public Administration Research and Theory* 20 (1): i21–i40.

Berwick, E., and F. Christia. 2018. "State Capacity Redux: Integrating Classical and Experimental Contributions to an Enduring Debate." *Annual Review of Political Science* 21: 71–91.

Besley, T., R. Pande, and V. Rao. 2007. "Political Economy of Panchayats in South India." *Economic and Political Weekly* 42 (8): 661–666.

Besley, T., and T. Persson. 2014. "The Causes and Consequences of Development Clusters: State Capacity, Peace, and Income." *Annual Review of Economics* 6 (1): 927–949.

Betancourt, R., and S. Gleason. 2000. "The Allocation of Publicly Provided Goods to Rural Households in India: On Some Consequences of Caste, Religion and Democracy." *World Development* 28 (12): 2169–2182.

Béteille, T. 2015. "Fixers in India's Teacher Labor Markets: Behind the Scenes." *Asian Survey* 55 (5): 942–968. doi: 10.1525/as.2015.55.5.942.

Béteille, T., G. Kingdon, and M. Muzammil. 2016. "Teacher Unions in India: Diverse and Powerful." In *The Comparative Politics of Education: Teachers Unions and Education Systems around the World*, edited by S. Wiborg and T. Moe, 239–268. New York: Cambridge University Press.

Bevir, M. 2010. *Democratic Governance*. Princeton, NJ: Princeton University Press.

Bhat, P. N. M., and S. I. Rajan. 1990. "Demographic Transition in Kerala Revisited." *Economic and Political Weekly* 25 (35–36): 1957–1980.

Bhatt, G. S. 2010. *Cult, Religion, and Society: Polyandrous People of Western Himalaya*. New Delhi: Rawat Publications.

Bhattacharjee, G. 2016. *Special Category States of India*. New Delhi: Oxford University Press.

Bhatty, K. 2008. "Social Equality and Development: Himachal Pradesh and Its Wider Significance." Ph.D. thesis, London School of Economics and Political Science.

Bhavnani, R., and A. Lee. 2018. "Local Embeddedness and Bureaucratic Performance: Evidence from India." *Journal of Politics* 80 (1): 71–87.

Bicchieri, C. 2016. *Norms in the Wild: How to Diagnose, Measure, and Change Social Norms*. New York: Oxford University Press.

Bohman, J. 1996. *Public Deliberation: Pluralism, Complexity, and Democracy*. Cambridge, MA: MIT Press.

Boix, C. 2003. *Democracy and Redistribution*. New York: Cambridge University Press.

Bordia, A., and A. Kaul. 1992. "Literacy Efforts in India." *The Annals of the American Academy of Political and Social Science* 520 (1): 151–162.

Bourdieu, P. 1986. "The Forms of Capital." In *Handbook of Theory and Research for the Sociology of Education*, edited by J. G. Richardson, 241–258. New York: Greenwood.

Braithwaite, V., and M. Levi. 2003. *Trust and Governance*. New York: Russell Sage Foundation.

Brass, P. 1965. *Factional Politics in an Indian State: The Congress Party in Uttar Pradesh*. Berkeley: University of California Press.

Brass, P. 1974. *Language, Religion and Politics in North India*. Cambridge: Cambridge University Press.

Brass, P. 2004. "Elite Interests, Popular Passions, and Social Power in the Language Politics of India." *Ethnic and Racial Studies* 27 (3): 353–375. doi: 10.1080/0141987042000189187.

Brehm, J., and S. Gates. 1999. *Working, Shirking, and Sabotage: Bureaucratic Response to a Democratic Public*. Ann Arbor: University of Michigan Press.

Brinkerhoff, D., and J. Brinkerhoff. 2015. "Public Sector Management Reform in Developing Countries: Perspectives beyond NPM Orthodoxy." *Public Administration and Development* 35 (4): 222–237.

Brinks, D. M. 2006. "The Rule of (Non)Law: Prosecuting Police Killings in Brazil and Argentina." In *Informal Institutions and Democracy: Lessons from Latin America*, edited by G. Helmke and S. Levitsky. Baltimore, MD: Johns Hopkins University Press.

Brodkin, E. 1997. "Inside the Welfare Contract: Discretion and Accountability in State Welfare Administration." *Social Service Review* 71 (1): 1–33.

Brodkin, E. 2008. "Accountability in Street-Level Organizations." *International Journal of Public Administration* 31 (3): 317–336.

Brodkin, E. 2016. "Street-level Organizations, Inequality, and the Future of Human Services." *Human Service Organizations: Management, Leadership and Governance* 40 (5): 444–450.

Brown, D. 1999. "Reading, Writing, and Regime Type: Democracy's Impact on Primary School Enrollment." *Political Research Quarterly* 52 (4): 681–707.

Brown, D., and W. Hunter. 2004. "Democracy and Human Capital Formation." *Comparative Political Studies* 37 (7): 842–864. doi: 10.1177/0010414004266870.

Brown, J. 1994. *Modern India: The Origins of an Asian Democracy*. Oxford: Oxford University Press.

Bruch, S., and J. Soss. 2018. "Schooling as a Formative Political Experience: Authority Relations and the Education of Citizens." *Perspectives on Politics* 16 (1): 36–57.

Brulé, R. 2020. *Women, Power, and Property: The Paradox of Gender Equality Laws in India*. New York: Cambridge University Press.

Brun, D., and L. Diamond, eds. 2014. *Clientelism, Social Policy, and the Quality of Democracy*. Baltimore, MD: Johns Hopkins University Press.

Bruns, B., I. H. Macdonald, and B. R. Schneider. 2019. "The Politics of Quality Reforms and the Challenges for SDGs in Education." *World Development* 118: 27–38.

Brysk, A. 2000. "Democratizing Civil Society in Latin America." *Journal of Democracy* 11 (3): 151–165.

Bueno de Mesquita, E., and M. Stephenson. 2007. "Regulatory Quality under Imperfect Oversight." *American Political Science Review* 101 (3): 605–620.

Busemeyer, M. 2014. *Skills and Inequality*. New York: Cambridge University Press.

Busemeyer, M., and C. Trampusch. 2011. "Review Article: Comparative Political Science and the Study of Education." *British Journal of Political Science* 41 (2): 413–443.

Bussell, J. 2019. *Clients and Constituents: Political Responsiveness in Patronage Democracies*. New York: Oxford University Press.

CAG. 2015. *Performance Audit of Mid Day Meal Scheme (2009–10 to 2013–14)*. New Delhi: Comptroller and Auditor General of India, Government of India.

Cammett, M. C., and L. M. MacLean. 2014. *The Politics of Non-state Welfare*. Ithaca, NY: Cornell University Press.

Campbell, A. 2005. *How Policies Make Citizens: Senior Political Activism and the American Welfare State*. Princeton, NJ: Princeton University Press.

Canales, R. 2011. "Rule Bending, Sociological Citizenship, and Organizational Contestation in Microfinance." *Regulation & Governance* 5 (1): 90–117.

Canales, R. 2014. "Weaving Straw into Gold: Managing Organizational Tensions between Standardization and Flexibility in Microfinance." *Organization Science* 25 (1): 1–28.

Capoccia, G., and R. D. Kelemen. 2007. "The Study of Critical Junctures: Theory, Narrative, and Counterfactuals in Historical Institutionalism." *World Politics* 59 (3): 341–369.

Carpenter, D. 2001. *The Forging of Bureaucratic Autonomy: Reputations, Networks, and Policy Innovation in Executive Agencies, 1862–1928*. Princeton, NJ: Princeton University Press.

Carpenter, D., and G. A. Krause. 2014. "Transactional Authority and Bureaucratic Politics." *Journal of Public Administration Research and Theory* 25 (1): 5–25.

Case, A., and A. Deaton. 2020. *Deaths of Despair and the Future of Capitalism*. Princeton, NJ: Princeton University Press.

Centre of Development Studies. 2000. *Swajal Capacity Building Programme 1999–2000*. Nainital: UP Academy of Administration.

Centeno, M. A., A. Kohli, D. J. Yashar, and D. Mistree. 2017. *States in the Developing World*. New York: Cambridge University Press.

Chakrabarti, R. 2013. *Bihar Breakthrough: The Turnaround of a Beleaguered State*. New Delhi: Rupa Publications.

Chambers, R. 1994. "The Origins and Practice of Participatory Rural Appraisal." *World Development* 22 (7): 953–969. doi: 10.1016/0305-750x(94)90141-4.

Chand, V. 2006. *Reinventing Public Service Delivery in India: Selected Case Studies*. New Delhi: Sage Publications.

Chandra, B. 2003. *In the Name of Democracy: JP Movement and the Emergency*. New Delhi: Penguin Books.

Chandra, K. 2004. *Why Ethnic Parties Succeed: Patronage and Ethnic Headcounts in India*. New York: Cambridge University Press.

Chandra, K. 2014. "Patronage, Democracy and Ethnic Politics in India." In *Clientelism, Social Policy, and the Quality of Democracy*, edited by D.A. Brun and L. Diamond. Baltimore, MD: Johns Hopkins University Press.

Chaudhury, N., J. Hammer, M. Kremer, K. Muralidharan, and F. Rogers. 2006. "Missing in Action: Teacher and Health Worker Absence in Developing Countries." *Journal of Economic Perspectives* 20 (1): 91–116.

Chetty, R., J.N. Friedman, N. Hilger et al. 2011. "How Does Your Kindergarten Classroom Affect Your Earnings? Evidence from Project STAR." *Quarterly Journal of Economics* 126 (4): 1593–1660.

Chhibber, P. 1995. "Political Parties, Electoral Competition, Government Expenditures and Economic Reform in India." *Journal of Development Studies* 32 (1): 74–96.

Chhibber, P. 2001. *Democracy without Associations: Transformation of the Party System and Social Cleavages in India*. Ann Arbor: University of Michigan Press.

Chhibber, P. 2014. *Religious Practice and Democracy in India*. New York: Cambridge University Press.

Chhibber, P., and I. Nooruddin. 2004. "Do Party Systems Count?" *Comparative Political Studies* 37 (2): 152–187. doi: 10.1177/0010414003260981.

Chhibber, P., S. Shastri, and R. Sisson. 2004. "Federal Arrangements and the Provision of Public Goods in India." *Asian Survey* 44 (3): 339–352.

Chibber, V. 2002. "Bureaucratic Rationality and the Developmental State." *American Journal of Sociology* 107 (4): 951–989.

Chibber, V. 2003. *Locked in Place: State-Building and Late Industrialization in India*. Princeton: Princeton University Press.

Chin, A. 2005. "Can Redistributing Teachers across Schools Raise Educational Attainment? Evidence from Operation Blackboard in India." *Journal of Development Economics* 78 (2): 384–405.

Chophy, G. K. 2019. "Agents of the Godlings: An Ethnographic Account of Folk Hinduism in Himachal Pradesh." *Journal of the Anthropological Survey of India* 68 (1): 123–134.

Cilliers, J., B. Fleisch, J. Kotze, N. Mohohlwane, S. Taylor, and T. Thulare. 2022. "Can Virtual Replace In-Person Coaching? Experimental Evidence on Teacher Professional Development and Student Learning." *Journal of Development Economics* 155: 102815.

Clarke, P., and J. Jha. 2010. "Rajasthan's Experience in Improving Service Delivery in Education." In *Public Service Delivery in India: Understanding the Reform Process*, edited by V. Chand. New Delhi: Oxford University Press.

Cohen, J. 1989. "Deliberation and Democratic Legitimacy." In *The Good Polity: Normative Analysis of the State*, edited by A. Hamlin and P. Pettit, 17–34. New York: Basil Blackwell.

Cohen, J. 1996. "Procedure and Substance in Deliberative Democracy." In *Democracy and Difference: Contesting the Boundaries of the Political*, edited by S. Benhabib. Princeton, NJ: Princeton University Press.

Cohen, J., and C. Sabel. 1997. "Directly-Deliberative Polyarchy." *European Law Journal* 3 (4): 313–342. doi: 10.1111/1468-0386.00034.

Colclough, C., and A. De. 2010. "The Impact of Aid on Education Policy in India." *International Journal of Educational Development* 30 (5): 497–507.

Coleman, J. 1988. "Social Capital in the Creation of Human Capital." *American Journal of Sociology* 94 (Supplement): S95–S120.

Collins, J. E. 2021. "Does the Meeting Style Matter? The Effects of Exposure to Participatory and Deliberative School Board Meetings." *American Political Science Review* 115 (3): 790–804.

Corbett, A. 2002. "Secular, Free and Compulsory: Republican Values in French Education." In *Education in France*, edited by A. Corbett and B. Moon, 23–39. London: Routledge.

Corbridge, S. 2007. "The (Im) possibility of Development Studies." *Economy and Society* 36 (2): 179–211.

Corbridge, S., G. Williams, M. Srivastava, and R. Véron. 2005. *Seeing the State: Governance and Governmentality in India*. New York: Cambridge University Press.

Cornwall, A., and J. Gaventa. 2000. "From Users and Choosers to Makers and Shapers Repositioning Participation in Social Policy." *IDS Bulletin* 31 (4): 50–62.

Corrales, J. 1999. "The Politics of Education Reform: Bolstering the Supply and Demand; Overcoming Institutional Blocks." *Country Studies: Education Reform and Management Publication Series* 2 (1).

Corrales, J. 2005. "The State Is not Enough: The Politics of Expanding and Improving Schooling in Developing Countries." In *Global Educational Expansion: Historical Legacies and Political Obstacles*, edited by A. Benavot, J. Resnik and J. Corrales. Cambridge, MA: American Academy of Arts and Sciences.

Coslovsky, S. 2011. Relational Regulation in the Brazilian Ministério Publico: The Organizational Basis of Regulatory Responsiveness." *Regulation & Governance* 5 (1): 70–89.

Crato, N., ed. 2021. *Improving a Country's Education: PISA 2018 Results in 10 Countries*. Cham, Switzerland: Springer.

Dahlström, C., and V. Lapuente. 2017. *Organizing Leviathan: Politicians, Bureaucrats, and the Making of Good Government*. New York: Cambridge University Press.

Das, A. 1986. "Landowners' Armies Take over 'Law and Order'." *Economic and Political Weekly* 21 (1): 15–18.

Das Gupta, J. 1970. *Language Conflict and National Development: Group Politics and National Language Policy in India*. Berkeley: University of California Press.

Das Gupta, J. 1978. "A Season of Caesars: Emergency Regimes and Development Politics in Asia." *Asian Survey* 18 (4): 315–349. doi: 10.2307/2643398.

Das, J., J. Hammer, and K. Leonard. 2008. "The Quality of Medical Advice in Low-Income Countries." *The Journal of Economic Perspectives* 22 (2): 93–114.

Das, M. B., S. Kapoor-Mehta, O. Tas Emcet, and L. Zumbyte. 2015. *Scaling the Heights: Social Inclusion and Sustainable Development in Himachal Pradesh.* Washington, DC: World Bank.

Dasgupta, A. 2018. "Technological Change and Political Turnover: The Democratizing Effects of the Green Revolution in India." *American Political Science Review* 112 (4): 918–938.

Dasgupta, A., and D. Kapur. 2020. "The Political Economy of Bureaucratic Overload: Evidence from Rural Development Officials in India." *American Political Science Review* 114 (4): 1316–1334.

Datta, U. 2015. "Socio-economic Impacts of JEEViKA: A Large-Scale Self-Help Group Project in Bihar, India." *World Development* 68: 1–18.

Davies, E. 2018. "From Universalization to Privatization: Drift in Indian Education Policy". Working Paper, Harvard Graduate School of Education.

Davies, E., and T. Falleti. 2017. "Poor People's Participation: Neoliberal Institutions or Left Turn?" *Comparative Political Studies* 50 (12): 1699–1731.

Denzin, N. 2012. "Triangulation 2.0." *Journal of Mixed Methods Research* 6 (2): 80–88.

Desai, M. 2001. "Party Formation, Political Power, and the Capacity for Reform: Comparing Left Parties in Kerala and West Bengal, India." *Social Forces* 80 (1): 37–60.

Desai, M. 2005. "Indirect British Rule, State Formation, and Welfarism in Kerala, India, 1860–1957." *Social Science History* 29 (3): 457–488. doi: 10.1017/S0145553200013018.

Deva, S. 1985. "The 'New Education Policy'." *Economic and Political Weekly* 20 (39): 1647–1649.

Dewey, J. 1927. *The Public and Its Problems*. Athens: University of Ohio Press.

Dhaliwal, I., and R. Hanna. 2017. "The Devil Is in the Details: The Successes and Limitations of Bureaucratic Reform in India." *Journal of Development Economics* 124: 1–21.

DiIulio, J. D. 1994. "Principled Agents: The Cultural Bases of Behavior in a Federal Government Bureaucracy." *Journal of Public Administration Research and Theory* 4 (3): 277–318.

DiMaggio, P., and W. Powell. 1983. "The Iron Cage Revisited: Institutional Isomorphism and Collective Rationality in Organizational Fields." *American Sociological Review* 48 (2): 147–160.

Dixit, A. 2002. "Incentives and Organizations in the Public Sector: An Interpretative Review." *Journal of Human Resources* 37 (4): 696–727.

Dixit, A. 2012. "Bureaucracy, Its Reform and Development." *Review of Market Integration* 4 (2): 135–157.

Dobbins, M. 2017. "Teacher Unionism in France: Making Fundamental Reforms an Impossible Quest?" In *The Comparative Politics of Education: Teachers Unions and Education Systems around the World*, edited by T. Moe and S. Wiborg. New York: Cambridge University Press.

Dobbins, M., and K. Martens. 2012. "Towards an Education Approach à la finlandaise? French Education Policy after PISA." *Journal of Education Policy* 27 (1): 23–43.

Douglas, M. 1966. *Purity and Danger: An Analysis of Concepts of Pollution and Taboo*. London: Routledge.

Downs, A. 1965. "A Theory of Bureaucracy." *American Economic Review* 55 (1/2): 439–446.

Doyle, A. M. 2021. "Twenty Years on – What Can PISA Tell Us about Educational Inequality in France and England?" *Compare: A Journal of Comparative and International Education* 1–15.

Drèze, J., and H. Gazdar. 1996. "Uttar Pradesh: The Burden of Inertia." In *Indian Development*, edited by J. Drèze and A. K. Sen. New Delhi: Oxford University Press.

Drèze, J., and A. Goyal. 2003. "Future of Mid-Day Meals." *Economic and Political Weekly* 38 (44): 4673–4683.

Drèze, J., and G. Kingdon. 2001. "School Participation in Rural India." *Review of Development Economics* 5 (1): 1–24.

Drèze, J., and J. Loh. 1995. "Literacy in India and China." *Economic and Political Weekly* 30 (45): 2868–2878.

Drèze, J., and A. Sen. 1989. *Hunger and Public Action*. Oxford: Clarendon Press.

Drèze, J., and A. Sen. 2002. *India: Development and Participation*. New York: Oxford University Press.

Drèze, J., and A. Sen. 2013. *An Uncertain Glory: India and Its Contradictions*. New Delhi: Penguin Books Limited.

Du Gay, P. 2000. *In Praise of Bureaucracy: Weber-Organization-Ethics*. London: Sage.

Du Gay, P. 2005. "Bureaucracy and Liberty: State, Authority, and Freedom." In *The Values of Bureaucracy*, edited by P. Du Gay, 41–62. Oxford: Oxford University Press.

Dubnick, M., and C. O'Kelly. 2005. "Accountability through Thick and Thin: Moral Agency in Public Service." In *Ethics in Public Management*, edited by H. Frederickson and R. Ghere, 139–164. London: Routledge.

Duflo, E., R. Hanna, and S. P. Ryan. 2012. "Incentives Work: Getting Teachers to Come to School." *American Economic Review* 102 (4): 1241–1278.

Duncan, I. 1999. "Dalits and Politics in Rural North India: The Bahujan Samaj Party in Uttar Pradesh." *Journal of Peasant Studies* 27 (1): 35–60.

Dunleavy, P., and C. Hood. 1994. "From Old Public Administration to New Public Management." *Public Money & Management* 14 (3): 9–16.

Duru-Bellat, M., and B. Suchaut. 2005. "Organisation and Context, Efficiency and Equity of Educational Systems: What PISA Tells Us." *European Educational Research Journal* 4 (3): 181–194.

Echeverri-Gent, J. 1992. "Public Participation and Poverty Alleviation: The Experience of Reform Communists in India's West Bengal." *World Development* 20 (10): 1401–1422.

Elmore, M. 2016. *Becoming Religious in a Secular Age*. Berkeley: University of California Press.

Elster, J. 1989. *The Cement of Society: A Study of Social Order*. Cambridge: Cambridge University Press.

Elster, J., ed. 1998. *Deliberative Democracy*. New York: Cambridge University Press.

Ertman, T. 1997. *Birth of the Leviathan: Building States and Regimes in Medieval and Early Modern Europe*. New York: Cambridge University Press.

Esping-Anderson, G. 1990. *The Three Worlds of Welfare Capitalism*. Princeton, NJ: Princeton University Press.

Evans, P. 1989. "Predatory, Developmental, and Other Apparatuses: A Comparative Political Economy Perspective on the Third World State." *Sociological Forum* 4 (4): 561–587.

Evans, P. 1995. *Embedded Autonomy: States and Industrial Transformation*. Princeton, NJ: Princeton University Press.

Evans, P. 1996. "Government Action, Social Capital and Development: Reviewing the Evidence on Synergy." *World Development* 24 (6): 1119–1132.

Evans, P. 2004. "Development as Institutional Change: The Pitfalls of Monocropping and the Potentials of Deliberation." *Studies in Comparative International Development* 38 (4): 30–52. doi: 10.1007/bf02686327.

Evans, P. 2015. "Bringing Deliberation into the Developmental State." In *Deliberation and Development: Rethinking the Role of Voice and Collective Action in Unequal Societies*, edited by P. Heller and V. Rao. Washington, DC: World Bank Group.

Evans, P., and P. Heller. 2015. "Human Development, State Transformation and the Politics of the Developmental State." In *The Oxford Handbook of Transformations of the State*, edited by S. H. Leibfried, H. Evelyne, M. L. Lange, D. Jonah, F. Nullmeier and J. D. Stephens, 691–713. Oxford: Oxford University Press.

Evans, P., E. Huber, and J. Stephens. 2017. "The Political Foundations of State Effectiveness." In *States in the Developing World*, edited by M. A. Centeno, A. Kohli, D. J. Yashar and D. Mistree. New York: Cambridge University Press.

Evans, P., and J. E. Rauch. 1999. "Bureaucracy and Growth: A Cross-National Analysis of the Effects of 'Weberian' State Structures on Economic Growth." *American Sociological Review* 64 (5): 748–765. doi: 10.2307/2657374.

Eynde, O. 2016. "Military Service and Human Capital Accumulation: Evidence from Colonial Punjab." *Journal of Human Resources* 51 (4): 1003–1035.

Falleti, T. 2009. "Infiltrating the State: The Evolution of Health Care Reforms in Brazil, 1964–1988." In *Explaining Institutional Change: Ambiguity, Agency, and Power*, edited by J. Mahoney and K. Thelen, 38–62. New York: Cambridge University Press.

Falleti, T. 2010. *Decentralization and Subnational Politics in Latin America*. New York: Cambridge University Press.

Falleti, T., and J. Lynch. 2009. "Context and Causal Mechanisms in Political Analysis." *Comparative Political Studies* 42 (9): 1143–1166.

Falleti, T., and T. Riofrancos. 2018. "Endogenous Participation: Strengthening Prior Consultation in Extractive Economies." *World Politics* 70 (1): 86–121.

Fenno, R. 1978. *Home Style: House Members in Their Districts*. Boston: Little, Brown.

Filmer, D., and L. Pritchett. 1999. "The Impact of Public Spending on Health: Does Money Matter?" *Social Science & Medicine* 49 (10): 1309–1323.

Fischer-Tiné, H., and M. Mann. 2004. *Colonialism as Civilizing Mission: Cultural Ideology in British India, Anthem South Asian Studies*. London: Anthem Press.
Fisher, J., ed. 1978. *Himalayan Anthropology: The Indo-Tibetan Interface*. The Hague: Mouton Publisher.
Forrester, D. B. 1966. "The Madras Anti-Hindi Agitation, 1965: Political Protest and Its Effects on Language Policy in India." *Pacific Affairs* 39 (1/2): 19–36.
Fox, J. 2007. *Accountability Politics: Power and Voice in Rural Mexico*. New York: Oxford University Press.
Fox, J. 2015. "Social Accountability: What Does the Evidence Really Say?" *World Development* 72: 346–361.
Fox, J. 2020. "Contested Terrain: International Development Projects and Countervailing Power for the Excluded." *World Development* 133: 104978.
Frankel, F. R. 2005. *India's Political Economy, 1947–2004: The Gradual Revolution*. New Delhi: Oxford University Press.
Freire, P. 1970. *Pedagogy of the Oppressed*. New York: Continuum.
Fukuyama, F. 2013. "What Is Governance?" *Governance* 26 (3): 347–368.
Fung, A. 2006. *Empowered Participation: Reinventing Urban Democracy*. Princeton, NJ: Princeton University Press.
Fung, A., and E. O. Wright. 2001. "Deepening Democracy: Innovations in Empowered Participatory Governance." *Politics and Society* 29 (1): 5–41.
Fung, A., and E. O. Wright, eds. 2003. *Deepening Democracy: Institutional Innovations in Empowered Participatory Governance*. New York: Verso.
Gailmard, S., and J. W. Patty. 2012. "Formal Models of Bureaucracy." *Annual Review of Political Science* 15: 353–377.
Gauri, V. 2009. "Public Interest Litigation in India: Overreaching or Underachieving?" World Bank Policy Research Working Paper No. 5109.
Geddes, B. 1990. "Building ' state' Autonomy in Brazil, 1930–1964." *Comparative Politics* 22 (2): 217–235.
Geddes, B. 1994. *Politician's Dilemma: Building State Capacity in Latin America*. Berkeley: University of California Press.
Geertz, C. 1973. *The Interpretation of Cultures*. New York: Basic Books.
George, A. L., and A. Bennett. 2005. *Case Studies and Theory Development in the Social Sciences*. Cambridge, MA: MIT Press.
Gerring, J. 2004. "What Is a Case Study and What Is It Good for?" *American Political Science Review* 98 (02): 341–354. doi: 10.1017/S0003055404001182.
Gibson, C., and M. Woolcock. 2008. "Empowerment, Deliberative Development, and Local-Level Politics in Indonesia: Participatory Projects as a Source of Countervailing Power." *Studies in Comparative International Development* 43 (2): 151.
Giddens, A. 1973. *Capitalism and Modern Social Theory: An Analysis of the Writings of Marx, Durkheim and Max Weber*. New York: Cambridge University Press.
Gift, T., and E. Wibbels. 2014. "Reading, Writing, and the Regrettable Status of Education Research in Comparative Politics." *Annual Review of Political Science* 17 (1): 291–312. doi: 10.1146/annurev-polisci-080911-131426.
Goel, S. 2013. "Sardar Vallabhbhai Patel and Public Administration." *Indian Journal of Public Administration* 59 (2): 247–258.

Goetz, A. M., and R. Jenkins. 2005. *Reinventing Accountability: Making Democracy Work for Human Development*. New York: Palgrave Macmillan.

Goffman, E. 1959. *The Presentation of Self in Everyday Life*. Garden City, NY: Doubleday Anchor Books.

Government of Himachal Pradesh. 2018. *Economic Survey of Himachal Pradesh, 2017–18*. Shimla, India: Government of Himachal Pradesh.

GoI. 2005. Himachal Pradesh Development Report. In State Development Report Series. Delhi: Government of India.

Goldin, C., and L. Katz. 2009. *The Race between Education and Technology*. Cambridge, MA: Harvard University Press.

Gouldner, A. W. 1954. *Patterns of Industrial Bureaucracy*. New York: Free Press.

Government of India. 1992. *Education for All: The Indian Scene*. New Delhi: Department of Education, Ministry of Human Resource Development.

Granovetter, M. 1985. "Economic Action and Social Structure: A Theory of Embeddedness." *American Journal of Sociology* 91 (3): 481–510.

Grindle, M. S. 1980. *Politics and Policy Implementation in the Third World*. Princeton, NJ: Princeton University Press.

Grindle, M. S. 1997. "Divergent Cultures? When Public Organizations Perform Well in Developing Countries." *World Development* 25 (4): 481–495.

Grindle, M. S. 2004. "Good Enough Governance: Poverty Reduction and Reform in Developing Countries." *Governance* 17 (4): 525–548.

Grindle, M. S. 2012. *Jobs for the Boys*. Cambridge, MA: Harvard University Press.

Guha, R. 2000. *The Unquiet Woods: Ecological Change and Peasant Resistance in the Himalaya*. Berkeley: University of California Press.

Gupta, A. 2012. *Red Tape: Bureaucracy, Structural Violence, and Poverty in India*. Durham, NC: Duke University Press.

Gutmann, A. 1999. *Democratic Education*. Princeton: Princeton University Press.

Gutmann, A., and D. Thompson. 1990. "Moral Conflict and Political Consensus." *Ethics* 101 (1): 64–88.

Habermas, J. 1994. "Three Normative Models of Democracy." *Constellations* 1 (1): 1–10.

Habermas, J. 1998. *Between Facts and Norms: Contributions to a Discourse Theory of Law and Democracy*. Cambridge, MA: MIT Press.

Habib, S. I., ed. 2010. *Maulana Abul Kalam Azad and the National Education System*. New Delhi: National University of Educational Planning and Administration.

Hacker, J. 2004. "Privatizing Risk without Privatizing the Welfare State: The Hidden Politics of Social Policy Retrenchment in the United States." *American Political Science Review* 98 (2): 243–260.

Hacker, J. 2006. *The Great Risk Shift: The Assault on American Jobs, Families, Health Care and Retirement and How You Can Fight Back*. Oxford: Oxford University Press.

Haggard, S. 2018. *Developmental States*. New York: Cambridge University Press.

Hajer, M. A., and H. Wagenaar. 2003. *Deliberative Policy Analysis: Understanding Governance in the Network Society*. New York: Cambridge University Press.

Hall, P., and M. Lamont. 2009. *Successful Societies: How Institutions and Culture Affect Health*. New York: Cambridge University Press.

Hall, P., and D. Soskice, eds. 2001. *Varieties of Capitalism: The Institutional Foundations of Comparative Advantage*. Oxford: Oxford University Press.

Hall, P., and R. Taylor. 1996. "Political Science and the Three New Institutionalisms." *Political Studies* 44 (5): 936–957.

Hammersley, M., and P. Atkinson. 1995. *Ethnography: Principles in Practice*. Abingdon: Routledge.

Hanson, J. K., and R. Sigman. 2013. "Leviathan's Latent Dimensions: Measuring State Capacity for Comparative Political Research." *Journal of Politics* 83 (4): 1495–1510.

Hanushek, E.A. 2002. "Publicly Provided Education." In *Handbook of Public Economics, Volume* 4, edited by A.J. Auerbach and M. Feldstein, 2045–2141. Amsterdam: Elsevier.

Hanushek, E. A. 2010. "How Well Do We Understand Achievement Gaps." *Focus* 27 (2): 5–12.

Hanushek, E. A., and L. Woessmann. 2011. "The Economics of International Differences in Educational Achievement." In *Handbook of the Economics of Education: Volume 3*, edited by E. A. Hanushek, F. Welch, S. Machin, and L. Woessmann, 89–200. Amsterdam: Elsevier.

Harding, R., and D. Stasavage. 2014. "What Democracy Does (and doesn't do) for Basic Services: School Fees, School Inputs, and African Elections." *Journal of Politics* 76 (1): 229–245.

Harlow, B., and M. Carter, eds. 2004. *Archives of Empire, Volume I: From the East India Company to the Suez Canal*. Durham: Duke University Press.

Harriss-White, B. 1991. *Child Nutrition and Poverty in South India: Noon Meals in Tamil Nadu*. New Delhi: Concept Publishing.

Hasan, Z. 1989. "Power and Mobilization: Patterns of Resilience and Change in Uttar Pradesh Politics." In *Dominance and State Power in Modern India: Decline of a Social Order*, edited by F. R. Frankel and M. S. A. Rao. New Delhi: Oxford University Press.

Hasan, Z. 1998. *Quest for Power: Oppositional Movements and Post-Congress Politics in Uttar Pradesh*. Oxford: Oxford University Press.

Hasan, Z. 2002. "Representation and Redistribution: The New Lower Caste Politics of North India." In *Transforming India: Social and Political Dynamics of Democracy*, edited by F. R. Frankel, Z. Hasan, R. Bhargava, and B. Arora. New Delhi: Oxford University Press.

Hayek, F. A. 1944. *The Road to Serfdom*. Chicago, IL: University of Chicago Press.

He, B. 2006. "Western Theories of Deliberative Democracy and the Chinese Practice of Complex Deliberative Governance." In *The Search for Deliberative Democracy in China*, edited by E. J. Leib and B. He, 133–148. New York: Palgrave Macmillan.

He, B. 2014. "Deliberative Culture and Politics: The Persistence of Authoritarian Deliberation in China." *Political Theory* 42 (1): 58–81.

He, B., and M. E. Warren. 2011. "Authoritarian Deliberation: The Deliberative Turn in Chinese Political Development." *Perspectives on Politics* 9 (2): 269–289.

Heclo, H. 1974. *Modern Social Politics in Britain and Sweden*. New Haven: Yale University Press.

Heilmann, S. 2008a. "From Local Experiments to National Policy: The Origins of China's Distinctive Policy Process." *The China Journal* 59: 1–30. doi: 10.1086/tcj.59.20066378.

Heilmann, S. 2008b. "Policy Experimentation in China's Economic Rise." *Studies in Comparative International Development* 43 (1): 1–26.

Heilmann, S., and E. Perry. 2011. *Mao's Invisible Hand: The Political Foundations of Adaptive Governance in China*. Cambridge, MA: Harvard University Press.

Heller, P. 1999. *The Labor of Development: Workers and the Transformation of Capitalism in Kerala, India*. Ithaca, NY: Cornell University Press.

Heller, P. 2000. "Degrees of Democracy: Some Comparative Lessons from India." *World Politics* 52 (4): 484–519.

Heller, P. 2001. "Moving the State: The Politics of Democratic Decentralization in Kerala, South Africa, and Porto Alegre." *Politics & Society* 29 (1): 131–163. doi: 10.1177/0032329201029001006.

Heller, P. 2005. "Reinventing Public Power in the Age of Globalization: The Transformation of Movement Politics in Kerala." In *Social Movements in India: Poverty, Power, and Politics*, edited by R. Ray and M. F. Katzenstein. New Delhi: Oxford University Press.

Heller, P., K. Harilal, and S. Chaudhuri. 2007. "Building Local Democracy: Evaluating the Impact of Decentralization in Kerala, India." *World Development* 35 (4): 626–648.

Heller, P., and V. Rao, eds. 2015. *Deliberation and Development: Rethinking the Role of Voice and Collective Action in Unequal Societies*. Washington, DC: World Bank Group.

Helmke, G., and S. Levitsky. 2004. "Informal Institutions and Comparative Politics: A Research Agenda." *Perspectives on Politics* 2 (4): 725–740. doi: 10.1017/S1537592704040472.

Henderson, J., D. Hulme, H. Jalilian, and R. Phillips. 2007. "Bureaucratic Effects: 'Weberian' State Agencies and Poverty Reduction." *Sociology* 41 (3): 515–532.

Henningham, S. 1983. "Bureaucracy and Control in India's Great Landed Estates: The Raj Darbhanga of Bihar, 1879 to 1950." *Modern Asian Studies* 17 (1): 35–57.

Herbst, J. 2000. "Economic Incentives, Natural Resources and Conflict in Africa." *Journal of African Economies* 9 (3): 270–294.

Herd, P., and D. P. Moynihan. 2018. *Administrative Burden: Policymaking by Other Means*. New York: Russell Sage Foundation.

Herring, R. 1983. *Land to the Tiller: The Political Economy of Agrarian Reform in South Asia*. New Haven, CT: Yale University Press.

Herring, R. 1999. "Embedded Particularism: India's Failed Developmental State." In *The Developmental State*, edited by M. Woo-Cumings. Ithaca, NY: Cornell University Press.

Hess, F. 1999. *Spinning Wheels: The Politics of Urban School Reform*. Washington, DC: Brookings Institution.

Hicken, A. 2011. "Clientelism." *Annual Review of Political Science* 14 (1): 289–310.

Hicken, A., and J. Simmons. 2008. "The Personal Vote and the Efficacy of Education Spending." *American Journal of Political Science* 52 (1): 109–124.

Hickey, S., K. Sen, and B. Bukenya, eds. 2015. *The Politics of Inclusive Development: Interrogating the Evidence*. Oxford: Oxford University Press.

Hirschman, A. O. 1970. *Exit, Voice, and Loyalty: Responses to Decline in Firms, Organizations, and States*. Cambridge, MA: Harvard University Press.

Holmstrom, B., and P. Milgrom. 1991. "Multitask Principal-Agent Analyses: Incentive Contracts, Asset Ownership, and Job Design." *Journal of Law, Economics, & Organization* 7: 24–52.

Honig, D. 2018. *Navigation by Judgment: Why and When Top Down Management of Foreign Aid Doesn't Work*. New York: Oxford University Press.

Honig, D., and L. Pritchett. 2019. "The Limits of Accounting-Based Accountability in Education (and Far Beyond): Why More Accounting Will Rarely Solve Accountability Problems." Research on Improving Systems of Education (RISE), Working Paper No. 19–030.

Hooghe, L., and G. Marks. 2003. "Unraveling the Central State, But How? Types of Multi-Level Governance." *American Political Science Review* 97 (02): 233–243.

Horowitz, D. L. 1989. "Incentives and Behaviour in the Ethnic Politics of Sri Lanka and Malaysia." *Third World Quarterly* 11 (4): 18–35.

Hossain, N. 2010. "Rude Accountability: Informal Pressures on Frontline Bureaucrats in Bangladesh." *Development and Change* 41 (5): 907–928.

Houtzager, P. P., and A. K. Acharya. 2011. "Associations, Active Citizenship, and the Quality of Democracy in Brazil and Mexico." *Theory and Society* 40 (1): 1–36. doi: 10.1007/s11186-010-9128-y.

Huber, E., C. Ragin, and J. Stephens. 1993. "Social Democracy, Christian Democracy, Constitutional Structure, and the Welfare State." *American Journal of Sociology* 99 (3): 711–749.

Huber, J., and C. Shipan. 2002. *Deliberate Discretion? The Institutional Foundations of Bureaucratic Autonomy*. New York: Cambridge University Press.

Hull, M. 2012. *Government of Paper: The Materiality of Bureaucracy in Urban Pakistan*. Berkeley: University of California Press.

IIM-A. 2014. *Mahila Samakhya 2014: A National Review*. Ahmedabad: Ravi J. Matthai Centre for Educational Innovation, Indian Institute of Management-Ahmedabad.

Isaac, T., and R. Franke. 2000. *Local Democracy and Development: People's Campaign for Decentralized Planning*. New Delhi: Leftword Books.

Isaac, T., and P. Heller. 2003. "Democracy and Development: Decentralized Planning in Kerala." In *Deepening Democracy: Institutional Innovations in Empowered Participatory Governance*, edited by A. Fung and E.O. Wright. New York: Verso.

Iversen, T., and J. Stephens. 2008. "Partisan Politics, the Welfare State, and Three Worlds of Human Capital Formation." *Comparative Political Studies* 41 (4–5): 600–637.

Iversen, V., R. Palmer-Jones, and K. Sen. 2013. "On the Colonial Origins of Agricultural Development in India: A Re-examination of Banerjee and Iyer, 'History, Institutions and Economic Performance'." *Journal of Development Studies* 49 (12): 1631–1646.

Iyer, L. 2010. "Direct versus Indirect Colonial Rule in India: Long-Term Consequences." *Review of Economics and Statistics* 92 (4): 693–713.

Iyer, L., and A. Mani. 2011. "Traveling Agents: Political Change and Bureaucratic Turnover in India." *Review of Economics and Statistics* 94 (3): 723–739.

Jaffrelot, C. 1998. "The Bahujan Samaj Party in North India: No Longer Just a Dalit Party?" *Comparative Studies of South Asia, Africa and the Middle East* 18 (1): 35–51.

Jaffrelot, C. 2000. "The Rise of the Other Backward Classes in the Hindi Belt." *Journal of Asian Studies* 59 (1): 86–108. doi: 10.2307/2658585.

Jaffrelot, C. 2003. *India's Silent Revolution: The Rise of the Lower Castes in North India*. New York: Columbia University Press.

Jaffrelot, C., and S. Kumar, eds. 2012. *Rise of the Plebeians? The Changing Face of the Indian Legislative Assemblies*. New Delhi: Routledge.

Jain, S. 1984. "Women and People's Ecological Movement: A Case Study of Women's Role in the Chipko Movement in Uttar Pradesh." *Economic and Political Weekly* 19 (41): 1788–1794.

Jandhyala, K. 2014. "From Sanghas to Federations: Empowering Processes and Institutions." In *Cartographies of Empowerment: The Mahila Samakhya Story*, edited by V. Ramachandran and K. Jandhyala. New Delhi: Zubaan Books.

Jannuzi, F. T. 1974. *Agrarian Crisis in India: The Case of Bihar*. Austin: University of Texas Press.

Jaoul, N. 2015. "A Strong Law for the Weak: Dalit Activism in a District Court of Uttar Pradesh." In *Regimes of Legality: Ethnography of Criminal Cases in South Asia*, edited by D. Berti and D. Bordia. New Delhi: Oxford University Press.

Jayal, N. 2013. *Citizenship and Its Discontents: An Indian History*. Ranikhet: Permanent Black.

Jeffrey, C. 2002. "Caste, Class, and Clientelism: A Political Economy of Everyday Corruption in Rural North India." *Economic Geography* 78 (1): 21–41.

Jeffrey, C., and J. Lerche. 2000. "Stating the Difference: State, Discourse and Class Reproduction in Uttar Pradesh, India." *Development and Change* 31 (4): 857–878. doi: 10.1111/1467-7660.00180.

Jeffrey, R. 1975. The Decline of Nair Dominance: Society and Politics in Travancore 1847–1908. New Delhi: Manohar.

Jeffrey, R. 1987. "Governments and Culture: How Women Made Kerala Literate." *Pacific Affairs* 60 (3): 447–472.

Jeffrey, R. 1992. *Politics, Women and Well-Being: How Kerala Became "a Model."* New York: Palgrave Macmillan.

Jenkins, R. 2010. "NGOs and Indian Politics." In *The Oxford Companion to Politics in India*, edited by N. G. Jayal and P. B. Mehta. Oxford: Oxford University Press.

Jensenius, F. R. 2017. *Social Justice through Inclusion: The Consequences of Electoral Quotas in India*. New York: Oxford University Press.

Jha, H. 2018. "Emerging Politics of Accountability." *Economic and Political Weekly* 53 (10): 47.

Jha, S., V. Rao, and M. Woolcock. 2007. "Governance in the Gullies: Democratic Responsiveness and Leadership in Delhi's Slums." *World Development* 35 (2): 230–246.

Jha, S. N. 1970. "Caste in Bihar Politics." *Economic and Political Weekly* 5 (7): 341–344.

Jodhka, S. 2004. "Sikhism and the Caste Question: Dalits and Their Politics in Contemporary Punjab." *Contributions to Indian Sociology* 38 (1–2): 165–192.

Johnson, C. 1982. *MITI and the Japanese Miracle: The Growth of Industrial Policy, 1925–1975*. Palo Alto: Stanford University Press.

Joshi, A., and M. Moore. 2004. "Institutionalised Co-production: Unorthodox Public Service Delivery in Challenging Environments." *Journal of Development Studies* 40 (4): 31–49. doi: 10.1080/00220380410001673184.

Joshi, D. 2005. "Misunderstanding Gender in Water: Addressing or Reproducing Exclusion." In *Gender, Water and Development*, edited by A. Coles and T. Wallace. New York: Berg Publishers.

Joshi, P. C. 1995. *Uttarakhand: Issues and Challenges*. New Delhi: Har-Anand Publications.

Kanwar, P. 2003. *Imperial Simla: The Political Culture of the Raj*. New Delhi: Oxford University Press.

Kapur, D. 2020. "Why Does the Indian State Both Fail and Succeed?" *Journal of Economic Perspectives* 34 (1): 31–54.

Kapur, D., and P. Mukhopadhyay. 2007. "Sisyphean State? Why Poverty Programmes in India Fail and yet Persist." Working Paper, Presented at the Annual Meeting of the American Political Science Association.

Kapur, D., P. Mukhopadhyay, and A. Subramanian. 2008. "The Case for Direct Cash Transfers to the Poor." *Economic and Political Weekly* 43 (15): 37–43.

Kapur, D., C. B. Prasad, L. Pritchett, and D. S. Babu. 2010. "Rethinking Inequality: Dalits in Uttar Pradesh in the Market Reform Era." *Economic and Political Weekly* 45 (35): 39–49.

Karpowitz, C. F., and C. Raphael. 2014. *Deliberation, Democracy, and Civic Forums: Improving Equality and Publicity*. New York: Cambridge University Press.

Kassel, D. S. 2008. "Performance, Accountability, and the Debate over Rules." *Public Administration Review* 68 (2): 241–252.

Kaufman, D. 2005. "10 Myths about Governance and Corruption." *Finance and Development* 42 (3): 41–43.

Kaufman, H. 1967. *The Forest Ranger: A Study in Administrative Behavior*. Baltimore, MD: Johns Hopkins University Press.

Keane, J. 2009. *The Life and Death of Democracy*. London: Simon & Schuster.

Keefer, P. 2007. "Clientelism, Credibility, and the Policy Choices of Young Democracies." *American Journal of Political Science* 51 (4): 804–821. doi: 10.1111/j.1540-5907.2007.00282.x.

Keefer, P., and S. Khemani. 2004. "Why Do the Poor Receive Poor Services?" *Economic and Political Weekly* 39 (9): 935–943.

Keefer, P., and S. Khemani. 2005. "Democracy, Public Expenditures, and the Poor: Understanding Political Incentives for Providing Public Services." *World Bank Research Observer* 20 (1): 1–27.

Kennedy, D. K. 1996. *The Magic Mountains: Hill Stations and the British Raj*. Berkeley: University of California Press.

Khan, M. 2010. "Political Settlements and the Governance of Growth-enhancing Institutions." Research Paper Series on Governance for Growth. SOAS, University of London.

Khan, M. H. 2018. "Political Settlements and the Analysis of Institutions." *African Affairs* 117 (469): 636–655.

Khemani, S. 2015. "Buying Votes versus Supplying Public Services: Political Incentives to Under-invest in Pro-Poor Policies." *Journal of Development Economics* 117: 84–93.

Khemani, S. 2019. "What Is State Capacity?" World Bank Policy Research Working Paper No. 8734.

King, D., and R. Lieberman. 2009. "Ironies of State Building: A Comparative Perspective on the American State." *World Politics* 61 (3): 547–588.

Kingdon, G. 2020. "The Private Schooling Phenomenon in India: A Review." *The Journal of Development Studies* 56 (10): 1795–1817.

Kingdon, G., and R. Banerji. 2009. "Addressing School Quality: Some Policy Pointers from Rural North India," *RECOUP Policy Brief*, 5. Cambridge: University of Cambridge.

Kingdon, G., and M. Muzammil. 2003. *The Political Economy of Education in India: Teacher Politics in Uttar Pradesh*. New Delhi: Oxford University Press.

Kingdon, G., and M. Muzammil. 2012. "The School Governance Environment in Uttar Pradesh, India: Implications for Teacher Accountability and Effort." *Journal of Development Studies* 49 (2): 251–269.

Kitschelt, H., and S. Wilkinson, eds. 2007. *Patrons, Clients, and Policies: Patterns of Democratic Accountability and Political Competition*. New York: Cambridge University Press.

Klitgaard, R. 1988. *Controlling Corruption*. Berkeley: University of California Press.

Kohli, A. 1987. *The State and Poverty in India: The Politics of Reform*. New York: Cambridge University Press.

Kohli, A. 1990. *Democracy and Discontent: India's Growing Crisis of Governability*. New York: Cambridge University Press.

Kohli, A. 2004. *State-Directed Development: Political Power and Industrialization in the Global Periphery*. Cambridge: Cambridge University Press.

Kohli, A. 2012. *Poverty Amid Plenty in the New India*. New York: Cambridge University Press.

Kohli, A. 2019. *Imperialism and the Developing World: How Britain and the United States Shaped the Global Periphery*. New York: Oxford University Press.

Kornberger, M., R. Meyer, C. Brandtner, and M. Höllerer. 2017. "When Bureaucracy Meets the Crowd: Studying 'Open Government' in the Vienna City Administration." *Organization Studies* 38 (2): 179–200.

Kosack, S. 2012. *The Education of Nations: How the Political Organization of the Poor, Not Democracy, Led Governments to Invest in Mass Education*. New York: Oxford University Press.

Kothari Commission. 1966. *Education and National Development: Report of the Education Commission 1964–66*. Delhi: Government of India.

Kothari, R. 1964. "The Congress 'System' in India." *Asian Survey* 4 (12): 1161–1173.

Kothari, R. 1974. "The Congress System Revisited: A Decennial Review." *Asian Survey* 14 (12): 1035–1054.
Kotter, J. P. 1992. *Corporate Culture and Performance*. New York: Free Press.
Kramon, E., and D. N. Posner. 2013. "Who Benefits from Distributive Politics? How the Outcome One Studies Affects the Answer One Gets." *Perspectives on Politics* 11 (2): 461–474.
Kremer, M., K. Muralidharan, N. Chaudhury, J. Hammer, and F. Rogers. 2005. "Teacher Absence in India: A Snapshot." *Journal of the European Economic Association* 3 (2–3): 658–667.
Krishna, A. 2003. *Active Social Capital: Tracing the Roots of Development and Democracy*. New Delhi: Oxford University Press.
Krishna, A. 2010. "Continuity and Change: The Indian Administrative Service 30 Years Ago and Today." *Commonwealth & Comparative Politics* 48 (4): 433–444.
Krishna, A. 2011. "Gaining Access to Public Services and the Democratic State in India: Institutions in the Middle." *Studies in Comparative International Development* 46 (1): 98–117.
Krishna, A., and G. Schober. 2014. "The Gradient of Governance: Distance and Disengagement in Indian Villages." *Journal of Development Studies* 50 (6): 820–838.
Kruks-Wisner, G. 2018. *Claiming the State: Active Citizenship and Social Welfare in Rural India*. New York: Cambridge University Press.
Kruks-Wisner, G. 2021. "Great Expectations, Great Grievances: The Politics of Citizens' Complaints in India." *Comparative Politics* 54 (1): 27–64.
Krumpal, I. 2013. "Determinants of Social Desirability Bias in Sensitive Surveys: A Literature Review." *Quality & Quantity* 47 (4): 2025–2047.
Kudaisya, G. 2002. "Constructing the 'heartland': Uttar Pradesh in India's Body-Politic." *South Asia: Journal of South Asian Studies* 25 (2): 153–181. doi: 10.1080/00856400208723480.
Kudaisya, G. 2006. *Region, Nation, "heartland": Uttar Pradesh in India's Body Politic*. New Delhi: Sage.
Kumar, A. 2009. *Community Warriors: State, Peasants and Caste Armies in Bihar*. New Delhi: Anthem.
Kumar, K., M. Priyam, and S. Saxena. 2001. "Looking beyond the Smokescreen: DPEP and Primary Education in India." *Economic and Political Weekly* 36 (7): 560–568. doi: 10.2307/4410292.
Kumar, P. 1999. "Dalits and the BSP in Uttar Pradesh: Issues and Challenges." *Economic and Political Weekly* 34 (14): 822–826.
Kumar, P. 2000. *The Uttarakhand Movement: Construction of a Regional Identity*. New Delhi: Kanishka Publishers.
Kumar, S. 2002. "Uttaranchal Assembly Elections: Marginal Difference." *Economic and Political Weekly* 37 (2): 1879–1882.
Kumar, S., and R. K. Chauhan. 2003. "Elections 2003: Understanding Complex Choices." *Economic and Political Weekly* 38 (28): 2927–2932.
Kumar, S., and R. Ranjan. 2009. "Bihar: Development Matters." *Economic and Political Weekly* 44 (39): 141–144.

Kumar, U., and A. Subramanian. 2012. "Growth in India's States in the First Decade of the 21st Century: Four Facts." *Economic and Political Weekly* 47 (3): 48–57.

Kumlin, S., and B. Rothstein. 2005. "Making and Breaking Social Capital: The Impact of Welfare-State Institutions." *Comparative Political Studies* 38 (4): 339–365.

Kurtz, M., and A. Schrank. 2007. "Growth and Governance: Models, Measures, and Mechanisms." *Journal of Politics* 69 (2): 538–554.

Lake, D., and M. Baum. 2001. "The Invisible Hand of Democracy: Political Control and the Provision of Public Services." *Comparative Political Studies* 34 (6): 587–621.

Landry, P. F. 2008. *Decentralized Authoritarianism in China: The Communist Party's Control of Local Elites in the Post-Mao Era*. Cambridge: Cambridge University Press.

Lange, M. 2005. "The Rule of Law and Development: A Weberian Framework of States and State–Society Relations." In *States and Development: Historical Antecedents of Stagnation and Advance*, edited by M. Lange and D. Rueschemeyer, 48–65. New York: Palgrave Macmillan.

Lanjouw, P., and N. Stern. 1998. *Economic Development in Palanpur over Five Decades*. Oxford: Oxford University Press.

Lawless, J., and R. Fox. 2001. "Political Participation of the Urban Poor." *Social Problems* 48 (3): 362–385.

Leonard, D. 2010. "'Pockets' of Effective Agencies in Weak Governance States: Where Are They Likely and Why Does It Matter?" *Public Administration and Development* 30 (2): 91–101.

Lerche, J. 1999. "Politics of the Poor: Agricultural Labourers and Political Transformations in Uttar Pradesh." *Journal of Peasant Studies* 26 (2–3): 182–241. doi: 10.1080/03066159908438707.

Lerman, A. E., and V. M. Weaver. 2014. *Arresting Citizenship: The Democratic Consequences of American Crime Control*. Chicago, IL: University of Chicago Press.

Levi, M. 1988. *Of Rule and Revenue*. Berkeley: University of California Press.

Levi, M., and A. Sacks. 2009. "Legitimating Beliefs: Sources and Indicators." *Regulation & Governance* 3 (4): 311–333. doi: 10.1111/j.1748-5991.2009.01066.x.

Levi, M., and R. Sherman. 1997. "Rational Compliance with Rationalized Bureaucracy." In *Institutions and Economic Development: Growth and Governance in Less-Developed and Post-Socialist Countries*, edited by C. Clague. Baltimore: Johns Hopkins University Press.

Levitsky, S., and M. V. Murillo. 2009. "Variation in Institutional Strength." *Annual Review of Political Science* 12 (1): 115–133. doi: 10.1146/annurev.polisci.11.091106.121756.

Lieberman, R. 2011. *Shaping Race Policy: The United States in Comparative Perspective*. Princeton, NJ: Princeton University Press.

Lieten, G. K. 1977. "Education, Ideology and Politics in Kerala 1957–59." *Social Scientist* 6 (2): 3–21. doi: 10.2307/3516681.

Lieten, G. K. 2002. "The Human Development Puzzle in Kerala." *Journal of Contemporary Asia* 32 (1): 47–68.

Lin, J. 1988. "The Household Responsibility System in China's Agricultural Reform: A Theoretical and Empirical Study." *Economic Development and Cultural Change* 36 (S3): S199–S224.

Lipset, S. M. 1959. "Some Social Requisites of Democracy: Economic Development and Political Legitimacy." *American Political Science Review* 53 (1): 69–105.

Lipsky, M. 1980. *Streel-Level Bureaucracy: Dilemmas of the Individual in Public Services*. New York: Russell Sage Foundation. Original edition, 1980.

Lipsky, M. 1984. "Bureaucratic Disentitlement in Social Welfare Programs." *Social Service Review* 58 (1): 3–27. doi: 10.1086/644161.

Little, A. W. 2010. *Access to Elementary Education in India: Politics, Policies and Progress*. London: Institute of Education, University of London.

Locke, R., M. Amengual, and A. Mangla. 2009. "Virtue Out of Necessity? Compliance, Commitment, and the Improvement of Labor Conditions in Global Supply Chains." *Politics & Society* 37 (3): 319–351. doi: 10.1177/0032329209338922.

Locke, R., and K. Thelen. 1995. "Apples and Oranges Revisited: Contextualized Comparisons and the Study of Comparative Labor Politics." *Politics & Society* 23 (3): 337–367.

Louis, P. 2002. *People Power: The Naxalite Movement in Central Bihar*. Delhi: Wordsmiths.

MacCormick, N. 1989. "The Ethics of Legalism." *Ratio Juris* 2 (2): 184–193.

MacLean, L. M. 2010. *Informal Institutions and Citizenship in Rural Africa: Risk and Reciprocity in Ghana and Cote d'Ivoire*. New York: Cambridge University Press.

Mahoney, J., and K. Thelen. 2010. *Explaining Institutional Change: Ambiguity, Agency, and Power*. New York: Cambridge University Press.

Mangla, A. 2018. "Elite Strategies and Incremental Policy Change: The Expansion of Primary Education in India." *Governance* 31 (2): 381–399. doi: 10.1111/gove.12299.

Mangla, A. 2022. "Social Conflict on the Front Lines of Reform: Institutional Activism and Girls' Education in Rural India." *Public Administration and Development* 42 (1): 95–105. doi: 10.1002/pad.1959.

Mangla, A., and V. Kapoor. 2021. "The Police in India: Institutional Design, Capacity and Performance." Working Paper, University of Oxford.

Mani, A., and S. Mukand. 2007. "Democracy, Visibility and Public Good Provision." *Journal of Development Economics* 83 (2): 506–529.

Mann, M. 1984. "The Autonomous Power of the State: Its Origins, Mechanisms and Results." *European Journal of Sociology* 25 (2): 185–213.

Mann, M. 2008. "Infrastructural Power Revisited." *Studies in Comparative International Development* 43 (3): 355–365.

Manor, J. 2000. "Small-Time Political Fixers in India's States: 'Towel over Armpit'." *Asian Survey* 40 (5): 816–835.

Manor, J. 2011. "The Congress Party and the 'Great Transformation'." In *Understanding India's New Political Economy: A Great Transformation?* edited by S. Ruparelia, S. Reddy, J. Harris, and S. Corbridge, 204–220. London: Routledge.

Mansbridge, J. 1992. "A Deliberative Perspective on Neocorporatism." *Politics & Society* 20 (4): 493–505.

Mansuri, G., and V. Rao. 2004. "Community-Based and -Driven Development: A Critical Review." *World Bank Research Observer* 19 (1): 1–39. doi: 10.1093/wbro/lkh012.

Mansuri, G., and V. Rao. 2013. *Localizing Development: Does Participation Work?* Washington, DC: The World Bank.

Mantzavinos, C., D. North, and S. Shariq. 2004. "Learning, Institutions, and Economic Performance." *Perspectives on Politics* 2 (01): 75–84. doi: 10.1017.S1537592704000635.

March, J. G., and J. P. Olsen. 1989. *Rediscovering Institutions: The Organizational Basis of Politics. New York*: Free Press.

March, J. G., and J. P. Olsen. 2013. "The Logic of Appropriateness." In *The Oxford Handbook of Political Science*, edited by R. E. Goodin. Oxford: Oxford University Press.

Marshall, T. H. 1950. *Citizenship and Social Class.* London: Cambridge University Press.

Mathew, E. 1999. "Growth of Literacy in Kerala: State Intervention, Missionary Initiatives and Social Movements." *Economic and Political Weekly* 34 (39): 2811–2820.

Mathew, S., and M. Moore. 2011. "State Incapacity by Design: Understanding the Bihar Story." *IDS Working Papers* 2011 (366): 1–31.

Mathur, K. 1972. *Bureaucratic Response to Development: A Study of Block Development Officers in Rajasthan and Uttar Pradesh.* Ann Arbor: University of Michigan.

Mathur, N. 2016. *Paper Tiger: Law, Bureaucracy and the Development State in Himalayan India.* New Delhi: Cambridge University Press.

Matland, R. E. 1995. "Synthesizing the Implementation Literature: The Ambiguity-Conflict Model of Policy Implementation." *Journal of Public Administration Research and Theory* 5 (2): 145–174. doi: 10.1093/oxfordjournals.jpart.a037242.

Mawdsley, E. 1996. "Uttarakhand Agitation and Other Backward Classes." *Economic and Political Weekly* 31 (4): 205–210.

Mawdsley, E. 1998. "After Chipko: From Environment to Region in Uttaranchal." *Journal of Peasant Studies* 25 (4): 36–54. doi: 10.1080/03066159808438683.

Mawdsley, E. 2002. "Redrawing the Body Politic: Federalism, Regionalism and the Creation of New States in India." *Commonwealth and Comparative Politics* 40 (3): 34–54.

Maynard-Moody, S., and M. Musheno. 2003. *Cops, Teachers, Counselors: Stories from the Front Lines of Public Service.* Ann Arbor: University of Michigan Press.

Maynard-Moody, S., and M. Musheno. 2012. "Social Equities and Inequities in Practice: Street-Level Workers as Agents and Pragmatists." *Public Administration Review* 72 (s1): S16–S23.

Mazumder, R. 2003. *The Indian Army and the Making of Punjab.* Delhi: Permanent Black.

McCubbins, M., R. Noll, and B. Weingast. 1987. "Administrative Procedures as Instruments of Political Control." *Journal of Law, Economics, & Organization* 3 (2): 243–277.

McDonnell, E. M. 2020. *Patchwork Leviathan: Pockets of Bureaucratic Effectiveness in Developing States*. Princeton, NJ: Princeton University Press.

Mehrotra, S. 2006. "Well-Being and Caste in Uttar Pradesh: Why UP Is Not Like Tamil Nadu." *Economic and Political Weekly* 41 (40): 4261–4271.

Mehta, G. 2000. "Development Planning and Strategy for Uttarakhand." In *Uttarakhand Statehood: Dimensions of Development*, edited by M. Sati and S. Sati. New Delhi: Indus Publishing Company.

Mehta, P. B., and M. Walton. 2014. "Ideas, Interests and the Politics of Development Change in India: Capitalism, Inclusion and the State." ESID Working Paper No. 36, University of Manchester.

Mehta, S. 2005. "Journey through the Unquiet Woods: Contested Resources and Protest Movements in Uttaranchal." In *Quality of Life in the Himalayan Region*, edited by L. R. Sharma. New Delhi: Indus Publishing Company.

Meier, K., and L. O'Toole. 2006. "Political Control versus Bureaucratic Values: Reframing the Debate." *Public Administration Review* 66 (2): 177–192.

Meltzer, A., and S. Richard. 1981. "A Rational Theory of the Size of Government." *Journal of Political Economy* 89 (5): 914–927.

Menon, D. M. 1994. *Caste, Nationalism and Communism in South India: Malabar 1900–1948*. New York: Cambridge University Press.

Metcalf, T. R. 1964. *Aftermath of Revolt: India 1857–1970*. Princeton, NJ: Princeton University Press.

Methi, S. N., and S. Jain. 1994. "The Shiksha Karmi Project in Rajasthan, India (SKP)." In *Beyond Jomtien: Implementing Primary Education for All*, edited by A. W. Little, W. Hoppers, and R. Gardner. London: Macmillan.

Mettler, S. 2002. "Bringing the State Back In to Civic Engagement: Policy Feedback Effects of the GI Bill for World War II Veterans." *American Political Science Review* 96 (2): 351–365.

Meyer, J., F. Ramirez, and Y. Soysal. 1992. "World Expansion of Mass Education, 1870–1980." *Sociology of Education* 65 (2): 128–149.

Meyer, R., I. Egger-Peitler, M. Höllerer, and G. Hammerschmid. 2014. "Of Bureaucrats and Passionate Public Managers: Institutional Logics, Executive Identities, and Public Service Motivation." *Public Administration* 92 (4): 861–885.

Mill, J. S. 1969 [1865]. "Auguste Comte and Positivism." In *The Collected Works of J. S. Mill (Volume 10)*, edited by J. M. Robson, 261–368. Toronto: University of Toronto Press.

Ministry of Education. 1985. *Challenge of Education: A Policy Perspective*. New Delhi: Government of India.

Moe, T. 1984. "The New Economics of Organization." *American Journal of Political Science* 28 (4): 739–777.

Moe, T. 1989. "The Politics of Bureaucratic Structure." In *Can the Government Govern?*, edited by J. E. Chubb and P. E. Peterson. Washington, DC: Brookings Institution Press.

Moe, T. 2011. *Special Interest: Teachers Unions and America's Public Schools.* Washington, DC: Brookings Institution Press.

Moe, T. 2015. "Vested Interests and Political Institutions." *Political Science Quarterly* 130 (2): 277–318.

Moe, T., and S. Wiborg, eds. 2017. *The Comparative Politics of Education: Teachers Unions and Education Systems around the World.* New York: Cambridge University Press.

Moffitt, S. L. 2014. *Making Policy Public: Participatory Bureaucracy in American Democracy.* New York: Cambridge University Press.

Møller, A. M. 2021. "Deliberation and Deliberative Organizational Routines in Frontline Decision-Making." *Journal of Public Administration Research and Theory* 31 (3): 471–488.

Monroe, P. 1940. *Founding of the American Public School System: A History of Education in the United States, from the Early Settlements to the Close of the Civil War Period, Vol. 1.* New York: Macmillan.

Moynihan, D. P., and J. Soss. 2014. "Policy Feedback and the Politics of Administration." *Public Administration Review* 74 (3): 320–332.

Mukherji, A., and A. Mukherji. 2013. "Sushasan: Governance and the New Bihar." In *The New Bihar: Rekindling Governance and Development*, edited by N. K. Singh and N. Stern. Noida, India: Harper Collins.

Mukherji, R. 2014. *Globalization and Deregulation: Ideas, Interests, and Institutional Change in India, Oxford International Relations in South Asia.* Oxford: Oxford University Press.

Mullen, R. D. 2011. *Decentralization, Local Governance, and Social Wellbeing in India: Do Local Governments Matter?* Oxford: Routledge.

Muralidharan, K., J. Das, A. Holla, and A. Mohpal. 2017. "The Fiscal Cost of Weak Governance: Evidence from Teacher Absence in India." *Journal of Public Economics* 145: 116–135.

Muralidharan, K., and N. Prakash. 2017. "Cycling to School: Increasing Secondary School Enrollment for Girls in India." *American Economic Journal: Applied Economics* 9 (3): 321–350.

Muralidharan, K., A. Singh, and A. J. Ganimian. 2019. "Disrupting Education? Experimental Evidence on Technology-Aided Instruction in India." *American Economic Review* 109 (4): 1426–1460.

Muralidharan, K., and V. Sundararaman. 2011. "Teacher Performance Pay: Experimental Evidence from India." *Journal of Political Economy* 119 (1): 39–77. doi: 10.1086/659655.

Murillo, M. V. 1999. "Recovering Political Dynamics: Teachers' Unions and the Decentralization of Education in Argentina and Mexico." *Journal of Interamerican Studies and World Affairs* 41 (1): 31–57. doi: 10.1111/j.1548-2456.1999.tb00083.x.

Myrdal, G. 1968. *Asian Drama, Volumes 1–3.* New York: Pantheon.

Nabatchi, T. 2010. "Addressing the Citizenship and Democratic Deficits: The Potential of Deliberative Democracy for Public Administration." *American Review of Public Administration* 40 (4): 376–399.

Naik, J. P. 1975. Policy and Performance in Indian Education, 1947–74, Dr. K. G. Saiyidain Memorial Lecture. Srinagar: Dr. K. G. Saiyidain Memorial Trust.

Naik, J. P. 1977. *Some Perspectives on Non-formal Education*. Bombay: Allied Publishers.

Naik, J. P. 1982. *The Education Commission and After*. New Delhi: APH Publishing.

Nandan, A., and R. Santhosh. 2019. "Exploring the Changing Forms of Caste-Violence: A Study of Bhumihars in Bihar, India." *European Journal of Cultural and Political Sociology* 6 (4): 421–447.

Narayan, D., and L. Pritchett. 1999. "Cents and Sociability: Household Income and Social Capital in Rural Tanzania." *Economic Development and Cultural Change* 47 (4): 871–897.

Narayan, K. 1997. *Mondays on the Dark Night of the Moon: Himalayan Foothill Folktales*. New York: Oxford University Press.

Neale, W. C. 1962. *Economic Change in Rural India. Land Tenure and Reform in Uttar Pradesh, 1800–1955*. New Haven, CT: Yale University Press.

Negi, J. 1995. *The Begār & Beth System in Himachal Pradesh: A Study of Erstwhile Shimla Hill States*. New Delhi: Reliance Publishing House.

Nelson, J. M. 2007. "Elections, Democracy, and Social Services." *Studies in Comparative International Development* 41 (4): 79–97.

NFHS-2. 2000. *National Family Health Survey* 2. Mumbai: International Institute for Population Sciences.

NFHS-4. 2015–16. *National Family Health Survey* 4. Mumbai: International Institute for Population Sciences.

Niedzwiecki, S. 2018. *Uneven Social Policies: The Politics of Subnational Variation in Latin America*. New York: Cambridge University Press.

Noonan, K., C. Sabel, and W. Simon. 2009. "Legal Accountability in the Service-Based Welfare State: Lessons from Child Welfare Reform." *Law & Social Inquiry* 34 (3): 523–568.

Nooruddin, I., and J. W. Simmons. 2015. "Do Voters Count? Institutions, Voter Turnout, and Public Goods Provision in India." *Electoral Studies* 37: 1–14. doi: http://dx.doi.org/10.1016/j.electstud.2014.10.006.

North, D. 1990. *Institutions, Institutional Change and Economic Performance*. New York: Cambridge University Press.

Nossiter, T. J. 1982. *Communism in Kerala: A Study in Political Adaptation*. Berkeley: University of California Press.

Novak, W. J. 2008. "The Myth of the 'Weak' American State." *American Historical Review* 113 (3): 752–772.

Nunn, N., and D. Puga. 2012. "Ruggedness: The Blessing of Bad Geography in Africa." *Review of Economics and Statistics* 94 (1): 20–36.

O'Brien, K., and L. Li. 1999. "Selective Policy Implementation in Rural China." *Comparative Politics* 31 (2): 167–186.

O'Brien, K., and L. Li. 2006. *Rightful Resistance in Rural China*. New York: Cambridge University Press.

O'Donnell, G. 1993. "On the State, Democratization and Some Conceptual Problems: A Latin American View with Glances at Some Postcommunist Countries." *World Development* 21 (8): 1355–1369.

O'Malley, L. S. S. 1931. *Indian Civil Service 1601–1930*. London: Frank Cass & Co.

Olsen, J. P. 2006. "Maybe It Is Time to Rediscover Bureaucracy." *Journal of Public Administration Research and Theory* 16 (1): 1–24.

Olsen, J. P. 2008. "The Ups and Downs of Bureaucratic Organization." *Annual Review of Political Science* 11 (1): 13–37. doi: 10.1146/annurev.polisci.11.060106.101806.

Ostrom, E. 1990. *Governing the Commons: The Evolution of Institutions for Collective Action*. New York: Cambridge University Press.

Ostrom, E. 1996. "Crossing the Great Divide: Coproduction, Synergy, and Development." *World Development* 24 (6): 1073–1087. doi: 10.1016/0305-750x (96)00023-x.

Ostrom, E. 2000. "Collective Action and the Evolution of Social Norms." *Journal of Economic Perspectives* 14 (3): 137–158. doi: 10.1257/jep.14.3.137.

Ostrom, V., C. M. Tiebout, and Robert R. Warren. 1961. "The Organization of Government in Metropolitan Areas: A Theoretical Inquiry." *American Political Science Review* 55 (4): 831–842.

Padgett, J. F., and C. K. Ansell. 1993. "Robust Action and the Rise of the Medici, 1400–1434." *American Journal of Sociology* 98 (6): 1259–1319.

Page, S. E. 2008. *The Difference: How the Power of Diversity Creates Better Groups, Firms, Schools, and Societies*. Princeton, NJ: Princeton University Press.

Paglayan, A. S. 2021. "The Non-democratic Roots of Mass Education: Evidence from 200 Years." *American Political Science Review* 115 (1): 179–198.

Pai, S. 2002. *Dalit Assertion and the Unfinished Democratic Revolution: The Bahujan Samaj Party in Uttar Pradesh*. New Delhi: Sage Publications.

Pai, S. 2007. *Political Process in Uttar Pradesh: Identity, Economic Reforms, and Governance*. New Delhi: Pearson Longman.

Paine, L. 1992. "The Educational Policy Process: A Case Study of Bureaucratic Action in China." In *Bureaucracy, Politics, and Decision Making in Post-Mao China*, edited by K. Lieberthal and D. Lampton. Berkeley: University of California Press.

Papola, T. 2000. "Contradictions in Development of Uttarakhand: Need for a Region-Specific and Autonomous Planning Framework." In *Uttarakhand Statehood: Dimensions of Development*, edited by M. Sati and S. Sati. New Delhi: Indus Publishing Company.

Parikh, J. 2011. "Hardships and Health Impacts on Women Due to Traditional Cooking Fuels: A Case Study of Himachal Pradesh, India." *Energy Policy* 39 (12): 7587–7594.

Parthasarathy, R., V. Rao, and N. Palaniswamy. 2019. "Deliberative Democracy in an Unequal World: A Text-as-Data Study of South India's Village Assemblies." *American Political Science Review* 113 (3): 623–640.

Pathak, S. 2020. *The Chipko Movement: A People's History*. New Delhi: Permanent Black.

Pepinsky, T., J. Pierskalla, and A. Sacks. 2017. "Bureaucracy and Service Delivery." *Annual Review of Political Science* 20: 249–268.

Perry, J., and W. Vandenabeele. 2015. "Public Service Motivation Research: Achievements, Challenges, and Future Directions." *Public Administration Review* 75 (5): 692–699.

Peters, B. G. 2017. "What Is So Wicked about Wicked Problems? A Conceptual Analysis and a Research Program." *Policy and Society* 36 (3): 385–396.

Peters, B. G. 2021. *Administrative Traditions: Understanding the Roots of Contemporary Administrative Behavior*. Oxford: Oxford University Press.

Piattoni, S. 2001. *Clientelism, Interests, and Democratic Representation: The European Experience in Historical and Comparative Perspective*. Cambridge: Cambridge University Press.

Piattoni, S. 2010. *The Theory of Multi-Level Governance: Conceptual, Empirical, and Normative Challenges*. Oxford: Oxford University Press.

Pierson, P. 1993. "When Effect Becomes Cause: Policy Feedback and Political Change." *World Politics* 45 (4): 595–628. doi: 10.2307/2950710.

Pierson, P. 2005. "The Study of Policy Development." *Journal of Policy History* 17 (1): 34–51.

Piore, M. 2011. "Beyond Markets: Sociology, Street-Level Bureaucracy, and the Management of the Public Sector." *Regulation & Governance* 5 (1): 145–164. doi: 10.1111/j.1748-5991.2010.01098.x.

Piore, M., and A. Schrank. 2008. "Toward Managed Flexibility: The Revival of Labour Inspection in the Latin World." *International Labour Review* 147 (1): 1–23. doi: 10.1111/j.1564-913X.2008.00021.x.

Pires, R. R. C. 2011. "Beyond the Fear of Discretion: Flexibility, Performance, and Accountability in the Management of Regulatory Bureaucracies." *Regulation & Governance* 5 (1): 43–69. doi: 10.1111/j.1748-5991.2010.01083.x.

Pons, X. 2016. "Tracing the French Policy PISA Debate: A Policy Configuration Approach." *European Educational Research Journal* 15 (5): 580–597.

Portes, A. 1998. "Social Capital: Its Origins and Applications in Modern Sociology." *Annual Review of Sociology* 24 (1): 1–24.

Posner, D. N. 2005. *Institutions and Ethnic Politics in Africa*. New York: Cambridge University Press.

Post, A. E., V. Bronsoler, and L. Salman. 2017. "Hybrid Regimes for Local Public Goods Provision: A Framework for Analysis." *Perspectives on Politics* 15 (4): 952–966.

Potter, D. 1989. "Jawaharlal Nehru and the Indian Civil Service." *South Asia Research* 9 (2): 128–144.

Potter, D. C. 1996. *India's Political Administrators: From ICS to IAS*. Oxford: Oxford University Press.

Pressman, J., and A. Wildavsky. 1984. *Implementation: How Great Expectations in Washington Are Dashed in Oakland*. Berkeley: University of California Press.

Pritchett, L. 2003. "'When Will They Ever Learn'? Why *All* Governments Produce Schooling." BREAD Working Paper No. 31.

Pritchett, L. 2009. "Is India a Flailing State? Detours on the Four Lane Highway to Modernization." Harvard Kennedy School of Government Working Paper.

Pritchett, L. 2013. *The Rebirth of Education: Schooling Ain't Learning*. Washington, DC: Center for Global Development.

Pritchett, L., and A. Beatty. 2012. "The Negative Consequences of Overambitious Curricula in Developing Countries." Center for Global Development Working Paper No. 293.

Pritchett, L., and M. Woolcock. 2004. "Solutions When the Solution Is the Problem: Arraying the Disarray in Development." *World Development* 32 (2): 191–212.

Pritchett, L., M. Woolcock, and M. Andrews. 2013. "Looking Like a State: Techniques of Persistent Failure in State Capability for Implementation." *Journal of Development Studies* 49 (1): 1–18.

PROBE. 1999. *Public Report on Basic Education in India.* New Delhi: Oxford University Press.

Provan, K. G., and P. Kenis. 2008. "Modes of Network Governance: Structure, Management, and Effectiveness." *Journal of Public Administration Research and Theory* 18 (2): 229–252.

Przeworski, A., and F. Limongi. 1997. "Modernization: Theories and Facts." *World Politics* 49 (2): 155–183.

Putnam, R. D., R. Leonardi, and R. Y. Nanetti. 1994. *Making Democracy Work: Civic Traditions in Modern Italy.* Princeton, NJ: Princeton University Press.

Raheja, G. G. 1988. *The Poison in the Gift: Ritual, Prestation, and the Dominant Caste in a North Indian Village.* Chicago, IL: University of Chicago Press.

Raina, J. L. 1993. "Nehru on Education." In *Nehru and Planning in India: Proceedings of the National Seminar on Pandit Jawaharlal Nehru, Planning Commission, and Planned Development in India, Ghaziabad, 1989.* New Delhi: Concept Publishing Company.

Ramachandran, V. 1997. "On Kerala's Development Achievements." In *Indian Development. Selected Regional Perspectives*, edited by J. Drèze and A. Sen. Delhi: Oxford University Press.

Ramachandran, V. 2014. "The Making of Mahila Samakhya: 1987–1992." In *Cartographies of Empowerment: The Mahila Samakhya Story*, edited by V. Ramachandran and K. Jandhyala. New Delhi: Zubaan Books.

Ramachandran, V., T. Béteille, T. Linden, S. Dey, and P. G. Chatterjee. 2018. *Getting the Right Teachers into the Right Schools: Managing India's Teacher Workforce.* Washington, DC: World Bank.

Ramamurti Committee. 1990. *Report of the Committee for the Review of National Policy on Education 1986.* Delhi: Government of India.

Raman, B. 2012. *Document Raj: Writing and Scribes in Early Colonial South India.* Chicago, IL: University of Chicago Press.

Rao, N. 1993. "Total Literacy Campaigns: A Field Report." *Economic and Political Weekly* 28 (19): 914–918.

Rao, V., and M. Walton, eds. 2004. *Culture and Public Action.* Stanford: Stanford University Press.

Rasul, I., and D. Rogger. 2018. "Management of Bureaucrats and Public Service Delivery: Evidence from the Nigerian Civil Service." *The Economic Journal* 128 (608): 413–446.

Rauch, J. E., and P. B. Evans. 2000. "Bureaucratic Structure and Bureaucratic Performance in Less Developed Countries." *Journal of Public Economics* 75 (1): 49–71.

Rawls, J. 1996. *Political Liberalism.* New York: Columbia University Press.

Reimers, F. M. 2021. *Primary and Secondary Education during COVID-19: Disruptions to Educational Opportunity during a Pandemic*. Cham, Switzerland: Springer.

Reyes, V. 2018. "Three Models of Transparency in Ethnographic Research: Naming Places, Naming People, and Sharing Data." *Ethnography* 19 (2): 204–226.

Rich, J. 2019. *State-Sponsored Activism: Bureaucrats and Social Movements in Democratic Brazil*. New York: Cambridge University Press.

Robinson, F. 1974. *Separatism among Indian Muslims: The Politics of the United Provinces' Muslims, 1860–1923*. Cambridge: Cambridge University Press.

Roll, M., ed. 2014. *The Politics of Public Sector Performance: Pockets of Effectiveness in Developing Countries*. New York: Routledge.

Ross, M. 2006. "Is Democracy Good for the Poor?" *American Journal of Political Science* 50 (4): 860–874. doi: 10.1111/j.1540-5907.2006.00220.x.

Rothstein, B. 2011. *The Quality of Government: Corruption, Social Trust, and Inequality in International Perspective*. Chicago, IL: University of Chicago Press.

Rothstein, B. 2015. "The Chinese Paradox of High Growth and Low Quality of Government: The Cadre Organization Meets Max Weber." *Governance* 28 (4): 533–548. doi: 10.1111/gove.12128.

Rothstein, B., and J. Teorell. 2008. "What Is Quality of Government? A Theory of Impartial Government Institutions." *Governance* 21 (2): 165–190.

Roy, I. 2013. "Development as Dignity: Dissensus, Equality and Contentious Politics in Bihar, India." *Oxford Development Studies* 41 (4): 517–536.

Roy, R. 1966. "Intra-party Conflict in the Bihar Congress." *Asian Survey* 6 (12): 706–715.

Roy, R. 1970. "Caste and Political Recruitment in Bihar." In *Caste in Indian Politics*, edited by R. Kothari. New Delhi: Orient Longman.

Rudolph, L. I., and S. H. Rudolph. 1987. *In Pursuit of Lakshmi: The Political Economy of the Indian State*. Chicago: University of Chicago Press.

Ruparelia, S. 2013. "India's New Rights Agenda: Genesis, Promises, Risks." *Pacific Affairs* 86 (3): 569–590.

Sabatier, P., and D. Mazmanian. 1979. "The Conditions of Effective Implementation: A Guide to Accomplishing Policy Objectives." *Policy Analysis* 5 (4): 481–504.

Sabatier, P. A. 1986. "Top-down and Bottom-up Approaches to Implementation Research: A Critical Analysis and Suggested Synthesis." *Journal of Public Policy* 6 (1): 21–48.

Sabel, C. 1994. "Learning by Monitoring." In *Handbook of Economic Sociology*, edited by N. J. Smelser and R. Swedberg, 137–165. Princeton, NJ: Princeton University Press.

Sabel, C. 2012. "Individualised Service Provision and the New Welfare State: Are There Lessons from Northern Europe for Developing Countries?" In *Promoting Inclusive Growth: Challenges and Policies*, edited by L. de Mello and M. A. Dutz, 75. Paris: OECD Publishing.

Sabel, C., A. Saxenian, R. Miettinen, P. Kristensen, and J. Hautamäki. 2011. Individualized Service Provision in the New Welfare State: Lessons from Special Education in Finland. In *SITRA*. Helsinki.

Sabel, C., and J. Zeitlin. 2008. "Learning from Difference: The New Architecture of Experimentalist Governance in the EU." *European Law Journal* 14 (3): 271–327. doi: 10.1111/j.1468-0386.2008.00415.x.

Sabel, C., and J. Zeitlin. 2012. "Experimentalist Governance." In *The Oxford Companion to Governance*, edited by D. Levi-Faur. Oxford: Oxford University Press.

Sadgopal, A. 2006. "A Post-Jomtien Reflection on the Education Policy: Dilution, Distortion and Diversion." In *The Crisis of Elementary Education in India*, edited by R. Kumar, 92–136. New Delhi: Sage Publications.

Sahlberg, P. 2007. "Education Policies for Raising Student Learning: The Finnish Approach." *Journal of Education Policy* 22 (2): 147–171.

Sanan, D. 2004. "Delivering Basic Public Services in Himachal Pradesh: Is the Success Sustainable?" *Economic and Political Weekly* 39 (9): 975–978.

Sandbrook, R., M. Edelman, P. Heller, and J. Teichman. 2007. *Social Democracy in the Global Periphery: Origins, Challenges, Prospects*. New York: Cambridge University Press.

Sanyal, P., and V. Rao. 2018. *Oral Democracy: Deliberation in Indian Village Assemblies*. New York: Cambridge University Press.

Sanyal, P., V. Rao, and S. Majumdar. 2015. *Recasting Culture to Undo Gender: A Sociological Analysis of Jeevika in Rural Bihar, India*. Washington, DC: World Bank.

Sarin, M. 2001. "Empowerment and Disempowerment of Forest Women in Uttarakhand, India." *Gender, Technology and Development* 5 (3): 341–364.

Sarup, A. 1986. "A Retrospective View of Formulating a New Education Policy." In *UNESCO in Asia and the Pacific: 40 Years On*, edited by B. Cahill. Bangkok: UNESCO Regional Office for Education in Asia and the Pacific.

Sati, M., and S. Sati, eds. 2000. *Uttarakhand Statehood: Dimensions of Development*. New Delhi: Indus Publishing Company.

Sax, W. 1991. *Mountain Goddess: Gender and Politics in a Himalayan Pilgrimage*. New York: Oxford University Press.

Saxena, N., and N. Mehrotra. 2014. "Addressing Girls' Education." In *Cartographies of Empowerment: The Mahila Samakhya Story*, edited by V. Ramachandran and K. Jandhyala. New Delhi: Zubaan Books.

Schleicher, A. 2018. *PISA 2018: Insights and Interpretations*. Paris: Organisation for Economic Cooperation and Development.

Schmidt, V. 1990. "Unblocking Society by Decree: The Impact of Governmental Decentralization in France." *Comparative Politics* 22 (4): 459–481.

Schmidt, V. 2008. "Discursive Institutionalism: The Explanatory Power of Ideas and Discourse." *Annual Review of Political Science* 11: 303–326.

Schneider, B. R. 2021. "Teacher Unions, Political Machines, and the Thorny Politics of Education Reform in Latin America." *Politics & Society* 50 (1): 84–116. doi: 10.1177/00323292211002788.

Schrank, A. 2009. "Professionalization and Probity in a Patrimonial State: Labor Inspectors in the Dominican Republic." *Latin American Politics and Society* 51 (2): 91–115. doi: 10.1111/j.1548-2456.2009.00049.x.

Schultz, T. W. 1961. "Investment in Human Capital." *American Economic Review* 51 (1): 1–17.

Scott, J. C. 1985. *Weapons of the Weak: Everyday Forms of Peasant Resistance*. New Haven: Yale University Press.

Scott, J. C. 1990. *Domination and the Arts of Resistance: Hidden Transcripts*. New Haven: Yale University Press.

Scott, J. C. 1998. *Seeing Like a State: How Certain Schemes to Improve the Human Condition Have Failed*. New Haven: Yale University Press.

Sen, A. 1997. "Indian Traditions and the Western Imagination." *Daedalus* 126 (2): 1–26.

Sen, A. 1999. *Development as Freedom*. New York: Alfred Knopf.

Sen, A. 2011. "Quality of Life: India vs. China." *New York Review of Books* 12 (2): 44–45.

Sen, G. 1992. "Social Needs and Public Accountability." In *Development Policy and Public Action*, edited by M. Wuyts, M. Mackintosh and T. Hewitt. Oxford: Oxford University Press.

Shani, O. 2017. *How India Became Democratic: Citizenship and the Making of the Universal Franchise*. New York: Cambridge University Press.

Sharma, A. 1995. "Political Economy of Poverty in Bihar." *Economic and Political Weekly* 30 (41/42): 2587–2602.

Sharma, A. 2005. "Agrarian Relations and Socio-Economic Change in Bihar." *Economic and Political Weekly* 40 (10): 960–972.

Sharma, A. 2008. *Logics of Empowerment: Development, Gender, and Governance in Neoliberal India*. Minneapolis: University of Minnesota Press.

Sharma, D., and R. Sudarshan. 2010. "Towards a Politics of Collective Empowerment: Learning from Hill Women in Rural Uttarakhand, India." *IDS Bulletin* 41 (5): 43–51.

Sharma, S. K. 2016. "Persisting Hierarchies, Perpetuating Inequalities, Historically Lived Realities of Dalits in Rural Himachal Pradesh." *Sociological Bulletin* 65 (1): 69–89.

Sharma, T. 2003. "Himachal Pradesh: Two Party Competition in a Small State." *Journal of Indian School of Political Economy* 15 (1): 173–188.

Sharma, T. R. 1999. "Local Configurations and National Parties in Himachal Pradesh." *Economic and Political Weekly* 34 (34/35): 2465–2471.

Sharma, U. 1980. *Women, Work and Property in North-West India*. London: Tavistock.

Sharpe, K. 1992. "Educational Homogeneity in French Primary Education: A Double Case Study." *British Journal of Sociology of Education* 13 (3): 329–348.

Sheingate, A. 2014. "Institutional Dynamics and American Political Development." *Annual Review of Political Science* 17: 461–477.

Shklar, J. N. 1964. *Legalism: Law, Morals, and Political Trials*. Cambridge: Harvard University Press.

Simola, H. 1993. "Educational Science, the State, and Teachers: Forming the Corporate Regulation." In *Changing Patterns of Power: Social Regulation and Teacher Education Reform*, edited by T. S. Popkewitz, 161. Albany: State University of New York Press.

Simola, H. 2005. "The Finnish Miracle of PISA: Historical and Sociological Remarks on Teaching and Teacher Education." *Comparative Education* 41 (4): 455–470.

Simon, H. A. 1965. *The Shape of Automation for Men and Management.* New York: Harper & Row.

Singh, C. 1998. *Natural Premises: Ecology and Peasant Life in the Western Himalaya, 1800–1950.* New Delhi: Oxford University Press.

Singh, N. K., and N. Stern. 2013. *The New Bihar: Rekindling Governance and Development.* Noida, India: Harper Collins.

Singh, P. 2011. "We-ness and Welfare: A Longitudinal Analysis of Social Development in Kerala, India." *World Development* 39 (2): 282–293. doi: 10.1016/j.worlddev.2009.11.025.

Singh, P. 2015. "Subnationalism and Social Development: A Comparative Analysis of Indian States." *World Politics* 67 (3): 506–562.

Singh, P. 2016. *How Solidarity Works for Welfare: Subnationalism and Social Development in India.* New York: Cambridge University Press.

Singh, P. 2017. "The Theoretical Potential of the Within-Nation Comparison: How Sub-National Analyses Can Enrich Our Understandings of the National Welfare State." *American Behavioral Scientist* 61 (8): 861–886.

Sinha, A. 2003. "Rethinking the Developmental State Model: Divided Leviathan and Subnational Comparisons in India." *Comparative Politics* 35 (4): 459–476.

Sinha, A. 2005. *The Regional Roots of Developmental Politics in India: A Divided Leviathan.* Bloomington: Indiana University Press.

Sinha, A. 2010. "Understanding Economic Reform of Public Services in a High Growth State of India." In *Public Service Delivery in India: Understanding the Reform Process*, edited by V. Chand. New Delhi: Oxford University Press.

Singh, N.K., and N. Stern. 2013. *The New Bihar: Rekindling Governance and Development.* Noida, India: Harper Collins.

Sitapati, V. 2016. *Half Lion: How P.V. Narasimha Rao Transformed India.* New Delhi: Penguin Books Limited.

Sivanandan, P. 1976. "Economic Backwardness of Harijans in Kerala." *Social Scientist* 4 (10): 3–28.

Skocpol, T. 1985. "Bringing the State Back In: Strategies of Analysis in Current Research." In *Bringing the State Back In*, edited by P. Evans, D. Rueschemeyer and T. Skocpol. New York: Cambridge University Press.

Skocpol, T. 1992. *Protecting Soldiers and Mothers: The Political Origins of Social Policy in the United States.* Cambridge, MA: Harvard University Press.

Skocpol, T., and E. Amenta. 1986. "States and Social Policies." *Annual Review of Sociology* 12: 131–157.

Slater, D. 2010. *Ordering Power: Contentious Politics and Authoritarian Leviathans in Southeast Asia.* New York: Cambridge University Press.

Slater, D., and E. Simmons. 2010. "Informative Regress: Critical Antecedents in Comparative Politics." *Comparative Political Studies* 43 (7): 886–917.

Slater, D., and D. Ziblatt. 2013. "The Enduring Indispensability of the Controlled Comparison." *Comparative Political Studies* 46 (10): 1–27.

Small, M., and J. Cook. 2021. "Using Interviews to Understand Why: Challenges and Strategies in the Study of Motivated Action." *Sociological Methods & Research* 1–41.

Snehi, Y. 2011. "Diversity as Counter-hegemony: Reet and Gender Relations in Himachal Pradesh." In *Recognizing Diversity: Society and Culture in the Himalaya*, edited by C. Singh, 75–97. New Delhi: Oxford University Press.

Snehi, Y. 2016. "Changing Economic Formation of Himachal Pradesh: From Feudalism to State Developmentalism." *Economic and Political Weekly* 51 (26–27): 101–110.

Snyder, R. 2001. "Scaling Down: The Subnational Comparative Method." *Studies in Comparative International Development* 36 (1): 93–110. doi: citeulike-article-id:5980296.

Soifer, H. 2015. *State Building in Latin America*. New York: Cambridge University Press.

Soifer, H., and M. vom Hau. 2008. "Unpacking the Strength of the State: The Utility of State Infrastructural Power." *Studies in Comparative International Development* 43 (3–4): 219–230.

Sood, A. 2003. "Himachal Pradesh: Critical Issues in Primary Education." *Economic and Political Weekly* 38 (25): 2460–2470.

Soss, J. 1999. "Lessons of Welfare: Policy Design, Political Learning, and Political Action." *American Political Science Review* 93 (2): 363–380.

Soss, J. 2005. "Making Clients and Citizens: Welfare Policy as a Source of Status, Belief, and Action." In *Deserving and Entitled: Social Constructions and Public Policy*, edited by H. Ingram, 291–328. Albany: State University of New York Press.

Srivastava, P. 2013. *Low-fee Private Schooling: Aggravating Equity or Mitigating Disadvantage? Oxford Studies in Comparative Education*. Oxford: Symposium Books.

Stasavage, D. 2005. "Democracy and Education Spending in Africa." *American Journal of Political Science* 49 (2): 343–358. doi: 10.1111/j.0092-5853.2005.00127.x.

Stokes, E. 1986. *The Peasant Armed: The Indian Revolt of 1857*. Oxford: Clarendon Press.

Stokes, S. C., T. Dunning, M. Nazareno, and V. Brusco. 2013. *Brokers, Voters, and Clientelism: The Puzzle of Distributive Politics*. New York: Cambridge University Press.

Sugiyama, N. B., and W. Hunter. 2013. "Whither Clientelism? Good Governance and Brazil's Bolsa Família Program." *Comparative Politics* 46 (1): 43–62.

Suleiman, E. N. 1974. *Politics, Power, and Bureaucracy in France: The Administrative Elite*. Princeton, NJ: Princeton University Press.

Swidler, A. 1986. "Culture in Action: Symbols and Strategies." *American Sociological Review* 51 (2): 273–286.

Swidler, A. 2013. *Talk of Love: How Culture Matters*. Chicago, IL: University of Chicago Press.

Taub, R. P. 1969. *Bureaucrats under Stress: Administrators and Administration in an Indian State*. Berkeley: University of California Press.

Teets, J. C. 2012. "Reforming Service Delivery in China: The Emergence of a Social Innovation Model." *Journal of Chinese Political Science* 17 (1): 15–32.

Tendler, J. 1997. *Good Government in the Tropics*. Baltimore, MD: Johns Hopkins University Press.

Tendler, J., and S. Freedheim. 1994. "Trust in a Rent-Seeking World: Health and Government Transformed in Northeast Brazil." *World Development* 22 (12): 1771–1791.

Thachil, T. 2014. *Elite Parties, Poor Voters: How Social Services Win Votes in India*. New York: Cambridge University Press.

Thachil, T., and E. Teitelbaum. 2015. "Ethnic Parties and Public Spending: New Theory and Evidence from the Indian States." *Comparative Political Studies* 48 (11): 1389–1420. doi: 10.1177/0010414015576743.

Tharakan, P. K. M. 1984. "Socio-economic Factors in Educational Development: Case of Nineteenth Century Travancore." *Economic and Political Weekly* 19 (45): 1913–1928.

Tharakan, P. K. M. 2004. "Ernakulam Revisited: A Study of Literacy in the First Totally Literate District in India." In *Paradigms of Learning: The Total Literacy Campaign in India*, edited by M. Karlekar. New Delhi: SAGE Publications.

Thelen, K. 2004. *How Institutions Evolve: The Political Economy of Skills in Germany, Britain, the United States, and Japan*. New York: Cambridge University Press.

Thelen, K. 2009. "Institutional Change in Advanced Political Economies." *British Journal of Industrial Relations* 47 (3): 471–498.

Tilak, J. 2007. "The Kothari Commission and Financing of Education." *Economic and Political Weekly* 42 (10): 874–882. doi: 10.2307/4419340.

Tillin, L. 2013. *Remapping India: New States and Their Political Origins*. Oxford: Oxford University Press.

Tillin, L. 2016. "Asymmetric Federalism." In *Oxford Handbook of the Indian Constitution*, edited by S. Choudhry and M. Khosla, P. Bhanu, 540–559. Oxford: Oxford University Press.

Tilly, C. 1986. *The Contentious French*. Cambridge, MA: Harvard University Press.

Tilly, C. 1992. *Coercion, Capital and European States: AD 990–1992*. Oxford: Blackwell.

Tilly, C. 2004. "Reasons Why." *Sociological Theory* 22 (3): 445–454.

Tooley, J., and P. Dixon. 2006. "'De facto' Privatisation of Education and the Poor: Implications of a Study from sub-Saharan Africa and India." *Compare: A Journal of Comparative and International Education* 36 (4): 443–462.

Tsai, K. 2006. "Adaptive Informal Institutions and Endogenous Institutional Change in China." *World Politics* 59 (1): 116–141.

Tsai, L. 2007. *Accountability without Democracy: Solidary Groups and Public Goods Provision in Rural China*. New York: Cambridge University Press.

Tyler, T. 1990. *Why People Obey the Law*. New Haven: Yale University Press.

UNDP. 2002. *Himachal Pradesh Human Development Report*. Shimla: Planning Department, Government of Himachal Pradesh.

UNDP. 2015. *The Millennium Development Goals Report 2015*. New York: United Nations.

UNESCO. 2002. *Education for All Global Monitoring Report, 2002: Is the World on Track?* Paris: UNESCO.

UNESCO. 2021. *The State of the Global Education Crisis: A Path to Recovery*. Paris: UNESCO.

Uphoff, N., ed. 1994. *Puzzles of Productivity in Public Organizations*. San Francisco, CA: Institute for Contemporary Studies.

USN. 2001. *The Balwadi: Binding the Himalayan Village*. Almora, Uttarakhand: Uttarakhand Seva Nidhi.

Vaishnav, M. 2017. *When Crime Pays: Money and Muscle in Indian Politics*. New Haven, CT: Yale University Press.

Vaishnav, M., and R. Swanson. 2015. "Does Good Economics Make for Good Politics? Evidence from Indian States." *India Review* 14 (3): 279–311.

Van Maanen, J. 1988. *Tales of the Field: On Writing Ethnography*. Chicago, IL: University of Chicago Press.

Van Meter, D. S., and C. E. Van Horn. 1975. "The Policy Implementation Process." *Administration & Society* 6 (4): 445–488. doi: 10.1177/009539977500600404.

Varshney, A. 1998. *Democracy, Development, and the Countryside: Urban–Rural Struggles in India*. New York: Cambridge University Press.

Varshney, A. 2002. *Ethnic Conflict and Civic Life: Hindus and Muslims in India*. New Haven: Yale University Press.

Varshney, A. 2007. "Mass Politics or Elite Politics? Understanding the Politics of India's Economic Reforms." In *India's Economic Transition: The Politics of Reforms*, edited by R. Mukherji. New Delhi: Oxford University Press.

Varshney, A. 2014. *Battles Half Won: India's Improbable Democracy*. New Delhi: Penguin Books Limited.

Vasan, S. 2001. "Community Forestry: Historical Legacy of Himachal Pradesh." *HIMALAYA, the Journal of the Association for Nepal and Himalayan Studies* 21 (2): 8.

Verma, R., S. Gupta, and R. Birner. 2018. "Can Vigilance-Focused Governance Reforms Improve Service Delivery? The Case of Integrated Child Development Services (ICDS) in Bihar, India." *Development Policy Review* 36 (52): O786–O802.

Verma, R. K. 1991. "Caste and Bihar Politics." *Economic and Political Weekly* 26 (18): 1142–1144.

Verma, V. 1995. *The Emergence of Himachal Pradesh: A Survey of Constitutional Developments*. New Delhi: Indus Publishing Company.

Véron, R. 2001. "The 'New' Kerala Model: Lessons for Sustainable Development." *World Development* 29 (4): 601–617.

Wade, R. 1982. "The System of Administrative and Political Corruption: Canal Irrigation in South India." *Journal of Development Studies* 18 (3): 287–328. doi: 10.1080/00220388208421833.

Wade, R. 1990. *Governing the Market: Economic Theory and the Role of Government in East Asian Industrialization*. Princeton, NJ: Princeton University Press.

Weber, E. 1976. *Peasants Into Frenchmen: The Modernization of Rural France, 1870–1914*. Stanford, CA: Stanford University Press.

Weber, E., and A. Khademian. 2008. "Wicked Problems, Knowledge Challenges, and Collaborative Capacity Builders in Network Settings." *Public Administration Review* 68 (2): 334–349.

Weber, M. 1947. *The Theory of Social and Economic Organization*. New York: Free Press.

Weiner, M. 1962. *The Politics of Scarcity: Public Pressure and Political Response in India*. Chicago, IL: University of Chicago Press.

Weiner, M. 1967. *Party Building in a New Nation: The Indian National Congress*. Chicago, IL: University of Chicago Press.

Weiner, M. 1991. *The Child and the State in India: Child Labor and Education Policy in Comparative Perspective*. Princeton, NJ: Princeton University Press.

Weitz-Shapiro, R. 2014. *Curbing Clientelism in Argentina: Politics, Poverty, and Social Policy*. New York: Cambridge University Press.

Wiborg, S. 2017. "Teachers Unions in the Nordic Countries: Solidarity and the Politics of Self-Interest." In *The Comparative Politics of Education: Teachers Unions and Education Systems around the World*, edited by T. Moe and S. Wiborg. New York: Cambridge University Press.

Williams, M. 2017. "The Political Economy of Unfinished Development Projects: Corruption, Clientelism, or Collective Choice?" *American Political Science Review* 111 (4): 705–723.

Williamson, O. 2000. "The New Institutional Economics: Taking Stock, Looking Ahead." *Journal of Economic Literature* 38 (3): 595–613.

Wilson, J. Q. 1978. *Varieties of Police Behavior: The Management of Law and Order in Eight Communities*. Cambridge, MA: Harvard University Press.

Wilson, J. Q. 1989. *Bureaucracy: What Government Agencies Do and Why They Do It*. New York: Basic Books.

Wilson, K. 1999. "Patterns of Accumulation and Struggles of Rural Labour: Some Aspects of Agrarian Change in Central Bihar." *Journal of Peasant Studies* 26 (2–3): 316–354.

Witsoe, J. 2011. "Corruption as Power: Caste and the Political Imagination of the Postcolonial State." *American Ethnologist* 38 (1): 73–85.

Witsoe, J. 2013. *Democracy against Development: Lower-Caste Politics and Political Modernity in Postcolonial India*. Chicago, IL: University of Chicago Press.

Woessmann, L. 2016. "The Importance of School Systems: Evidence from International Differences in Student Achievement." *Journal of Economic Perspectives* 30 (3): 3–32.

Woo-Cumings, M., ed. 1999. *The Developmental State*. Ithaca, NY: Cornell University Press.

Woolcock, M. 1998. "Social Capital and Economic Development: Toward a Theoretical Synthesis and Policy Framework." *Theory and Society* 27 (2): 151–208.

Woolcock, M., and D. Narayan. 2000. "Social Capital: Implications for Development Theory, Research and Policy." *World Bank Research Observer* 15 (2): 2225–2249.

World Bank. 2003. *World Development Report 2004: Making Services Work for Poor People*. Washington, DC: World Bank.

World Bank. 2007. Himachal Pradesh: Accelerating Development and Sustaining Success in a Hill State. New Delhi: World Bank Poverty Reduction and Economic Management Unit.

World Bank. 2018. *World Development Report 2018: Learning to Realize Education's Promise*. Washington, DC: World Bank.

Xu, C. 2011. "The Fundamental Institutions of China's Reforms and Development." *Journal of Economic Literature* 49 (4): 1076–1151.

Yadav, Y. 2002. "Understanding the Second Democratic Upsurge." In *Transforming India: Social and Political Dynamics of Democracy*, edited by F. Frankel, Z. Hasan, R. Bhargava, and B. Arora. New Delhi: Oxford University Press.

Yanow, D. 1996. *How Does a Policy Mean? Interpreting Policy and Organizational Actions*. Washington, DC: Georgetown University Press.

Zacka, B. 2017. *When the State Meets the Street: Public Service and Moral Agency*. Cambridge, MA: Harvard University Press.

Ziblatt, D. 2008. "Why Some Cities Provide More Public Goods Than Others: A Subnational Comparison of the Provision of Public Goods in German Cities in 1912." *Studies in Comparative International Development* 43 (3–4): 273–289.

Index

Abers, Rebecca, 296, 337
Acemoglu, Daron, 16
active citizenship, 64, 169, 340
  social apathy and, 340
adaptive governance, 313
  in China, 302
administrative burdens, 32, 62–63, 166–167, 214–215
  bureaucratic norms and, 18, 71–72, 334–335, 339–340
  how marginalized groups experience, 63–64
  in HP, 214–215
  in UP, 148, 152–158, 166–167, 169
  in Uttarakhand, 247–248, 257–258
  village collective action and, 82
administrative tasks, 37–38. *See also* task
  complexity of, 40–42
  for primary education, 40
AEC. *See* Alternative Education Center
agrarian economy
  caste politics in UP and, 127–128, 130–131
  child labor and, 83
  state-building in HP and, 176–177, 183–184
  in Uttarakhand, 219
Ahuja, Amit, 72, 132
Aiyar, Yamini, 293, 294 333, 347
Almora, 222, 234, 237
  teachers in, 238–245
  school accountability in, 245–248
  village primary education in, 248–259
Ambedkar, B. R., 92
Ambedkar School in UP, 162
Ambedkar Village Program (AVP), 143
  inspection process created by, 146
  policy implementation impacted by, 145
  clientelistic politics and, 143–148
  in Saharanpur, 146
  in Sitapur, 147
Andhra Pradesh, 95–96, 102
Andrews, Matt, 40, 74, 344–345
Ang, Yuen Yuen, 314–316
Anganwadi centers, 230
Anganwadi workers, 212–213, 231
Annual Status of Education Report (ASER), 42
  measures for policy implementation, 42–46
Ansell, Ben, 9, 75–76, 101
Appadurai, Arjun, 65, 84, 340
ASER. *See* Annual Status of Education Report
auditing, 58
  of schools, 57–58, 262
  practices in French bureaucracy, 323
Auerbach, Adam, 79, 339, 341
authoritarian deliberation in China, 312–313
autonomy, 69–70
  in legalistic bureaucracy, 275–276
  of MSUP, 275–277
  of SSA, 136–137
  of Weberian bureaucracy, 73–74

AVP. *See* Ambedkar Village Program
Ayres, Ian, 58
Azad, Maulana, 89–91
Azim Premji Foundation, 114, 287–288

Bahujan Samaj Party (BSP), 80, 130, 269–270
  Ambedkar Village Program and, 143, 145, 146
  dignity politics and, 161
  political leadership in UP, 134
  political mobilization of Dalits and, 131, 290–295
  relationship to bureaucracy, 80, 132–133
  village governance and, 161
Bai, Gowri Parvathi, 304
Baiocchi, Gianpaolo, 64–65
balwadi program, 235–236, 246–247, 254–255
Banerjee, Abhijeet, 10, 16, 79–80, 343, 345–346
Banerji, Rukmini, 284–287
Bardach, Eugene, 58
Bardhan, Pranab, 316–317
Basic Shiksha Adhikari, 137, 139–140. *See also* District Education Officers
Bates, Robert, 15
begar (forced labor), 174–175
BEP. *See* Bihar Education Project
Berreman, Gerald, 222–224
beth (compulsory labor), 174–175
Bharat Gyan Vigyan Samiti (BGVS), 189
Bharatiya Janata Party (BJP)
  primary education reforms under, 109–110
  in HP, 178–179, 181–183
  in Uttarakhand, 227–228
Bihar, 24–25, 42–43, 171–173, 261–263, 347
  bureaucratic norms in, 279–280, 297
  caste system in, 262, 281
  clientelism in, 297
  corruption in, 283–284
  Cycle Scheme for girls' education, 286–287, 297
  education quality reforms in, 290–295
  electoral politics in, 281–282, 285–286
  as Jungle Raj, 283–284
  learning outcomes in, 45–46
  legalistic bureaucracy in, 278–295, 297
  Mission Gunvatta in, 290–292, 295
  primary education in, 27, 278–295
  primary school expansion in, 286–290
  reforms in, 262, 279, 280–286, 290–291, 295
  zamindari in, 280–281
Bihar Education Project (BEP), 103–104
Bihar Lokayukta Act, 284–285
Bihar Special Courts Act (2009), 284–285
BIMARU states, 280–281
BJP. *See* Bharatiya Janata Party
Block Development Officers, 125, 197–198, 201–202
Block Resource Coordinators (BRCs), 140, 192
Bohman, James, 55
Bolsa Família, 346
Bordia, Anil, 96–97, 105, 114–115
Bourdieu, Pierre
  on primary education, 9–10
  on social capital, 10
Braithwaite, Valerie, 58
Brass, Paul, 93–94
Brazil, 48–49, 60, 64–65, 296, 337, 346
BRCs. *See* Block Resource Coordinators
Brehm, John, 38
Brinks, Daniel, 48, 352–353
Brodkin, Evelyn, 30, 50–51, 63
Brown v. *Board of Education*, 11
BSA. *See Basic Shiksha Adhikhari*
BSP. *See* Bahujan Samaj Party
bureaucracy. *See also specific topics*
  defining, 3–4, 7, 328–329
  emergence of, 67
  frontline public services and, 351–365
  importance of, 328–331
  principal–agent approach to, 49
  regional differences in, 329
  relational approaches to, 50
  understandings and behaviors, 56–60
  varieties of, 69–73
bureaucratic activism, 296
bureaucratic discretion, 20–21
bureaucratic ethos, 46–47
bureaucratic norms, 31, 46–50, 69, 327–328, 352–353
  causal mechanisms of, 50–51
  changes in, 30, 295–297
  defining, 17, 48
  in developmental state research, 48–49
  divergence of, 35–36

education and, 7
endurance of, 30
evolution of, 7–8
officials bound by, 21
policy implementation and, 77
policy implications of, 343–349
political origins of, 67–69
state formation and, 69
at subnational level, 68
theoretical scope conditions and, 73–76
typology for, 17, 52, 66–67, 84
unique characteristics of, 47–48
bureaucratic overload, 294–295
bureaucratic understandings, 56–60
Bussell, Jennifer, 79, 341

CABE, 103. *See also* Central Advisory Board of Education
cabinet secretaries, list of, 126
Cammett, Melani, 325–326, 335–336
capability-centered approach, of Sen, 19–20
Carpenter, Daniel, 50, 330–331
case selection, 24–30
demographic indicators of, 26
socioeconomic indicators in, 26
caste reservations, 128–130, 132–133, 158–160, 227
caste system, 16, 25–27, 81–82, 245, 295. *See also specific topics*
in Bihar, 262, 281
community mobilization of lower castes, 262
in HP, 184–186
in Kerala, 305
lower-caste representation, 132–133
mobilization of lower castes, 127–135
political culture and, 82–83
in UP, 122, 127–135, 269–270
upper divisions of, 130–131
in Uttarakhand, 227
Yadav, L. P., on, 282–283
CCP. *See* Chinese Communist Party
Ceará, Brazil, 48–49
Central Advisory Board of Education (CABE), 94–95
centralization, 94, 115–116
Chandra, Kanchan, 28–29, 78
on patronage democracy, 132, 134
Chauhan, R. K., 3–4
Chhibber, Pradeep, 81, 315–316
Chibber, Vivek, 71, 79–81, 333–334
child labor, 82–83, 145
China, 33, 74–75, 334
adaptive governance in, 302
agricultural reforms in, 314–315
authoritarian deliberation in, 312–313
decentralization in, 313–314
deliberative bureaucracy in, 310–317
directed improvisation in, 314
household responsibility system in, 314–315
India compared with, 311
policy implementation in, 50
primary education in, 311–312
Chinese Communist Party (CCP), 312–313
Chipko movement, 224–225
Christian missionaries, 304, 307–308
schools, 89
citizenship
active forms of, 64, 169, 340, 341. *See also* active citizenship
defined as a bundle of rights, 9–10
legalistic bureaucracy in India and, 124–125
policy feedback and, 60–61
societal feedback during implementation and, 64–65
civic associations, 81
civic-judicial activism, 112–115
classrooms, 143
clientelism, 76–79, 132, 281, 328–329
in Bihar, 297
coping with, 143–147
defining, 76
in India, 35, 79
in legalistic bureaucracy, 143–147, 262–263
policy implementation and, 78
in UP, 78
Cluster Resource Centre Coordinators (CRCCs), 288–289
inspection by, 289–290
TaRL methods of, 291–292
codifiable tasks, 40, 42–43. *See also* administrative tasks; task complexity
indicators for, 43–44
Cohen, Joshua, 54–55
Coleman, James, 10
on social capital, 80–81

collective action, 51–52, 336–337
bureaucratic norms, 335–336
legalism and, 157–162
public agencies as institutional sites of, 50
in Uttarakhand, 222–225
in study villages, 81–82
colonialism
education and, 82–83, 89, 175
in HP, 174–175
in UP, 121–124
in Uttarakhand, 222–224
public administration in India and, 67–68
Communist Party of India (Marxist), West Bengal, 306
Communist Party of India (Marxist), Kerala, 305–306, 308
community mobilization. *See also* collective action
of lower castes, 262
in Uttarakhand, 225
complaints, 64
complex tasks, 40–42, 45. *See also* administrative tasks; task complexity
indicators for, 43–44
compulsory labor. *See beth*
Congress Party, 86–87, 89–91
in Bihar, 281–282
centralization of authority, 94–95
electoral strategy, 89–91
in HP, 175–177, 181–182
national leadership, 262
primary education policy and, 39, 213–217
in UP, 124–127
in Uttarakhand, 281–282
coproduction, 19–20, 51–52, 71, 331
power relations and, 39
conflictual patterns of, 336–337
inclusive, 207–217
institutionalized forms of, 39
in primary education, 39, 213–217
regimes of, 335–337
Corbridge, Stuart, 51–52, 64, 339
Corrales, Javier, 40
corruption, 28–29, 329–330
Weberian bureaucracy and, 54
in Bihar, 283–284
in UP, 132
in Uttarakhand, 233–234
Covid-19 pandemic, 343, 347–349
education reform and, 347–349
CPM. *See* Communist Party of India (Marxist)
CRCCs. *See* Cluster Resource Centre Coordinators

Dakar Framework for Action, 107–109
Dalits, 72–73, 79–80, 128–130, 143, 146, 152, 265, 271, 305. *See also* Scheduled Castes
harassment of, 272–273
in HP, 182–186
mistreatment of, 133
mobilization of, 130–132
patriarchy challenged by, 269
political assertiveness of, 269–270
in UP, 138–139
women, 154–155
Dasgupta, Aditya, 128, 294–295
Davies, Emmerich, 169, 336, 339
decentralization, 23. *See also* panchayats
in China, 313–314
in Finland, 321
in France, 324–325
in India, 23, 149–150, 199, 232, 309–310
Dehradun, 222, 227–228
teachers in, 238–245
deliberation and democracy, 344–345
authoritarian, 312–313
defining, 52
developmental state and, 331–338
frontline workers and, 266–267
goals of, 7–8
in legalistic bureaucracy, 275–278
policy implementation and, 58–59
primary education and, 186
among teachers, 190–192
in UP, 263–278
in women's associations, 267–268, 205, 206
women's empowerment and, 268–269
deliberative bureaucracy, 7–8, 17, 21, 32, 33, 35, 54–56, 71–72, 78–79
in the absence of democracy, 310–317
in China, 310–317
communication in, 59–60
downsides of, 59–60
gender inequality combated by, 264–270
in HP, 186–200, 217–218, 337–338
in Kerala, 302–310
legalistic bureaucracy compared with, 35, 66–67, 275–278
marginalized groups in, 65, 66
in MSUP, 264–270, 295–296
policy implementation and, 18, 58–59

primary education and, 187–200
in social movements, 303–310
societal feedback in, 64–65, 74–75
state formation and, 176–186
women's empowerment and, 264–270
democracy, deliberative conceptions of, 54–55
Dewey on, 55–56
human well-being and, 5–6, 11
patronage, 28–29, 78, 132
procedural, 54–55
Sen on, 5–6
societal feedback in, 74–75
stability of, 11
Third Wave of, 5–6
in UP, 316–317
Denmark, 73–74
Deobandi community, 273–274
Department of Women and Child Development, 230
developing countries
distributive politics in, 76
policy implementation in, 35
primary education in, 75
principal–agent approach in, 50
public policy in, 34–35
societal participation in, 61, 64–65
state-building in, 67
developmental state, 20, 69–70
bureaucratic norms in, 48–49
defining, 331–332
deliberation and, 331–338
inclusive development, 331, 334–335
industrial growth and, 331
informal features of, 70
Japan's MITI as an example of, 69–70
societal feedback in, 334–335
Dewey, John, 55–56. *See also* pragmatism
influence on Maoist thought, 313
DIETs. *See* District Institutes of Education and Training
DISE. *See* District Information System for Education
District Annual Work Plans, 139–140
District Education Officers, 112, 230. *See also* Basic Shiksha Adhikaris
District Information System for Education (DISE), 109–110
District Institutes of Education and Training (DIETs), 109–110, 355
District Primary Education Program (DPEP), 103–106, 109–111
World Bank on, 106
Dixit, Avinash, 49
DPEP. *See* District Primary Education Program
Du Gay, Paul, 53–54
Duflo, Esther, 343
Dwarahat, 242, 257, 258

economic growth, in India, 12–13, 15
economic liberalization, 86–87
policy expansion under, 101
EdTech, 348–349
education. *See also specific topics*
bureaucratic norms and, 7
as constitutional and fundamental right, 4–5, 112–113
gender gap in, 4–5
of marginalized groups, 89
private, 5, 346–347
public spending on, 6, 87, 95, 97–100, 107, 304
schooling goals and, 40
sociology of, 10
in South Asia, 4–5
in sub-Saharan Africa, 4–5
in the United States, 11
as valence issue, 75–76, 86–87
Education for All program. *See* Sarva Shiksha Abhiyan
elite capture, 156
elite decisions, 24
in policy implementation, 37
Elster, Jon, 46–47
embeddedness, 39, 72–73, 334–335
esprit de corps, 53–54, 332
in Indian Administrative Service, 125–127
ethnic particularism thesis, 78–79
ethnographic fieldwork, 31. *See also* research design; research methods
Evans, Peter, 20, 69–71
exclusionary norms, 39, 81. *See also* caste; untouchability
access to education and, 86–87, 131
the state and, 20
exit, from public education, 5
coproduction and, 335–336
in Uttarakhand, 221
in UP, 164–168

Falleti, Tulia, 23, 25–27, 169, 339, 342–343
federalism, 89–93
in India, 23

federalism (cont.)
  social policy and, 23
field methods, 30. *See also* research design; research methods
Finland, 33
  bureaucratic norms in, 317–321
  decentralization in, 321
  education reform in, 302, 320–321
  primary education in, 302, 319
flailing state, 70, 332–333
focus group discussions, 357–362
forced labor. *See begar*
Forest Act (1927), 224
Fox, Jonathan, 63, 335–336, 345–346
France, 33
  bureaucratic norms in, 317–319, 321–325
  decentralization in, 324–325
  legalism and Napoleonic administration in, 323
  legalistic bureaucracy in, 323–325
  primary education in, 302, 321–323
  teachers in, 324–325
  Third Republic of, 9
frontline institutions, 82
frontline monitoring, 58–59, 74
  in legalistic bureaucracy, 57–58
frontline public services, bureaucracy and, 351–365

Gandhi, Indira, 93–95, 224–225, 282–283
Gandhi, M. K., 92–93
Gandhi, Rajiv, 95–97, 103
Gangetic plains, 42–43, 261–262, 336–337
Garhwal Rifles, 222
Gates, Scott, 38
Gaya district, 288, 291–292, 364
gender inequality, 25–27. *See also* patriarchy; women's associations; women's empowerment
  domestic violence and, 267
  double marriage and, 274–275
  deliberative bureaucracy combating, 264–270
  education and, 4–5, 103–104
  in HP, 184–186, 207
  in UP, 152–157, 264–270
Gerring, John, 24, 27–29
Gibson, Christopher, 65
globalization, education and, 101–104
Goetz, Anne-Marie, 63
good governance
  economic growth and, 20
  policy agenda, 36
Gouldner, Alvin, 47
governance
  coproduction and, 39
  deliberation and, 54–55
  legalism and, 52–53
  participatory forms of, 61
  vertical dimension of, 23
Granovetter, Mark, 47
Grindle, Merilee, 6–7, 20–21, 25–27, 37–38, 48–49, 70, 329, 343
Gujjar community, 3–4, 152
  education in, 4
  mobile schooling for, 194–196
Gupta, Akhil, 62–63, 169, 329–330

Habermas, Jürgen, 54–55
Haggard, Stephan, 20, 70
Hanushek, Eric, 10–11, 318
Harding, Robin, 78, 294
HDI. *See* Human Development Index
He, Baogang, 312–313
Heilmann, Sebastian, 313–314
Heller, Patrick, 72–73, 309–310
Herbst, Jeffrey, 15
Herd, Pamela, 62–63, 340
Herring, Ronald, 127–128, 332–333
HGVS. *See* Himachal Pradesh Gyan Vigyan Samiti
Hicken, Allen, 76
hierarchy. *See also* caste system; women's empowerment
  in India, 264–265
  in Kerala, 305
  in Weberian bureaucracy, 46–47
higher education, 10–11, 75–76, 89–91, 102
Himachal Pradesh (HP), 3–4, 14, 16, 24–25, 229–230, 315–316, 364
  caste system in, 184–186
  centrally sponsored schemes in, 177–178
  colonialism in, 174–176
  creation of, 175–176
  Dalits in, 182–186
  deliberative bureaucracy in, 173–200, 217–218, 337–338
  demographics of, 171–173, 183–184
  Department of Education in, 212
  Devta Committees in, 184–185, 207–208
  disadvantaged children in, 190–196

electoral dynamics in, 182
Finance Commission in, 177–178
gender norms in, 184–186, 200–207
history of, 171–176
language politics in, 175–176
learning outcomes in, 45–46
local needs in, 187–190
MDM Program in, 202–203
party competition in, 181–182
party system in, 181–182
patronage-based systems in, 199–200
Planning Commission in, 177–179
political culture in, 83–84
primary education in, 13–14, 171, 187–200
school access in, 42–43
socioeconomic features of, 183–184
Special Category Status, 177–178
state formation, 176–186
state government leadership in, 181
State Planning Department, 178, 200–201
student participation in, 44–45
study map of, 173
Uttarakhand compared with, 29
women's associations in, 184–185, 201
Himachal Pradesh Gyan Vigyan Samiti (HGVS), 189–190, 212
Hindi belt states, 13, 340
Hindi language, education debate and, 92–93
Hirschman, Albert, 221
Honig, Dan, 58, 345
Hossain, Naomi, 64, 169
HP. *See* Himachal Pradesh
Huber, Evelyne, 20
human capital, 9
Human Development Index (HDI), on India, 11
Hunter Commission, 89
hygiene, enforcement in MDM Program in UP, 150, 152–157, 169

IAS. *See* Indian Administrative Service
ICS. *See* Indian Civil Service
IMF. *See* International Monetary Fund
Implementation. *See* policy implementation
incentive schemes, 345
inclusive development, 331
state capacity for, 19–21
India. *See also specific topics*
bargaining power in, 23
China compared with, 311
clientelism in, 35, 79
colonialism in, 67–68
economic growth in, 12–13, 15
federalism in, 23
HDI, 11
heterogeneity of states in, 362
hierarchy in, 264–265
inequality in, 12–13, 335–336
local study sites in, 362–365
policy implementation in, 23
primary education in, 11–14, 311
public services in, 6–7, 12–13
public spending in, 95
social movements in, 337–338
as soft state, 332–333
subnational comparison in, 23
voter–politician relationships in, 35
World Bank and, 103–104
Indian Administrative Service (IAS), 124, 306, 180
esprit de corps in, 125–127
lottery for, 28
officers in, 27–28
Indian Civil Service (ICS), 122–123
Indian Institutes of Technology, 106–107
Indian National Congress (INC). *See* Congress Party
Indian state, conceptualizations of, 333–334
flailing state, 70, 332–333
Indonesia, 91–92
industrial bureaucracy, 47
inequality, 39. *See also* caste system; gender inequality; hierarchy; patriarchy; *zamindari*
in India, 12–13, 335–336
informal institutions, 341
informal networks, 81
infrastructural power
defining, 6
Mann on, 37–38
input provision for schooling, 40–44
instrumental rationality, 46–47
Integrated Child Development Services, 285, 346–347
intensive tasks, 40–41, 74. *See also* task complexity
indicators for, 43–44
International Monetary Fund (IMF), 103
interviews, 353–355, 357–362. *See also* research design; research methods
Iyer, Lakshmi, 16

Jammu and Kashmir, 177, 229–230
Janata Dal United (JDU), 128–130, 284–286
Jeevika Program, 287
JDU. *See* Janata Dal United
Jeffrey, Craig, 28–29, 306–307
Jehanabad, 290–291, 293
Jenkins, R., 63
Jomtien Conference, 105–106
Joshi, Murali Manohar, 109–110
Joshi, Puran Chand, 227
J-PAL. *See* MIT Jameel Poverty Action Lab

Kagan, Robert, 58
Kanshi Ram, 130
Kapur, Devesh, 131, 294–295, 333–334
Kasturba Gandhi Balika Vidyalaya (KGBV), 270–275
  launch of, 270–271
  programming in, 271–273
  teaching models of, 271–272
  vocational training at, 278
Kaufman, Herbert, 48
Kerala, 13–14, 33, 72–73, 83, 119–120, 171–173, 325–326
  bureaucratic norms in, 307–308
  Campaign for Democratic Decentralization, 309
  caste system in, 305
  Communist government in, 305–306
  decentralization in, 309–310
  deliberative bureaucracy in, 302–310
  demographics of, 304
  geography of, 304
  hierarchy in, 305
  literacy programming in, 189
  Panchayati Raj Institutions in, 309
  political mobilization in, 306
  primary education in, 303–304, 306
  private schooling in, 306–307
  public spending in, 307–308, 310
  social movements in, 302
  subnationalism in, 305–306
Kerala Education Act, 308
Kerala model of social development, 303–310
Kerala Sastra Sahitya Parishad (KSSP), 189
  creation of, 309
  institutionalization of, 309–310
KGBV. *See* Kasturba Gandhi Balika Vidyalaya
Khan, Mushtaq, 78
Khanduri, Bhuwan Chandra, 220
Kingdon, Geeta Gandhi, 202, 346–347
Kinnaur, 180
Kohli, Atul, 20, 67–68, 75
Kosack, Steve, 79–80, 83
Kothari, Daulat Singh, 93
Kothari Commission, 93–97
KPPC. *See* Kerala Provincial Congress Committee
Krause, George, 50
Krishna, Anirudh, 15, 81, 82
Kruks-Wisner, Gabrielle, 51, 64, 169, 339, 340
KSSP. *See* Kerala Sastra Sahitya Parishad
Kumaon Regiment, 222
Kumar, Nitish, 80, 284–285, 287–288, 294

labor
  child, 82–83, 145
  by women, 158–160, 184–185, 237
Lahaul–Spiti, 180
land reform, 75–76. *See also ryotwari*; *zamindari*)
language politics, 93–94
  education and, 91–92
law and order bureaucracy, 28–29, 67–68. *See also* legalistic bureaucracy
  in Bihar, 262, 284–285, 286–287
  in UP, 122–124, 127–135
learning outcomes, 45. *See also* Annual Status of Education Report (ASER)
  in Indian states, 45–46
  in OECD countries, 317–318. *See also* PISA
legalism, 57–58, 156–157
  in Bihar, 297
  collective action and, 157–162
  defining, 7–8, 52
  in France, 323
  in liberal legal tradition, 52–53
  reinforcement of, 229–234
  rules-based accountability and, 54
  in UP, 134–148
  in Uttarakhand, 229–234
  Weber on, 53
legalistic bureaucracy, 17–18, 52–54, 56, 64, 71
  autonomy in, 275–276
  in Bihar, 292–295
  bureaucratic understandings from, 56

civil society experience of, 234–237
clientelism in, 143–147, 262–263
deliberation in, 275–278
deliberative bureaucracy compared with, 35, 66–67, 275–278
distance in, 231–232
in France, 323–325
frontline monitoring in, 57–58
policy implementation from, 18, 58
public services and, 63–64
reforms under, 297
in Saharanpur, 168
school infrastructure provision and, 134–148
in Sitapur, 168
societal monitoring and, 62–63
SSA and, 135–138
in UP, 28–29, 121–135, 168
in Uttarakhand, 32, 82, 229–237, 259–260
Weberian bureaucracy distinguished from, 64
legalized bureaucracy, societal feedback and, 74–75
Levi, Margaret, 21, 48, 332
liberal legal tradition, legalism in, 52–53
Lindvall, Johannes, 9, 75–76
Lipsky, Michael, 20, 47–48, 71, 341–342
literacy rates, 89
census enumeration and, 303, 359
in China, 311
in Indian states, 189, 220
local bureaucracy, in China, 314
local participation, in MDM Program, 151
lower-level bureaucrats, 27–28, 147, 173–174
Lucknow, 169, 227
community ownership in, 151
MDM Program in, 148–152
Lynch, Julia, 25–27

Macaulay, Lord 89
MacLean, Lauren, 221, 325–326, 335–336, 339, 341
Mahabharata, 246
Mahadalits, 284
mahila mandals. *See* women's associations
Mahila Samakhya program, 30, 32–33, 104, 261–263, 295–296, 336–337, 339–340, 342–343
in UP, 263–278
Mahila Samakhya Uttar Pradesh (MSUP), 275
autonomy of, 275–277
deliberative bureaucracy in, 264–270, 295–296
frontline workers, 266, 278, 295, 296
gender-sensitive teaching models of, 271–272
organizational identity of, 296–297
program, 263–278
policy interpretation of, 266
sanghas created by , 265–267, 273, 277–278 *See also* women's associations
Mandal, B. P., 23, 128–130, 282
Mandal Commission, 128–130. *See also* caste reservations
Mann, Horace, 6
on infrastructural power, 37–38
on primary education, 9–10
Mao Zedong, 313
March, James, 7, 48
marginalized groups, 63
in deliberative bureaucracy, 65, 66
education of, 89
Marshall, T. H., 9–10
Mathew, Santhosh, 283
Mathur, Nayanika, 233–234
Mathura, 274–275
Mayawati, 80, 130, 132–133, 146, 161, 271
McDonnell, Erin, 275–276, 332
MDGs. *See* UN Millennium Development Goals
MDM. *See* Midday Meal Programme
Members of the Legislative Assembly (MLAs), 188
metis, 58–59
Mexico, 56, 63, 346
MG Program. *See* Mission Gunvatta Program
MHRD. *See* Ministry of Human Resource Development
microfinance, 56
Midday Meal [MDM] Programme, 12–13, 42, 87, 148–158, 204, 216, 241, 252, 259, 288–290, 339–342
expansion of, 105
grievance procedures, 151–152
in HP, 202–203
hygiene requirements in, 150, 152–157, 169
community participation in, 151
MDM Authority, 149–151

Midday Meal [MDM] (cont.)
meal preparation, 154
monitoring, 293–294
public scrutiny of, 148–149
service delivery in, 150–152
supervision of, 149
in UP, 148–158
VEC management of, 112, 150
military
state-building and, 67
education, 16, 29, 186
Ministry of Human Resource Development (MHRD), 95–96, 103, 107–112, 235
Macaulay's *Minute on Indian Education* (1860), 89, 175. *See also* colonialism; education
Mission Gunvatta (MG) program, 290–292, 295
teachers under, 290–291
missionary schools, 89
MIT Jameel Poverty Action Lab (J-PAL), 290
MLAs. *See* Members of the Legislative Assembly
mobile schooling, 4
for Gujjar community, 194–196
mobilization. *See* community mobilization; political mobilization
modernization, 15
bureaucracy in Europe and, 53
primary school expansion and, 87–88
Moe, Terry, 10
Moffitt, Susan, 58–59, 65
Mohini Jain v. *State of Karnataka*, 113
Moore, M., 283
Mother Teacher Associations (MTAs), 200–203, 207, 341–342
creation of, 202–203
deliberation in, 205, 206
primary school monitoring by, 204–207
Moynihan, Donald, 62–63, 340
MSUP. *See* Mahila Samakhya Uttar Pradesh
MTAs. *See* Mother Teacher Associations
multilevel comparative analysis, 22–24. *See also* research design
multilevel governance, 22–24
methodological advantages of, 24
multilevel field research, 351–357. *See also* research methods
Muslims, education programming for, 92–93, 265–266, 273–274
Myrdal, Gunnar, 332–333
NAFRE. *See* National Alliance for the Fundamental Right to Quality Education and Equity
Naik, J. P., 93–94, 96–97
Namboodiripad, E. M. S., 305–306
National Alliance for the Fundamental Right to Quality Education and Equity (NAFRE), 113–114
National Commission for the Protection of Child Rights (NCPCR), 114
National Commission on Education, 93
National Council of Educational Research and Training (NCERT), 94–96
National Development Council (NDC), 95–96
National Policy on Education (1986), 234
National Policy on Education (2020), 346–347
National Elementary Education Mission (NEEM), 103–104, 107–109
national identity, 91–92
National Literacy Mission, 189, 309
National Policy on Education (NPE) 1968, 93–94, 97–100
National Policy on Education (NPE) 1986, 95–100, 264–265
National Policy on Education (NPE) 2020, 346–347
National Rural Employment Guarantee Scheme, 233–234
Navodaya Vidyalaya program, 96–97
NCERT. *See* National Council of Educational Research and Training
NCPCR. *See* National Commission for the Protection of Child Rights
NDC. *See* National Development Council
NEEM. *See* National Elementary Education Mission
Nehru, Jawaharlal, 89–93, 124
New Delhi, 112, 127–128, 177
New Institutional Economics, 37
New Public Management, 323
nongovernmental organizations (NGOs), 74, 81, 236, 237, 287–288
Nooruddin, Irfan, 79–80
norms
defined, 46–47
theoretical characteristics of, 47
NPE. *See* National Policy on Education

OBCs. *See* Other Backward Classes
O'Donnell, Guillermo, 15
Olsen, Johan, 7, 48, 328–329
Operation Blackboard, 97–100
oral histories, 341, 356–357. *See also* research methods
Ostrom, Elinor, 19–20, 39, 46–47
Other Backward Classes (OBCs), 23, 127–130, 132–133, 227, 282
  political mobilization of, 282–283
  political representation of, 281–282

Pahari communities, 29, 83–84
Pahari dissatisfaction, in Uttarakhand, 225–229
Pahari linguistic identity in HP, 175–176
panchayats, 210–211, 356
  deliberation and, 207, 161
  elite capture and, 150, 156
  involvement in primary education, 203, 161, 246–247, 255–256
  in HP, 203, 209–211
  in Kerala, 309
  in UP, 160–161
  in Uttarakhand, 222–224
  women's participation in, 207
Panchayati Raj Institutions, 23
Pande, Lalit, 234
Parmar, Yashwant Singh, 176–182
participant observation, 355
participation, chain of, 65, 340
Participatory Rural Appraisal (PRA), 356, 361
party systems
  in Indian states, 181–182, 220, 227–228
  public spending and, 79–80, 327–328
Paswan, Ram Vilas, 284
Patel, Sardar, 124
Patna district, 364, 288
patriarchy, 265, 268–269. *See also* gender inequality
patronage. *See also* clientelism
  in Indian democracy, 29, 76–78, 132, 134
peasant resistance, in Uttarakhand, 222–225
Perry, Elizabeth, 313
Perry, James, 313, 345
Peters, B. Guy, 323
PISA. *See* Programme for International Student Assessment
police agencies, 123–124, 134, 193, 333
policy feedback, 21
  in societal feedback, 60–61
policy implementation, 31, 32, 85
  bureaucratic norms and, 17–19, 50–52, 76–79
  causal mechanisms for, 50–52, 56–67
  in China, 50
  clientelism and, 78
  conceptualization of, 36–39
  context in study of, 25–27
  defining, 35–36, 38
  deliberation and, 58–59
  from deliberative bureaucracy, 18, 58–59
  in developing countries, 35
  elite decisions in, 37
  in India, 23
  from legalistic bureaucracy, 58
  operationalization of, 40–42
  politics of, 38–39, 339
  rule interpretation in, 37
  in rural UP, 138–143
  scholarship on, 37–38
  school infrastructure and, 196–200
  social welfare and, 37–38
  societal feedback and, 339–341
  society in, 39
  the state and, 36
  street-level bureaucracy and, 342–343
political competition. *See also* party systems
  in Indian states, 178–179, 181–182, 306
  public goods provision and, 78, 311–312
political culture, 82–84
  caste system and, 82–83
  subnational comparison of, 83–84
  Weiner on, 82–83
political mobilization, 79–80. *See also* community mobilization
  in Bihar, 282–283
  in Kerala, 306
  public spending on education and, 79–80
  societal feedback and, 80
  in UP, 80, 130
Posner, Dan, 38–39
PRA. *See* Participatory Rural Appraisal
pragmatism, 55
  in Dewey's political philosophy, 55–56
  in Maoist thought , 313
Praja Mandal movement, 175

Pratham, 42, 285–288, 290–291, 294
predatory bureaucracies, 6, 78
preschool services, 231
primary education, 36, 64, 71, 82, 86–88
  administrative tasks for, 40
  in Bihar, 27, 278–295
  as career path, 105–106
  case selection, 24–30
  in China, 311–312
  comparative indicators for, 42–46
  completion rates, 109
  coproduction in, 39, 213–217
  deliberation and, 186
  deliberative bureaucracy and, 187–200
  in developing countries, 75
  economics of, 10
  expansion of, 115
  explanations for outcomes in, 14–16
  in Finland, 302, 319
  fiscal responsibility for, 106–107
  in France, 302, 321–323
  goals of, 9
  in HP, 13–14, 171, 187–200
  implementation of, 8–11, 346–348
  in India, 11–14, 86–116, 311
  inequality and, 9–10
  in Kerala, 303–304, 306
  politics of, 10–11, 75–76
  schools, 197
  social capital and, 81–82
  social welfare and, 9–10
  timeline of Indian government policies on, 98–100
  in UP, 27, 105, 120
  in Uttarakhand, 220–221
  Weiner on, 105–106
primary school monitoring, by MTAs, 204–207
principal–agent framework, 49
  applied to bureaucracy, 49
  applied to developing countries, 50
  multidimensional complexity and, 49
Pritchett, Lant, 10–11, 40, 58, 70, 74, 332–333, 344–345
private schooling, 5, 346–347
  in Kerala, 306–307
  RTE Act and, 114–115
  in UP, 161–162
  in Uttarakhand, 257–258
PROBE report, 12–13, 202–203
procedural democracy, 54–55
Programme for International Student Assessment (PISA), 317–319, 321–322
Progresa, 346
public agencies, as collective action sites, 7, 50
public apathy, 157–158, 167–168, 340
public goods provision
  community social capital and, 183–184
  and credit claiming, 78
  clientelism and, 76–79, 132
  geography and, 15, 171
  and state embeddedness, 72
  spending on, 79–80
public infrastructure
  in UP, 226
  in Uttarakhand, 226
public policy. *See also* policy implementation
  implementation of, 6
  and institutional performance, 38
  in developing countries, 34–35
public reason, 55
public services
  implementation of, 6, 7, 17, 51–52
  in India, 6–7, 11–14
  NGO involvement in, 113
  the state as actor in, 22
  subnational differences in, 13
public spending, 5–6
  on education, 6, 87, 95, 97–100, 107, 304
  in India, 95
Pulse Polio campaign, 231
Punjab Hills, 173–176
Putnam, Robert, 80–81

racial discrimination, 11
Ramachandran, Vimala, 111–112, 264
Ramamurti Committee, 102
Rao, P. V. Narasimha, 95–96, 101, 102, 109–110
Rao, Vijayendra, 20, 21, 64–65, 81
Rashtriya Janata Dal (RJD), 283–284
rationalization, of teachers in Uttarakhand, 238–248
Rawls, John, 55
redistribution, 75–76
relational approach, to bureaucracy, 50
research design, 22
  case selection and, 24–30
  generalizability of, 28–29

multilevel comparative analysis, 22–24
research methods, 22, 30–31
ethnographic fieldwork, 31
focus group discussions, 357–362
interviews, 353–355, 361–362
multilevel field research, 351–357
oral histories, 356–357
positionality and, 360, 361
qualitative data and, 357–362
responsive regulation, 58
Revenue villages, in AVP, 144
Rich, Jessica, 337
Right to Education [RTE] Act, 12–13, 42–43, 78, 87
civic and judicial action for, 113
rights-based agenda and, 112–113
criticism of, 114–115
infrastructure standards stipulated by, 42
passage of, 112–115
RJD. *See* Rashtriya Janata Dal
Robinson, James, 16
Roorkee, 161–162, 222
RTE Act. *See* Right to Education Act
rule interpretation
of MSUP, 266
in policy implementation, 37
rule of law, 52–54, 63, 315–316
rules-based accountability, 259
legalism and, 54
rules-based protocols, 61–62
Ruparelia, Sanjay, 112–113
ryotwari, 16

Sabel, Charles, 59, 319–320
Saharanpur, 138–139, 141–142, 144, 146, 151, 156–157, 161–166, 186, 362–364
AVP in, 146
legalistic bureaucracy in, 168
MSUP in, 273–274
Samajwadi Party (SP), 128–130, 132–133
Samyukt Socialist Party, 23, 282
Sant Ravidas, 158
Sanyal, Paromita, 64–65, 81
Saraswati Shishu Mandir, 252–253
Sarva Shiksha Abhiyan (SSA), 12–13, 87, 109–112, 167, 198–199, 245–246, 286–287
advantages of, 135–136
autonomy of, 136–137
history of, 135
legalistic bureaucracy and, 135–138
program rule-bending, 199
reporting of, 140
VECs and, 203
Save the Children, 113–114
Scheduled Castes (SCs), 130–131, 133, 227
Scheduled Tribes, 227
school access, 42
in HP, 42–43
school infrastructure
legalistic bureaucracy and provision of, 134–148
policy implementation and, 196–200
schooling, education goals compared with, 40
Scott, James, 58–59, 65, 344
SCs. *See* Scheduled Castes
SC-ST Prevention of Atrocities Act, 247
SDGs. *See* UN Sustainable Development Goals
SEED. *See* Society for Environmental and Rural Development
Self Help Groups (SHGs), 152, 265–266, 287. *See also* women's associations
Sen, Amartya
capability-centered approach of, 19–20
on democracy, 5–6
Seva Mandir, 105
Shani, Ornit, 124–125
Sharpe, K., 323–324
Sherman, Richard, 21, 48, 332
SHGs. *See* Self Help Groups
Shimla, 6–7, 175, 180, 204, 205, 210, 212
Shiksha Karmi Program, 105
Shklar, Judith, 52–53
SIDA. *See* Swedish International Development Agency
Singh, Charan, 127–128
Singh, Manmohan, 101, 113–114, 148–149
Singh, Prerna, 157–158, 279, 301–302, 305–306
Singh, V. P., 128–130
Sinha, A., 23, 69
Sitapur, 138–139, 167–168, 186, 273, 362–364
AVP in, 147
legalistic bureaucracy in, 168
sanghas in, 277
SSA in, 140
Skocpol, Theda, 20
Slater, Daniel, 69
Smith, Adam, 38
social capital, 80–82

social capital (cont.)
definition of, 80–81
primary education and, 81–82
in study villages, 81–82
in Uttarakhand, 259–260
social development, Kerala model of, 303–310
social movements. *See also* collective action; community mobilization; political mobilization
deliberative bureaucracy in, 303–310
in India, 337–338
in Kerala, 302
social programs, 23
Social Uplift Through Rural Action (SUTRA), 201
social welfare, 8–11
policy implementation and, 37–38
primary education and, 9–10
Social Work and Research Center (SWRC), 105
societal feedback, 60–67, 71
defining, 21, 51–52
deliberative bureaucracy and, 64–65, 74–75
in democracy, 74–75
in developmental state, 334–335
legalistic bureaucracy and, 74–75
as a form of policy feedback, 60–61
policy implementation and, 339–341
political mobilization and, 80
society
in policy implementation, 39
the state and, 39
Society for Environmental and Rural Development (SEED), 252, 254–255
Somanathan, Rohini, 79–80
Soss, Joe, 9, 51, 60–61, 339–340
South Korea, 75
SP. *See* Samajwadi Party
SSA. *See* Sarva Shiksha Abhiyan
Stasavage, David, 78, 294
the state. *See also* bureaucracy; developmental state; Indian state
as actor in public service provision, 22
bureaucratic norms and formation of, 69
policy implementation and, 36
relational treatment of, 24
society and, 39
state capacity, 22, 36–38, 63
bureaucratic norms and, 70
for inclusive development, 19–21
state-building, 69, 344–345
and the origins of bureaucratic norms, 67–69
in UP, 121–135
in HP, 173–186
States Reorganisation Act, 92
States Reorganisation Commission of 1953, 92
Stern, Nicholas, 279
street-level bureaucracy, 7, 17–18, 70, 71
collective welfare institutions and, 341–343
policy implementation and, 342–343
student participation, 44
in HP, 44–45
in Uttarakhand, 44–45
Student Welfare Group (SWG), 320
subnational comparison, 22, 31
of bureaucratic norms, 68
in India, 23
pitfalls in, 25–27
of political culture, 83–84
sub-Saharan Africa, education in, 4–5
SUTRA. *See* Social Uplift Through Rural Action
Swedish International Development Agency (SIDA), 104
Swidler, Anne, 84

Tamil Nadu, 83, 93–94, 105, 119–120
TaRL. *See* Teaching at the Right Level
task complexity, 37–38. *See also* codifiable tasks; intensive tasks; complex tasks
indicators for, 43–44
teachers, 4
absence of, 44–45
under Bihar's MG program, 290–291
deliberation among, 190–192
in France, 324–325
local politicians and, 244
main duties of, 292
politicization of, 275–276
training, 190–192, 243
rationalization policy in Uttarakhand, 238–248
teachers' unions, 4, 39, 75, 111, 321, 324–325
negotiation of in Uttarakhand, 241–244
Teaching at the Right Level (TaRL), 290–292, 347

adoption of, 291–292
teaching input indicators, 44
Teets, Jessica, 313
Teitelbaum, Emmanuel, 79–80, 327–328
Tendler, Judith, 48–49, 346
Thachil, Tariq, 79–80, 327–328
Tharakan, P. K. M., 306–307
Thelen, Kathleen, 37, 88, 342–343
thin accountability, 58
Tilly, Charles, 323
trust-building, 361
Tsai, Lily, 50, 316–317
on embeddedness, 72–73
on state accountability, 72

Uganda, 294
UKD. *See* Uttarakhand Kranti Dal
UN Millennium Development Goals (MDGs), 4–5, 107–109
UN Sustainable Development Goals (SDGs), 343
UNDP. *See* United Nations Development Program
UNESCO, 103, 106
UNICEF, 103, 113–114
United Nations Development Program (UNDP), 11
United States
administrative burden in, 63
education in, 11
Forest Service, 48
policy feedback in, 60–61
state capacity in, 330–331
Unni Krishnan v. *The State of Andhra Pradesh*, 113
untouchability, 174–175, 130–131, 281, 305. *See also* caste system
Midday Meal Programme in UP and, 149, 152–157
UP. *See* Uttar Pradesh
USN. *See* Uttarakhand Seva Nidhi
Uttar Pradesh (UP), 14, 24–25, 32, 119–120, 262–263, 315–316, 362–364
caste system in, 122, 127–135, 269–270
clientelism in, 78
colonial state, 122–124
common rules in, 137
Dalits in, 138–139
deliberation in, 263–278
democracy in, 316–317
demographics of, 28–29
elections in, 137
electoral dynamics in, 182
formation of, 122
geography of, 28–29
government leadership of, 128–129
Jat belt, 186
law and order bureaucracy in, 122–124, 127–135
learning outcomes in, 45–46
legalistic bureaucracy in, 28–29, 121–131, 135, 168–169
literacy rate, 120
lower-caste political mobilization in, 127–135
Mahila Samakhya in, 263–278
MDM Program in, 149
policy implementation in rural, 138–143
primary education in, 27, 105, 120
public order in, 123–124
public services in, 13
socioeconomic indicators in, 139
Uttarakhand separation from, 29, 220
Village Education Committees in, 345–346
zamindari in, 122
Uttar Pradesh Hill Development Department, 225
Uttarakhand, 13–16, 24–25, 42–43, 92–93, 186, 220, 232–233, 364
caste system in, 227
collective action in, 222–225
community mobilization in, 222–225
creation of, 222–229
decentralization in, 232
electoral politics in, 227–228
exit in, 221
geography of, 222
HP compared with, 29
learning outcomes in, 45–46
legalism in, 229–234
legalistic bureaucracy in, 32, 82, 229–234, 259–260
literacy rate, 220
Pahari identification in, 225–229
peasant resistance in, 222–225
primary education in, 220–221
public infrastructure in, 226
social capital in, 259–260
student participation in, 44–45
study map of, 222
teachers in, 238–248
UP separation from, 29, 220

Uttarakhand (cont.)
  voice in, 221
Uttarakhand Kranti Dal (UKD), 227
Uttarakhand Seva Nidhi (USN), 234, 235, 237
Uttaranchal, 227. *See also* Uttarakhand

Vajpayee, Atal Bihari, 109–110
Varieties of Capitalism, 10–11, 318–319
Varshney, Ashutosh, 128
VECs. *See* Village Education Committees
Village Education Committees (VECs), 61–62, 150–151, 163, 255–256, 287, 336–337
  accountability and, 345–346
  on MDM Programme, 112, 150
  monitoring, 237
  SSA and, 203
  in UP, 345–346
  women's associations in, 256
village governance, in Dharmaur, 209–213
vocational training, 10–11
voice, in Uttarakhand, 221
voter–politician relationships, 76–78
  in India, 35

Warren, Mark, 312–313
Weber, Max
  on bureaucracy and ethos, 332
  on legalism, 53
Weberian bureaucracy, 6, 20–21, 48–49, 70, 332
  autonomy of, 73–74
  formal structures of, 54
  hierarchical design of, 46–47
  insulated from society, 64, 64
  legalistic bureaucracy distinguished from, 64
Weiner, Myron, 34
  on policy implementation, 34–35
  on political culture, 82–83
  on primary education, 105–106
welfare, 8–11. *See also* social welfare
Wiborg, Susanne, 10, 320–321
wicked problems, 41–42
Wilson, James Q., 38, 47–48
Woessmann, Ludger, 10–11, 318
women's associations, 156, 237. *See also* Self Help Groups
  in Bihar, 287
  in HP, 184–185, 201, 211–215
  in Uttarakhand, 246–247, 251, 254–257, 304
  in UP, 265–267, 273, 277
  deliberation in, 267–268 *See also* Mahila Samakhya UP
women's empowerment, 264–265. *See also* women's associations; Mahila Samakhya UP; Uttarakhand Seva Nidhi
  deliberation and, 268–269
  deliberative bureaucracy for, 264–270
Woolcock, Michael, 40, 65, 70, 74, 80, 344–345
World Bank, 12–13, 36, 88, 103
  on DPEP, 106
  India and, 103–104
  Swajal Project, 237
World Education Forum in Dakar, 107–109

Yadav, Lalu Prasad, 284–286
  on caste system, 282–283
Yadav, Mulayam Singh, 132–133, 143, 227
Yanow, Dvora, 50–51

Zacka, Bernardo, 50–51
zamindari, 122, 127, 130–131, 183–184, 280–281
  collective action and, 16

Milton Keynes UK
Ingram Content Group UK Ltd.
UKHW030424191124
451136UK00009B/61

9 781009 258043